D1263304

THE LICENSING ACT
OF 1737

During the last few days of the session in the spring of 1737, Parliament
quickly considered and passed a law establishing government censorship over British drama and creating a government-regulated
monopoly in the theaters. The Licensing Act and the similar laws that
succeeded it profoundly restricted British literature and the theaters for
more than two centuries, until the Theatres Act of 1968 put an end to
prior censorship of all new plays. This study examines, for the first
time, the intricate social, legal, and political factors underlying the passage of the Licensing Act. Vincent J. Liesenfeld tells the story with an
immediacy and style that will make reading it a pleasure not only for
scholars of eighteenth-century theater or social history, but for all who
have an active interest in the dynamic interrelationships between literature and historical events.

The Licensing Act. The original act in the custody of The House of Lords Record Office. Reproduced by permission of the Clerk of the Records.

VINCENT J. LIESENFELD

THE LICENSING ACT OF 1737

THE UNIVERSITY OF WISCONSIN PRESS

Library
L.U.P.
Indiana, Pa

344.42097 L625L
C.1

Published 1984

The University of Wisconsin Press
114 North Murray Street
Madison, Wisconsin 53715

The University of Wisconsin Press, Ltd.
1 Gower Street
London WC1E 6HA, England

Copyright © 1984
The Board of Regents of the University of Wisconsin System
All rights reserved

First printing

Printed in the United States of America

For LC CIP information see the colophon

ISBN 0-299-09810-9

To Marge

CONTENTS

Contents

PREFACE

Enemies of the state, particularly Jacobites, manipulated the London stage during 1736 and 1737 as part of their larger plan to create disaffection in Britain and overthrow the government and ultimately the Crown itself. The Licensing Act was one of several countermeasures taken by the government in the face of the conspiracy that threatened it. This view of the circumstances surrounding the passage of the act is repeatedly displayed by government apologists in the press, by ministerial records, and by the pattern of the government's reactions to other events from the summer of 1736 through the autumn of 1737.

Opposition propagandists, other official and private documents, and the pattern of criticisms directed against the government during the same period, however, suggest that the Licensing Act was one of several measures designed by Walpole to suppress all vestiges of dissent and to permit him to exercise dictatorial authority without regard for the constitutional limitations of his office. Critics of the government insisted that its avowed concern for protecting national liberties from a Jacobite conspiracy was nothing but a mask for its intention to suspend those liberties. The government, on the other hand, argued that its critics' patriotism was merely an expedient disguise for their sympathy towards those who would weaken the political stability on which the exercise of those liberties depended.

Literary historians have tended to favor the views of the government's critics. By focusing primarily—sometimes exclusively—on the dramas that preceded passage of the Licensing Act, they have highlighted the hostility to Walpole that most of those plays exhibit. At the same time, however, the political, economic, legal, and social influences that contributed to the passage of the act have been neglected.

Although it has been recognized that the act was affected by political as well as literary pressures, these elements usually have been considered only insofar as they overlapped. Political dramatic satire seemed in the nineteenth century to have been so crucially important a factor in the passage of the law, for example, that the parliamentary committee considering a new Theatres Act during the summer of 1832 heard testimony that "Fielding's Pasquin was the sole cause of the Licensing Act."[1] A modern study of dramatic satire in the period concludes that the personal attacks on

Walpole in *Pasquin* and *The Historical Register* "combined with the many specific dramatic satires on his Excise scheme and Gin Act gave him a convenient excuse for the Licensing Act."[2]

Emphasis on the importance of political drama, particularly Fielding's, to the passage of the act is well founded, but in the absence of other perspectives that emphasis distorts the nature of the act and the purposes it was intended to serve. The Licensing Act, which aimed its effects at literature, was not exclusively or even primarily a literary event. It was, rather, a product of particular social, legal, economic, and political conditions, as well as of the reactions to literary works that, in turn, were dominated by those same complex issues.

This study examines those issues and thereby attempts to establish other perspectives from which the Licensing Act can better be understood, but it cannot pretend to offer any clear answers to the most important questions that those perspectives raise. Jacobitism and satire personally offensive to Walpole and the king, for example, were both demonstrably significant factors in the passage of the act, but whether the government was actually imperiled by those threats, or in what degree, cannot be determined except on the basis of contemporary testimony, most of which is self-serving and all of which should be suspect in this regard. What can be demonstrated is that these and other major factors—theatrical, social, political, economic, and legal—created a coalition of mutual interests in the spring of 1737 that favored official restrictions on playhouses and prior censorship of new plays.

ACKNOWLEDGMENTS

For their helpful criticisms of earlier versions of this study and for their encouragement at every stage I am grateful to Phillip Harth, Merritt Y. Hughes Professor of English, and Eric Rothstein, Edgar W. Lacy Professor of English, University of Wisconsin—Madison; Richard B. Schwartz, Professor of English and Dean of the Graduate School, Georgetown University; and Professor Malcolm Kelsall, University College, University of Cardiff. I also wish to thank Shirley Strum Kenny, Professor of English and Provost of Arts and Humanities, University of Maryland, who read and commented on the entire manuscript.

A major part of the research for this study was supported by a Fulbright-Hays grant. I am grateful to Mr. J.O.A. Herrington, past Executive Director of the United States–United Kingdom Educational Commission, for his help and good counsel during and since the tenure of that scholarship.

I wish to thank George Hugh Cholmondeley, sixth Marquess of Cholmondeley, for permission to publish the contents of several manuscripts in the Cholmondeley (Houghton) Collection in the Cambridge University Library.

Transcripts and photographic reproductions of documents in the custody of the House of Lords Record Office are published by permission of the Clerk of the Records (Crown copyright).

Extracts from and transcripts of Crown-copyright records in the Public Record Office appear by permission of the Controller of Her Majesty's Stationery Office.

Photographs of two prints in the Department of Prints and Drawings are published with the permission of the Trustees of the British Museum.

Extracts from the Oxford University Archives are published by permission of Mr. T. H. Aston, Keeper of the Archives.

Extracts from and transcripts of other manuscripts listed in the bibliography are published by permission of the Cambridge University Archives, Lincoln's Inn Library, the Harvard Theatre Collection, and the Folger Shakespeare Library.

I also wish to acknowledge the special help provided by Miss M.E.A. Pamplin and Mr. A. G. Purvis, Manuscripts Room, Cambridge University Library; Mr. D. J. Johnson, Assistant Clerk of the Records, the House of Lords Record Office; Miss E. S. Leedham-Green, Assistant to the Keeper, Cambridge University Archives; Mr. R. Walker, Librarian, Lincoln's Inn Library; Miss B. R. Masters, Deputy Keeper of the Records, Corporation of London Records Office; Miss J. Coburn, Head Archivist, Greater London Record Office; M. M. de La Fourniere, Directeur des Archives et de la Documentation, Ministère des Affaires Étrangères; Mr. W. Kellaway, Secretary and Librarian, Institute of Historical Research, University of London; and the staffs of the reading rooms of the British Library, the Sterling and Goldsmith Libraries of the University of London, the Bodleian Library, the William Andrews Clark Memorial Library, and the Columbia University Library.

Marge and our children Patricia and Peter have helped patiently in countless ways, and to them I owe thanks without measure.

THE LICENSING ACT
OF 1737

INTRODUCTION

The Licensing Act of 1737 has been characterized as a "central historical event" of the period.[1] Its effects on eighteenth-century drama were incalculable. Its most controversial provision, requiring government censorship prior to the performance of new plays, was extended (in a revised form) by the Theatres Act that replaced it in 1843, and continued in force until the Theatres Act of 1968.[2] Next to the laws protecting copyright, the 1737 act has probably had the most profound influence on English literature of any official measure in the last three centuries, and has been in many respects the model censorship device in modern Western society.

The Licensing Act was the result of several sets of conditions that bred hostility towards the drama and theaters. The religious opposition to dramatic entertainments, for example, that had helped to close the theaters from 1642 to 1660 and had rallied to Jeremy Collier's *Short View of the Immorality and Profaneness of the English Stage* in 1698 was still widespread in the 1730s. Furthermore, despite plays like Lillo's *London Merchant*, tradesmen and merchants tended to disapprove of playhouses, and a significant number of London citizens felt the city would be improved by their extermination, or at least by their removal from the surrounding area. These sentiments survived the passage of the Licensing Act they had encouraged. Writing in 1738, an anonymous defender of the stage cited objections that were still being raised against it: the stage nourished and fomented the passions, said its critics, indulging audiences' craving for vice and thereby encouraging public licentiousness.[3] Even the managers of some theaters advocated government regulation of their activity, viewing such control as a means of insuring a profitable monopoly in London. Walpole's government itself had given evidence (beginning in 1728 with the ban on Gay's *Polly*) that it wished to prevent the performance of certain plays.

During the early 1730s the traditional methods the government had relied on to regulate the theaters and the plays they produced collapsed. Until late in 1733, Walpole had been able, either through the power of the Lord Chamberlain or the Treasury or justices of the peace, to exercise some measure of control over the playhouses. But for nearly four theatrical seasons thereafter, until the Licensing Act went into effect, the theaters were free from all but the most inconsequential restraints (chiefly the laws against profanity, which remained in effect but were apparently not actively enforced after about 1725).

During the same four-year period new conditions developed that influenced the passage of the Licensing Act. One of the most important proved to be the growing insecurity of Walpole's government. The increase in satiric attacks aimed at him from the stage was part of a rising discontent not only with the first minister but with the king himself, who was also frequently ridiculed. The widening split in the royal family between the Prince of Wales and his parents, and the rise in Frederick's popularity at the same time that his father's was falling, were exploited by the Opposition and playwrights alike to undermine Walpole's position. The king was dissatisfied with Walpole's management of this sensitive domestic issue; at the same time, he was annoyed at unrest in the nation at large, and was more annoyed when Walpole's attempts to silence it seemed instead to increase it; and, like the Opposition, he frequently disagreed with the foreign policy of avoiding hostilities that Walpole and his brother were pursuing. All of these difficulties made Walpole's position less and less secure, particularly when, in one form or another, they became the subject of plays that drew packed houses and exposed the ministry and the royal family to public derision. The increase in the frequency and severity of these dramatic attacks coincided with the collapse of legal and traditional methods of regulating the stage and contributed to the gradual erosion of the king's confidence in his first minister to manage national affairs. Under these circumstances it is not surprising that Walpole took a more intense interest in theatrical activities than he had earlier in his administration.[4]

Walpole tried to cope with growing public attacks in several ways. He maintained an effective system, inherited from former governments, for dealing with printed libels on the king and his ministers. After circumstances deprived him of the legal means to silence objectionable dramatic performances (which evidently were not within the scope of libel laws), he looked for an opportunity to enact new legislation. Such an occasion arose in 1735, but although the government had a hand in drafting the bill introduced that year, it contained no provision for the censorship of plays, and it was dropped when the government tried to amend it to include one. Parliament's willingness to abandon popular legislation regulating the theaters in order to deprive the ministry of a vehicle for the imposition of dramatic censorship provoked another, more spectacular rise in the prominence of explicit political satire on the London stage. Criticisms of the government or of the king that had to be disguised when they appeared in print, and even then were liable to legal prosecutions, were presented openly and with impunity in dramatic performances. Two theatrical seasons played under conditions of freedom unparalleled in the history of British theater were enough to exhaust the tolerance of Parliament, and when the matter was reconsidered in 1737, the legislature acted swiftly.

During 1735, social, religious, and economic conditions had been favorable to a bill regulating the theaters but insufficient to overcome widespread resistance to censorship. Two years later, while those same conditions continued to favor a theaters bill, political conditions had changed so radically that a more restrictive bill, creating arbitrary prior censorship not subject to appeal, passed with only a few voices raised in opposition.

Walpole managed matters more skillfully in 1737 than he had in 1735. Only when he was able to demonstrate convincingly the need for official censorship did he have the bill introduced. In order to secure evidence for his demonstration, he made secret arrangements with the two independent theaters operating in London to alert him when they received offensive plays, and thereby acquired the infamous farce *The Golden Rump*. In part because the scurrility of the play (aimed primarily at the king) made opposition to the bill inexpedient, in part because another bill, dealing with theaters in Cambridge and Oxford, had already made explicit the principle of government authority over the stage, the bill moved quickly to passage. The Licensing Act constituted a revival and coalescence of the two methods of theatrical regulation that had disappeared earlier in the decade: it reinstated the legal basis of official control by amending a vagrancy statute enacted a quarter-century earlier to make it once more effective, and it firmly established the Lord Chamberlain's authority by giving it the force of law. The act made a most favorable impression on the king and apparently helped to renew his confidence in his first minister. As a result, the stability of the government, threatened at once from above and from below, was restored.

I

REGULATION OF
DRAMATIC ENTERTAINMENTS
BEFORE 1737

1

DEREGULATION OF THE THEATERS, 1729–1734

From 1660 until about 1730, theatrical activities in Britain were affected by legal restrictions and royal prerogatives that had developed more or less independently of each other. Patents granted by the Crown authorized the operation of theaters and the formation of companies; laws against vagrancy restricted the activities of players; the Lord Chamberlain exercised wide control over theaters, companies, and plays. The process of regulation was simple in theory but complex and inconsistent in practice. It was these two defects that led to its breakdown during the 1733–34 season, a year before Parliament first considered a bill to regulate theatrical activities directly.

THE LORD CHAMBERLAIN AND THE MASTER OF THE REVELS

When the theaters were reestablished after the Restoration, their operations were under the nominal control of the king's Lord Chamberlain. His authority was founded on traditions, many of them imprecisely defined. It extended directly to the management of the theaters, particularly their relationships with actors and actresses. The drama itself appears to have come under his control through another court official, the Master of the Revels, who by 1660 had become his subordinate and thereby brought the drama under his jurisdiction.

Edmund Tilney, the third Master of the Revels, seems to have been the first to exercise the power of licensing and "correcting" plays intended for public performance. The duties of his office had been generally limited to the supervision of court dramas, although in 1574 the queen's patent to the Earl of Leicester's players required their plays to be "seen and allowed" by the Master of the Revels as a condition of their public performance in London.[1] After Tilney's appointment in 1579 and his authorization to license plays for public performance in 1581, moreover, the Master of the Revels seems regularly to have reviewed plays prior to their performance, ordered revisions or excisions, and signed the manuscripts of plays to indicate his

9

approval. At the same time, however, other authorities, including municipal officers of towns, justices of the peace, the Lord Mayor of London, and even the Lord Chamberlain, could intervene to control or prohibit the performance of plays.[2]

From 1610, when Sir George Buck assumed the post on the death of Tilney, his uncle, until 1623, the authority of the Master of the Revels declined, although his fee for licensing rose to £1 for each play. Buck's successor, Sir Henry Herbert, however, not only demanded (and received) up to £4 as his fee, but also claimed the right to license plays, and occasionally books of verse, for publication.[3] This additional authority (which was recognized after the Restoration but which apparently fell into disuse in 1663, when Herbert turned the post over to deputies) was based on the application of statute law, not on royal prerogative exercised by patent. The Printing Acts constituted the Company of Stationers as a publishing monopoly, and it in turn agreed to print only those plays and other dramatic entertainments that had been approved for publication by the Master of the Revels. When the last Printing Act expired in 1694, the legal basis on which the Lord Chamberlain and the Master of the Revels could regulate the publication of plays disappeared.[4]

After the Restoration the authority of the Master of the Revels, and of the Lord Chamberlain more generally, to regulate the content of plays was repeatedly and often successfully called into question. Herbert was reappointed as master by Charles II, but almost immediately his power to license plays for performance was threatened by the patents the king granted to Thomas Killigrew and Sir William Davenant, which authorized them to act as censors of plays performed by their companies. The Lord Chamberlain then ordered local officials throughout the country to suppress every play performed without a license from the Master of the Revels, and Herbert entered two lawsuits against Davenant to recover the fees he claimed were due him (and which he estimated would bring him £4,000 a year). The court decisions were inconclusive, but Killigrew apparently settled the dispute by agreeing voluntarily to pay Herbert his regular fees; in return, Herbert promised him the reversion of the office. Killigrew became Master of the Revels on Herbert's death in 1673, and Killigrew's son, Charles, in turn held the post from his death (in March 1682/83) until January 1724/25.

The close association of the stage with the court of Charles II and the continuing role of the Killigrews in theatrical management seem to have led to a neglect of the practice of submitting plays regularly to the Master of the Revels for official approval. From the time that Charles Henry Lee succeeded to the office in 1725 until the Licensing Act of 1737, the Master of the Revels seems to have exercised control only over plays that were voluntarily submitted to him by managers.[5]

This decline in the authority of the Master of the Revels was interrupted several times by his attempts, or attempts of the Lord Chamberlain or other court or government officials, to revive the practice of licensing plays for performance. Interest in official control of the drama often increased during periods of political instability. From 1678 to 1682, for example, at the time of the Popish Plot, the Lord Chamberlain acted against Lee's *Lucius Junius Brutus*, Tate's *Sicilian Usurper*, Crowne's *First Part of Henry the Sixth* and *The City Politiques*, Shadwell's *Lancashire Witches*, and Dryden's *Duke of Guise*, either by forbidding their performance or silencing them after they reached the stage. Restrictions were also enforced during the reign of James II and immediately thereafter, again coinciding with periods of political tension.[6]

After 1688, official attention began to turn to passages in plays that displayed debauchery or profanity, an emphasis that reflected rising public criticisms of the stage for its influence on contemporary manners. Although plays continued to be censored because of their political implications (the suppression of the first act of Colley Cibber's revision of *Richard III* at the turn of the century is the most famous example),[7] their immorality became a more serious concern. To insure that potentially offensive passages were suppressed in due time, the Lord Chamberlain sent messages to the theaters and to the Master of the Revels in January 1703/04 reminding them that plays were to be examined and licensed before they were given out in parts to the companies.[8]

How scrupulously these instructions were carried out thereafter has never been clearly determined.[9] In 1715, however, Richard Steele refused to submit plays to the Master of the Revels for licensing or to pay the 40s. fee he demanded for each new play acted by Steele's company at Drury Lane. When Cibber was sent to Killigrew "to enquire into the Right of his Demand, and to make an amicable End of our Dispute," the Master of the Revels was unable to support the right he claimed to license dramas except by reference to custom. From "that Time," Cibber notes, "neither our Plays, or his Fees, gave either of us any farther trouble."[10]

ROYAL PATENTS

The authority of the Lord Chamberlain to prevent, even in advance, the performance of a play, seems to have had no more basis in law than that traditionally exercised by his subordinate. Unlike the Master of the Revels, however, the Lord Chamberlain could enforce his proscriptions by imposing a variety of penalties on an uncooperative theater. His power was related to the special legal status enjoyed by the patent theaters, which simultaneously protected them in common as a theatrical monopoly and subjected them to his authority, the extent of which was vaguely defined by tradition. The history of patents before about 1730 indicates that theaters operating under them were usually required to obey the directions of the Lord Chamberlain regarding the plays they performed, their financial operations, their seating practices, and most other activities.[11]

In 1714, a patent for Drury Lane was issued to Robert Wilks, Colley Cibber, Thomas Doggett, Barton Booth, and Richard Steele, to expire three years after Steele's death, and it was under the terms of this grant that the patentees in 1715 successfully resisted demands by the Master of the Revels to review plays before their performance and to collect fees for reading them. The authority of the grant, however, proved insufficient to withstand a later challenge from the Lord Chamberlain: in 1720 the patent was revoked (apparently as a result of Steele's opposition to a bill in Parliament affecting the power to create new peers), and a new license was issued to Wilks, Cibber, and Booth.

The Drury Lane managers were not the only patentees to feel the power of the Lord Chamberlain. At about the time that Steele received his patent, John Rich had opened the renovated theater in Lincoln's Inn Fields under patents issued by Charles II to Sir William Davenant and Thomas Killigrew (one of which his father had owned, one of which he had purchased).[12] Late in 1728 the Lord Chamberlain ordered Rich not "to suffer any Play to be rehears'd upon his stage till it had been first of all supervis'd by his Grace."[13] The play Rich was about to put into rehearsal was Gay's *Polly*. Five days after it was submitted to the Duke of Grafton for his inspection, it was suppressed at the request of Sir Robert Walpole, who, according to Lord Hervey, objected to being characterized as a highwayman in the play. Although Gay turned the ban to his advantage by printing the play in the spring of 1729 and reportedly realized in subscriptions four times what he might have expected to earn by having it acted, the official prohibition effectively prevented its performance.[14]

It was clear that every company operating under a patent or license risked the imposition of a variety of sanctions, including an order silencing the theater, for failure to obey instructions from the Lord Chamberlain. These directives often stipulated players' salaries, or enjoined one manager from permitting an actor from another theater to perform on his stage,[15] and frequently limited the autonomy of the theaters for the sake of protecting and stabilizing the monopoly they shared. By prohibiting players from moving to another theater without his permission, for example, the Lord Chamberlain prevented managers from trying to outbid one another for talented actors.

With the exception of some periods, usually times of special political or moral sensitivity, enforcement of the requirement that plays be sent to the Lord Chamberlain for approval was admittedly lax. Nevertheless, it appears that managers not only obeyed (as Rich did) when they were ordered to submit plays for licensing, but sometimes sent them voluntarily to the Lord Chamberlain for his approval before their performance. Although the reasons for these apparently unpredictable variations in licensing practices are by no means clear, managers may have believed that a play that had passed the Lord Chamberlain's inspection enjoyed special legal protection.

LEGAL RESTRICTIONS ON PLAYS

Before 1737, several laws prohibited "indecent expressions" in dramatic performances (see App. A-1). Prosecutions for violations of these statutes seem to have been most frequent during periods of widespread concern over the immorality of the stage, but the laws could be invoked at any time. In the summer of 1724, for example, John Harper, Anthony Aston, and several others were indicted in the Court of King's Bench by Philip Yorke, the newly appointed attorney general, for their parts in *The Prodigal Son; or, Libertine Reclaimed*, a play that was said "to ridicule and thereby the . . . Holy Scripture to vilify and Contemn."[16] Actors, not managers or playwrights, were prosecuted whenever these laws were enforced, and for the general safety of the company, managers apparently chose to send some potentially offensive plays to the Lord Chamberlain for whatever protection his approval might afford. Despite these precautions, players were occasionally prosecuted for speaking passages in plays that had been approved by the Master of the Revels or the Lord Chamberlain: in many of those cases the accused petitioned the Crown to stay their prosecutions on that ground, but such requests were seldom honored.[17]

Official scrutiny of plays during the decade before the Licensing Act, however, had a different emphasis: it was intended primarily to prevent performances that Walpole and the ministry believed would have unfavorable political consequences. No existing laws specifically forbade the performance of plays critical of the government or even of the Crown except insofar as they might be attacks on the church. The government might—and did—act to silence politically embarrassing plays in theaters operating under royal patents or licenses, but enforcement of such bans was effective only so long as there remained a credible threat that the Lord Chamberlain could close an uncooperative theater. Seemingly the only remedy in law available to the ministry against a politically offensive play lay in the statutes against seditious libel.

According to a legal view widely accepted in 1730, "general Misrepresentations of the Government, or the State of the Nation, or mutinous Hints tending to excite Discontent and Sedition in the People" were considered seditiously libelous, and as such were punishable by harsh fines and imprisonment.[18] In a famous case in 1704, cited repeatedly as a precedent in the eighteenth century, it had been established that a "pamphlet, reflecting on the Government and asserting that its officers are corrupt, ignorant and incapable, is a libel and punishable as a crime, although no particular member of the Government and no individual officer is mentioned or referred to."[19] The Lord Chief Justice concluded that "to say that corrupt officers are appointed to administer affairs is certainly a reflection on the government. If men should not be called to account for possessing the people with an ill opinion of the government, no government can subsist."[20]

By these standards, Gay's *Beggar's Opera* and *Polly*, many of Fielding's plays, and the satires of other dramatists during the 1720s and 1730s might have been considered seditious libels. The law of libel gave little weight to transparent protestations of satirists that the literal meaning of their words was innocent: "It is a ridiculous Absurdity," observed one of the leading legal authorities of the century, "to say, That a Writing which is understood by every the meanest Capacity, cannot possibly be understood by a Judge and Jury."[21]

As a matter of practice, however, it was sometimes difficult before the Juries Act of 1730 to convict persons accused of libel on the basis of words the literal meaning of which was not defamatory, or the application of which was not immediately apparent. After the Juries Act produced "special" juries empaneled under government influence, it became easier to obtain convictions:[22] in 1738 this political reality was demonstrated by the conviction of the printer of the *Craftsman* for his involvement in producing a paper consisting largely of passages from Shakespearean plays.

The government was alert to discover and, when it deemed it advisable, to prosecute those responsible for publishing seditiously libelous matter. Walpole's government maintained a small bureaucracy inherited from earlier administrations to detect libels, determine which of them deserved action, and apprehend and prosecute those responsible. During Walpole's ministry, the system, which had continued after the Printing Acts lapsed in 1694, included two "messengers of the press" who bought copies of "all the printed Pamphlets and News Papers" published in England, noted on them when and from whom they were purchased, and delivered them to the Solicitor to the Treasury (Anthony Cracherode until the end of 1730, then Nicholas Paxton). The solicitor perused the papers and observed "upon them to his Maj^ty Secretarys of State when the King or Governm^t are traduced or Slandred thereby."[23] It was not directly to the secretaries of state that the Treasury solicitor delivered his opinion, but rather to the Duke of Newcastle's under secretary, Charles Delafaye, who played a significant role in all government matters relating to Jacobitism. (After 1734, opinions went to his successor, Andrew Stone.)[24] After consultation with the attorney general, one of the secretaries of state would issue a warrant for the arrest of the author, printer, or publisher of the material, or, when these persons could not be identified, a general warrant for the arrest of anyone who might be discovered to have had a hand in it. This procedure was sometimes used against persons whom the government had no expectation of convicting, or even of bringing to trial, but who would be put to the trouble and expense of bonds and sureties after their arrest.[25] Yet there seems to be no evidence that any dramatic performance was ever prosecuted under the libel laws. The explanation may lie in the difficulty the government would be likely to encounter in proving publication, an essential part of the charge of libel. Unless the prosecution was able to obtain the actors' parts or "sides," it would presumably be unable to secure a conviction. Spoken words by themselves could constitute little more than slander, an offense that fell far short of libel and for which it was far more difficult to win a conviction.[26]

For whatever reason, dramatic performances seem never to have come under prosecution for seditious libel, even at a time when many were more defamatory than the newspapers and pamphlets that were being effectively prosecuted on that charge.[27] Instead, the government employed another legal device to counter attacks from the stage.

VAGRANCY LAWS

Until about 1730, the Lord Chamberlain seems to have been able to use the threat of closing a theater to enforce bans on the performance of certain plays. This threat extended only to the patent companies, whose authority to act derived from a royal grant and whose activities were therefore subject to the nominal control of the Crown, and to the practical control of the ministry.

During the 1729–30 theatrical season, however, circumstances arose that diminished the credibility of that threat. At the end of September 1729, Thomas Odell announced that he intended to open a new theater in Ayliffe Street in Goodman's Fields and was "obtaining Letters Patents" for that purpose. Early in October the venture, which at first had seemed to attract little comment, met with the sort of opposition that was to become increasingly common during the next decade:

Great Numbers of Gentlemen and substantial Merchants and Tradesmen, residing in and near the said Street, . . . applied to His Majesty's
Justices of the Peace, acting for the Division of the Tower . . ., and set
forth to them the Evil Consequences that will necessarily attend the
Carrying on such a Design. The Justices . . . were so thoroughly
convinced, that the Erecting the said Theatre . . . will draw away
Tradesmens Servants and others from their lawful Callings, and corrupt
their Manners, and also occasion great Numbers of loose, idle, and
disorderly Persons, as Street-Robbers, and common Night-Walkers, so
to infest the Streets, that it will be very dangerous for His Majesty's
Subjects to pass the same, . . . [that they] ordered Caveats to be enter'd in
the proper Offices, to prevent the Gentlemen obtaining Letters Patents
for Erecting the said Theater.

Despite this opposition, Odell opened the theater on 31 October, and
performances continued in the face of growing criticism during the winter.[28]

Finally, on 28 April 1730, the City of London (which itself had no jurisdiction over the district where the theater was located) petitioned the king "to
give . . . Orders for the Suppressing an Evil of so Dangerous a
Consequence."[29] The king's response was immediate. In an order dated the
same day, the Lord Chamberlain, Charles Fitzroy, the Duke of Grafton,
wrote to Odell: "In Obedience to His Majesty's commands I do, by Vertue of
my Office of Chamberlain of His Majesty's Household Silence and Strictly
Charge you, or any Person, or Persons listed in your Service not to presume
to Act or Represent any Comedies Tragedies or other Theatrical performances for the future, as you will answer ye contrary at your Peril."[30] The
manager visited court the next day and appealed to the king for permission
to continue performances, but to no avail.[31]

For nearly two weeks the playhouse in Goodman's Fields was silent.
Then, acting on the advice of his attorneys, Odell reopened the theater on
11 May, played for the rest of the season, resumed operations on 16
September, and continued to offer performances regularly during the
1730–31 season.[32] Odell's "peril" proved to have been little more than an
empty threat by the Lord Chamberlain. If a manager wished to operate a
theater without the sanction of letters patent, and even under the disapproval of the Lord Chamberlain, there was no remedy at law available to the
Crown or to others who opposed him.

Odell's theater may not have been the first to operate independently of
permission granted by the Crown. In the last days of 1720, John Potter
opened a new theater in the Haymarket, and although it was said about a
year later that it was operating under a patent "obtain'd in the late Reign for
twenty Years, nine of which are already elapsed," no record of such a grant

has been discovered.[33] For most of the decade, however, Potter's theater was used by foreign companies and loosely organized English groups, and then only intermittently. While it operated in this fashion, the house seems to have been tolerated by the patent companies, whose common monopoly it did not seriously threaten, and by the residents living in the new neighborhoods to the west of London. The Little Theatre in the Haymarket did not make a significant mark on the theatrical life of the capital until the spring of 1730, when from the end of April until well into June it offered two of Fielding's most successful plays, *The Author's Farce* and *Tom Thumb*.[34]

In 1732, about the time that the Haymarket's "patent" would have expired, Potter insisted that Walter Aston have his play *The Restauration of King Charles II* approved by "a Gentleman of the *Treasury*, and another of the *Exchequer*" before it could be performed; Aston instead consulted "a particular Friend of the aforementioned Gentlemen." A newspaper account of 20 May 1732 reported the problem that then arose: the play "contain'd some Expressions which several of His Majesty's Justices of the Peace thought too scurrilous to be represented on the Stage, and in order to stifle the Performance of a Thing that carried with it such an evil Tendency they proposed to have issued out Warrants for taking up all the Players, upon which it was laid aside."[35]

Potter's caution was the result of similar warrants issued against his company during the summer of 1731 that effectively closed it until mid-February 1731/32. The government had acted to stop the production of a play or plays it considered seditious, but it had proceeded neither through the Lord Chamberlain's office nor through prosecutions under the libel laws. Instead, it had directed its attack against the actors themselves under the provisions of a law dealing with vagrancy passed in the last year of Queen Anne's reign. The actors apparently escaped only by abandoning the theater after learning of a warrant issued for their arrest: the ministry's strategy was successful even though no prosecutions ensued.

The plays involved in 1731 were *The Fall of Mortimer* (usually attributed to William Hatchett) and perhaps Fielding's *Welsh Opera*, later revised as *The Grub-Street Opera*. *The Fall of Mortimer*, a revival of an old tragedy, used the parallel history of Edward III to attack Robert Walpole (Mortimer) and his "Brother-Devil" Horatio for conspiring with the queen to dupe the king and bleed the country for their personal gain.[36] It had its premiere on 12 May and was joined after a week by Fielding's *Welsh Opera*, in which Squire Apshinken, intimidated throughout the play by his wife, who manages the house and servants; their troublesome (and probably impotent) son, Owen; and Robin, the butler, ridiculed respectively the king, queen, Prince of Wales, and Robert Walpole. The revision, *The Grub-Street Opera*, was promised for 11 June but was never performed: most historians contend that it was "suppressed," although convincing evidence for that conclusion has never been presented.[37]

The main play, however, provoked the authorities to action. By 24 June the players at the Haymarket had "been forbid acting any more *The Fall of Mortimer*," and on 7 July the Middlesex grand jury delivered a presentment to the Court of King's Bench, finding the recently published version of the play to be "a false, infamous, scandalous, seditious, and treasonable libel, written, acted, printed, and published, against the peace of our Sovereign Lord the King, his crown and dignity."[38]

It was not under this presentment, however, that the government proceeded against the Haymarket company, which still continued to perform the play. During the evening on Tuesday, 20 July, the night before another performance was scheduled, the justices of Westminster "met to consider of the Act of Parliament of the 12: of the late Queen in order to suppress the New Theatre in the Hay-Market." The statute (12 Anne 2, ch. 23) was titled "An Act for reducing the Laws relating to Rogues, Vagabonds, Sturdy Beggars and Vagrants, into One Act of Parliament; and for the more effectual punishing such Rogues, Vagabonds, Sturdy Beggars and Vagrants, and sending them wither they ought to be sent."[39] Like its predecessors, the 1714 act defined a wide variety of persons, including "Common Players of Interludes," as "Rogues and Vagabonds" subject to arrest, whippings, and commitment to hard labor in a house of correction. It was the latest in a long series of vagrancy acts that had been designed at least in part to prevent the acting of stage plays by "unauthorized" performers (see App. A-2). During the reign of Elizabeth the protection of a nobleman had made members of his company immune from prosecution under such acts. After 1660 the king's patents had granted similar immunity: without such protection any person acting in a dramatic performance might be arrested as a vagrant or a beggar. It is almost certainly this legal principle that lay behind Gay's characterization of the author of his most famous play.[40]

The practical application of the law was open to question, however. While the definition in the statute seemed simple on its face, it actually assumed that actors were vagrants, vagabonds, and beggars, "wandering abroad" from place to place without any fixed residence or lawful occupation. A member of a London theatrical company might be considered a common player of interludes and at the same time be an established resident in a particular neighborhood of the capital. In fact, according to Nicholas Paxton's letter to Walpole describing the meeting on 20 July, one of the justices considering action against members of the Haymarket company concluded that the law did not apply to them and immediately left the meeting. But the other justices had no such reservations and "granted a Warrant for apprehending the several Players ag[t] whom Information was given, who were all those that acted in the Fall of Mortimer."

On Wednesday morning the warrant was given to the high constable of Westminster, who went with a posse to the playhouse twice that day but was unable to find any of the actors. The Treasury solicitor, however, was still confident that "some of those Fellows will soon be taken and handled as they deserve." The government appears to have been vitally concerned in the matter: Paxton closed his letter with the request that Walpole "communicate this to his Grace [the Duke of Newcastle] and likewise my Lord Harrington [the other secretary of state], who was very desirous of knowing what was done before he went out of Town."[41]

The solicitor continued to harass the Little Theatre in the Haymarket by sending men, armed with the warrant, to seize the actors during other performances. As Paxton reported to the Commissioners of the Treasury in October, these efforts had put him "at great Expense in suppressing the New Play house in the Hay Market on Acco[t] of some most seditious Plays Acted & attempted to be acted there."[42] Again on Friday, 20 August, for example, constables of Middlesex and Westminster tried to apprehend members of the company at a performance of Samuel Johnson's innocuous—if not nonsensical—*Hurlothrumbo*, but the players again escaped.[43] The government appears to have taken no interest in Johnson's play itself, and was instead retaliating for plays the theater had offered earlier in the summer by making it impossible for it to continue to operate.[44] The campaign against the theater seems to have been a success, at least temporarily.

The effectiveness of this law as an instrument of censorship was soon destroyed by legal action from another quarter. While the government was content to harass the Little Theatre in the Haymarket in order to prevent the performance of certain kinds of plays, the patentees at Drury Lane, together with Rich (who had recently moved his company to the new theater in Covent Garden), prosecuted actors at the Haymarket under the same law with the avowed intention of protecting their traditional monopoly.

During 1732, Wilks, Cibber, and Booth had applied for a renewal of their patent at Drury Lane. Although Rich challenged their request in Chancery, new letters patent, to take effect on 1 September, were drawn up on 28 April and passed the Privy Seal on 3 July.[45] Before the patent took effect, however, the management of the theater was reorganized,[46] and by May 1733 John Highmore, "a wealthy young gentleman with theatrical propensities" but evidently little managerial capacity, owned a one-half share in the patent; Mary Wilks, the widow of Robert Wilks, and her agent, John Ellys, controlled one-third; and Hester Booth, Barton Booth's widow, owned one-sixth.[47] Management of the theater was complicated by the fact that none of the patentees had a legal interest in the ownership of the theater building itself. In May 1733 Theophilus Cibber, the actor, persuaded a majority of the leaseholders of the building to sublet Drury Lane to him and nine others (eight of whom were also actors there) for fifteen years, at a rent of £4 4s. for each acting night. When the band of actors, led by the young Cibber, attempted to take possession of the theater on 26 May, the patentees locked them out. Cibber and most of the company played at Bartholomew Fair during the summer, and then began the regular season at the Little Theatre in the Haymarket on 26 September.[48]

A series of legal maneuvers followed. Cibber and his company began ejectment proceedings against the Drury Lane patentees (who were represented by none other than Nicholas Paxton, Walpole's Solicitor to the Treasury), while Highmore brought action against the players at the Haymarket under the vagrancy act for performing without a patent. Cibber's suit was successful: on 13 November 1733 Yorke, who had been appointed chief justice of the Court of King's Bench two weeks earlier, ruled against the patentees and ordered them to surrender Drury Lane Theatre to Cibber and the other parties to the sublease.[49]

Meanwhile, Highmore had been attempting unsuccessfully to force the rebelling company back to Drury Lane under his terms. At first, he had sought to persuade the Lord Chamberlain to intervene, "as in former Days, to support the King's Patent," but after several weeks spent in "Levee-haunting, . . . [h]e was told at last, he could have no Aid from that Quarter, and that he must apply to the Law for the Support of his Patent; and by Way of Comfort, a Hint, at the same Time was given him that the *Act against Vagrants* would effectually serve him!"[50] Before undertaking legal action, Highmore, with John Rich, wrote to the actors at the Haymarket threatening "to proceed in such a manner as the law directs" if they continued to perform there. Theophilus Cibber replied that "he had been advised that his action was legal, that he knew it to be reasonable, and that he declined to change his present condition for servitude."[51]

The patentees then moved quickly—and, as the event proved, hastily. Rich and Highmore issued summonses to John Mills and Henry Giffard to appear before Sir Thomas Clarges, a justice of the peace for Middlesex, to answer a charge of vagrancy under the act of Queen Anne for performing without a patent. The suit offered a way for the plaintiffs to make the legality of nonpatent theaters itself a judicable issue. The case was argued on 5 November, but the justices (for reasons that are not clear, but which probably had something to do with Giffard's status as the new owner of one-sixth of the Drury Lane patent) dismissed it when they could not be satisfied of the validity of the summonses.[52]

A week later, on 12 November, Highmore had John Harper, one of the principal actors at the Haymarket, arrested on a charge of vagrancy. He was immediately committed by Clarges to Bridewell, to be put at hard labor. The case was heard on 20 November in the Court of King's Bench. Against the charge of vagrancy Harper's attorneys offered the defense that "the Act applied only to players *wandering* abroad. He was a freeholder in Surrey, and had a house in Westminster valued at 50*l*."[53] Highmore's attorneys argued that the circumstance of being a "housekeeper" resident in Westminster was immaterial to the application of the act in respect to actors, and "that it was in the Power of the greatest Subject in *England* to be guilty of an Action of Vagrancy; and that the only Point to be disputed there was, whether *Harper*'s performing in the *Haymarket* Theatre was committing that Act?"[54]

Harper was then released on his own recognizance. When the issue came to trial (evidently on 28 November), Yorke, who had a decade earlier prosecuted the same actor in the same court for using profanity on stage, found in his favor and dismissed the case. Harper was "conducted through . . . [Westminster] Hall, amidst the triumphant Acclamations of his theatric Friends."[55]

Highmore had been defeated on all sides. On 24 January 1733/34 Charles Fleetwood purchased his share of the patent for £2,250 and Mary Wilks' for £1,500, thereby acquiring five-sixths of the patent.[56] The new manager negotiated with the company, the actors returned to Drury Lane on 8 March, and the united company gave its first performance four days later.

The act that had once seemed a scourge to dissuade theaters from performing plays inimical to the government and to enforce a monopoly established by custom was defeated, at least in its application to the London theaters, by Harper's acquittal. Players and managers were quick to realize the implications of Yorke's decision: nonpatent theaters could no longer be effectively regulated by recourse to existing vagrancy statutes. While Giffard's company at Goodman's Fields continued "playing against all the Opposition that could be made to it, against the Power of the City of *London*, and even their Remonstrances to the Court that it was a Nusance . . ., it was not then [i.e., after Harper's trial] thought in the Power of the Crown to suppress a Playhouse, though acting without Royal Licence and Permission, because it was not evidently an illegal Thing."[57]

The outcome of Harper's case was the most important legal factor in the series of events that led to the passage of the Licensing Act. Yorke's decision destroyed the foundation on which the monopolistic theatrical patent system and the government's system of regulating the drama rested. The last legal obstacle to independent theaters had been removed, and with it went the only legal obstacle to the performance of seditious plays. Not surprisingly, when the ministry finally moved to suppress the political satires that were filling the theaters three seasons later, the new law it proposed took the form of an amendment to the same vagrancy act that Yorke's decision had nullified.

After the return of Cibber's company to Drury Lane, an uncertain equilibrium developed among the London theaters. Drury Lane and Covent Garden continued to be the strongest houses, but the power of their managers was held in check by the possibility that their actors could leave for another theater. The way remained open for the creation of new theaters, which could attract players from the established houses. Such a possibility caused apprehension not only among theatrical managers but among the London authorities and residents who disapproved of playhouses, existing or contemplated, and who now had no legal means to oppose them. Pressure mounted immediately for new controls: during the next theatrical season Parliament considered, and almost passed, a bill to regulate the theaters.

2

THE BILL TO RESTRAIN THE
NUMBER OF PLAYHOUSES, 1735

By the mid-1730s it was clear that traditional methods of regulation of the theaters were no longer effective. The decline in official control was accompanied by a rise in public criticism of theaters and plays. Charges of immorality against the drama, of the unhealthy effects of theaters on their neighborhoods, and of the corruption of the London lower classes by these two influences reflected a growing uneasiness at the unchecked proliferation of theaters. Since the direct authority of the Crown and the indirect authority of the law courts had failed to curb the spread of playhouses in and near London, and since the powers of the Lord Chamberlain and the Master of the Revels had declined to the point that even ritual regulations could be ignored with impunity, the problem of the theaters became, almost by default, a matter of parliamentary concern.

In these circumstances it is not surprising to find a report that the House of Commons took up the question of regulation of the theaters late in the spring of 1733. The only first-hand account of this action appears in a letter from Charles Howard, an administration member from Carlisle, to Lord Carlisle:

> Col. the Hon. Charles Howard to [Lord Carlisle].
>
> [1733,] May 24. —I send you the list Mr. Brougham has drawn out for the Commission of Peace. . . . The Princess's jointure of fifty thousand pounds came into the House of Commons, and a Bill to regulate the Playhouses read the first time; a debate of about two hours upon it, but no Division. Never was there more occasion for it sure than at present, for the Stage is scurrilous to the last degree.[1]

Since publication of the letter in 1897, this two-hour debate has been cited repeatedly as the first parliamentary move in a campaign that culminated in passage of the Licensing Act in 1737,[2] but the absence of evidence to corroborate the information in the letter makes it open to suspicion. The *Journals of the House of Commons*, for example, which scrupulously record every stage of every bill considered by the House, mention none concerning the theaters in the spring of 1733.

Apparently on the basis of Howard's reference to the "Princess's join-ture," the Historical Manuscripts Commission editor added the year "1733" to the date in the manuscript because he thought Parliament had voted money for the Princess Royal on the occasion of her marriage to the Prince of Orange in the spring of 1733. The royal marriage, however, was per-formed on 14 March 1733/34. Parliament took up the bill(later 7 Geo. II, ch. 13) to provide for the Princess Royal, not on 24 May 1733, but on 8 April 1734; and the measure called for an annuity of £5,000, not a jointure of £50,000.[3] Moreover, the assignment of the letter to the year 1733 is inconsis-tent with the status indicated for its author, since it was not until 1734 that Howard, after repeated applications, was appointed to the rank of colonel as an aide-de-camp to the king.[4]

From internal evidence it appears that his letter must have been written in 1737, not 1733. The "Princess's jointure" to which it refers is "a Bill for enabling his Majesty to settle a Revenue for supporting the Dignity of her Royal Highness the Princess, in case she shall survive His Royal Highness the Prince, of *Wales*" (later 10 Geo. II, ch. 29), a jointure of £50,000. It was ordered in the House on 24 May 1737, the day on which the bill that was to become the Licensing Act had its first reading.[5]

ORIGINS OF THE PLAYHOUSE BILL

Parliament did not consider legislation dealing with the theaters until 1735, when Sir John Barnard, an independent member from London who had led the efforts to defeat Walpole's excise bill in 1733 and who had for some time been especially concerned with the interests of small merchants and trades-men in London, introduced a bill to limit the number of playhouses. His call for a new law reflected the increasing hostility among many citizens to existing theaters and was proposed in reaction to an announcement of the imminent appearance of yet another playhouse in London.

Public criticism of the stage in 1735 continued to involve the issues of immorality, violence, and the decay of neighborhoods that had provoked antitheatrical sentiment in the late 1720s and to focus on the same target, the theater in Goodman's Fields. Moral decay in society was still attributed to the influence of the drama: Arthur Bedford's sermon, for example, which had so thoroughly examined "The Evil and Mischief of Stage-Playing" in 1729, was reprinted without change late in March or early in April 1735.[6] Playhouses were also accused of bringing higher rents, liquor, and prostitu-tion into their neighborhoods. Sir John Hawkins described the process of decline in the area near the theater in Goodman's Fields: "Its contiguity to the city, soon made it a place of great resort, and what was apprehended

Library
I.U.P.
diana, Pa

344.42097 L625l
c. 1

from the advertisement of plays to be exhibited in that quarter of the town, soon followed: the adjacent houses became taverns, in name, but in truth they were houses of lewd resort . . . ; and the former occupiers of them, useful manufacturers and industrious artificers, were driven to seek elsewhere for a residence."[7]

During the month in which Parliament was considering Barnard's theater bill, the *Universal Spectator, and Weekly Journal* presented a similar analysis of the effects of the theaters on their neighborhoods:

> What will ensue from *new Play-houses* being erected may be seen by that at *Goodman's-Fields*: The Street were [sic] it is built used formerly to be inhabited by *Silk-Throwsters, Riband-Weavers*, and others whose *Trades* employ'd the *industrious Poor*; immediately on setting up this *Play-house*, the Rents of the Houses were raised, as the Landlords could then lett them to more *profitable* Tenants, and now there is a *Bunch* of *Grapes* hanging almost at *every Door*, besides an adjacent *Bagnio* or two; an undoubted Proof that *Innocence* and *Morality* are not the certain Consequences of a *Play-house*.[8]

Physical and economic symptoms of the spiritual pollution they allegedly spread became an important element in attacks against the theaters in the mid-thirties, when there were frequent efforts to correct problems of crime and urban decay in London. The increase in public awareness of the need to rehabilitate certain neighborhoods and to prevent the decline of others gave impetus to the more specific, and therefore more effective, alarms raised against the playhouses.

Areas near other theaters displayed conditions even more appalling than those the *Universal Spectator* had decried in Goodman's Fields. The streets around the two patent houses, for example, were notorious. Commenting in April 1735 on the charge that the theaters were "the great Resort of Lewd Women," Samuel Richardson contended that the description was entirely justified

> if we consider what the Play-houses in *Drury-Lane* and *Covent-Garden* have done for their adjacent Neighbourhoods. The *Hundreds of Drury*, the *Covent-Garden Gout, &c.* are common Observations, in every one's Mouth, upon the Iniquities of those Places. *Salisbury Court, Fleet-street*, when the Playhouse was there, had hardly a Tenement unoccupied by Inhabitants of this Class; and on its Remove, this Sort of Gentry have also removed, and the Place has as reputable Inhabitants as any other Part of the City.[9]

Violence was becoming a problem for the theaters themselves as personal safety and morality were put in equal peril in their neighborhoods. Lacy Ryan, an actor and Rich's play-producer at Covent Garden, for example, was so badly injured in an attack by street robbers on 16 March 1734/35 that he had to give up his roles for a time.[10]

Assaults also occasionally occurred within the theaters. On the evening of 8 February 1734/35, a riot erupted in the King's Theatre in the Haymarket, in the presence of the king and queen, "occasion'd by the Footmen's coming into the Passages with their lighted Flambeaux, which gave Offence to the Ladies, &c. in the House; whereupon the Footmen were order'd out, but they refus'd to go, and attack'd the Centinels, but a stronger Guard coming to their Assistance, with their Bayonets fix'd, drove them out; in the Fray one of the Footmen was stabb'd in the Groin, and in the Body, and its thought will die of the Wounds."[11] Even dramatic performances could provoke violence, as many a playwright made it a practice to send his friends to the theater, "ready with their hands and sticks, to support his Muse in case her charms should prove insufficient. . . . The consequence of this is, the house is filled with uproar, and the play not heard as it ought to be."[12]

But disorders in and near the theaters were not the most important issue for opponents of the playhouses. Instead, complaints of violence, immorality, and neighborhood decay became subordinate parts of an argument for increased public control of the theaters aimed at correcting their immediate and direct economic effects. The mischief of the drama threatened trade as much as body or soul, and the protection of all three became the crusade of those who advocated new controls on the theaters. Just as it had in the autumn of 1729, this focus provided a rallying point for tradesmen and merchants opposed to another new theater in London.

Bedford had included "Idleness" in his list of "particular Vices" encouraged by the stage, and it was this threat to industry more than any other single factor that provoked attacks on the theaters in 1735. Critics alleged that the increasing number of playhouses was making it impossible to maintain a climate in which apprentices and clerks could work. After several reports of plans for a new theater had appeared in the newspapers, *Hooker's Weekly Miscellany* (8 March 1734/35) published "A Letter humbly offered to the trading Citizens of London," which objected to the erection of another theater because "with us, whose trade is the support of this opulent city, it must be very detrimental, by too much taking off the thoughts of our youth from business, and planting in their green minds luxury and debauchery."[13] Barnard had been actively concerned about the pernicious effects of the drama on trade, and especially on London apprentices, before 1735. Hawkins reports that after the opening of Odell's theater,

> the merchants of London, then a grave sagacious body of men, found that it was a temptation to idleness and to pleasure that their clerks could not resist: they regretted to see the corruptions of Covent-garden extended, and the seats of industry hold forth allurements to vice and

debauchery. The principal of these was Sir John Barnard, a wise and venerable man, and a good citizen: he, as a magistrate, had for some time been watching for such information as would bring the actors at Goodman's-fields playhouse within the reach of the vagrant laws; but none was laid before him that he could, with prudence, act upon.[14]

The immediate occasion for raising the matter of the theaters in Parliament early in March 1734/35 appears to have been the project for erecting, by subscription, a new theater in St. Martins le Grand. A proposal for the new house was advertised in the *Daily Courant* on 6 January 1732/33, with the claim that £1,500 had already been subscribed: the notice was repeated in an advertisement in the *Daily Post* on 21 February 1734/35. These notices directed interested subscribers to communicate with "A. B." by leaving a letter at St. Dunstan's coffeehouse in Fleet Street, in reply to which they would receive particular information about the proposal.[15]

Evidently nothing came of this somewhat mysterious proposal except Barnard's bill. In fact, soon after the playhouse bill had been dismissed in Parliament, Aaron Hill insinuated that the advertisements for the new playhouse had been nothing but a provocation deliberately fabricated to inspire government action in the patentees' interests:

> I will not undertake for the truth of a report which yet seems likely enough to deserve the credit it meets with among thinking men—that the advertisement concerning a design to build, by subscription, a new theatre, near the heart of the city, was a manager's stratagem to alarm and incense its magistrates, and pave the way for success of his own modest purpose to establish his throne (and that of his brother monarch) in the Empire of Nonsense, by a Parliamentary exclusion of all other pretenders.[16]

It is impossible to say how much credit should be given to Hill's suspicions. (If the announcement was simply a maneuver by one of the patentees, however, there are some grounds for believing that it was executed with Walpole's connivance. It may not be merely coincidental that the first notice of the new theater appeared in the *Daily Courant*, one of the papers closely associated with, and secretly subsidized by, the government until June 1735, when it merged with the *London Journal* and the *Free Briton* in a new publication supporting the ministry, the *Daily Gazetteer*.)[17] Whether the proposal for a new theater was legitimate or a ruse of one of the patentees, it provided a sufficient incentive for Barnard to introduce the issue of the theaters in Parliament.

On Wednesday, 5 March 1734/35, Barnard rose in the House of Commons to ask for new, more effective regulation of the theaters. He emphasized "the Mischief done to the City of London by the Play-Houses, in corrupting the Youth, encouraging Vice and Debauchery, and being prejudicial to Trade and Industry; and how much these Evils would be increas'd, if another Play-House should be built in the very Heart of the City."[18] Many in the House "seem'd to smile" at Barnard's speech, and "at first, it seem'd to be receiv'd with a Sort of Disdain," but it was supported by several members, most of them associated with the Opposition, and "at length . . . it was spoke for both by Young and Old."[19] His motion for leave to bring in a bill dealing with the theaters was seconded by Samuel Sandys, who had followed Pulteney into Opposition in 1725 and was at this time Pulteney's closest associate. Others who spoke in support of the motion included Sir Thomas Saunderson, another Opposition member; and the Master of the Rolls, Sir Joseph Jekyll, an independent; as well as Pulteney himself.

James Erskine, the brother of Lord Mar (who had led the rebellion in 1715), also argued in favor of the motion, decrying the increase in the number of playhouses as a threat to the national character:

> It is no less surprizing than shameful, to see so great a Change for the worse in the Temper and Inclinations of the *British* Nation; which, tho' chearful and facetious formerly, yet was sedate and solid; but now so extravagantly addicted to lewd and idle Diversions, that the Number of Play-Houses in *London* was double to that at *Paris*; so that now we exceed in Levity our fluttering, fiddling Masters the *French*, from whom we had learned these and many other Impertinencies, as much unsuitable to the Mein and Manner of an *English* or *Scotchman*, as they were agreeable to the Air and Lightness of a Monsieur. It is astonishing . . . to all *Europe*, that *Italian* Eunuchs and Signora's should have set Salaries equal to those of the Lords of the Treasury and Judges of *England*, besides the vast Gains which these Animals make by Presents, by Benefit Nights, and by performing in private Houses; so that they carry away with them Sums sufficient to purchase Estates in their own Country, where their Wisdom for it is as much esteem'd, as our Vanity and foolish Extravagance, laugh'd at and despis'd.[20]

Erskine's speech hit squarely at the evils of idleness and social depravity generally attributed to the theaters. The target of his attack on the French was probably the company then performing at the Haymarket on Wednesdays and Fridays, in contempt of the traditional ban on dramatic plays on those days in Lent. His irritation at the "Gains" of Italian eunuchs was almost certainly a reference to Farinelli's income, estimated to have been £4,000 in 1735, and specifically to a benefit for the singer set for 15 March at which it was estimated about £2,000 was raised.[21]

Despite the reports that Barnard's motion was ridiculed, there is no record of anyone speaking against it, and the official journal of the House shows that leave was given *nemine contradicente* to bring in a bill to control the theaters. Moreover, although the debate seems to have focused exclusively on the need to limit the number of theaters in London, the unanimous consent of the House was given "to bring in a Bill or Bills for restraining the Number of Houses for playing of Interludes, and for the better regulating common Players of Interludes."[22] At this point, therefore, it appears that there was no opposition to the idea of increased controls over either the number of theaters or the activities of their players. In fact, when the bill was introduced in the House nearly a month later, one of its most important provisions made players at nonpatent theaters and, for the first time, their managers as well liable to prosecution as vagrants.

On the basis of published reports of the debate, it appears that those members who spoke for Barnard's motion were nearly all associated with the Opposition. The notable exception was Sir Robert Walpole himself, who "warmly supported" the motion.[23] When the committee was selected to prepare and bring in the bill, however, several members from both sides of the House were included. The committee consisted of a dozen members: "Sir *John Barnard*, the Master of the Rolls [Sir Joseph Jekyll], Mr. Chancellor of the Exchequer [Sir Robert Walpole], Sir *Thomas Sanderson*, Mr. *Sandys*, Mr. *Pulteney*, Sir *Edward Stanley*, Mr. *Talbot*, Mr. *Erskine*, Mr. Attorney-General [Sir John Willes], Mr. Solicitor-General [Dudley Ryder], and the Lord *Gage*."[24] Many of those named had spoken in debate in favor of the bill. Among the others, Stanley was an Opposition member from Lancashire, Willes was one of Walpole's allies and Gage one of Newcastle's, and the Honorable John Talbot of Lincoln's Inn was an Old Whig who consistently supported the ministry.[25] In view of the political diversity represented by the committee, and in view of the unusual unanimity of the House in ordering the bill brought in, it would be unreasonable to assume that Barnard's bill was initially a partisan or controversial parliamentary issue.[26]

What is less clear, however, is whether Barnard's measure was considered at this stage to be a public or a private bill—that is, whether it represented official government policy or not. The bill seems to have been written originally as a private measure, since it contained a clause declaring "that this Act shall be deemed a publick Act," a formula that, paradoxically, is never found in public bills.[27] But the manner in which the bill was introduced strongly suggests that it was being treated as a public measure. All available records agree that Barnard's motion on 5 March was made on his own initiative, a procedure which would have violated the standing order of the House that required each private bill to be brought in, not by motion, but by a petition signed by the suitors for the bill. The petition had to be presented in three stages, each marked by a formal question to the House.[28] There is no record that any part of this procedure, required for all private bills, was followed in the case of the theater bill. Two other points in the progress of the bill in the House also suggest that it was not treated as a private bill but, rather, as an expression of government policy. According to a standing order of the House of 12 November 1705, all private bills had to be printed and copies distributed to members before first reading. The special order on 3 April, *after* its first reading, that Barnard's bill be printed indicates that it was not being handled routinely as private legislation at that stage.[29] More significant may be the fact that while one full week's public notice, posted in the House lobby, was required between the second reading of a private bill and the first sitting of the committee named to examine it, Barnard's bill had its second reading on 10 April and was heard first in committee four days later.[30]

Whatever its status, the presence of Walpole, the Master of the Rolls, the attorney general, and the solicitor general on the committee named to draw up the bill suggests that the government took an active interest in the terms in which it was formulated. Other evidence indicates that the role of the ministry in the drafting and sponsorship of the bill was more substantial than has hitherto been recognized.

About three weeks after the House appointed the committee to bring in the bill, the Treasury board agreed to assume the expense involved in preparing it. The meeting at which this decision was made occurred in the Treasury chambers in Whitehall on Thursday, 27 March, when Walpole and William Clayton approved payment to Nicholas Paxton for the costs involved in two parliamentary measures: "Mr Paxtons Memorial 27th March 1735 apprizing My Lords of the Expence of preparing a Bill for limiting Playhouses, and of Expences on the King's behalf on acco^t of a peticon now in the House of Lords by James Mackgill Claiming the Title of Visco^t Oxfurd and Lord Mackgill is read and agreed to."[31]

Paxton's request probably represented a charge to the government for his work in drafting the legislation. As Solicitor to the Treasury, Paxton was the officer through whom government business in the House of Commons was conducted.[32] His involvement meant that the bill to regulate the theaters was written by the man who had been in charge of the ministry's systematic scrutiny of the activities of the press for nearly a decade, and who had been intimately involved in recent attempts to suppress the Little Theatre in the Haymarket. When it was brought before the House on 3 April, the bill was still ostensibly under the sponsorship of an independent member from London, but it represented public policy to a degree that most private bills did not.

Four weeks elapsed between the time the House ordered the bill and the day of its first reading. During that interval the regulation of the theaters became the subject of frequent comment in the newspapers.

The first mention of the bill appeared in the *Daily Advertiser* of 6 March. Although very brief, the report recognized that under the measure, official control of the theaters would derive from a new source: "We hear that Sir John Barnard has offer'd a Proposal limiting the Number of Playhouses, and for putting them under the Regulaton of Parliament."[33] The last phrase was prophetic of the enthusiasm with which many parties in the controversy would recommend that Parliament, or someone it appointed, ought to become a manager of last resort for the theaters.

On Saturday, 8 March, "A Letter humbly offered to the trading Citizens of London" written by "Tradelove" appeared in *Hooker's Weekly Miscellany*.[34] The letter, dated 3 March, pointed out the temptations to vice that prevailed in theater audiences, and especially the corruption of young people that could be anticipated if a playhouse near the center of the city (and therefore more convenient to their places of employment) were to be erected as advertised. He noted the lack of success London citizens had had in petitioning against the theater in Goodman's Fields and the failure of the Crown to silence the Little Theatre in the Haymarket as evidence of the need for parliamentary intervention. In a reference to the legal problem at the center of efforts to regulate the theaters, "Tradelove" alluded unfavorably to the practice of the Haymarket of paying £10 annually in rent (scot and lot), thereby frustrating any attempts to charge its members under the vagrancy act.

In an essay in the *Prompter* on Friday, 21 March, Aaron Hill also expressed the hope that parliamentary action would restore effective regulation of the stage. Hill was skeptical, however, of reports that "the extent of the bill . . . [could] be so narrow as some people represent it." Despite the need to "restrain, with regard to *number*, the increase of corrupt and ridiculous theatres," "schools of public effeminacy and corruption," it would be far "nobler . . . to correct and new model the old" patent theaters by removing from the present managers their absolute power over theatrical affairs. Hill argued that since

> there are a few players from whose conversation a Member of Parliament would not be apprehensive that his son might gather manners and sentiments which he would not wish him to propagate, does it not amount to an inconsistency to suppose the same cautious father consenting to leave in the hands of those players [i.e., unqualified managers] the choice and direction of plays and thereby the tuition and, in some measure, formation of the noblest youths in the kingdom?

Hill was especially critical of the managers' timidity in presenting topically satiric pieces: "There are proofs without number of these people *excepting* against the most necessary and most seasonable satire, upon no nobler a foundation than their fear of disobliging people of condition and thereby reducing their audiences."

This criticism must be kept in mind in considering Hill's concluding suggestion for broadening the projected bill to include a panel of state officers to be responsible for the selection of plays: "I dare believe with whatever regret the good people of this nation look up to the increase of state officers and commissions, there would be a general concurrence for approbation of one new appointment, and since censors of the public manners were found necessary by the Roman Senate, would to Heaven as we have, already, Commissioners of Trade, we might hear of some such establishment as Commissioners of Taste also!"[35] In other words, Hill recommends a board of taste whose members would protect playwrights and the public from the current practice of censorship by cowardly theater managers. Official selection of plays in his view would mean greater, not less, freedom for the stage.

Much the same sort of general supervision of managers was the substance of one provision of an act of Parliament proposed in the *Grub-Street Journal* on 27 March: managers would be forbidden to reject good plays or to replace them with others that were supported only by influence. In addition to putting the selection of plays in the hands of the ministry, the bill suggested in the *Grub-Street Journal* would limit the number of theaters, regulate prices, allow authors to air their complaints and provide remedies for them, protect managers against excessive demands by actors, and protect actors against those by managers. A letter to the paper by "Modulus" also alludes to a threat of another players' revolt similar to the one led by Theophilus Cibber that had ended only a year earlier. The House's order for a bill to regulate the theaters, he reports, "has given a terrible panic to some of those ingenious gentlemen [i.e., players]; and to my knowledge, quashed a very hopeful scheme for the present, framed by certain fertile heads, and designed to have been played off at a proper season, by way of obliging the Town with another Theatrical Revolution, built on the same democratical principles with the former, but I assure you, on a much more solid and lasting foundation."[36]

Whatever the reliability of this report (for which there is no corroboration), a "panic" was certainly spreading among players over the anticipated effects of the bill. The wording of the House's order for the bill implied the imposition of restrictions that would be to the advantage of the patentees at the expense of other managers and of actors in general. Just how severe those restrictions would be was not clear until the provisions of the bill were made public after its first reading. At that point a deluge of petitions began pouring into the House, and corresponding "cases"—printed statements intended for distribution outside Parliament—were circulated in the city. The original issues of public morality and trade were quickly overshadowed by questions of theatrical competition and of the competence and fairness of theater managers. As a result, the House of Commons became the forum for an extensive debate on the business and labor practices of the London theaters.

Sir John Barnard presented his bill "for restraining the Number of Houses for playing of Interludes, and for the better regulating common Players of Interludes" to the House on Maundy Thursday, 3 April 1735. Although its first reading may have been timed deliberately to coincide with the end of Passion Week in order to emphasize its religious overtones, it is unlikely that the preparation of the bill had been completed much before the 27 March Treasury board meeting at which payment for Paxton's expenses was approved. For the first time in two years, however, and probably not coincidentally, no plays were staged in London during the week before Easter, although musical productions (which had been tolerated officially for some time) were performed on Tuesday, Wednesday, and Thursday at several theaters.[37]

There is no evidence that the bill was debated on its first reading: no division occurred, and there is no mention of any discussion in any of the reports of parliamentary deliberations. The simple resolution of the House, "that the Bill be read a Second time," indicates that support for the bill at this stage was certainly still general, if not unanimous, since a formal order setting a specific day for the second reading was always made in cases of bills opposed or otherwise considered of special importance.[38]

THE BILL'S PROVISIONS

On 3 April the House also directed that Barnard's bill be printed, an order that was made specifically for public bills only, since private ones were supposed to be printed before first reading according to a standing order. The three known surviving copies of the printed bill are the only reliable source of information about its provisions as they stood before the second reading (see App. B-1).[39]

The specific powers granted and restrictions imposed by each theatrical patent then in effect are enumerated in a two-page preamble to the bill. It recognizes three distinct patents, in addition to that which incorporated the Royal Academy of Music in 1731, and names the individuals in whom they were currently vested: the Killigrew and Davenant patents held by John Rich, and the patent originally granted to Wilks, Cibber, and Booth, held by Charles Fleetwood and Henry Giffard. The preamble also notes that Rich's

patents both declare that all other "Companies of Players . . . should be
silenced and suppressed, and that no Play should be acted . . . containing any
prophane, obscene or scurrilous Passage, or other Passage offensive to Piety
or good Manners." The preamble ends with the complaint that

> diverse ill-disposed and disorderly Persons, have of late taken upon
> themselves, without any legal Authority, to act and represent Tragedies,
> Comedies, Plays, Operas, and other Entertainments of the Stage . . . ; for
> which Purposes, several Theatres, Play-houses, or other Houses, have
> been erected for carrying on the same, in Defiance of the Laws of the
> Land; by Reason whereof great Mischiefs have already arisen, and much
> greater are likely to ensue, unless the same be timely prevented; and
> the Laws now in being, have been found insufficient for preventing this
> great and growing Evil.

In order to correct this situation, "and to the End that an Effectual Stop
may be put to these pernicious and illegal Practices," the bill prohibits
everyone except those in whom the existing letters patent are vested to offer
theatrical "Entertainment of the Stage, for Gain, Hire or reward." No restriction is put on free performances, but if liquor is sold on the premises the
entertainment is to be treated as one for which money is taken.

A clause later in the bill prohibits the performance of "any Tragedies,
Comedies, Operas, Plays, or other Entertainments of the Stage . . . which
shall contain any prophane, obscene, or scurrilous Passage, or any Passage
offensive to Piety, or good Manners." While the bill does not directly give
the force of law to existing letters patent, then, it does formally enact two of
their principal provisions. In addition, the bill forbids any person to "take or
receive . . . any more or greater Price [for admission] . . . than what hath
hitherto been usually and customarily taken and received for the same,
upon common and ordinary Occasions."

Suppression of unauthorized companies of players and of offensive
performances as well as the regulation of admission prices were the traditional responsibilities of the Lord Chamberlain and the Master of the Revels;
if Barnard's bill had passed, these three areas of control over the theaters
would have become instead the business of mayors, bailiffs, and other local
government officials. It is clear, despite the lacunae in the bill, that somewhat different penalties are attached to these different classes of violations.
Anyone presenting an offensive performance, for example, is to be fined
(the amount is unspecified). The bill in its printed form does not include
details of the penalty for setting unusually high admission prices; space is
left blank immediately after that prohibition to accommodate the wording
of a penalty to be formulated in committee.

Although a lacuna also follows the central prohibition against performances by companies not authorized by letters patent, the nature of the penalty is clear. This passage (like the phrase "diverse ill-disposed and disorderly Persons" in the preamble and the phrase later in the bill describing remedies against officials who fail to apprehend violators) was a standard formula from the vagrancy acts: persons offending against that provision "shall, notwithstanding any Settlement, be deemed adjudged and taken as [*blank space*]." In one of the surviving copies of the bill, a contemporary (almost certainly a member of the House) has added in this space "Rogues Vagabonds and Sturdy Beggars within the intent," part of the standard conclusion to this clause.

Despite the importance of the two clauses forbidding offensive plays and excessive admission prices, it is this prohibition, in law, against activity by persons not authorized by letters patent, and the penalty which would classify offenders as vagrants, that lie at the heart of the bill. These provisions would have overturned the court decision in the prosecution Highmore had brought against Harper by making all players except those protected by the patentees liable to the penalties for vagrancy and by completely eliminating residency as a defense. Enactment of the bill would have made continued performances at the nonpatent theaters illegal and thereby ended all independent theatrical competition.

These provisions would also have frustrated plans for another theater in St. Martins le Grand unless its sponsors could obtain new letters patent from the king. Even if he had been inclined to grant one, however, the king would have been prevented by the bill from issuing a patent for another theater, at least for the time being. The bill makes it lawful for the king to grant new patents only "whenever any of the [existing] Letters Patents shall expire or be determined, . . . so that there shall not exceed the Number of [*blank*] Theatres or Play-houses, at one and the same Time." The bill further restricts royal prerogative by limiting the still unspecified number of theaters to a certain, but also unspecified, geographical area. The context of the provision, however, stipulates that patents may be granted only for "Theaters or Playhouses . . . which shall be situate within [*blank*] thereof, and not elsewhere": in the annotated copy of the bill, the lacuna has been filled in with the phrase "the City of Westminster or the Liberties." The only exception is for the performance of plays in "any of his Majesty's Royal Palaces, during such Time as his Majesty, or any of the Royal Family shall reside therein."

Barnard's bill, then, was originally designed to fix by law the number and location of theaters, and touched upon the drama only secondarily. Houses and companies not constituted under letters patent were declared illegal, and persons violating that prohibition were to be treated as vagrants regardless of their residency. The location and number of theaters were to remain constant, since new patents could be granted only to replace those then in force and only for theaters in and near Westminster. Rich, Fleetwood, and Giffard (in his capacity as a shareholder in the Drury Lane patent, but not as the manager of the theater in Goodman's Fields, at the suppression of which Barnard's bill was directed) were guaranteed an incontestable theatrical monopoly and the full weight of the vagrancy law to enforce it. In addition, admission prices were to be stabilized; and—in the only clause aimed directly at the drama as well as the theaters—persons involved in offensive performances were to be fined. From the point of view of those opposed, for whatever reason, to the spread of theaters in and near London, the bill must have seemed an ideal solution.

The next day, Good Friday, the essay in the *Prompter* criticized the proposed restrictions on theaters. "There is a Kind of *Stupidity*," the *Prompter* said, "in the Supposition of any Prospect of *suppressing* Theatres, or indeed of any over-narrow *Restraint* of such *Diversions*, in a Country like ours, where the gloomy Dispositions of People stand so visibly in need of all the liveliest Inducements to shake off *Sourness*, and *Melancholy*. Persons who *hang*, or *drown* themselves with so natural a Propensity, should have no *Checks* to a more social Vivacity of Spirit *thrown in their Way by their Governours.*" The essay also assails the reprinting of Bedford's sermon and defends Giffard's theater in Goodman's Fields as the best managed of all the playhouses: to close it, the essay contends, would simply drive audiences, especially apprentices, to more distant theaters.[40]

Nevertheless, the first petition to Parliament relating to the bill shows wholehearted support for shutting Giffard's theater permanently. This petition is a simple restatement of the complaint against that playhouse that more than five years earlier had sparked widespread opposition to the theaters. The petition, from the "Justices of the Peace . . . and others, of the *Tower* Division" in Middlesex, was heard in the House of Commons on the Wednesday after Easter, the day before Barnard's bill came up for second reading. The petition alleges "that the Play-house, erected in *Goodman's-fields*, is a great Nusance, the Attempts to prevent the same having been hitherto ineffectual," and therefore prays that the bill under consideration will pass into law.[41] In view of Hawkins' observation that Barnard, in his capacity as a magistrate, had "for some time" been trying to find grounds for action against the theater in Goodman's Fields, and in view of the speed with which the Middlesex justices and the other petitioners brought their statement to the House, it is possible that the petition had been composed and the signers canvassed, perhaps by Barnard himself, sometime before the first reading of the bill. Although the petition was ordered to "lie upon the

Table, until the . . . Bill be read a Second time," the point after which petitions were usually received by the House,[42] it was not taken up for consideration until the crucial committee meeting of 21 April.

On Thursday, 10 April, one week after its introduction in the House, Barnard's bill had its second reading. Except for the final motion that a bill pass, this was the most important step in the progress of any bill. The second reading was the customary occasion for the main debate, if there was to be any, on the nature of the bill as a whole. Since it was considered out of order either to mount opposition to or attempt to change the principle of a bill in committee, commitment usually signified approval by the House of its basic character.[43]

According to the *Journals*, no division occurred on the second reading or on the motion to commit, and the amount of business conducted in the House that day suggests that debate, if there was any at all, must have been short: the bill was sent to a Committee of the Whole House, which was ordered to sit the following Monday morning.[44] A month after it had voted unanimously to consider a bill to regulate the theaters, the House agreed, apparently without significant objection, to the basic principle of Barnard's bill.

PUBLIC CONTROVERSY OVER THE BILL

While overt opposition to the bill within the House of Commons may have been negligible at this stage, it was growing rapidly among other groups who intended to argue their objections both publicly and in Parliament. Petitions, nearly all of them opposing the bill, began to stream into the House immediately after the bill was committed on 10 April, and cases corresponding to them were distributed in London. These petitions and cases did much more than restate long-standing arguments over the theaters. In effect, they reformulated the debate by focusing it on issues of internal theatrical economy and business practices rather than on the purported damage to public morals and to the trade and industry of society in general. Five of the eight petitions presented to the House before the bill was first considered in committee on 14 April were concerned primarily with the effects the legislation was likely to have on theatrical businesses and companies. In number and tone, this initial group of petitions accurately represented the intensity and extent of criticism that was to be raised against Barnard's bill by those who would be most directly affected by it.

Like the petition received in the House on 9 April, the three presented after the bill was committed on Thursday dealt with the theater in Goodman's Fields. The first was from twenty-three persons who had contributed to pay for the construction of Giffard's new theater there in 1731. The subscribers register no explicit complaint against the bill, but simply state that they "apprehend, That . . . their Properties may be greatly affected" by it. The House referred their petition to the consideration of the Committee of the Whole House and—in a step unusual except in cases of election bills—approved the request of the petitioners that their counsel be allowed to present oral arguments to the committee.[45] A printed case corresponding to their petition was evidently published before the bill itself came up for first reading (see App. B-2). The case expresses the subscribers' hope that anything threatening the survival of their theater would be excluded from the bill before it was introduced in the House. The tone of the case is less reserved than that of the petition because, ostensibly at least, cases were addressed to the public rather than to members of Parliament. The case emphasizes the economic basis of the subscribers' argument in language similar to that usually found in cases and petitions from merchants whose financial interests might be injured by a bill under discussion in Parliament:

> That in regard the said Subscribers are by the LAW *of the Land* entituled to, and interested in the said Theatre, and Performances therein exhibited, (nothing being there exhibited contrary to Law) they humbly presume and hope, from the Honour and Justice of Parliament, that nothing will be inserted in the said Bill, which may destroy their *Legal Right* by suppressing the said Theatre, especially inasmuch as there is no Precedent where the private Interest of any Subject has been taken away by Parliament, without an Equivalent being given for the same.[46]

Most of the subsequent petitions and cases against the theater bill contain similar arguments. Citing provisions in the bill (usually the one which would outlaw nonpatent theaters), other petitioners argue that the bill would deprive them of income to which they are legally entitled; and, like merchants threatened by bills restricting trade, they pray "that the House will grant them such Relief. as to the House shall seem meet." The subscribers to the theater in Goodman's Fields may have hoped to thwart the central purpose of the bill; when their case proved unsuccessful, they tried by petition to persuade the House directly to relax the proposed restrictions.

Henry Giffard, the manager of the theater in Goodman's Fields, also petitioned the House on 10 April, and just as it had in the case of the petition from the subscribers to the theater, the House referred his petition to the Committee of the Whole House for its consideration and authorized Giffard or his counsel to appear before it. According to Giffard (who was named in the bill itself as a privileged party), passage of the legislation would "be the utter Ruin of him and his Family" in spite of the protection it would afford to his interests in the Drury Lane patent.[47]

Unlike the subscribers' petition, Giffard's does contain one circumspect claim to a legal right which the bill threatened to abridge. His design in managing a theater in Goodman's Fields, Giffard contends, is one "which, as he conceived, and was informed, was not contrary to any Law then in being." The legality of his activity, only hinted at in his petition, forms the central issue in "The Case of Henry Giffard" that corresponds to it, in which he defends the theater in Goodman's Fields against the principal objections that had been raised against it since it opened in 1729 (see App. B-3).

He begins the case with a review of the legal question Odell had faced when the Lord Chamberlain had ordered his new theater shut in response to complaints made to the king by the Lord Mayor and the Court of Aldermen. Odell, Giffard reports, was advised by "several of the most eminent Lawyers" that he "had a *Right by the Law of the Land*, to proceed in his . . . Undertaking," and he therefore ignored the order by continuing his business ("without any *Complaint* or *Interruption*") until 1731, when he sold the theater to Giffard. Having established the legality of his activity, Giffard goes on (in words very similar to those used by the subscribers in their case) to ask for more than simply the "Relief" he seeks in his petition: "He hopes, from the Honour and Justice of Parliament, . . . that he may be protected in his *Legal Property*, and follow this his Business and Employment therein; if not, he hopes an Equivalent will be made him, as has always been done where Property has been taken away." Giffard's objection, in other words, was not so much to the principle of the bill as to the fact that its protection did not extend to his theater.

At the end of his case Giffard answers the social and economic criticisms that had inspired the attacks on his playhouse. Just as he is blatantly self-serving in his assertions that no opposition whatsoever was raised against the playhouse between 1729 and 1735, so he argues equivocally that his theater cannot be accused of exercising a pernicious influence on apprentices. "If it be suggested," Giffard remarks innocently, "that this House may be a Detriment, by Apprentices frequenting the same, the Answer, it is presumed, is obvious, That such Apprentices as will frequent Play-Houses contrary to their Master's Intentions, will not go to this House, where they may be seen either by the Masters, or some of the Master's Acquaintance; but will go to those at the other End of the Town, where they are less liable to be known."[48]

The third petition read in the House of Commons on 10 April uses a nearly identical argument in defense of the same playhouse by asserting that apprentices and servants would patronize a distant theater even if Giffard's was suppressed. The petitioners (merchants, shopkeepers, and tradesmen) go so far as to commend the local theater for its role in improving the moral character of the neighborhood. The House of Commons was not persuaded, however, and rejected their petition out of hand, probably on account of the relative triviality of the "injury" the petitioners apprehended from the bill.[49]

Two undated cases without corresponding parliamentary petitions also relate to the theater in Goodman's Fields. Both are by the players belonging to the theater, and both ask for Parliament's help in averting the economic catastrophe with which Barnard's bill threatens them.[50]

One is "The Case of the Comedians, &c. belonging to the *Theatre* in *Goodman's-Fields*, In Relation to a Bill for Restraining the Number of Play-Houses, &c."(see App. B-4). The players make no specific plea for assistance, but simply apply, "IN this *melancholly* Exigence, . . . to those HONOURABLE MEMBERS, who compose THAT AUGUST ASSEMBLY, whose *Humanity*, as well as *Justice*, may find out some *Expedient* to *relieve* those, who in such Case, have the *Certainty* of being *Undone*, and, as they conceive, without even the *Prospect* of the *least Advantage*, accruing to *any Person*." The case makes it clear that those involved in the theater had no illusion either about the real purpose of the bill or that Giffard's share in the patent granted to Wilks, Cibber, and Booth would in any way protect his own playhouse: the "*Suppression* of the *Theatre* in *Goodman's–Fields* is intended," and if that should occur, say the players, it "would absolutely deprive above 300 Persons of the *Common Necessaries* of *Life*, whose *sole Dependance* is upon the *Existence* of the *said Theatre*, not having been bred to any other Business."

The other case, "To the Honourable House of Commons. The Case of the Company of *Comedians*, belonging to the *Theatre* in *Goodman's-Fields*" (see App. B-5), proposes an alternative to the sudden unemployment they anticipate. The players "will be deprived of the Means of Life," argues the case, "unless the known *Justice* and *Humanity* of this HONOURABLE HOUSE should immediately interpose, by admitting a Clause or Clauses, for tolerating them, the present *Actors* of *Goodman's-Fields*, to Act in some of the several Counties of *England*, and thereby enable them to Support Themselves and Families, in the Manner they have hitherto done." Giffard had insinuated a request that Goodman's Fields be included in the bill as one of the authorized theaters in London, but his actors suggest only that a clause be inserted to permit them to perform somewhere else in England.

Yet another undated case for which there is no corresponding parliamentary petition complains that the bill would cause unnecessary financial hardships. In this instance, however, the complainant is John Rich, the patentee at Covent Garden and owner of Lincoln's Inn Fields, in whom both the Davenant and Killigrew patents were vested (see App. B-6). Although he, like Giffard, is protected by name in the bill, he says that he will lose the benefits from one of his two theaters (while still being bound to pay the expenses connected with both of them) if "the Bill should take away one of the Patents." The basis for this fear is unclear (the bill as originally printed provided for no such revocation), but it may have been connected with the clause that would limit the simultaneous operation of theaters in London to a specific number irrespective of the number of patents then in force.

On Friday, 11 April, two more petitions dealing with the theater bill were presented to the House. The first was by "his Majesty's Companies of Comedians of the Theatres Royal in *Drury-lane*, and *Covent-garden*," but although the petitioners were associated with the theaters protected by the bill, their petition is formulated in terms identical to those of the cases and petitions from the theater in Goodman's Fields. The players recite their belief that acting is an entirely legal profession, and referring to their lease of Drury Lane theater, they claim that their rights and property would be "greatly affected" by the bill. The House ordered this petition to "lie upon the Table" indefinitely, a mark of disfavor that denied the petitioners' request to be heard in committee and effectively disposed of their petition without rejecting it outright.[51] The refusal of the House to consider the petition may have been prompted by the apparent triviality of its grounds of complaint and the uncertain character of the injury it anticipated from the bill.

The paradox that companies belonging to the patentees' theaters would petition against Barnard's bill is explained by a case of twenty-two actors and actresses "in Behalf of *Themselves* and the *Rest* of the *Comedians* of the *Theatres-Royal* of *Drury-Lane* and *Covent-Garden*" which probably appeared at about this time (see App. B–7). The argument parallels that of the petition, but in the case the grounds of the players' complaint and the injury they anticipated from the bill are clear. They object to the bill because, they contend, it would deny them any alternative to working under the arbitrary demands of their managers, and so would encourage the kind of unfavorable labor practices on the part of the patentees that in 1733 had caused most of the company to revolt from Drury Lane. As a protection against the power of a theatrical monopoly, the players suggest the creation of a panel of arbitration, made up of "*Men* of *Fortune, Learning,* and *Ability* . . . appointed as the Legislature shall think fit," to settle "any *Differences* or *Disputes* . . . between the *Patentees* and *Actors*." Such a board would give the players a degree of bargaining power by offering them an impartial court of appeal against decisions of the patentees.

Some of the players involved in the case—the two Millses, Johnson, Miller, Cibber, Harper, Griffin, Milward, Heron, and Butler—faced a problem more serious than the general effects of another London theater monopoly. These eight actors and two actresses had the lease of Drury Lane,[52] but Barnard's bill made it clear that control of the playhouse building in no way constituted legal authority to use it for performances. Ironically, the players were threatened by the possibility that the patentees would abandon them, just as they had earlier abandoned the patentees, to the financial burdens of a theater from which little or no income could be derived.

The other petition read to the House of Commons on 11 April was by John Potter, proprietor of the Little Theatre in the Haymarket, who also cites the threat of financial ruin as the grounds of his complaint against the bill. He notes that he had laid out £1,200 for the construction of the theater itself, and that, like Giffard, he had invested heavily (£500) in equipment and had taken a lease of sixty-one years on the theater property in the Haymarket. The House referred his petition, as it had Giffard's, to the consideration of the Committee of the Whole House and instructed that Potter's counsel should be allowed to testify before it.[53]

The next day the *Universal Spectator, and Weekly Journal* printed a letter from "Dramaticus" that defended the idea of a strong theater bill against an attack in the *London Daily Post* of 31 March. The *Post* article had recommended ancient Athens as a precedent to show that tolerance or outright support of theaters was more characteristic of a free people than attempts to suppress the stage. While admitting the precedent, the letter in the *Universal Spectator* points out that in Athens the stage was under government supervision: "Dramaticus" advocates official control of the drama as well as of the theaters. In a comment following the letter, "Henry Stonecastle" says he feels "Dramaticus" is too harsh in his judgment of players, but he endorses legislative action to avert the threat of yet another London theater. "Stonecastle" goes on to suggest that if new theaters are built they will create conditions as bad as those already existing in the neighborhood of Goodman's Fields Theatre. Finally, a hasty postscript to these comments demands quick and effective legislative action to stop the proliferation of theaters, which are spreading so rapidly in London that they threaten to engulf the country like a plague: "Since the above was sent to the Press I have receiv'd Information that a great Number of *Apprentices* and *Gentlemen* . . . have form'd a *new Company* at *York-Buildings*, which shews the Necessity for the *Number* of *Players* and *Playhouses* to be *regulated*, or else the whole Nation may degenerate into a Set of *Stage-Players*."[54]

Shortly thereafter, the debate over the bill served as the subject of a thirty-two-page pamphlet published anonymously but probably written by Samuel Richardson sometime after 10 April.[55] *A Seasonable Examination of the Pleas and Pretensions of the Proprietors of, and Subscribers to, Play-Houses, Erected in Defiance of the Royal Licence* (London: T. Cooper, 1735) attempts to refocus the debate once again on the larger public problems associated with the theaters. Just as he had in *The Apprentice's Vade Mecum* two years earlier, Richardson in his new pamphlet attacks London theaters generally for their pernicious influence on trade. In 1735, however, his purpose is not simply to caution apprentices but also to recommend that the theaters not permanently silenced by Barnard's bill be strictly controlled by the government.

Richardson immediately directs his attack at Giffard's theater in Goodman's Fields, which had been erected and successfully operated "in Defiance of the Prerogative of the Crown, which had always, till then, been allow'd to have an indisputable Right to licence the Persons who pretended to act or perform Interludes, Plays, or other Entertainments of the Stage: And in Defiance of the City-Magistracy, to avoid whose Cognizance and Controul, it was contrived to be set up just without the Limits of the City" (p. 4). As a result, the traditional instrument of control over all theaters had been weakened, and Richardson sees no alternative but parliamentary action to provide an effective remedy.

Richardson argues that some of the chief objections to Barnard's bill are nothing but fabrications designed to obstruct its passage. For example, pointing to Giffard's own petition in which the manager anticipates financial ruin, Richardson insists that Giffard will actually benefit if the bill passes, even though—or rather, because—it will close his theater in Goodman's Fields, since it will thereby proportionally strengthen the Drury Lane playhouse, in which Giffard has a major interest as one of the patentees (p. 11).

More generally, Richardson sees the moral contamination spread by the theaters as a consequence of the lack of effective management. Instability in the theaters has led to a deterioration in the quality of plays selected for production. As a remedy, he proposes supervision of the theaters by a neutral panel whose powers and object would go far beyond the board of arbitration suggested by the players in their petition: such a panel would "judge, not only of the Merits and Performances of the Patentees and Actors, but of the Pieces to be brought upon the Stage, and . . . [control] in some measure . . . the Taste of the Town, so much vitiated by the execrable Management both of the one and the other" (pp. 29–30).

Although these proposals are similar to those that were offered in the *Prompter* and the *Grub-Street Journal* in March, Richardson's emphasis is more specifically on granting government appointees the power of prior restraint over the production of plays "offensive to Piety, good Manners and Virtue." So important does he consider the need to legislate an end to performances containing "prophane, obscene, or scurrilous" passages that he advocates enactment of Barnard's bill for the sake of that proscriptive clause alone (pp. 22–23).

Richardson's pamphlet contains the most explicit and detailed argument for censorship presented during the public debate over the theater bill in April. It attempts to shift that debate from the question of controlling the increase in the number of London theaters (the principle around which Barnard's bill was written) to the essentially different issue of the need to review the content of plays before their performance. His recommendation was prophetic of the attempt in Parliament later in the month to alter the principle of the theater bill.

PARLIAMENTARY DEBATE

Before the House began its first committee hearing on the bill on Monday, 14 April, it received two more petitions opposing the measure. The first was from Anthony Aston, an itinerant comedian and father of Walter Aston, the author of *The Restauration of King Charles II*. The elder Aston asked permission "to be heard, personally, he being poor, and having no Money to fee Counsel," and the House agreed to his request.[56]

The second petition was from Charles Lee, Master of the Revels, and Lestrange Symes, Controller, who expressed their fear that the bill would adversely affect their interests and authority (for the corresponding case, see App. B-8). With a somewhat reckless disregard for the fact that traditional control over the theaters had already broken down, they complain that the bill would deprive them of the very powers they need in order to continue to regulate playhouses and their companies, especially their power to license "Players of Interludes, Drolls, Country Shews and Entertainments." The grounds of the petition are ostensibly financial, inasmuch as each license issued by these officials was subject to stamp duty. In addition, however, the petition expresses concern for the principle of royal prerogative, a principle that Barnard's bill would confound by giving preeminent jurisdiction over the theaters to statute law instead of to the Crown. The petition was referred to the Committee of the Whole House for consideration, and the House then resolved itself into the committee to consider Barnard's bill.[57]

By tradition, the chairman of such a committee was the member who had introduced the bill or a member closely connected with it. Since the chairman was not permitted to take part in the debate in committee or to propose motions, it was occasionally more convenient for the sponsor of the bill to have another supporter act as chairman. In this case, however, Sir John Barnard, in accordance with custom, took the chair of the committee.[58] There are usually no official records of what transpired in committees other than the summary account given to the House by the chairman from the bar after the Speaker resumed the chair: on 14 April, Barnard simply reported that the committee "had considered the several Petitions to them referred; and had heard Counsel upon the Petition of the several Persons, whose

Names are thereunto subscribed, and others, upon whose Subscription the Theatre in *Goodman's-fields* hath been built; and also upon the Petition of *Henry Giffard*; and also upon the Petition of *John Potter*; and had heard Antony Aston upon his Petition."[59]

Aston's presentation to the committee was apparently a theatrical exhibition in its own right, "operating on the risible Muscles of the Gay, and Good-natured."[60] His speech, published in May as a twelve-page pamphlet with an elaborate title page and dedication, burlesques the self-effacing tone and extravagant claims of many of the other petitions presented in opposition to the theater bill (see App. B-9).[61] In addition to ridiculing the pomposity of other petitioners against the bill, however, Aston also raises a genuine objection to it on behalf of players and audiences outside London, all of whom would be deprived of the benefits of the theater if the bill were to pass. The country gentry would have to come to London to see a play, a situation that "would put them to a vast Expence and Inconveniency" considerably more substantial than the "Great Charge and Inconvenience" dreaded by the London tradesmen. As for itinerant performers throughout England, the bill would mean their ruin: "If all Country Actors must promiscuously suffer by this Act, I question if there is Wood enough in *England*, to hang them all on; What Recourse for their Bread must most of them take, who, for many Years, have addicted themselves solely to Acting, and especially those who from their Infancy have been trained up to it? If silenc'd, 'they cannot dig, and to beg they'll be ashamed,' being capable in no other way to subsist honestly." Moreover, even the amateur actor would be deprived of an innocent exercise of his talent: "What an Outcry would there be through all the Counties in *England*, if Sister *Abigail*, Cousin *John*, and *Cicely*, &c. should be hinder'd at Marts, Fairs, Horse Races, and Cock Matches, of their usual Dramatic Diversion?"

To prevent the absolute prohibition of theatrical performances outside London, Aston had evidently offered an amendment which Sir Edward Stanley presented to the other members of the committee named to prepare the bill. Aston alludes to this "Memorial" in his speech and suggests that the House reconsider its proposed total ban on dramatic performances outside the two London patent houses. There is some reason to believe that Aston may have succeeded in persuading the House to adopt the amendment he proposed. The argument of the last petition presented to the House on Barnard's bill implies that by that time (28 April) the bill allowed for performances outside the London area. Theophilus Cibber later observed that Aston "fairly laughed [the bill] out of the House," and Charles Dibdin suggested that the bill "was got rid of through [Aston's] arguments," but there seems to be no evidence to support these conclusions.[62]

After the committee's deliberations on the fourteenth, Barnard reported that in addition to considering the petitions and hearing oral presentations, his committee "had made a Progress in the Bill," but it is impossible to determine with any certainty what portions of the bill, if any, were debated or amended that day. The House resolved to sit again as a Committee of the Whole House on Barnard's bill "upon Friday Morning next" (18 April).[63]

The next day, Tuesday, 15 April, another issue of the *Prompter* appeared dealing with the theater bill. Using arguments similar to those in Hill's essay of 21 March, William Popple enthusiastically recommends the proposal from the case of the twenty-two players from Drury Lane and Covent Garden for an independent board of arbiters to settle disputes between actors and managers. While he criticizes the monopoly that would be created by Barnard's bill, the independent group he suggests is more than a panel to safeguard the rights of players who would no longer be able freely to leave one manager in favor of another: "It would not be amiss to extend their commission as far as authors, whose plays would stand a fairer chance if gentlemen of fortune, learning and ability, instead of the present judges [the managers], were to examine their merit and reject or receive them." This role for the board is nearly identical to the one Hill had recommended in March, but Popple is more insistent that public taste rather than the mismanaged theaters ought to be the central target for reformation by Parliament. "Restraining the number of playhouses is confining the evil but not rooting it out, and the stage will want as much regulation then as it does now, while public taste is no better than it is." He cautions that without more effective regulation of the drama itself "perhaps some future inconveniencies may arise, more pernicious than those now proposed to be regulated."[64]

Two days later the *Grub-Street Journal* took up the call for an independent board to arbitrate differences between managers and actors and to review plays. The anonymous letter in the issue for Thursday, 17 April, is far more specific in what it recommends than Hill or Popple had been. It proposes the appointment of one or more persons, with substantial salaries from the state, to "judge and determine betwixt Proceedings of the Managers of the Theatres, and the exorbitant Claims of the Actors; with a Power to punish both by pecuniary Mulcts; and upon their Perseverance, either in Neglect of Business, or scandalous Abuse of Morals, to exclude and cut off the Offender as a rotten Member of the Society, not to be re-admitted but upon a reasonable Prospect of Amendment." In addition, the letter recommends "that all Plays, &c. be examined and authorized by the said Officer, so that all Plays, or such Parts of them, as any way tend to Corruption of Manners, be excluded the Theatre."[65] These suggestions combine reforms sought by disgruntled players as well as by citizens crusading against the immorality of the stage. The similarities between the letter and earlier proposals for a supervisory board are less striking than the new and radically different role the letter proposes for it: the basis for the reform which the theaters require lies not in limiting their number but in attacking the evil at its root, putting plays under official scrutiny and allowing the performance only of those found, or rendered, inoffensive. The letter is based on a principle essentially different from Barnard's bill, but very similar to that which Walpole would try in the following week to add to it.

On the day that the anonymous letter appeared in the *Grub-Street Journal*, Parliament received another petition opposing Barnard's bill. Francis Forcer, the proprietor of Sadler's Wells, complained that the bill failed to exempt his house from its penalties, although the Wells had "been, for upwards of Forty Years, a Place of Reputation, nothing immoral, or indecent, being represented there." Moreover, Forcer suggests that since his performances consist "in Music, Rope Dancing, Ground Dancing, and other Activities of Body, concluding with a short Pantomime Entertainment, all in Dumb Show," and since his season does not coincide with that of the regular theaters, the Wells should not come under the jurisdiction of the bill. Forcer's emphasis on the dates of his regular season suggests that he saw the bill as a measure designed to benefit the patentees by eliminating their competitors.

Forcer complains, just as Giffard and Potter had, that the bill would unfairly injure him financially by making his investments worthless and leaving him under an expensive lease. The bill provided that a house in which liquor was sold was subject to its penalties if plays were performed there, even if no charge was made for the performance, and Forcer objects that such a clause could be used unfairly against his business.

The House considered letting the petition lie upon the table, perhaps because Forcer had been so insistent that any prosecution of the Wells would have been simply unwarranted harassment. For the first time, however, a question related to the theater bill was disputed and brought to a vote in the House. The motion was made to leave the petition on the table, the question was put, the motion defeated, and the petition rejected.[66] This division should not be interpreted as evidence that members disagreed on the merits of Forcer's petition, although such disagreement may have existed. The vote indicates only that the House was not unanimous in its decision to reject the petition, but since there was little if any practical difference between dismissing a petition outright and letting it lie on the table indefinitely, the vote might be taken as a suggestion that most members were becoming impatient with what may have seemed an endless stream of repetitious petitions.

The next day, Friday, 18 April, two more petitions were presented to the House, one from the Middlesex justices of the peace, the other from the Lord Mayor, aldermen, and Common Council of London. Both petitions support the theater bill in nearly identical arguments and language. They catalogue the offenses of which the theaters had been repeatedly accused and charge that playhouses tend "greatly to the Corruption of Youth, and Encouragement of Vice, Lewdness, and all manner of Immorality." Since "the Laws, now in being, have been found insufficient for preventing so growing an Evil," they express the hope that the House will act to correct these conditions. Both petitions were referred to the Committee of the Whole House, which had been ordered to convene that morning to consider the bill.[67]

The committee failed to meet that day, however. When the order of the day was read for the House to resolve itself into committee, a motion was made to postpone the committee until the following Monday at noon, the hour at which important debates were usually scheduled,[68] and the motion passed on a division.

It is difficult to assess the significance of the vote and division on this question. Votes against the motion to postpone the committee until Monday were not necessarily votes against the bill itself. On the contrary, in the absence of any other evidence indicating a shift in members' general attitude to Barnard's bill, it would appear that there was still widespread support for the measure itself.[69] Votes for the motion, on the other hand, were not necessarily meant to obstruct passage of the bill. Inasmuch as Barnard himself was chosen as one of the tellers for the yeas, it is likely that he supported the motion and may even have been its sponsor.[70] The fact that the question was brought to a division and the small margin by which it was passed indicate that the delay may have been disputed for tactical reasons. In view of the controversial move by the government in the following week to modify Barnard's bill, it is possible to speculate that the opposition to the motion on 18 April was motivated by a desire on the part of the ministry to have a sympathetic House in which to propose a new clause, either later that same day (18 April), or on some day other than the following Monday.

The motion "that this House will, upon Monday next, at Twelve of the Clock, resolve itself into a Committee of the whole House, to consider further of" the theater bill, was passed on the division, ninety-seven to eighty-six.[71] The closeness of the vote indicates that whatever the issue may have been in this procedural dispute, the House was almost evenly split on it.

On Monday, 21 April, before the House resolved itself into a Committee of the Whole House to consider the bill, the last petition to be presented in opposition to Barnard's bill was read. In it, Hannah Lee explained that for thirty years she had offered entertainments, "according to ancient Custom," at Southwark Fair in booths that "have always been Nurseries for the greatest Performers that ever acted on the *British* Stage," and she asks that she be heard, by her counsel, against the bill. As it had Forcer's, the House rejected Lee's petition,[72] and no more petitions opposing the theater bill were presented thereafter.

After the order of the day was read for the House to consider the bill again in committee, the House turned to the petition from the justices of the peace of the Tower Division in Middlesex, the first petition presented to the House, and ordered it referred to the consideration of the committee. It is difficult to explain why the House let the petition lie so long on the table, especially since it had tabled it only "until the . . . Bill be read a Second time." Perhaps by returning to a statement of the principal purpose of the bill the House hoped to counteract the effects of the intervening petitions which had complained of its injustices; perhaps some members, anticipating the clause Walpole apparently proposed during the committee that day, hoped to focus attention on the need simply to limit the number of playhouses; perhaps the delay in considering the petition was nothing more than an oversight. In any case, the House went into committee with Barnard again as its chairman, and after its deliberations ordered the committee to meet "upon Friday next, at Twelve of the Clock."[73] The House, however, never reconvened in committee on Barnard's bill, and the second meeting proved to have been the last.

There is, again, no record of what took place in this meeting of the committee. Nevertheless, on the basis of contemporary reports, it is possible to reconstruct what probably occurred during the session: Robert Walpole attempted to add to the bill a provision which would give the Lord Chamberlain the power to censor plays. In its original form, of course, Barnard's bill included a prohibition against plays containing "any prophane, obscene or scurrilous Passage, or any Passage offensive to Piety and good Manners," and a penalty by fine for violations, but Walpole's proposal evidently would have required plays to be approved by a government official before they could be performed. Although the new clause would have answered some of the objections raised against the bill by Lee and Symes in their petition on the fourteenth, and might have satisfied those like the author of the letter in the *Grub-Street Journal* who had advocated reform of the drama as well as of the theater, "the worthy Gentlemen who promoted the Bill" in the House found the idea unacceptable and preferred to drop the bill altogether rather than agree to the measure.[74]

A report of proceedings in the House published in 1742 suggests that Walpole's proposal took the form of "a Clause . . . for enlarging the Power of the Lord Chamberlain, with Regard to the Licensing of Plays."[75] Writing half a century later, William Coxe offers a more complete description of the proposal and the manner in which it was presented; according to his account, Walpole conceived the deliberations on Barnard's bill "to be a

favourable opportunity of checking the daring abuse of theatrical representations, which had arrived to a most extravagant height. It was proposed
to insert a clause, to ratify and confirm, if not enlarge the power of the lord
chamberlain, in licensing plays, and at the same time insinuated to the
house, that unless this addition was made, the king would not pass it."[76]
Although the proposed clause has not survived, contemporary manuscript
notations on one copy of the bill are suggestive. In the section setting
penalties for the performance of any play "containing any prophane,
obscene or scurrilous Passage, or any Passage offensive to Piety and good
Manners," the word "seditious" has been inserted above the words
"obscene or," a caret has been inserted between the words "or" and "any,"
and in the adjacent margin are the words "Ld Chamberlains power." It
appears that this may have been the point at which Walpole tried to add a
clause empowering the Lord Chamberlain to censor plays.[77]

There are at least two possible explanations for the timing of Walpole's
proposal and for his attempt to make the licensing clause the price of royal
assent to the bill. The ministry had been involved in the preparation of the
bill from the beginning and had had the opportunity to include the clause in
the original draft. Walpole may have suspected, however, that Barnard and
many others who supported limiting the number of theaters would oppose
censorship of the drama. By waiting to introduce such a clause until the
House had all but passed the original bill, and then announcing that the
king's assent was contingent on it, Walpole may have believed that a majority
in the House would accept his clause rather than abandon a bill of which
they otherwise approved. The event proved he had miscalculated.

It is possible that the king himself was responsible for the timing of
Walpole's proposal, but it is difficult to see why in mid-April the king might
suddenly or spontaneously seek to impose censorship on the drama. From
all appearances, none of the theaters presented plays during March or April
that might, even remotely, have been cause for royal or official concern.[78]
On the other hand, Barnard's bill threatened to deny to the king the power
to issue new letters patent except under conditions set by law and to
supersede the traditional royal prerogative still further by putting the
theaters under statutory regulation. The king's desire to reaffirm his prerogatives through the Lord Chamberlain may have led him to insist that
Walpole introduce a "saving Clause" of the kind Lee and Symes had petitioned for.

Walpole's proposal may have involved serious violations of House procedure. The new clause threatened to make a fundamental change in the
principle of Barnard's bill, the kind of change which should have been
made before the second reading and which was out of order in committee.[79]
Moreover, members were reportedly very sensitive to the impropriety of

introducing the name of the king in debate or of attempting to use knowledge of the king's opinion to influence deliberations in the House,[80] so Walpole's attempt to change the bill might have been received coolly in the House for that reason alone.

Whatever the motives that lay behind it, Walpole's attempt to intimidate the House was self-defeating. According to Coxe, his proposal was opposed by Barnard, who "strongly objected" to it: Barnard "declared that the power of the lord chamberlain was already too great, and had been often wantonly exercised, particularly in the prohibition of Polly. He should therefore withdraw this bill, and wait for another opportunity of introducing it, rather than establish by law a power in a single officer so much under the direction of the crown, a power which might be exercised in an arbitrary manner, and consequently attended with mischievous effects."[81]

Barnard refused to allow his bill to be used as the vehicle for giving the force of law to the Lord Chamberlain's traditional authority over plays, and there proved to be enough members like him who preferred throwing out the bill to establishing a censor under law. Although nearly ten days intervened between the last committee meeting and the vote that ended deliberation on Barnard's bill, the outcome was probably a foregone conclusion on the twenty-first. At Giffard's theater that night the dancer Excell sang a new song addressed to the city titled "Goodman's Fields Theatre": its contents cannot even be guessed, although it would be tempting to speculate on whether its tone was conciliatory or teasing, and whether Giffard realized that although the bill was still formally before the House, his and the other nonpatent theaters were no longer in danger.[82]

On Friday, 25 April, the House put off until *"Wednesday* Morning next" the committee on the theater bill that had been ordered for noon. The postponement almost certainly occurred after five o'clock, and since the meeting was rescheduled without any recorded opposition, the delay was probably owing simply to the time taken by other business.[83] Members opposed to Walpole's clause did not try to use the motion for postponement to force the matter to a vote.

In fact, the House took no final action on Barnard's bill until Wednesday, 30 April. In the meantime, on the twenty-eighth, the last petition to be received on the bill was presented from the city of Exeter describing a situation similar to the one in London immediately after the opening of Goodman's Fields Theatre. It complains of the new theater "erected within the said City . . . in Defiance of the Magistrates and Government . . . ; their Authority, by reason of some Deficiency in the Laws, not being thought sufficient to suppress it." The city asks the House to grant it the same relief that Barnard's bill promised to provide in the capital.[84] Either the Exeter Common Council was not aware that Barnard's bill prohibited all theatrical performances outside London and hoped to persuade the House to give the city legal authority to close playhouses within its jurisdiction, or the bill had been amended in committee, perhaps as a result of Aston's petition and speech, so that its provisions applied only to the London area, and the Exeter council was attempting to restore some of its original scope. In any event the House referred the petition to committee, giving no indication that it was about to dismiss the bill without further consideration.

THE REJECTION OF THE PLAYHOUSE BILL

As the last item of business on Wednesday, 30 April, the order of the day was read for the House to resolve itself into a Committee of the Whole House on the theater bill. A motion was then made to delay the committee until "To-morrow at Twelve of the Clock." The result of the voice vote on the motion was disputed and the House divided, those in favor of postponement going out of the chamber and those against, remaining on the benches. The motion to delay was defeated, ninety to seventy-four.[85] Instead of resolving itself into the committee as ordered, however, the House then agreed, without a division and apparently without opposition, to postpone the committee until "this Day Fortnight," 14 May, the day before Parliament was prorogued and on which no substantive business could be conducted.[86] This action indicates that a majority in the House had voted against the motion because they favored putting off the committee for two weeks, not out of a desire to sustain the order of the day, and that a vote against the motion had been equivalent to a vote against any further consideration of the bill.

It is therefore misleading to take literally the comment by Coxe that Barnard decided to "withdraw" his bill: such an action would have precluded the vote in the House and would have been permitted under the rules only with unanimous consent.[87] Delaying consideration of a bill beyond the end of the working period of a session was a tactic frequently used to kill private legislation and relatively unimportant public bills.[88] The vote at the end of April clearly constituted outright rejection of Barnard's bill by the House: in defeating the motion, the majority of members were registering opposition to any further consideration of the bill, not objection to a one-day delay.

This conclusion is supported by unofficial reports of the action. They indicate that the bill was dropped chiefly on account of Walpole's ultimatum, and that Barnard himself preferred to discard the bill rather than allow it to become the means of establishing a censor under the direction of the Crown.[89] Although the evidence is not conclusive, it would seem that the ministry itself may also have supported the long "postponement," and so voted against the motion. On Tuesday, 6 May, Robert Hunter Morris, a twenty-two-year-old New Yorker then visiting London with his father, wrote in his diary, "My father went to the Rainbow, where he was told that [Sir Robert Walpole] had but a majority of 16 in the house of Commons."[90] The only recorded division in the House in March, April, or May showing a sixteen-vote margin for either side was the vote on the motion to postpone the theater bill committee on 30 April. Morris's information may, of course, refer to a division in a Committee of the Whole House (committee divisions were not recorded in the *Journals*), or it may be inaccurate. If it refers to the division on the motion to postpone the theater bill committee, however, it means that Walpole himself preferred to have the bill thrown out rather than allow Parliament to settle the issue of the theaters by an act that did not also establish a system of censorship.

The vote may not, then, have represented simply a victory by those who opposed censorship of the drama, although that is the interpretation it has usually been given.[91] It may instead have been the consequence of a dead-lock, in which Barnard refused to provide the government with a vehicle of censorship, and the government refused to allow a theater bill to pass unless it established censorship. The elements in the coalition that killed the bill are described in Edward Harley's parliamentary diary, which also indicates that allegations in the press that the patentees were actively supporting the bill were not without foundation:

> April 30: Bill for regulating the Play Houses flung out by appointing a long day for going into the Comee to consider further on the Bill. The opposition was by the young people of the House, + by Ld Baltimore + other freinds to Sʳ Wm Lemmon who was the ground Land-Lord of Goodmans fields playhouse. The other Play Houses were for the Bill that They only might be established by law. See the coming in of the Bill + the Progress of it + the Several Pettions for + agnst it.[92]

Unlike the members who opposed Walpole's clause, those who voted to protect Leman's financial interests had almost certainly been against Barnard's bill from the beginning, but they apparently reserved their objections until the issue of censorship created a wider base of opposition. Leman's friends could never have stopped the bill in the face of the general support it obviously had in the House until Walpole introduced his proposal.[93] In view of the relatively close vote on the thirtieth, on the other hand, it also seems unlikely that there were enough members opposed to Walpole's proposal to defeat the bill without the aid of those who wanted to protect the business of the theater in Goodman's Fields. Barnard's original motion for the bill had been supported inside and outside the House by a coalition of persons motivated variously by moral, economic, and religious concerns; it was defeated by another coalition formed by political and economic interests.

Nothing more is heard in the House of Barnard's bill or of the theaters before Parliament was prorogued on 15 May. The day after the crucial vote, however, the *Grub-Street Journal* printed a "Petition of the Actresses and Female Dancers" at Drury Lane and Covent Garden, a mock appeal to Parliament to amend the clause in Barnard's bill related to performances in places where liquor was sold. The petitioners complain "that it will be impossible for us to perform our parts with any spirit" if Parliament approves the clause, which they say reads: " 'That no Tragedy, Comedy, &c. shall be acted in any house or place where wine, ale, beer, and other liquors shall be sold.' " This citation is almost certainly a deliberate misquotation, since the printed bill does not prohibit performances where liquor is sold but only says that such sale constitutes the performances as ones for "Gain, Hire, or Reward," and thereby restricts them to the patent theaters. (Francis Forcer's petition on 17 April had quoted the clause in its original form, and there is no evidence that it was subsequently amended.) The petition concludes with "Conundrum's" epigram: "Were *Drams* to these deny'd, we soon should see,/That less *dramatic* would each *Drama* be."[94] The flippant tone of the petition may suggest that the Grub-Street correspondent knew that by the time the paper appeared, Barnard's bill would no longer need to be taken seriously as a threat to the theaters.

Two days after the bill was dropped, a select committee presented a report that was to influence the form of the Licensing Act adopted twenty-five months later. The committee, which consisted of fifty-seven members (among them Lord Gage, Sandys, Barnard, Stanley, Walpole, and Talbot, all of whom had been named to prepare the theater bill that session), had been appointed on 27 March to consider existing laws relating to the maintenance and settlement of the poor, and to consider what further provisions might be necessary for their better relief and employment. On Friday, 2 May, William Hay delivered to the House the resolutions his committee had formulated, which the House agreed to on the following Wednesday.[95] Although the report came too late for any legislative action that session, the resolutions suggested the issues that for the next several years would dominate attempts in Parliament to reform laws relating to the poor and would in the meantime affect the terms of the Licensing Act. The vagrancy laws had been used as legal instruments of control over the theaters until the court decision in the Harper case made them ineffective for that purpose; Barnard's bill had been designed to make all the members of nonpatent companies once again subject to prosecution as vagrants; the Licensing Act that was finally to accomplish that reform in the law in 1737 was conceived during a period in which Parliament was reviewing and preparing to redefine the complicated system of vagrancy laws and poor laws then in effect, a process that began with the work of Hay's committee in 1735.

A suggestion for just such a redefinition appeared in the *Prompter* on the day that Hay reported the resolutions of his committee to the House. Hill recommends that "the Statute of Elizabeth against common Strollers and Players of Interludes" should have been revised by the addition to Barnard's bill of a clause "declaring all . . . managers to be *Vagrants*, and liable to the merited correction."[96]

The *Prompter* returned to the subject of theater legislation three times in the next two weeks. On Tuesday, 6 May, Popple expressed the hope that Parliament would renew its interest in the theaters and enact a new law regulating them in the following session, but in contrast with his earlier proposal for extensive official regulation, he recommends that the legislature avoid interfering with the internal management of the playhouses.[97] A week later Hill again discussed the difficulties of regulating the theaters by the use of vagrancy laws. He recalls that at least one manager had been at pains to prove his actors were vagrants, referring to Highmore's suit two years earlier. But Hill contends—much as Aston had before the House—that under the original statute (39 Eliz., ch. 4; see App. A-2) plays do not come under the definition of "interludes" nor actors under that of "common players," both of which terms in the act referred to disreputable itinerant groups and their occasional performances at country fairs: modern acting companies, he argues, have nothing in common with strollers.

Hill insists that attempts to apply the old legal framework of vagrancy laws to the modern theater would lead to the ludicrous conclusion that the king's companies (at the patent houses) were bands of "rogues and vagabonds" in all but name. Instead, he proposes the revocation of all existing patents and the appointment of competent managers; the current patentees, he insinuates, had concocted the proposal for a theater in St. Martins le Grand to provoke parliamentary action that would restore their monopoly.[98]

The day after Parliament was prorogued, the *Prompter* returned to the subject of a future theater bill. Hill again contends that Barnard's bill had been solicited by the patentees; limiting the number of theaters, he argues, would only enrich them and (in an analogy prophetic of Jekyll's Gin Act of the next session) would no more improve morality than reducing the number of taverns would lower the incidence of drunkenness. Competition, on the other hand, would help to improve the theaters. Hill recommends a new bill that would encourage competition and at the same time give officially authorized theaters a financial advantage: it should prohibit the performance at unauthorized playhouses of all forms of entertainments except tragedy and comedy, and permit "the acting of . . . farce, Harlequinery, buffoonery, . . . dancing, singing, dumb or deserving-to-be dumb entertainment" and other amusements only in the royal and licensed theaters.[99]

Barnard's bill continued to be a subject of comment after Parliament was prorogued. The effects it would have had on London theater companies were represented in a satiric print titled *The Player's Last Refuge; or, The Strollers in Distress*, printed for "B. Dickenson at Inigo Iones's Head against Exeter Change in yᵉ Strand" (Fig. 1). The print shows the ruin of players that had been predicted by the companies of Goodman's Fields, Drury Lane, and Covent Garden in their petitions and cases, and later by Anthony Aston in his speech to the House, as a consequence of Barnard's bill. The design of the print and the verses that accompany it (see App. B-10) suggest that the engraving was probably finished sometime after 21 April: the figure of "a *strolling* Sophonisba" seems to be the person described in the verses below the print as "Mʳˢ L—e," and her relative prominence in the scene suggests that it was engraved after Hannah Lee's petition was presented in Parliament.[100]

The print illustrates the opposition to the theaters that Sir John Barnard mounted not only in Parliament but also in the city government of London. Since the prorogation, Barnard had led the London Court of Aldermen to order the suppression of the theatrical performances traditionally held (and often forbidden by the local authorities) during Bartholomew Fair at the end of August,[101] and the print refers to the miseries of players at the fair in the first tableau.

Hannibal, the male figure in the second, and central, tableau may have been meant to represent an actor from one of the patent theaters (perhaps Samuel Stephens from Covent Garden, who had the part of Hannibal there on 15 March).[102] The print shows him supported on either side by emblematic representations of Despair and Poverty, who urge him to accept a *"Masque and Pistols"* offered by *"the Ghost of* Lunn [Rich] *executed at Kingston with a Halter about his Neck."* Hannibal is shown at the point of choice, considering and apparently rejecting the fate of Sophonisba (on the left) and preparing to take up the theatrical props, an act which would return him to his profession, but now as nothing more than *"a Strolling"* player, presumably liable to prosecution as a vagrant. The threat allegedly posed to the patent theaters is represented again in the third tableau, in which *"the Corps of* Pistol," Theophilus Cibber from Drury Lane, is borne away. The print, then, portrays the ruin of actors from Covent Garden and Drury Lane, and, in the figures of Lunn and Orpheus Harlequin, even of John Rich, one of the patentees.

Two other figures are depicted prominently in the print: *"H—pp—ly a* Retailer *of* Coffee, [and] *F—d—g a* Retailer *of* Wine," are the *"chief Mourn-*

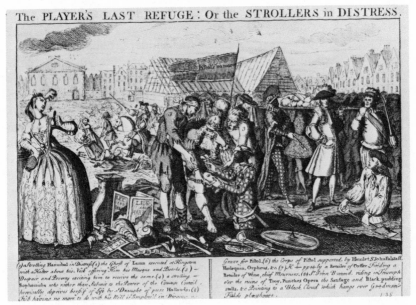

The Player's Last Refuge. Reproduced by permission of the Trustees of the British Museum.

ers" in Pistol's funeral procession. Hippisley, who had a coffeehouse in Newcastle Court, Butcher Row, and owned theaters in Bristol and Bath, had taken the part of Peachum in Gay's *Beggar's Opera* in 1728, and by the 1735–36 season was a highly paid actor at Covent Garden, second only to Stephens: the print shows him just behind Hannibal, both of them now in distress on account of Barnard's attacks on the stage.[103] The only figure in the print shown weeping is "*F——g Whom once did Gods with* Nectar *cheer* [but who now]/*Pawns his full Bottom for a* Pot *of* Beer." This is Timothy Fielding, an actor who retired from Drury Lane in the autumn of 1733 to open the Buffalo Tavern in Bloomsbury Square but who continued to operate a theatrical booth at the London fairs for several years.[104]

The print suggests the disarray with which Barnard's bill and his actions through the London Court of Aldermen threatened all the theaters in 1735. The bill would have suppressed all the nonpatent theaters, redefined vagrancy and revived its legal penalties, and reduced the relatively few players still acting to a choice between personal ruin and acceptance of whatever conditions of employment their managers wished to impose. Actors excluded from the companies of the two protected theaters, and those who, like the younger Cibber and his fellow revolters, refused to accept the will of the patentees, would face arrest if they continued to perform. But the prophecy was not fulfilled, and the independent theaters survived as competitors for the players, plays, and audiences of the patent houses.

But the failure of Barnard's bill, like the failure of Highmore's suit, had consequences that profoundly affected the theaters. The limitation of the number of playhouses in and near London had been a matter of extensive public controversy since Odell had opened his theater in Goodman's Fields in the autumn of 1729. Highmore's action against Harper in 1733 had promised to settle that controversy by making it legally impossible for nonpatent theaters to assemble acting companies. The failure of his suit effectively granted legal recognition and even protection to unauthorized theaters, since their players could no longer be prosecuted as vagrants. The independent theaters were thereby assured of far greater security and freedom by the dismissal of Highmore's suit than they could have had if the application of the vagrancy law had never been thoroughly tested. As long as the legal ambiguity of their position existed, it had evidently acted as a restraint on the managers and players in the nonpatent theaters; when litigation resolved all doubts, their caution was no longer necessary.

The defeat of Barnard's bill in Parliament had similar, but more far-reaching, effects. Restrictions on the theaters had been concretely formulated in a bill; it was debated and apparently all but agreed upon in the House of Commons; and then it was suddenly rejected at the end of April. With the Lord Chamberlain evidently powerless and the courts unwilling to act, Parliament's refusal to control the playhouses meant that the only remaining threat against the nonpatent theaters had disappeared. Whatever consideration their managers had given to the danger of prosecution under the vagrancy acts became unnecessary after the autumn of 1733, and whatever fear they may have had that their newly recognized freedom might provoke action by the legislature, the only source of control they had not yet confronted, seemed to be removed by the defeat of Barnard's bill. Despite the hopes Hill and Popple entertained for parliamentary action in the next session, the rejection of Barnard's bill indicated that legislative control of the theaters had become a dead issue. The result could only be the strengthening of the nonpatent theaters. Their new strength, in turn, would create a more equal balance in bargaining power between the managers of patent theaters and their companies, since the players could withdraw without hindrance to another theater, or even start one of their own, if conditions under the patentees became intolerable.

Had Barnard's bill been exclusively a question of the control of the number of theaters in London, its defeat would probably have meant no more than an increase in the intensity of theatrical competition for players, audiences, and plays and a realignment of the relative strengths of the playhouses into another equilibrium of the kind that had been established during the 1733–34 season. But the theater bill had been dismissed from Parliament chiefly on account of a censorship clause, not simply because it imposed a limitation on the number of theaters. The fact that the House rejected the bill for this reason was to have more serious consequences than a refusal to limit the number of theaters alone might have had.

At the end of April Parliament voted against creating an official censor to review the contents of plays. Even timid managers like those Hill had criticized in the *Prompter* could find in the House's action the courage to accept what he described as "the most necessary, and most seasonable, *Satire*." Just as Highmore's suit, at first a threat to theatrical competition, had by its failure given that competition protection and encouragement, so Walpole's failure to establish official supervision of the drama gave protection and encouragement to the very plays and playwrights the ministry found objectionable. The defeat of Walpole's proposal seemed to remove the necessity for whatever caution and deference managers might have exercised in their choice of plays. No single factor was as responsible for the sudden rise in dramatic political satire over the next two years as Parliament's rejection of Walpole's censorship clause at the end of April.

But the parallel between the effects of Highmore's defeat in the courts and Walpole's in Parliament extended to long-term consequences as well. As the increased stability of the nonpatent theaters after Highmore's defeat had inspired them to open and aggressive competition, their success itself became the provocation for renewed attempts to suppress them, and their opponents had no alternative but to seek decisive action by the legislature to close them permanently. The defeat of Walpole's clause encouraged managers and playwrights to produce satiric pieces with impunity. When the new plays became intolerable, those offended by them seemed to be left with no alternative except to seek an equally decisive action in the legislature, one which would extirpate offending theaters and dramatists alike.

3

POLITICS, SOCIETY, AND
THE THEATERS, 1736

The Licensing Act has always been recognized as a device intended by Walpole to halt dramatic performances he considered to be seditious. About a week before the bill was introduced in Parliament, Fielding attributed to the *Daily Gazetteer*, the government's newspaper, the charge that his drama aimed at "the overthrow of the M——y."[1] The assumptions that his plays and those of others were somehow threatening the government, and that as a result Walpole designed legislation to protect himself from dramatic attacks, are not open to serious challenge. But because the act has seldom been considered in relation to other political events in the 1730s, it is less clear how theatrical performances by themselves could have effectively endangered a ministry. However deeply Walpole might have resented satires directed against him,[2] his position as first minister continued to depend more directly on the support of the king (and, consequently, of the queen) than on national or even parliamentary popularity.

The literary and political contexts in which the Licensing Act arose indicate that dramatic satires against Walpole himself were not the only, and perhaps not even the primary, threat the stage posed to his position. His ministry was jeopardized by a variety of other problems associated with the theaters, many of which might have been inconsequential except for the political and social circumstances that existed in the spring of 1737. It was because of these circumstances that Walpole could argue persuasively that the drama endangered the security not only of his government but of the nation itself and thereby win Parliamentary endorsement of the Licensing Act.

The most important of these circumstances was the virulence of dramatic attacks on members of the royal family, particularly the king. There is substantial evidence to suggest that some of these personal satires, which opponents of the Licensing Act also condemned, infuriated the king even more than they did Walpole, and that Walpole hoped that the act would placate the king and thereby make his own position more secure. That position had become precarious during the 1737 parliamentary session, chiefly because of the king's disagreements with Walpole over the issue of the Prince of Wales' allowance and over the policy to be adopted in dealing with the city of Edinburgh after the Porteous riots. The theaters contributed to the problems Walpole faced as the significance of these two issues continued to grow.[3] Besides sometimes offering plays that ridiculed the king, the theaters exploited his quarrel with the prince in a way that seemed to encourage sympathy with Frederick's cause. Moreover, a number of serious disturbances occurred in the playhouses during the 1736–37 season, at a time when many, especially Walpole, were apprehensive of general rioting that threatened to plunge the nation into anarchy. In view of these and other political and social conditions in May of 1737, the Licensing Act seems to have been a part of a larger strategy of Walpole's ostensibly designed to restore national stability and to reduce the threat that the ministry perceived of an impending Jacobite revolution.

CIVIL DISORDERS IN 1736

There were ample grounds for the suspicion that the nation was on the verge of revolution in 1737, at least in Walpole's view. During the previous summer, Hervey observed, "a licentious, riotous, seditious, and almost ungovernable spirit in the people showed itself in many tumults and disorders, in different shapes, and in several parts of the kingdom."[4] In the midst of widespread disorders throughout the country, London witnessed major violence or the threat of it on three separate occasions during the summer and early autumn of 1736, and on their account Walpole took extraordinary measures to preserve order in the capital.

The first was an incident that seemed to be a prelude to an imminent physical attack on the seats of government power. In the early afternoon on Wednesday, 14 July 1736, an explosion occurred without warning in Westminster Hall while all the courts were sitting and caused "the utmost confusion . . . , everybody concluding it was a plot to blow up the Hall."[5] The explosion was triggered by chemically treated octavo sheets of white and brown paper which were thrown about the Hall by the explosion, and on which were printed announcements of the public burning of five "Libels, called Acts of Parliament" that were "Destructive of the Product, Trade, and Manufacture of this Kingdom" and that tended "to the utter Subversion of the Liberties and Properties thereof."[6] In this incident, as in most others that threatened or seemed to threaten the civil order, Walpole saw a Jacobite conspiracy at work; he wrote his brother Horace, who was still with the king in Hanover, that "there is no reason to doubt but the whole was projected and executed by a set of low Jacobites."[7]

The perpetrator, Robert Nixon, was quickly apprehended and convicted of seditious libel for ridiculing five acts of Parliament and for defaming the king by styling him *"a Foreign Prince."* During the trial the attorney general emphasized the government's leniency in thus prosecuting as a case of libel a crime that amounted to treason. The government repeatedly claimed that since Nixon had attacked the king, he must have been acting in support of the Pretender.[8]

Less than two weeks after the incident in Westminster Hall, more serious disturbances occurred in east London, in Shoreditch and Spitalfields, over the presence of what were considered to be unusually large numbers of immigrant Irish workers employed there in the place of regular English laborers and at cheaper wages. Rioting began in the evening of Monday, 26 July, and for the next two nights officers in the Tower dispatched guards to quell mobs that numbered about four thousand. Walpole "sent several persons both nights to mix with the mob, and to learn what their cry and true meaning was," and discovered that "although the complaint of the Irish was the first motive, the Jacobites are blending with it all other discontents, endeavouring to stir up the distillers and gin retailers, and to avail them-selves of the spirit and fury of the people." "These lower sorts of Jacobites," Walpole warned his brother, "are very industrious, and taking advantage of every thing that offers, to raise tumult and disorder among the people." Their primary target was thought to be "to influence the people, and to raise great tumults upon Michaelmas-day, when the Gin-act takes place," a threat Walpole perceived as early as the last week in July, two months before the provisions of the law were to take effect.[9]

It is estimated that there were over six thousand dramshops in London in 1736, dispensing in excess of 5.5 million gallons, with the result that, as Hervey described it, "the drunkenness of the common people was so universal, . . . that the whole town of London . . . swarmed with drunken people of both sexes from morning to night, and [was] more like a scene of a Bacchanal than the residence of a civil society."[10] To reduce the availability of gin, Parliament in the spring of 1736 passed a bill (9 Geo. II, ch. 23) sponsored by Sir Joseph Jekyll, Master of the Rolls, to increase the fee for a liquor retailer's license from £20 to £50, and the tax on a gallon of gin from 5s. to £1.[11]

In anticipation of the implementation of the act, the Little Theatre in the Haymarket presented an anonymous "Heroic Comi-Tragical Farce," *The Deposing and Death of Queen Gin,* on 2 August.[12] Although little is known about its reception (there is no record of another performance), it could not have failed to attract the attention of the government.

Frequent (and, in the suspicious eyes of the beleaguered ministry, in-terrelated) disorders were not limited to the capital. In the midst of deep official anxiety over the threat of rioting in London in August and September, large detachments of the army had to be called out in at least three other sections of the country to deal with rioting directed against turnpikes and toll gates.[13] Disaffection with the government was widespread in the country, and it produced a sense of general unrest that the ministry feared might breed further, and more serious, disorders. Early in September, Walpole's fears were realized when an incident occurred that was to have serious effects on the stability of his ministry. The event, in fact, grew out of an earlier riot, during which John Porteous, an army captain, killed eight people when he fired on an Edinburgh crowd protesting the execution of a smuggler. The city mob for a time threatened to take its own revenge, but after Porteous was himself sentenced to death for murder, the danger of rioting seems to have diminished. Several months later, however, a group of armed men invaded and effectively seized the city of Edinburgh and lynched Porteous, whose execution had been postponed by the queen after she received a petition for clemency signed by many of the Scottish nobility and gentry. Five days later, on 12 September, a foot regiment had to be ordered to Edinburgh to preserve the peace.

The incident was less a riot than a well-executed act of insurrection. The insult to the queen's authority and the contempt for London rule it displayed were compounded in the public silence by which the participants were protected: despite the £200 reward offered by the queen for information about those involved, no one was apprehended. The affair showed that mob action might be conducted with impunity and that the national authority could be openly and successfully flouted.[14]

Walpole was especially apprehensive of the repercussions the incident might have later in September among those disposed to riot when the unpopular Gin Act took effect. Throughout the month "infinite care [was] taken to observe and watch all . . . [the] motions" of Jacobites in London, and although, as Walpole wrote to his brother, "upon the turn that the Spitalfields riots took, . . . the whole spirit was at once dashed and seemed to have been totally laid aside[,] . . . upon the contrary success at Edinburgh, the fire kindled anew."[15] According to one of Walpole's informers, "great discontents and murmurings" were spreading "through all this Mobbish part of the Town" on account not only of the Gin Act but of the Smuggling Act and the Westminster Bridge Act, three of the five unpopular acts Nixon had attacked in his libel.[16]

The government immediately took steps to discourage rioting. On the queen's orders, horse and guards were "posted and appointed to patrol day and night some time before and long after Michaelmas Day, throughout all the streets of London and Westminster."[17] London began to take on the appearances of an occupied city. When Michaelmas arrived (29 September), retailers of liquor draped their signs with black and organized mock lyings-in-state and funeral processions for "Madam Geneva," re-creating publicly the action of the farce performed at the Little Theatre in the Haymarket almost two months earlier, while Covent Garden offered *The Funeral; or, Grief a la Mode.*[18] Otherwise the day and night passed uneventfully, and none of the serious disturbances Walpole had feared materialized.[19]

The king presumably was notified through letters from London of the steps being taken by the queen and his chief minister to deal with threats of riot or rebellion during his absence, but there is no evidence that he was alarmed by them. In fact, he seemed unconcerned that his protracted visit to Hanover was itself becoming a major grievance among London mobs. The king's long absence from London was only one factor in the civil unrest that pervaded the capital during the autumn and winter, but its consequences were to prove central in the satires that helped to provoke the Licensing Act in the spring.

By the time George II had left London on 22 May 1736, two days after Parliament rose, he had grown "so inordinately peevish" at the delay of the end of the session that, as Hervey observed, "everybody about him wished him gone almost as much as he wished to leave them."[20] To the attraction that Madame Walmoden, his German mistress, held for him had been added a son (whose paternity could only be presumed), born to her earlier that spring, whom the king was most anxious to see. The postponement of his visit for nearly a month caused him, and in turn those close to him, considerable irritation, and a general sense of relief marked his departure. Nevertheless, in the face of general unrest and rioting during the summer, efforts had to be made to convince the king to return to England. Walpole, Hervey, and even the queen (who governed by commission during his absence) wrote to urge him to bring Madame Walmoden with him if that would hasten his return.[21]

When he was still in Hanover on his birthday at the end of October and had given no evidence that he intended to return, the queen finally "writ him a very pathetic letter, acquainting him with the daily increase of disaffection."[22] The court was becoming unpopular; citizens argued that their trade was being ruined by the king's lavish spending abroad; tradesmen complained that because of the king's absence, fewer people were coming to town for the winter; and the mob adopted the cry *"No gin, no King."* Throughout the town rumors were avidly circulated—that Madame Walmoden was the natural daughter of George I by his German mistress; that Madame Walmoden's husband had demanded and received fifty thousand pounds from the king for his wife, was later discovered in bed with her by the king, subsequently infected his wife, and thereby successfully "poxt" the king, and (among the mob) that "the late King is still alive . . . [and] that the present will never return."[23]

It was estimated that by early December the king had drawn between £600,000 and £700,000 from the Treasury. His demands for money so depleted the Treasury that by the third week of November funds were no longer sufficient to pay pensions, a circumstance that reportedly put Walpole into a fit of swearing. Public reaction against the king's extravagance was similarly intense: the question commonly proposed was "if he thought Parliament had given him a greater civil-list than any of his predecessors only to defray the extraordinary expenses of his travelling charges, to support his Hanover bawdy-houses in magnificence, and enrich his German pimps and whores."[24] Feelings against him ran so high that the queen, who had been the subject of widespread sympathy earlier in the autumn, gradually became herself a target of ridicule: in mid-November she was publicly hissed at the opera.[25]

While the queen's popularity declined along with the king's, the Prince of Wales' rose. The king had attempted to insure that his son would remain subordinate to the queen during his absence, but despite these precautions, the prince set up a separate residence soon after the king's departure, pleading his wife's "illness" to explain their remaining in London while the queen moved to Richmond. In the autumn, when "the Queen declared she intended to stay at Kensington till the King came,"[26] the prince arranged to spend most of his time in London and at Kew, only keeping a levee at Kensington one morning each week. The prince's behavior seemed calculated to increase his popularity at the expense of his absent parents', and accounts of his conduct reportedly angered the king in Hanover.[27]

Frederick used the theaters to publicize his independence from his parents. Between the end of August and mid-December, he and the princess commanded or attended a total of ten performances at London theaters without the queen or other members of the royal family, including the performance of *The Conscious Lovers* at Drury Lane that opened the regular season by their command. Later in the season, Henry Giffard held "an elegant Supper and a Concert of Musick" to mark the princess' birthday on 19 November, just a few days after the queen had been publicly humiliated at the opera. The queen, in the same four-month period, attended only four performances, three of them operas. Only once did the Prince and Princess of Wales and the queen appear at a performance together, on 10 November, when they attended the second performance of Handel's opera *Alcina* at Covent Garden (which had been first presented by their command on 6 November) and occupied a box elaborately decorated in their honor.[28]

While the town displayed its affection for her son, it became increasingly cool towards the queen as weeks passed and the king remained abroad. When she made her way to St. James's at the end of the first week in December to take up her winter residence and prepare for the king's return, people stood sullenly in the streets, refusing even to remove their hats as she passed.[29]

As the queen was experiencing the general disaffection in the capital against the throne, the government was proving that it was still capable of acting effectively against persons who bred that disaffection. On 7 December, "M[r] Nixon . . . was Convicted in being concern'd in Composing the Libel & blowing it up in Westminster-Hall, with the 5 Acts of Parliament; for w[ch] he was condemned to pay 200 Marks, & suffer 5 Years Imprisonment; & to be brought before y[e] Courts at Westminster, wth a Parchment round his Head declaring his Offence."[30] The trial was heard before Philip Yorke by a special jury that Paxton had described as "a very good one" in a letter to Newcastle when it was struck about a week earlier: the jury confirmed his expectations by reaching its verdict "in Two Minutes Time, the Gentlemen not going out of Court."[31] At least in the law courts, if not always elsewhere, the government could act successfully against libelers whom it wished to silence.

THE THEATERS AND THE KING'S RETURN TO LONDON

Disturbances continued to plague London theaters during the autumn. At Lincoln's Inn Fields, performances of the main play, *Cato*, were interrupted on 28 October and again on 30 October (the king's birthday): "Four or five Persons (amongst whom two were known to belong to the Attorney of a neighbouring Manager) attended" and, after trying unsuccessfully to persuade those in the middle gallery to leave ("insinuating there was nothing worth seeing . . . there"), first "tried to stampede the audience by shouting 'Fire,' " and finally were content to hiss each time the rest of the audience applauded. These disturbances were probably caused by Charles Fleetwood's belligerence toward his competitor. Henry Giffard, who had taken over management of Lincoln's Inn Fields, later connected the Drury Lane manager with them, and Fleetwood was to become notorious shortly thereafter for having hired "Bravoes and Bullies, to go to the Theatre, to the Nuisance of Society, [and] the Disturbance of his Majesty's Liege Subjects in their innocent Diversions."[32]

Giffard had opened his season, on the eve of the implementation of the Gin Act, not at the Goodman's Fields Theatre where he and his company had performed for seven years, but at the much more capacious Lincoln's Inn Fields, which had not seen a regular season since Rich had left it for his new theater in Covent Garden in December 1732. Although Giffard's company had appeared at Lincoln's Inn Fields in June, his intentions were apparently not settled until well into the autumn.[33] Late in July an auction of various properties belonging to him was announced, and in mid-September the lease for the "late Theatre in Goodman's Fields" that still had "upwards of 50 Years to come" was reportedly put up for sale. Yet about two weeks after Giffard opened Lincoln's Inn Fields it was announced, with some assurance, that he would "very shortly open the Theatre in Goodman's-Fields, notwithstanding the many false and invidious Reports of his having intirely left that part of the Town." It was not until 13 November that Giffard advertised his intention to remain at Lincoln's Inn Fields by carrying on performances there through subscriptions, a proposal he revised about a week later. Giffard's proposals suggest that he may have found his move to the new theater less successful than he had anticipated.[34] In fact, from its opening on 28 September until 23 October, Lincoln's Inn Fields played only every other night, always in competition with Drury Lane but never with Covent Garden (whose manager, Rich, still owned the theater Giffard was managing), and thereafter its performances competed with Rich's only on Saturdays until early November. Fleetwood probably viewed with disfavor any success on the part of a new company nearby, and when Giffard offered *Cato* as the main play at the end of October, the night after the same play had opened at Drury Lane, Fleetwood may have employed his "Bravoes and Bullies" to try to ruin the competing enterprise.[35]

Reactions to the afterpiece at Lincoln's Inn Fields may have aggravated the disorders. *Harlequin Shipwreck'd: With the Loves of Paris and Oenone*, performed after every play by Giffard's company from 21 October to 1 December, may have been seen as a morbid prediction of the king's fate if he tried to return to England.[36] When he did, the play assumed more portentous significance. On Tuesday, 14 December, after the winds finally seemed favorable for the king's embarkation from Helvoetsluys and it was generally assumed in England that he had set sail, a violent storm suddenly developed during the night and persisted for four days, during which there was no word of the king's safety.

During this period, the Prince of Wales took extraordinary pains to show that he felt no anxiety at the possibility that his father might be a victim of the continuing storm. The queen said that she overheard the prince talking "of the King's being cast away with the same sang-froid as you would talk of a coach being overturned, and that my good son strutted about as if he had been already King."[37] Many near the prince reportedly advised him to " 'think right and act accordingly'—in other words to attempt a coup," but he was content for the moment to receive noncommittally the assurances of their "service" from the leaders of the Opposition.[38] "Popularity always makes me sick," the queen told Hervey on this occasion, "but Fritz's popularity makes me vomit." That same night, when Hervey dined at Walpole's, he found the first minister's reactions to the prince's behavior and to the state of the nation almost equally severe: Walpole described Frederick as a "poor, weak, irresolute, false, lying, dishonest, contemptible wretch, that nobody loves, that nobody believes, that nobody will trust, and that will trust everybody by turns, and that everybody by turns will impose upon, betray, mislead, and plunder. And what then will become of this divided family, and this divided country, is too melancholy a prospect for one to admit conjecture to paint it." Hervey suggested that at least the queen would still have some influence over him, but Walpole "interrupted . . . , very eagerly, [to say that] 'he would tear the flesh off her bones with hot irons. . . . the notion he has of her great riches, and the desire he would feel to be fingering them, would make him pinch her and pinch her again, in order to make her buy her ease, till she had not a groat left.' "[39]

The prince showed his disregard for the queen's feelings even more dramatically the next day. He brought her a letter, purportedly written to a Mrs. Cowper by an unidentified person at Harwich, that reported sounds of guns at sea in the middle of the previous night which were thought to be signals of distress from the king's ships. That evening, however, while the queen was at the opera house in the Haymarket, a messenger, who had landed at Yarmouth after three perilous days at sea, arrived with a letter from the king, saying he had never stirred out of Helvoetsluys.[40]

The queen's relief was to be short-lived. Less than forty-eight hours later, late Sunday night and in the early hours on Monday, 20 December, the storm abated, the wind shifted, and there was no doubt, according to Hervey, that the king had finally embarked. Monday night the wind changed once again, "a most prodigious storm" arose, greater than the previous one; and fear for the king was renewed. There was no word of the king until the end of the week, when the master of a sloop that had been shattered on the English coast reported that he had sailed with the king from Helvoetsluys Monday morning, had seen the royal yacht tack about when the storm developed, but had then lost sight of it.

Throughout the capital it was generally believed that the king was at the bottom of the sea, but that possibility did little to soften the minds of the people toward him. A "thousand impertinent and treasonable reflections were thrown out against him every day publicly in the streets," and the king's "damnation" was publicly toasted in at least one alehouse about this time.[41]

It was not until Sunday, 26 December, while the queen was in her chapel, that her apprehension was relieved. A message arrived from the king saying that he had, with the greatest difficulty, regained the port at Helvoetsluys in mid-afternoon on Monday. Not only had the storm been extremely violent, the king reported, but he was then very ill, and had only embarked Monday morning in the face of the storm on the insistence of Sir Charles Wager.[42] The "great discontents at the King's long absence" continued into the new year despite the news of his narrow escape from the storm and of his illness.[43] While the winds and disease held him in Helvoetsluys, the prince's popularity continued to grow in London and served as a catalyst for the general disaffection directed against his father. On 30 December, during a performance of Shakespeare's *King Henry the Eighth* at Drury Lane presented by the command of the prince and princess, some in the audience reportedly acclaimed the prince with general shouts of "Crown him! crown him!"[44] A similar incident occurred during the night of 4 January, which the prince spent in helping to extinguish a great fire in the Inner Temple and distributing money to those who were fighting it with him: he "exerted himself so much there, that . . . several of the mob cried out: 'Crown him! crown him!' "[45] A week later the prince distinguished himself, and ingratiated himself still further with the people, by granting £500 to the Lord Mayor to be applied to releasing "poor Freemen of yᵉ City of London from Prison."[46]

The king at last embarked from the Continent at noon on Thursday, 13 January, after five weeks of danger, uncertainty, and illness, and twenty-four hours later landed safely at Leastoff (Lowestoft). Saturday morning at about four o'clock a messenger arrived at St. James's to announce the king's arrival. The news found the queen herself ill, sleepless, and evidently distressed over the imminent reunion with her husband after his eight months' absence. At nine, Walpole met the prince in the queen's antechamber on his way to visit her and spent most of the morning in conference with him and Princess Emily, reportedly in attempts to persuade Frederick to avoid quarrels with his father in the future. Finally, the queen awakened from a short sleep, called them in, and prepared to meet the king, who had left Stratford St. Mary in Suffolk for London at 6 A.M. He arrived in the capital a little after noon, and as he made his way through the city most in the streets either ignored him or hissed as he passed. But when he arrived at St. James's at about two in the afternoon he bestowed kisses and smiles on all his family and lost no time in taking the queen off to bed.[47]

In an ironic celebration of the king's return, two theaters offered satires to coincide with his arrival in London. On Saturday, just a few hours after the king and queen were reunited, Giffard offered *Harlequin Shipwreck'd* as the afterpiece for the first time in more than two weeks; it continued to appear at the end of each performance for a week. The Little Theatre in the Haymarket (which had been used only four times previously that season) began a more or less regular schedule of performances on the eve of the king's arrival in London with two political satires, *The Defeat of Apollo; or,*

Harlequin Triumphant, a "Dramatick Entertainment," and *The Fall of Bob, Alias Gin*, "A Mock-Tragedy."[48] The two plays seem to have been characteristic of the fare Fielding and his company offered at the Haymarket over the next five months, and at least one theater historian has discovered in them the same sort of politically dangerous drama that led directly to the Licensing Act.[49]

It is not clear why the theaters in the Haymarket and Lincoln's Inn Fields failed to offer a full schedule of plays during January, but it may have been due at least in part to economic pressures created by competition among the four theaters for a smaller than normal London audience. Although theater managers and merchants may have expected the town to fill in anticipation of the opening of Parliament after the king's return, their expectations were disappointed. Parliament met briefly on Friday, 21 January, as scheduled, but was immediately prorogued to Tuesday, 1 February, on account of the king's illness, which had evidently kept him indisposed since shortly after his return to England.[50] Despite—or perhaps because of—his father's illness, the prince conspicuously involved himself in entertainments during the last week in January, attending the opera at the King's Theatre on Tuesday, commanding a performance (of *Hamlet*) at Drury Lane on Thursday, and attending a performance of Handel's *Parthenope* at Covent Garden on Saturday, the eve of the anniversary of the "martyrdom" of Charles I. During the evening "a great Disturbance" broke out in the presence of the prince and princess, and of "Centinels attending at Covent-Garden-Play-house." Although the reasons for the presence of sentinels and for the disorder in Rich's theater are not clear, the incident provided another timely example of the riots that had afflicted the ministry during the preceding six months.[51]

II

THE MAKING OF
A NEW ACT OF PARLIAMENT

4

DOMESTIC CRISES, SPRING 1737

THE OPENING OF PARLIAMENT

Before the government took action against the rioters at the theater in Covent Garden, it turned its attention to the general spirit of insurrection it believed pervaded the nation. On Tuesday, 1 February, three days after the disturbance at the playhouse, the Parliament that was to pass the Licensing Act as one of its last pieces of business was opened by an address from the king that condemned all "disturbers of the public repose." The speech, composed with the advice of the chief ministers, was presented by the Lord Chancellor, Charles Talbot, for the commission appointed to open the session on behalf of the king, who found that it was "not convenient" to attend. After commenting briefly on foreign affairs, Talbot turned to the matter of the "sedition" of those responsible for "the many contrivances and attempts carried on in various shapes, and in different parts of the nation, tumultuously to resist and obstruct the execution of the laws and to violate the peace of the kingdom." Even as he spoke, an army detachment was dispatched from Exeter to Tiverton in anticipation of serious rioting there.[1]

Parliament replied to the king's speech with the customary addresses of thanks. The Commons deplored "the spirit of faction and sedition, which has lately manifested itself," and registered its "abhorrence of the many wicked and detestable practices, which the disturbers of the public repose have secretly fomented and openly carried on."[2] The suggestion of a conspiracy underlying the recent disturbances reflected the ministry's view of them as evidence of the Jacobite threat to the nation.

While Parliament prepared to consider new measures directed at "the deluded enemies of the public peace,"[3] the government continued its campaign against the disorders under existing laws. At the direction of the king, Lord Harrington, the secretary of state, instructed Nicholas Paxton on 8 February to "prosecute, at [the king's] Expence, the Persons who lately insulted the Centinels attending at Covent-Garden-Play-house, in a most audacious manner."[4] Presumably following the lead of the king, Harrington pointedly made no mention of the affront the riot may have given to the prince and princess.

When the Lords met on 10 February, Carteret led the Opposition speakers in condemning the riot in Edinburgh and succeeded in a motion to order the city's provost, bailiffs, and the commanders of the city guards and of the king's forces, to appear in a month's time before the bar of the House for questioning.

In the course of the initial debate over the Porteous incident, Lord Bathurst raised a theme that was to be repeated later in the session during consideration of the theaters. "The general Method," he pointed out, "of stirring the People up to Sedition, is by spreading false and seditious Libels or Reports against their Magistrates, and every one knows how easy it is to prosecute the Authors of such, and how severely they are punished, by the Laws of this Kingdom."[5] Evidence for his conclusion was immediately at hand: while the debate was underway that day, Robert Nixon was walking through Westminster Hall and visiting the four law courts there in turn, displaying on his forehead, according to the terms of his sentence, a paper declaring his offense; he was then returned to prison to serve his five-year sentence.[6] But while Opposition speakers dismissed Nixon's crime as the act of a madman, they repeatedly stressed the legitimate motives of those responsible for most of the disorders: "The People seldom or never assemble in any riotous or tumultuous manner," Lord Granville argued on 10 February, "unless they are oppressed, or at least imagine they are oppressed." Similarly, Bathurst pointed out that "Riots and Tumults generally proceed from Oppression, or from Neglect in the Civil Magistrate."[7]

In adopting its strategy of scrutinizing the circumstances of the Edinburgh riot, the Opposition was doing more than simply following the tradition of exploiting disorders as evidence of the nation's disapproval of the government. While the ministry preferred to examine the Porteous affair as one aspect of a "general inquiry" into the causes of unrest throughout the country, the Opposition intended to force the administration to deal harshly with Edinburgh, hoping that the sixteen Scottish peers normally committed to Walpole would then waver or defect from their support of the government. Walpole himself was put in an unusually precarious position by the attitude of the king and queen, who adamantly insisted that the city be punished for tolerating an act of insurrection that had directly challenged the authority of the Crown. If the city were punished, Walpole's power in Parliament would be jeopardized; if it were not, the king was determined to replace Walpole with a chief minister more willing to avenge the insult to the queen.[8]

Walpole's position also came under attack from other quarters during February. On the first of the month country interests allied with the Opposition defeated those of the City of London by electing Daniel Lambert, who had been a vigorous opponent of the excise, to the London Court of

Aldermen. As a result, the balance of the Court of Aldermen thereafter shifted to the interests opposed to Walpole and the ministry.[9]

This erosion of support in London for the chief minister was associated with an increase in the prince's popularity. The public displays of adulation offered to Frederick during the preceding weeks were indications of a growing disaffection over what was seen as the king's lack of effective leadership, a feeling that was manifested in the London election. In Parliament, support for the prince also became an indication of opposition to his father's ministers, and there the issue was to come to a climax later in February that threatened Walpole's leadership even more directly than did the issue of parliamentary response to the Edinburgh riot.

Frederick had been associated privately with the Opposition since his arrival in England in 1728/29. In part because of that alliance, Walpole and the king restricted the prince to an annual allowance of less than £34,000, about £10,000 of it from the Duchy of Cornwall, and the rest "in small sums without account," although Parliament had assumed that his father would grant him £100,000, the income the king himself had received while he was Prince of Wales. When Frederick and the seventeen-year-old Princess Augusta were married late in April 1736, the king had substituted a more secure income (from the civil list) of £50,000 in place of the prince's direct allowance of £24,000, but the amount was still only half of what the king had been permitted.[10]

Early in February the prince, with the encouragement of the Opposition, decided to make his relationship with his father a public issue by allowing the question of his allowance to be raised in Parliament, an action he had threatened to take as early as 1734, when Bolingbroke had advised it as a first step toward total independence from the king.[11] The prince's interest in obtaining a larger allowance was based on necessity as much as on a desire to embarrass his father. Frederick's expenses had for some time exceeded his regular income, and he was badly in debt: a year later, in 1738, after borrowing a total of £30,000 from three London bankers and discharging only his most pressing debts, he was left with less than £5,000. Moreover, during the preparations for bringing the allowance before Parliament, the prince obliged himself to many of his potential supporters with promissory notes to be paid upon his succession. He had evidently borrowed money before on the same terms, a practice that Hervey had complained of to the queen several months earlier: "There are some who deal with the Prince for money payable at the King's death with most extortionate interest, who would want nothing but a fair opportunity to hasten the day of payment; and the King's manner of exposing himself a thousand different ways would make it full as easy for these fellows to accomplish such a design as their conscience would to form it."[12]

The terms of these loans, which had so alarmed Hervey in the autumn, became even more significant during February, when there were signs that nature, with only a little prompting by the Opposition, might hasten the day of payment. While it was being suggested that the king would dissolve Parliament if he faced an address from it regarding the prince's allowance with which he could not, or would not, comply, the Opposition anticipated a quite different outcome before that dissolution could be made. The king's health had been poor since his return to England, and the condition that had prevented him from presiding over the opening of Parliament at the beginning of February continued to afflict him; Egmont recorded almost daily in his diary that his health did not seem to improve noticeably. The king's condition was to be the focal point of the play that assured swift passage of the Licensing Act later in the spring, but in February the nature of the king's problem was not widely known. The public accounts indicated that he was still "indisposed by [the] . . . fatiguing tempestuous Passage from Holland," and even at court little was said of his condition.[13] The Opposition, "knowing the King's warm prompt temper," reportedly hoped, by introducing the question of the prince's allowance publicly in Parliament with little warning, "to put him in such a passion as, in his present weak condition, and which they thought weaker than it was, might go a good way towards killing him."[14] As long as his death seemed imminent, calculations generally suggested that the motion on the allowance would carry by a majority of about forty, but the king responded to treatments, and by the seventeenth had recovered sufficiently to hold his customary audience.[15] The king's appearance in public that Thursday reassured the court and helped to determine the outcome of the vote on the prince's allowance early in the following week.

On Friday, during the annual consideration of the provision for the army, Walpole defended the need for a large standing army by citing the disaffection of the nation, the internal threat from Jacobites, the frequent rioting over turnpikes, smuggling, and the Spitalfields and Edinburgh riots: moreover, "if a certain motion was to be made next week as he heard of," Walpole said, referring to the motion on the Prince of Wales' allowance, "there would be a stronger reason for keeping up the Army than any that had been mentioned." The government's army bill finally carried by a majority of eighty-one.[16]

Despite the government's success in the vote on Friday, Walpole remained apprehensive over the outcome of the vote to be taken on the prince's allowance, which he insisted was a test of whether Frederick or his father should be king.[17] On Monday, the day before the issue was to be raised in the House of Commons, Walpole and Hervey went to St. James's, where Walpole did his best to persuade the queen, and after her the king, to agree to a "treaty of composition," which, he hoped, would disarm the prince's allies. He proposed that the prince be granted an annual income of £50,000 (independently, not subject to the king's control) and that the king settle a jointure on the princess. After Walpole left the king, a message containing these proposals was taken to the prince by ten members of the cabinet council, who were received, heard, thanked, and told that the matter was already in other hands and no longer under his control. The king and queen, enraged at the prince's reply, reproached Walpole for his suggestions.[18]

The next day, 22 February, the king went in person to the House of Lords to give royal assent to a bill, showing the Lords and the members of the Commons who went up to hear his assent that his health was improved. As soon as the lower House returned to its business, Pulteney moved for an address to the king, "that He would be graciously pleased to settle 100,000 Pounds a Year upon His Royal Highness the Prince of Wales."[19] Walpole argued against it and told the House of the message presented to the prince the day before. In doing so he was clearly exceeding his own authority and jeopardizing his position as first minister: five months later, he admitted that he had received neither the king's nor the queen's consent for the "treaty" he had proposed to them. Consequently, his public announcement of it in Parliament, which could hardly be repudiated or amended as the private message to the prince might have been after the parliamentary crisis had passed, threatened to have the most serious consequences for his ministry.

What drove Walpole to this desperate move was the prospect of almost certain defeat, by a margin then variously expected to be between eight and ten. But when the vote finally came, at 1 A.M. on Ash Wednesday, half of the Tories abstained, and the motion failed, 204 to 234.[20] Although those close to the prince advised him not to encourage his supporters to introduce the same motion in the House of Lords, the Opposition in the Commons refused to bear all the odium of the ministry and the king; the motion was introduced the following Friday in the House of Lords and was again defeated, 40 to 103.[21] As a result of its support for the motions, however, the Opposition obliged the prince to a closer alliance, and so, paradoxically, the ministry faced an Opposition that was stronger after the defeat than it had been before.

After the allowance was defeated in Parliament, Walpole convinced the king and queen, much against their inclination, not to eject the prince from St. James's: he continued to live there until September (when, after the birth of his daughter, he was at last forbidden to live in his parents' house), but the queen never spoke to him and the king refused to acknowledge his presence.[22]

Walpole himself recognized that at least one of the purposes of the motion had been to discredit him in the eyes of the king. According to

Hervey, when the prince was warned that the motion would never succeed, he replied that "at least I shall show I can . . . turn out Walpole, and by showing I have weight enough to make my father change his administration, shall make a much better figure than I can do by being quiet." A contemporary observed, "Upon the whole this was looked upon as a stroke at the Ministry, and no pains or money was omitted to defeat the intent; it is said more was given to baffle this Motion than would have answered the demand made for the Prince."[23]

The consequences for Walpole in this respect were more serious than might at first be apparent. A few hours before the motion was raised in the Commons, the queen told Hervey that if it carried the king intended to dissolve Parliament and appoint a Tory administration. After the motion was defeated, Walpole himself admitted to the king that he would have had to resign if the vote had gone the other way, since he could have had a majority of a hundred on any other question and would therefore be in the untenable position of being able to carry his own points but not the king's. Egmont concluded that, privately, Walpole anticipated even more serious consequences if the motion had succeeded: "It was to be followed," he wrote, "by another to send him to the Tower."[24]

Despite his victory, Walpole's position was still precarious after the vote. The Opposition had managed to muster "an ominous number" of votes in the Commons (204), "being the same," Egmont observed, "by which the Excise scheme was lost three or four years ago, for the 204 was then the number of the minority, yet it proved so great a one that Sir Robert Walpole would not venture pushing that scheme, but dropped it, and no doubt the same number uniting on any occasion, but especially on so popular one as the procuring to the Prince what almost all men believe his due, must have put Sir Robert Walpole under apprehensions."[25] The king and queen, like Walpole, understood the equivocal nature of the ministry's success in defeating the motion. In addition to considering evicting the prince from St. James's after the vote, his parents contemplated removing Walpole and replacing his administration with one led by Carteret, Bishop Sherlock, Newcastle, and Philip Yorke, now Lord Hardwicke and the new chancellor, who during the debate over the Porteous riot had been laying plans to assume control of the government. Walpole reportedly offered to resign to make room for a new government.[26]

By the end of February, then, Walpole's position and the stability of the government were in grave jeopardy. Public dissatisfaction with recently enacted legislation, especially the Gin Act, continued, as did riots over turnpikes throughout the country. In Parliament, the debate over the Porteous riot threatened a prolonged battle in which the first minister would find himself beset on all sides—by the Opposition, his own supporters in Scotland, and the king. The king and queen gave only half-hearted support to Walpole's position as they felt their own undermined by widespread public defamation and by the rebellion of their son, both threats they expected Walpole to deal with but which he found himself practically powerless to extinguish. In each of these areas the king demanded severe countermeasures and was disappointed by compromises. Throughout the winter and spring the continuing crisis was perceived by the government in terms of a classic model of subversion, in which the problems that beset it from without, and the solutions that seemed inexorably to be forced upon it from within or above, threatened both its own stability and the security of the nation.

THE LONDON THEATERS

In these circumstances it is not surprising that the London theaters began to offer plays that alluded to contemporary political controversies and, at least in the government's view, tended to exacerbate them. On the same night that the riot broke out at Covent Garden in the presence of the Prince and Princess of Wales, for example, Robert Dodsley's afterpiece *The King and the Miller of Mansfield* had its first performance at Drury Lane. The play, which was given frequently throughout the spring, represents "the inherent equality of men" through a free-speaking, independent miller, and a king (Henry III) who restores his family to prosperity out of sympathy with the plight of his son, the victim of unjust accusations made by a nobleman who had seduced the son's sweetheart.[27] Partly on account of its democratic bias, partly on account of the occasional allusions in the songs and dialogue to bribes as the courtier's instrument of persuasion, the play was considered to be of a "decided political cast."[28] The prince and princess attended a command performance on Dodsley's first benefit night, 2 February 1736/37, and Frederick's presence may have given a special significance not only to the lines critical of the court but also to the relationships among the beneficent king, the independent miller, and his falsely accused son. "When he saw it," Egmont wrote, the prince "was much pleased and gave public approbation of it," and Egmont himself, after seeing a performance three nights later, called it "chiefly a satire on the Court and courtiers" and observed that it gave "good lessons to Kings."[29] Three months later, Fielding, in his Dedication to *The Historical Register*, cited a letter in the government's newspaper, the *Daily Gazetteer*, which, he said, accused Dodsley's play (as well as his own) of aiming at "the overthrow of the M——y."[30]

Francis Lynch's *Independent Patriot*, which first appeared on 12 February at Giffard's theater, was more explicitly political and at the same time less partisan than Dodsley's. The lead character, significantly named Medium, criticizes both the ministry and the Opposition, but his criticism of the first minister is tempered by sympathy: "Well," he concludes after "bewailing the fact that men are never what they seem," "of all Men living, I think a Premier Minister the most wretched—Let his Intentions be never so upright (Wou'd to Heaven I cou'd say that was the Case at present) he shall often find himself oblig'd to practice on the Passions of those whose Duty 'twou'd be to cooperate with him without Gratuity." Sanguine, on the other hand, a "nominal Patriot," righteously condemns "all Ribbands that shou'd seduce a Man from the Interest of his Country!" and then is discovered to be secretly in the minister's employ, feigning his scorn of reward in order to insinuate himself into the Opposition's council.[31] Less than a fortnight after Lynch's play was brought on at Lincoln's Inn Fields, Giffard produced John Hewitt's comedy *A Tutor for the Beaus; or, Love in a Labyrinth*, one of the few anti-Opposition plays.[32] In his preface to the play, published in 1737 and dedicated to "Miss Skerret," Hewitt complained that it had been rushed into production without adequate rehearsal;[33] the reason for the haste has not been explained, but it may have been connected in some way with the crucial debate on the prince's allowance that began in the Commons the next day.

The opening of Parliament and the king's improved health encouraged a return to the normal pace of public life in London, and by the end of February four playhouses and the opera house were operating with their regular schedule of performances. In addition, early in the month an advertisement had appeared that promised further growth in the number of theaters. On Friday, 4 February, the *Daily Advertiser* published an unsigned notice, dated two days earlier, announcing a plan "to erect a New Theatre for the exhibition of Plays, Farces, Pantomimes, &c." and asking interested persons to prepare designs for the structure to be submitted on 2 May at a time and place to be announced in the same paper on 30 April.

Although the project seems to have been carried no further (the end of April passed without any announcement), the same paper carried a letter from the "Agent for the Company" on Saturday, 19 February, claiming that the proposed new theater was intended for the use of "a Company of Comedians every day expected here, late Servants to their Majesties KOULI KAN and THEODORE, who in the mean time will entertain the Town in the true Eastern manner, at the New Theatre in the Hay-Market, with a celebrated Piece call'd A Rehearsal of Kings." The letter, presumably by Fielding or someone representing him, noted that the proposal for the new playhouse was thought "by some Wise Heads . . . to come from a certain Manager, in order to revive the Playhouse Bill this Session of Parliament."[34] The notice was apparently ignored in Parliament, but a few "Wise Heads" might have construed an action taken in the House of Commons on Monday, 14 February, as a preliminary step in a move "to revive" some degree of official control of the theaters. On that day the House gave leave to a select committee to bring in "a Bill for the more effectual punishing Rogues and Vagabonds,"[35] which could have included a new definition of vagrants aimed at reestablishing the strict statutory regulation of players that had been overturned in 1733. When the bill was brought in for its first reading in the middle of the second week in March, however, the definitions it contained were not essentially different from those of past bills of a similar nature.

In the meantime, Fielding was beginning his last season, not at the Haymarket, which had been open only four nights that month, but at Fleetwood's theater. *Eurydice; or, The Devil Henpeck'd*, was Fielding's first new play of the season, and it was rehearsed as an afterpiece for perform- ance on the evening of Saturday, 19 February (the day on which the letter from the "Agent" appeared in the *Daily Advertiser*), for the "Benefit [of] the Author of the Farce."[36]

The performance of the afterpiece that night was prevented by a disorder involving footmen in the audience. The footmen began arriving in the theater before three that afternoon in the customary way to hold places in the boxes for their masters or mistresses; they then were supposed to retire to what had been designated (since at least 1702) as their gallery, the upper gallery, where they were permitted to watch the performance without charge. But their behavior had frequently offended the rest of the audience, particularly at times when their "Noise and Turbulence" interfered with the performance. On 19 February the footmen provoked a major riot by in- solently interrupting the main play and insulting the audience generally: "The pit rose against the footmen in the boxes and drove them out of the theatre. The footmen, however, raised a disturbance outside, broke down a door, and rushed into their gallery. In the midst of the hubbub, young Cibber harangued the audience from the stage; and, failing to quell the gallery, summoned the High Sheriff of Westminster, who read the Riot Act, and with the aid of his posse made several arrests." The company managed to get through the main play, *Cato*, but " 'Euridice' . . . was drowned in hisses, whistles, and catcalls," making it impossible for the actors to continue.[37] Although Fielding's *Eurydice* was never performed in its original form, in April he produced at the Haymarket an afterpiece based on the fate of his farce at Drury Lane.

On Monday night, 21 February, another "great Riot" broke out, but this time Fleetwood was prepared. After he had locked the entrance to the gallery to prevent the footmen from repeating the previous disruption,

> a great Number of Footmen . . . assembled themselves . . . in a riotous Manner, with great Outcries of burning the House and Audience together, unless they were immediately admitted into . . . their Gallery; and in order to strike a Terror, they began to hew down the Door of the Passage which leads to the said Gallery; of which Colonel *De Veil*, (who was in the House) had immediate Notice, and thereupon came out where they were thus assembled, and notwithstanding they threatened to knock his Brains out, he read the Proclamation [the Riot Act] to them . . . and . . . they all went off in a few Minutes after the Proclamation was read.[38]

The two nights of rioting offered further evidence that outbreaks of civil disorder were a growing threat to public safety and confirmed the danger the ministry had emphasized repeatedly during the debate in the House of Commons on the army on Friday, 18 February.

After his disappointment at Drury Lane, Fielding apparently turned his attention to the Little Theatre in the Haymarket. On Ash Wednesday, 23 February, the *Daily Advertiser* carried an elaborate announcement of "a new Dramatic Comi-Tragical Satire of Three Acts, entitled *A REHEARSAL of KINGS or, The Projecting Gingerbread-Baker*: With the unheard-of Catastrophe of MacPlunderean, *King of* Rogusmania: And the ignoble Fall of *Baron* Tromperland, *King of* Clouts."[39] The play, which had been publicized by the "Agent for the Company" at the Haymarket in his letter to the paper on the previous Saturday, was scheduled for Wednesday, 9 March, but was prevented by still another disturbance.

Meanwhile, on Tuesday, 1 March—the queen's fifty-fourth birthday and the day before Samuel Johnson, with David Garrick, set out for London with great expectations of establishing himself as a tragic dramatist on the now flourishing stages in the capital[40]—Henry Giffard presented the premiere of "An Historical Play" written "In Imitation of Shakespeare" by William Havard. Giffard played the title role, and the author, an Irish actor at Lincoln's Inn Fields, took the part of Bishop Juxon in his own play. *The Tragedy of King Charles the First* had been announced in the *Daily Advertiser* on 8 February, but evidently was not finished until shortly before its first performance. Giffard, who had commissioned the play from Havard, reportedly had to lock the actor in a garret near Lincoln's Inn until he finished it, releasing him each day only after he had written a prescribed number of lines. The product of these unorthodox conditions proved to be the "best and most successful Play that was Acted" at the theater that season.[41] Its popularity may have been connected with the growing interest in Shakespearean drama, but it was probably more directly owing to the political significance audiences found in the play: *King Charles the First* was one of the two plays that Chesterfield, in his famous speech against censorship later in the spring, agreed the government should have suppressed.[42]

The theme of the tragedy, "majesty misled," was applied to contemporary affairs through lines that emphasized "the parallels between Charles I's reign and George II's." Although passages were dropped from the acting version (and then restored in the version published later the same month) that pointedly alluded "to Charles's having kept a Minister despite his monopoly of governmental power, his use of money stolen from the public treasury to buy popularity, and his refusal to protect English shipping from piratical foreigners,"[43] the underlying moral remains in the stage version: Charles, like George, had kept his father's corrupt ministers in power, and by doing so paved the way for his own destruction. Nevertheless, the blunting of the play's contemporary application in the stage version and the care with which Fairfax, a normative character, establishes early in the play the limitations subjects must recognize in seeking to oppose "Arbitrary Sway,"[44] suggest that both the playwright and the manager were conscious of the need for caution in criticizing the government and the king.

Despite these precautions and the play's success, *King Charles the First* provoked attacks against Giffard's theater—criticism that arose primarily from political and ideological grounds rather than out of the kind of economic or moral concerns that had sparked opposition to his theater in Goodman's Fields earlier in the decade. Half a century later, Sir John Hawkins cited a major objection to the effects of the play: it contained, he said,

> sentiments suited to the characters of republicans, sectaries and enthusiasts, and a scenical representation of the events of that prince's disastrous reign, better forgotten than remembered. Sober persons thought that the revival of the memory of past transactions of such a kind as these were, would serve no good purpose, but, on the contrary, perpetuate that enmity between the friends to and opponents of our ecclesiastical and civil establishment, which they had heretofore excited; and for suffering such representations as these, they execrated not so much the author as the manager.[45]

While Havard's play was evoking political interest at Giffard's theater, the footmen continued to afflict Drury Lane. In the afternoon of Saturday, 5 March, exactly two weeks after the first in the pair of disturbances had disrupted performances at the theater, the footmen sent a letter to Fleetwood threatening to mount another attack on his house unless certain conditions were met: "We are willing to admonish you before we attempt our Design; and Provide you will use us Civil, and Admitt us into our Gallery, which is our Property, according to Formalities; and if you think proper to Come to a Composition this way, you'll hear no further; and if not, our Intention is to Combine in a Body in Cognito, And Reduce the play house to the Ground, Valuing no Detection we are Indemnified." That night the footmen were "on account of their Rudeness . . . denyed entrance into the Gallery," upon which about three hundred of them "arm'd with offensive Weapons broke open the Doors of *Drury-Lane* Playhouse, . . . fought their Way to the Stage Door, and wounded 25 Persons."[46] Evidently by prearrangement with Fleetwood, Colonel De Veil was again present in the house, this time with "a small Guard to support him," but when he was called upon to read the Riot Act, "the Violence and Number of Footmen in this riotous Assembly" prevented him. Once again even the presence of the Prince and Princess of Wales "and others of the Royal Family" did nothing to temper the fury of the mob; Sir William Wyndham, one of the prince's closest advisers, fought hand-to-hand with one of the rioters. De Veil, apprehensive of "where this dangerous Attempt would end," finally was able to take several of the ringleaders into custody. They, and the wounded in the audience, were taken to "an adjacent Room to the Playhouse," where, "till Two o'Clock in the Morning," the footmen were examined by De Veil while a surgeon treated the injured.[47]

Three rioters were sent almost immediately to Newgate, but the fear of further violence remained. During the next week the riot became so popular a "Topick of publick Discourse" that efforts had to be made to deter the footmen from renewing their attacks on the theater and at the same time to allay general apprehensions that threatened to discourage audiences from attending Drury Lane. Accordingly, on Tuesday, 8 March, the *Daily Advertiser* announced that "all proper Care being taken, every thing was very quiet last Night, and 'tis believ'd will continue so." Fleetwood at the same time offered a reward for the discovery of the author or authors of the threatening letter. All was quiet until the performance on Thursday, 10 March, when there was a momentary outburst of shouting, but nothing came of it.[48] It was apparently not until the following Monday that the reason for the sudden calm was reported in the press: from 7 March until at least 14 March (and, in view of the way in which the report was presented, probably thereafter indefinitely), fifty armed soldiers stood guard at the playhouse during every performance, with a "Civil Power" (probably a justice, perhaps De Veil) in attendance each night as well, to read the proclamation and to order the guard into action if those steps became necessary.[49]

While Drury Lane was in a state of siege, an even more serious disruption occurred in Fielding's Little Theatre in the Haymarket. *A Rehearsal of Kings*, which had been announced in the press on 19 and 23 February, was advertised on 8 March for performance the next day, a Wednesday, at the Haymarket, along with an afterpiece "call'd the Historical Register, for the Year 1736, written by the Author of Pasquin." The advertisement itself, written in the style of the namesake of the afterpiece (a yearbook of foreign and domestic political events), suggested that Fielding, the "Great Mogul," had only at that moment "acceded to the Treaty" and agreed to install his company in Potter's theater for the season.[50]

The plan miscarried, and neither play was presented the next evening, on account of "some Persons taking clandestinely Possession of the Hay-Market Playhouse, who were about Eight o'Clock committed to Bridewell for the same. . . . Several hundred Persons were turn'd away."[51] The disruption may have been part of a theatrical dispute over use of the house similar to the one involving the company from Drury Lane in 1733–34. Plays had been offered at the Haymarket intermittently during January and February and early March, but nearly all of them had been benefit performances: the suggestion in the advertisement on 8 March that Fielding had recently concluded a formal agreement with the theater raises the possibility that another group of players may have been challenging the new arrangement. The third and last "N.B." to the elaborate advertisement in the *Daily Advertiser* two weeks earlier, on the other hand, warns against "all . . . who may *hire* or be *hir'd*, to do the Drudgery of Hissing, Catcalling, &c.," so there may have been threats of disruption calculated to prevent the performance on 9 March.[52]

When the *Daily Advertiser* on 10 March 1736/37 reported the seizure of the Haymarket theater, it added the assurance that the play would be performed on the following day; but on the eleventh it reported that "the Rehearsal of Kings . . . is put off, by an unforeseen Accident, 'till Monday next."[53] The "accident" was almost certainly the sudden intervention by the Duke of Grafton, the Lord Chamberlain, who moved to prevent dramatic performances at the Haymarket on Wednesdays and Fridays in Lent: "altho' the Patent Play-Houses pay a due Observance" to those days, "yet these Heathens had no respect to [them] . . . , but play'd on, and would continue to do (even in the *Passion* Week) had not they been expressly forbid by the Lord *Chamberlain*."[54]

The history of performances on these days in Lent shows that while the Haymarket theater took the lead in violating the traditional ban, the other theaters, even those managed by the patentees, had by 1737 abandoned their "due Observance" and followed their competitor. Beginning with seven performances in 1730, the Haymarket offered plays on some or all Wednesdays and Fridays each Lent. In 1733 the theater offered *The Beggar's Opera* on Ash Wednesday and continued in production during Passion Week, an innovation Fielding repeated the following year. By 1736 all the theaters were open on some of the forbidden days, and Fielding continued the run of *Pasquin* into Passion Week that year until ordered by the Lord Chamberlain to desist.

Despite that order, Fielding resumed offering plays on each Wednesday and Friday after Ash Wednesday (23 February) in 1737. The first, significantly, was *Pasquin*—and at advanced prices—on Friday, 25 February: on the same day Giffard offered a double bill at Lincoln's Inn Fields, while Drury Lane was dark; Covent Garden offered Handel's *Justin*, as it did on the following Wednesday (when the Prince and Princess of Wales were present) and Friday. But Fleetwood decided to follow the lead of Fielding and Giffard and offered a standard double bill on 2, 4, and 9 March.[55] It was then, on Thursday, 10 March, that the Lord Chamberlain moved again to halt performances at all the theaters on Wednesdays and Fridays. His orders, copies of which were sent separately to the managers of Drury Lane, Covent Garden, Lincoln's Inn Fields, and the Haymarket,[56] were obeyed at all the theaters. (Musical entertainments, which were not banned, continued at Covent Garden on the forbidden days until after Easter.) It is difficult to explain why the Lord Chamberlain's interdiction was so effective in controlling the playhouses in Lincoln's Inn Fields and the Haymarket. Whatever the reason, just ten weeks before the Licensing Act was ordered in Parliament, the traditional agent of official regulation of the theaters demonstrated that he still exercised some influence over patentees and independent managers alike.

On the same day that the seizure of the Haymarket theater forced postponement of *A Rehearsal of Kings*, the bill dealing with vagrancy that had first been discussed two years earlier was introduced in the House of Commons and had its first reading. It was intended "for the more effectual punishing Rogues and Vagabonds; and for the better Relief and Employment of such poor Persons as are therein mentioned,"[57] but it touched on a point of law to which theater managers and players were especially sensitive, and it became clear later in the month that many persons associated with the theaters viewed this vagrancy bill with considerable anxiety. Nevertheless, it was another bill, first mentioned in Parliament the next day (10 March), that marked a more important turning point in the relationship between the government and the playhouses.

THE UNIVERSITIES' BILL

On 10 March, the day that the Lord Chamberlain sent his order to the London theaters, another form of traditional regulation of the stage became an issue in Parliament. A new theater had opened despite the adamant opposition of officials who had traditionally regulated the activities of players. Unable to silence the new playhouse, the officials petitioned the House of Commons for a new law to reestablish their authority. Their petition, based on circumstances that corresponded to those prevailing in London, was a prelude to the Licensing Act introduced later in the spring.

The petitioners were the chancellor, masters, and scholars of the University of Cambridge, who found themselves unable to prevent theatrical performances at a playhouse recently built at Cambridge.[58] Since the reign of Queen Elizabeth the university had tried, with varying degrees of success, to prevent dramatic performances in or near the town during Stourbridge Fair,[59] usually the only time in which regular performances were attempted. But entertainments at the fair, which was held in September every year, had been limited to temporary stages erected in a cornfield next to the Cam two miles east of the Cambridge marketplace which were dismantled—or were supposed to be—when the fair ended after a fortnight. The new playhouse, on the other hand, was a permanent structure.[60]

Entertainers in the fair came under the jurisdiction of the town of Cambridge and of the vice-chancellor of the university. By a royal charter from Elizabeth the university's authority extended "an English Mile around the Town, to be measured ab extrimis Adificiys . . . yet for some Purposes the University has a larger Precinct: with respect to Higlers, Regrators, Purveyors, Plays and Torneaments, they may not be suffered within 5 Miles of the Town."[61] But the prohibition proved unenforceable almost from the beginning. Although at first persons responsible for the performances were charged and sentenced to pay the costs of the court and sometimes a fine, they regarded the expense merely "as the equivalent of a licensing fee."[62] Moreover, the lenient practice of the university in the seventeenth century had led to the assumption that its officers could grant licenses for dramatic entertainments: as late as 1713 it was "a Common . . . Opinion that the Vice-Chancellor may give Leave for Plays, Shows &c.," although "K. James in his Charter . . . expressly prohibited [him] . . . from giving such Leave."[63]

In 1701 the tolerant atmosphere changed. After "the Mayor and some of the Corporation . . . encouraged Stage players to act at Sturbridge Fair in contempt and violaton of the Rights and Privileges of this University . . . and against the express order of the Vicechancellor," Thomas Doggett (who had previously posted a bond for £500 "not to act during the Fair or in the liberties of Cambridge") performed on stage, evidently failed to fulfill his bond, and was sent to prison by the vice-chancellor, Richard Bentley.[64]

The university actively and sometimes vigorously opposed plays during the fair despite the permission often granted for them by the town authorities.[65] When "a Play Booth was . . . erected near Paper Mills in contempt & defiance of the Authority of the University" at the end of August

1730, the university senate charged the proctors to allow "no Member of this University of what standing or Degree soever . . . to be Present at any Plays or interludes" performed at the new booth: violators were to be fined "twenty Shillings for each Transgression," or, if they refused commitment to prison upon the command of any of the proctors, they were to "be proceeded against according to the utmost extremity of the Law."[66] Such attempts at controlling a temporary theater by acting against its potential audience through a primitive form of surtax on admission charges were not entirely successful, and plays of one sort or another continued to be performed during the fair in 1734 and 1735.[67]

In 1736 the university seems to have been more determined than it had been for some time to suppress theatrical entertainments. On 11 August, more than a month before the fair was to begin, the senate took notice of plans for another play booth and ordered "that if any Member of this University . . . shall presume to be present at any Play or Interlude there to be acted, he shall suffer the Penalty of Forty Shillings for each Transgression" (see App. C-1). Joseph Kettle, who had proposed to build the booth, evidently concluded that his audience would not be deterred from attending by the increased fine, since by 6 September his playhouse had been erected in anticipation of the fair, "notwithstanding the Vicechancellor & Heads of Colleges did discourage & to the Utmost of their Power endeavour to prevent" it.[68] But Kettle's theater, unlike all those that had been erected before the fair in previous years and then taken down after it, was a permanent structure that remained standing (and unused) through the autumn and winter of 1736–37. Early in March the university, which had been powerless to stop construction of the house, sought new authority from Parliament to remove it.

The university acted although the new playhouse was not used after the end of the fair in 1736, and although there were no plans to reopen it before September 1737. It may have been that officials, who had resigned themselves to performances during the fair when it became clear that they could not prevent them, saw a permanent theater as an encouragement to itinerant companies or resident players to offer performances between fairs and wished to take action before that practice became established. Other events in the town and the university's reactions to them early in March, however, indicate that the petition concerning the new playhouse was an afterthought, a corollary to the university's alarm over another danger that seemed to threaten its members—and its authority—even more seriously than stage plays.

The university's more immediate concern late in the winter of 1736–37 was over the same problem that had preoccupied London at the end of September in 1736: how to check the uncontrolled spread of shops selling liquor. The university had long enjoyed the exclusive right to license (or forbid) taverns and public houses in its vicinity. But during 1736, a local newspaper reported that a distiller had opened a new tavern in Trumpinton Street, not under a license from the univerity but "by Virtue of a Privilege given to the Distillers by a late Act of Parliament, of setting up or following any Business whatsoever in any City, Town, Corporate, &c." The report indicated that a similar development was expected in Oxford.[69] That the university's authority was no longer respected and that the number of taverns was definitely increasing were confirmed by the report in September that another distiller was setting up a tavern in Bridge Street under the same act.[70]

The "late Act of Parliament" to which both distillers owed their new privilege was the Gin Act. It authorized anyone who had been engaged in distilling for seven years to take up any other occupation anywhere in England after 29 September 1736, other laws or customs to the contrary notwithstanding. This provision of the Gin Act voided (apparently unintentionally) an act of 1553 that reserved to the two universities the exclusive right to license vintners and taverns in their vicinities, and limited the number of taverns in Oxford to three, and in Cambridge to four.[71]

Apprehensive about the possibility of an uncontrolled increase in the number of taverns, the chancellor, masters, and scholars of Cambridge University petitioned Parliament on Thursday, 3 March 1736/37, "to grant such Relief as to them in their great Wisdom shall seem meet" (see App. C-2).[72] Having requested restoration of its traditional authority over taverns, the university senate as an afterthought composed a similar petition to Parliament two days later, seeking a law under which it could act against Kettle's theater and prevent the erection of playhouses in the future (see App. C-3). This decision by the university on 5 March seems to have grown not out of its fear of imminent performances or of the establishment of additional playhouses so much as out of a more general intention to secure by statute its traditional prerogatives to protect students from immoral influences—the allurements first of taverns, and then of theaters.[73]

The petitions were presented to the House of Commons by the member for the university, Thomas Townshend, the son of Walpole's brother-in-law.[74] Although it seems unlikely that the petitions were sent to London at different times, Townshend presented them to the House separately. On Thursday, 10 March, he brought in the petition dealing with the new playhouse, the second of the two resolutions adopted in Cambridge the week before. It was not until nearly a week later that he introduced the first.

The reasons for presenting these petitions in a sequence the reverse of that in which they had been adopted, and for the long interval between their introductions, cannot be established conclusively. The effect of the procedure, however, was to give the question of theaters, not of taverns, priority in Parliament. After hearing the petition on 10 March, the House ordered the preparation of "a Bill for the more effectual preventing the unlawful Playing of Interludes within the Precincts of the University of Cambridge, and the Places adjacent," and Townshend and Robert Walpole were appointed to bring in the legislation.[75] It was only after drafting of the playhouse bill was under way that Townshend brought the petition dealing with taverns to the attention of the House. On Wednesday, 16 March (the same day that the new vagrancy bill had its second reading and was sent to a Committee of the Whole House for debate the following Wednesday), Townshend presented the other petition. After hearing it, the House moved to consider the section of a 1713 law (12 Anne, ch. 14) that had most recently guaranteed to the universities their traditional authority to regulate taverns, and then instructed Townshend and Walpole to insert in the bill they were preparing a clause to amend the Gin Act and restore to Cambridge University its exclusive authority over taverns.[76]

As a result of this sequence of events, the legislation dealing with the universities was from the start focused on the issue of theaters, to which the problem of taverns was always subordinate. The appointment of Townshend and Walpole on 10 March to draw up a bill to prohibit the performance of plays clearly marks the beginning of Parliament's concern over the theaters in 1737.

5

POLITICS, SOCIETY, AND THE
THEATERS, SPRING 1737

Outside Parliament, the theaters continued to promote new plays that focused on contemporary political affairs and personalities. Fielding finally produced the frequently advertised, long-awaited, and long-delayed *A Rehearsal of Kings; or, The Projecting Gingerbread-Baker* at the Haymarket on Monday, 14 March. Little is known about the play except from advertisements, which describe it as "a new Dramatic Comi-Tragical Satire of Three Acts" presented by "a Company of Comedians dropt from the Clouds, late Servants to their thrice-renown'd Majesties, Kouly Kan and Theodore." "Kouly Kan" (sometimes "Kuli Khan") was the Shah of Persia, whose imperialistic intentions towards his neighbors were notorious; "Theodore" was Theodore I, the title under which Baron Neuhoff had set up in 1736 as the self-appointed leader of a group of Corsican patriots fighting for the independence of their island from Genoa.[1]

The rehearsal format of the play presumably highlighted the same parallel between the stage and the state suggested by these names. There may also have been an instance of that parallel in the name of the country of one of the kings: "Macplunderkan, King of Roguomania" (or, in another notice, "Macplunderean, King of Rogusmania") is a monarch of "rogues," the class of petty criminals that had once included (and was soon to include again) actors as prominent members in its legal definition. The names of the other principal characters suggest a satire of considerable dimensions: "Mynheer Maggot, Mynheer Wiserman, . . . King of Clouts, King Bombardino, King Pamper-Gusto, King Lexoneris, King Taxybundus [or Taxyburndus], three Wandering Kings, Sardonides, Bandequimonti [or Bandiquamonti] and Crimerowky [or Crimcrowky], two Queens incog. Plutonibus and Companardicoff, Don Resinando's Ghost, and the Ghost of a Dutch Statesman." Although it is difficult to determine what its specific targets might have been, it was almost certainly aimed at the ministry (perhaps satirizing Walpole as Macplunderkan).[2] The play was offered at advanced prices again on Tuesday and Thursday, and then disappeared. That same Thursday a newspaper report criticized the play at the Haymarket when it appealed for public approval of a "new Tragi-Comedy, intitled The Free-Thinker" scheduled for mid-April, "tho' the Company of Players are not dropt down from the Clouds, nor does the Play libel the Government."[3]

On Friday, 18 March, most of the theaters were dark (as they had been on Wednesday) in compliance with the Lord Chamberlain's order: only Covent Garden among the regular playhouses was open, offering Handel's setting of Dryden's *Alexander's Feast*. On the same day the *Weekly Miscellany* published a condemnation of the "Impiety and Looseness . . . allow'd with Impunity to tread our Stage, and encouraged by Acclamations to debauch the People." The writer praises the drama of ancient Greece and Rome and argues that "it was the Judgment of Antiquity, that *National Security* cannot subsist without *National* Virtue, and that general Looseness and Prophaneness were the Seeds of Ruin to a State."[4]

Those "seeds" were clearly in evidence the next day: *The Beggar's Opera* appeared at Drury Lane, *King Charles the First* at Lincoln's Inn Fields, and *Pasquin* at the Haymarket. But the most shocking example of "looseness and prophaneness" that day was not in the theaters but in the press, in a fictional "vision" that was later to be adapted for the stage and in that form to become the immediate occasion for the Licensing Act.

"THE VISION OF THE GOLDEN RUMP"

The first part of the piece appeared on 19 March in *Common Sense*, a weekly periodical that had begun publication on 5 February, the first Saturday of the parliamentary session, under the editorship of Charles Molloy, an Irish Roman Catholic and attorney.[5] The new partisan journal was named by Lords Chesterfield and Lyttelton—under whose supervision it, like the *Craftsman*, was conducted—after the Queen in Fielding's *Pasquin*, to serve as a vehicle "to carry to a larger audience than could be reached by a London play the social and political ridicule which had been so effective on the stage of the Little Theatre in the Haymarket."[6] But behind Molloy, behind Chesterfield and the Opposition, the Old Pretender, James III, reportedly founded *Common Sense* "from abroad . . . as a paper which he could use for his own purposes, but which would not be overtly Jacobitical."[7] He had discussed plans for such a paper, to be edited by Molloy, in letters to his agent in Paris, Daniel O'Brien, at the end of August 1736, and to Colonel William Cecil, an English Jacobite, early in October. O'Brien sent details of the new journal to the Pretender on 4 February 1736/37, and indicated that Pope and Chesterfield were among those who were expected to contribute to it. Walpole was probably aware of the Pretender's involvement in the paper through information he regularly obtained from Cecil, whom he had somehow convinced, despite James's warnings to him to the contrary, that he was intent on restoring the Stuarts as soon as the proper occasion presented itself.[8]

The paper quickly became known for its "Scurrility and Defamation." According to a contemporary writing under the name "Marforio" (Pasquin's traditional counterpart) in 1740, "the first thing" of this sort "that brought it into request" was "The Vision of the Golden Rump," "a most impudent Satire upon the K—— and the . . . Q——, not to mention the Ministry and the Court."[9]

The satire opens on a large river that carries the writer, in a small canoe, to "a pleasant Meadow" that resembles Greenwich Park. The broadest avenue is filled with "Cavaliers all magnificently dressed" hastening "to a Temple" about a half a mile away. An elderly man in black greets the writer and begins to explain the scene: the cavaliers are "the *Noblesse* of the Kingdom . . . going to the Temple to celebrate the annual Festival of the GOLDEN RUMP," the name of the Pagod. He conducts the visitor to the temple, places him "in a Niche near the Altar," and points out the three celebrants: the Pagod, or idol, itself; the High Priestess, or Tapanta; and her Vicar General, the Chief Magician. (A satiric print representing the principal characters was published later in the spring: see Fig. 2.)[10]

The Pagod resembles a human figure, but with "Goats Legs and Feet," a "Head . . . made of Wood," and "his Body down to the Waist of Silver." He stands on the altar with his "Back . . . turned to the Congregation," the posture in which "he had placed himself . . . upon his first Entrance into the Temple, as well to shew his Politeness, as to testify his Respect and Gratitude to a Nation which had elected him into the Number of the *Diu majores*, or greater Gods."[11] This attitude displays "his Posteriors" to best advantage, "which were large and prominent, and from whence he derived his Title," inasmuch as they "were of solid Gold."

At the right hand of the idol stands "the TAPANTA" (a word perhaps related to the Spanish *tapar*, "to hide, conceal, or screen"), "dressed in the Habit of a *Roman* Matron." In one hand she holds a silver bell, and in the other a golden clyster-pipe, the bladder of which is full of "*Aurum potabile*, compounded with Pearl Powders, and other choice Ingredients. This Medicine," the visitor's guide explains, "at proper Season, was injected by the TAPANTA into the F——d——t of the PAGOD, to comfort his Bowels, and preserve his Complexion. It was likewise applied, upon extraordinary Occasions, to appease the IDOL, when he lifted up his cloven Foot to correct his Domesticks who officiated at the Altar." The Pagod was by nature "very cholerick," and "his Fury was sometimes so very sudden and unexpected," that he kicked those "who stood near him, ere the HIGH-PRIESTESS had time to apply

THE FESTIVAL OF THE GOLDEN RUMP.
Rumpatur, *quæquæ* Rumpitur *invidiâ*.

UNA EURU
NOTUSQ: RU
CREBERQ. PROCE
AFRICUS.

Designed by the Author of Common Sense   *Publish'd according to Act of Parliament 1737.*   *Price 1⁶*

The Festival of the Golden Rump. Reproduced by permission of the Trustees of the British Museum.

the golden Clyster." Similarly, at times "the Storm was so loud and violent, and the PRIESTESS met with such Opposition in those Parts to which she directed her Tube, . . . that she was unable to apply it at all."

To illustrate this condition, the writer quotes a line from the *Aeneid* (I.85) and refers the reader to "*Cotton*'s Translation . . . [which] will best explain my Meaning." Charles Cotton's "translation" of the first book of the *Aeneid* was a "Travestie" of Virgil titled *Scarronides*, first published in 1664 and reprinted in 1734. The verse, in its context, provides an eloquent explanation of the "Meaning":

> *AEol*, who all the while stood gaping
> At her fine Peacock's gawdy Trapping,
> Seeing her mount *Olympus* Stair-case,
> Began t'untruss, to ease his Carcase,
> Twice belch'd he loud from Lungs of Leather,
> To call his roaring Troops together;
> And twice (as who should say, we come)
> They roar'd "th' Concave of his Womb:
> With that he turns his Buttocks Sea-ward,
> And with a gibing kind of Nay-word,
> Quoth he, Blind Harpers, have among ye;

'Tis ten to one but I bedung ye.
At the same Word, lifting one Leg,
And pulling out his trusty Peg,
He let at once his gen'ral Muster
Of all that e'er could blow or bluster;
And (like a Coxcomb) in his Tuel
Left not one Puff to cool his Gruel.

. . . .

. . . when *AEol* pluck'd the Plug
From th' Muzzle of his double Jug,
The Winds burst out with such a Rattle,
As he had broke the Strings that twattle.[12]

Across from the Tapanta, at the Pagod's left hand, stands the Chief Magician, wearing under his blue robe a cassock of white satin embroidered "all over with flying Dragons," and bearing the words "AURI SACRA FAMES." The Magician was called "Gaster Argos" on account of "his Belly, which was as large and prominent as the PAGOD's Rump." In his hand the Magician carries "a Rod or Wand . . . , which he waved continually to and fro, like *Harlequin Faustus* in a modern Pantomime." The wand, the gentleman in black explains, changes itself into a serpent or dragon whenever the Magician casts it on the ground.

The Chief Magician represents Walpole, carrying the staff of his office and conjuring the dragon, the symbol in popular literature for the excise that Walpole had unsuccessfully proposed four years earlier.[13] The High Priestess is clearly meant to be the queen, whose "Vicar General" Walpole was and who (with Walpole) ministered to the needs and whims of the king.

The Pagod almost certainly represents George II. The term was used elsewhere to identify the king, as in Pope's imitation of "The Fourth Satire of Dr. John Donne" (1733), where in a vision the king's presence-chamber "seems, with things so richly odd, / The Mosque of *Mahound*, or some queer Pa-god." Even the initial letters of the idol's title are suggestive (George Rex). And the king's interest in gold was so strong that it sometimes got the better even of his interest in his mistresses.[14]

The posture assumed by the Pagod, and the specific focus on his most prominent attribute that consequently dominates the scene, may at first seem little more than gratuitous scurrility. This aspect of the idol and the nature of the dangers to which bystanders were exposed, however, would have been clearly understood by contemporaries as references to the king.

After he had returned to London in mid-January 1736/37, the king had been so ill that the opening of Parliament was first postponed and then had to be handled by a commission. His illness was partly owing to "a violent cold" he had contracted during his journey and that he had neglected after he arrived in London. Although those close to him tried to conceal the presence of another, more serious condition, it was soon a matter of conversation that he was "extremely out of order" from fever, shooting pains in his head, and an excruciating case of the piles complicated by a fistula in the same area. The disorders were a recurrence of those the king had suffered some two years earlier, and their causes were practically the same as they had been then. Hervey summarized the king's condition in 1735, after a journey much shorter and less demanding than that of 1736/37:

> By unreasonably hurrying himself to arrive in England, though he was as unreasonably sorry to return thither at all, he had made himself extremely ill; for whilst he travelled in this violent manner, day and night, and almost without any rest, only for the pleasure of bragging how quick he moved, he had so heated his blood that he was feverish for several days after he returned; and by sitting so long in his coach had brought upon himself such a severe fit of the piles, to which he was extremely subject, that he was in great pain, lost a great quantity of blood, and had . . . violent . . . inflammation and swelling.[15]

Although Walpole diagnosed the cause of the king's disorders in 1737 to be his "pining and fretting," and told the queen "that he would never be well till she would send for Madam Walmoden to nurse him,"[16] his surgeons treated the symptoms more directly. "The Vision" in *Common Sense* probably represents the queen (who was "from morning to night in the King's room" during his indisposition) in readiness to "nurse" the king in the absence of his mistress, using one of the common "fomentations" applied in cases of piles, some of which might have been characterized as "*Aurum potabile.*" One contemporary recipe for the remedy, for example, includes "two pennyworth of litharge of gold, an ounce of sallad-oil, a spoonful of white-wine-vinegar; put all into a new gallipot; beat it together with a knife, till it is as thick as an ointment, spread it on a cloth, and apply it to the place; if inward, put up as far as you can."[17] In extremely inward cases, presumably, the clyster-pipe would have provided a more forceful (and convenient) method of application.

The course of the king's recovery is difficult to determine with any precision because of the secrecy that surrounded his condition. On 22 February he went to the House of Lords to give royal assent to a bill and to show the Opposition, just before the question of the prince's allowance was moved in the Commons, that he had recovered.[18] Yet his condition remained a matter of concern for several weeks: in a letter dated 2 March, Roger Bradshaigh commented to Walpole on the king's recent "happy recovery," and as late as 22 April, John Byrom, when he saw the king in the park, felt it important to note that he was "smiling, and looked better."[19] The publication of the first part of "The Vision" in mid-March, then, would have been a most timely reminder of the king's recent indisposition.

The "visible marks" of the Pagod's "Fury" also had a counterpart in recent incidents involving the king, whose violent temper was notorious even while he was a young man at his father's court in Hanover: as Lady Mary Wortley Montagu observed at that time, "He looked upon all the men and women he saw as creatures he might kick or kiss for his diversion."[20] This tendency was aggravated in 1735 and again in 1737 by the king's physical disorders, with the result that while his illness continued, "everybody shared the warm and frequent sallies of his abominable temper, and everybody imputed them to what was the joint though not the sole cause of these eruptions, which was the affliction he felt for a change of a German life to an English one, with the society of a stale wife instead of a new mistress; and, what grated more than all the rest, the transition to limited from unlimited power." After his return to England in 1735, for example, "every-one who came near him . . . had some share of his bilious temper," and in at least one fit he evidently kicked Lord Harrington, one of his secretaries of state.[21]

Even before he left Hanover at the end of 1736, the king's temper created a similar incident, a report of which quickly reached England. "A jest is current in town and country," Egmont reported on 15 December, "that . . . his Majesty . . . came into the room of his mistress's mother, where he found Mr. [Horace] Walpole, and asking what they had been talking of, she replied he had been advising her, if she came to England, not to concern herself with public affairs, which put the King into such a passion that he kicked him. Upon this, people say Horace has got the length of the King's foot."[22]

The letters of Horace Walpole and Sir Charles Wager (who conveyed the king to and from Hanover) were also full of examples of the king's "insup-portable" impatience. It was only with the greatest difficulty that Wager was able to keep the king at Helvoetsluys during the storm: by threatening to set out across the Channel in a packet-boat without him, the king forced Wager to sail, but the weather proved so unfavorable that the admiral finally succeeded in persuading the king to agree to turn back to port.[23] During this incident the king was "supposed to have kicked his hat overboard" in "one of his paroxysms." The incident occasioned a " 'hieroglyphical' " print titled *Aeneas in a Storm* showing

> a ship in a storm, raised by young Winds, who are among the clouds; one of them is kicking a hat, another contumeliously salutes the ship. Neptune rises to allay the tumult. On the shore is Britannia, pointing to the ship, with these lines engraved before her feet:—"She, *While y* Outragious Winds y* Deep deform / Smiles on y* Tumult, & enjoys y* Storm.*" Under the engraving is:—"Tanta haec Mulier *potuit Suadere* Malorum."[24]

It may have been from this print that the author of "The Vision" in *Common*

Sense took the notion of a storm proceeding from the Rump: the line he cites from the *Aeneid* (I.85) to illustrate the "unnatural Sallies or Hurricanes" describes the consequence of Aeolus' sending a violent storm against Aeneas. Whatever the connection between the print and "The Vision," however, the Virgilian quotation in *Common Sense*, drawn as it is from the scene that the print parodies, would presumably have raised in the minds of readers a similar image of the king's behavior during the storm in January.

Having thus caricatured the three most powerful figures in Britain, "The Vision" continues with a speech from the Golden Rump (signaled by the sound of the Tapanta's silver bell and uttered in "an hollow, hoarse Voice") instructing all the nations to offer their people and "Vessels of Silver, Vessels of Gold." Following the Tapanta's signal, the Chief Magician returns an address (perhaps in a parody of parliamentary procedure) in the name of the congregation, promising to obey the Rump's commands.

The first part of "The Vision" concludes with three processions of the faithful. The first consists of 12 men in blue velvet and about 24 in red, the Knights of the Golden Rump, each with the same motto embroidered around a large rump on his vest: "RUMPATUR, *quisquis* RUMPITUR *invidiâ,*" which the visitor translates "*Whoever envies me, or whoever is not on my Side, let him be* RUMPED." The second procession consists of 22 knights dressed in "Party-coloured Robes of Black and White" called Castellans or Tapanta's Knights, and the third of about 250 "*Ecuyers*" of the Chief Magician, each of whom carries "a large Vessel of Gold on his Head, full of square Pieces of the same Metal, each about the Size of a Dye," which are set at the foot of the altar. After the High Priestess consecrates the vessels "in Form to the Service of the PAGOD," the Chief Magician casts his rod down, which immediately turns into "a monstrous Dragon" who "gulped them down . . . in less time than a Dunghill Cock would have pick'd up a dozen Barley-Corns from a Threshing Floor," and even seems to show an interest in "those Parts of the PAGOD which were formed of Gold." But the Chief Magician takes the dragon by the tail, and it resumes the shape of a wand.

One week later, on 26 March, *Common Sense* published the conclusion of "The Vision." The Chief Magician begins by stroking "the GOLDEN RUMP with the small End of his Rod," and as a result "that Part of the IDOL swelled to such an enormous Size, that . . . the unnatural Protuberance, or additional Weight of Gold, was sufficient to make a Statue as large as the Statue in *Grosvenor-Square*, Horse and all." This was almost certainly an uncomplimentary reference to the "doubly gilt" outsized equestrian statue of George I by Van Nort that had been put up by Sir Richard Grosvenor in 1726: ten years before "The Vision" was published, the statue was defaced and mutilated, presumably by Jacobites, but those responsible were never discovered.[25]

The Pagod was so pleased by this addition of gold that it "testified" its "Satisfaction by a loud Grunt," which in turn was answered by the universal acclamation of the congregation, and by another series of processions by Knights of the Golden Rump, Castellans, and Ecuyers. This time, however, those in attendance approach the altar to receive tickets from the Magician, who draws them from a silk bag delivered to him by the Tapanta. The Knights of the Golden Rump receive vellum tickets entitling them to certain privileges, but many of them are dissatisfied with their portions and demand "larger Appointments."

The Castellans' tickets bear the monosyllable "Trans" and "Plus," sometimes repeated two or three times, apparently standing for a certain sum of money. The gentleman in black remarks on the popularity of "Plus" tickets, but notes that

> some Years ago there was a general Assembly of *Castellans*; they made a Decree by which the Use of PLUS *Tickets* were forbidden, as being contrary to the original Constitution of their Order; but they inserted a Clause of Dispensation, in case the Claimant should be a Person of *distinguished Merit*. This Article rendered the Prohibition useless; for since that Day, every *Castellan* hath been a Person of *distinguished Merit*.

These remarks, if the rest of the scene did not, make it clear that Walpole's habit of bribery is here being burlesqued: the terms of the "Decree" are identical to those of an act against bribery adopted by Parliament in 1729 (2 Geo. II, ch. 24) and generally ignored thereafter.

The final procession consists of Ecuyers, who advance "without observing any Order; pressing, squeezing, treading on one another's Heels, and reaching over one another's Shoulders, to receive their *Tickets*." They show deference only to their "Leader— . . . an aukward, clumsy Person" named Sacoma, who "held a Pair of Gold Scales in his Right Hand, while his Left was employed to hold up his Breeches." Sacoma, the visitor learns, is the "*Weigh-Master*," whose "Office was to *weigh* the Power and Interest of the neighbouring Nations, and all the Words and Actions, and even the very Thoughts of their Rulers." As a result of his proficiency in defeating "all the Designs which have been formed against the Theocracy of the GOLDEN RUMP," the country has "no Occasion for Soldiers, or Garrison Towns; but wholly rel[ies] on the Skill of the excellent SACOMA, to whom we owe our present Security, and the flourishing Condition of this Country."

Sacoma, who "was in great Favour with the GOLDEN RUMP, and nearly related to the CHIEF MAGICIAN," represents Horatio (or Horace, as he was commonly called) Walpole, Robert's younger brother. Although he usually returned to London while Parliament was sitting to defend the government's foreign policy in the House of Commons, from 1724 he served on the Continent with a number of diplomatic responsibilities, the most important of which proved to be his role as chief negotiator in The Hague from April 1734 to November 1739, charged with keeping Britain out of the War of Polish Succession. His efforts in foreign policy led his critics to dub him the "Balance Master of Europe." Almost equally sensitive was his role as traveling companion and chaperon to the king during his visit to Hanover during 1736–37.[26]

The ambassador was one of the principal targets of Opposition caricature and satire, as much for his personal habits as for his role in foreign policy. That Horace Walpole was undignified in his manners and attire is well attested by popular ballads (in which he holds a place of distinction second only to his brother)[27] and by the revulsion of those who had close contact with him. The queen "used to complain of his silly laugh hurting her ears, and his dirty sweaty body offending her nose. . . . Sometimes she used to cough and reach as if she was ready to vomit with talking of his dirt; and would often bid Lord Hervey open the window to purify the room of the stink Horace had left behind him, and call the pages to burn sweets to get it out of the hangings."[28]

The employment to which Sacoma devotes his left hand would have been understood by contemporary readers as a direct reference to one of Horace Walpole's best-known traits. About a year after "The Vision" was published, a ballad titled "The Negotiators; or, Don Diego Brought to Reason" appeared, containing an almost identical reference:

> So without further Speeches,
> H[orace] tuck'd up his Breeches,
> (Pray note what great Patience *Negotiating* teaches). . . .

Milton Percival points out that this "particular action is so often mentioned in the satires of the day that it must be taken as indicating an actual habit."[29]

After the visitor's guide has explained Sacoma's character, the Tapanta again rings her bell, cueing the Magician to deliver a short speech to the congregation. He explains "that his *Pagod-ship* was engaged to sup with *Jupiter* that Evening in *AEthiopia*," and places his wand at the feet of the Pagod, where it again turns into a dragon that flies up through the roof of the temple with the Golden Rump astride it. The Tapanta blesses and then dismisses the congregation, and attended by the Magician departs for her apartment through a passage behind the altar. But after most of the congregation has left the temple, the gentleman in black explains to the visitor the real destination of the Pagod: "He never mounts the Dragon, but when he is in an amorous Fit," a condition that the guide implies arises with some frequency. Since "these Love Sallies sometimes produce very bad Effects, and even render the Divinity of our great PAGOD suspected," the Magician conceals the cause of his absence from the common people, just as Walpole tried to screen the king's sexual escapades and his special interests in visiting Hanover.[30]

In fact, at the time "The Vision" was published the king was planning another trip to see Madame Walmoden. On Sunday, 13 March, and again on 18 March, less than two months after his return to London, his chief ministers indicated that the king was preparing to leave for Hanover.[31] The prospects that he might again be out of Britain for two-thirds of the year had prompted one of the queen's personal servants several months earlier to observe that "if the king should go to Hanover [in 1737], it would be for good and all, for the people would be so exasperated they would never let him come back."[32] As May approached, the ministry settled on a strategy to keep the king in London. Having neglected the Opposition's bill that dealt harshly with Edinburgh in retaliation for the Porteous riot, the ministry "afterwards joined in it to keep the Parliament sitting to prevent the King from going abroad again."[33] In the event, the king did not visit Hanover in 1737, but the reason for his remaining in England may have been not so much the necessity of awaiting the end of the session as the persuasive charms of his new domestic mistress, Lady Deloraine, who claimed that the "country . . . was under a great obligation to her, for it was solely owing to her" that the king did not leave England that year.[34]

FIELDING'S PLAYS AND PARLIAMENTARY SUPPRESSION OF UNIVERSITY THEATERS

During the week between the publication of the first and second parts of "The Vision of the Golden Rump," two other events occurred in London that, along with the play dramatizing "The Vision," were to lead to the passage of the Licensing Act. The first of them took place on Monday, 21 March, in the Haymarket theater, when "the Great Mogul's Company of Comedians" offered for the first time Fielding's *Historical Register for the Year 1736* as an afterpiece to Lillo's *Fatal Curiosity*.[35] The second occurred on Thursday, 24 March, in the House of Commons, when the bill to suppress stage-playing in Cambridge was introduced.

The situation in the last scene of *The Historical Register*, much like that at the end of "The Vision," represents Walpole's bribery of members of Parliament, including the "Patriots," and their consequent willingness to support his measures. This conversion erases "the wide difference" (III.156) between them and the five politicians in the first scene. Their similarity may have been further emphasized by the identities of the actors since three of the five men who played the parts of the politicians in the first scene also appeared as the patriots in the last scene.

Although only these two scenes involve explicitly political characters, Fielding extends the significance of at least some of the other scenes into a political dimension. Before *The Historical Register* "begins," Sourwit (one of the visitors at the rehearsal) asks Medley to explain "what thread or connection" exists in "this history . . . , how is your political connected with your theatrical?" "Oh, very easily," Medley replies. "When my politics come to a farce, they very naturally lead to the playhouse where, let me tell you, there are some politicians too, where there is lying, flattering, dissembling, promising, deceiving, and undermining, as well as in any court in Christendom" (I.92–99). When Pistol (representing Theophilus Cibber) runs "mad and thinks himself a Great Man," Medley replies to Sourwit's objection that "this jest [is] a little overacted" by saying "we don't overact him half so much as he does his parts, though 'tis not so much his acting capacity which I intend to exhibit as his ministerial." He reiterates the parallel between the theatrical and political worlds just before Pistol, announced by drums and fiddles, enters with the mob (II.284–98). Later, Ground-Ivy (Colley Cibber), defends his "alteration" of Shakespeare's *King John* by telling the prompter, "I have seen things carried in the House against the voice of the people before today," and when Apollo remarks, "Let them hiss and grumble as much as they please, as long as we get their money" (an attitude shared by the politicians, as Medley had pointed out before Pistol's first appearance), Medley characterizes the line as "the sentiment of a Great Man, and worthy to come from the great Apollo himself" (III.117–23).

When Pistol *"enters and overturns his father,"* he is introduced "to no purpose at all," according to Medley (III.155), but his presence here is meant at least to continue the satire on the theatrical reign of the Cibbers, and perhaps to extend it to the political world by representing a similar situation in the royal family. Pistol's lines, spoken to Ground-Ivy, certainly suggest an analogy to the relationship between the prince and his father:

> Your pardon, sir, why will you not obey
> Your son's advice and give him still his way;
> For you, and all who will oppose his force,
> Must be o'erthrown in his triumphant course.
>   (III.136–39)

The Historical Register is episodic, with each scene (and sometimes individual lines) providing satiric cuts more or less independent of the others. Although it is therefore difficult to see a thoroughly consistent double pattern in the satire, in which each theatrical or political character stands allegorically for identifiable targets in both worlds, parallels between the theatrical and political targets underlie so much of the play that they tend to create a sense of coherence between the two levels. In addition, the play has a rough sort of symmetry in the arrangement of scenes: the first and last are openly and specifically political; the third (the auction scene) is a more general indictment of contemporary political principles; and the second (involving four London ladies discussing the opera) and the fourth and fifth (with Pistol, Apollo, and Ground-Ivy) are aimed primarily at the theaters. It is likely that the Haymarket audience, accustomed to applying satires to familiar targets, may have helped to "point" some of the lines and bits of business that today seem innocuous or only vaguely suggestive on the printed page. As the "first player" says before the "play" begins, satire requires little more than that a playwright name his target, "that's enough to set the audience a-hooting" (I.27–28).[36] The first minister, for example, could be discovered, by anyone inclined to look, lurking in at least five of the six scenes, labeled with some of the scores of fictional names under which he had been satirized during the previous twenty years: the "little gentleman" and Quidam in the first and last scenes; Pistol, the "Prime Minister theatrical," in the fourth and (with the prompter) in the fifth; Hen in the third, offering to sell interest at court; and perhaps even the "dancing-master," who is "practicing above the stairs" with one of the ladies and so delays their "council" in the second scene (there is also, as the prompter tells Apollo, an "abundance of dancing-masters in the house who do little or nothing for their money"). But despite the pervasive presence of the twin targets of Walpole and Cibber, the play is neither personal invective nor a partisan manifesto: its undertone of disillusionment is frequently tempered by antics of mild farce (e.g., I.95; III.284).

After being first mentioned in the advertisement for *A Rehearsal of Kings* on 8 March, and then, with a "short and very merry farce" called *The Damnation of Eurydice* on 15 March, *The Historical Register* was performed at the Haymarket on Monday, 21 March, at advanced prices. Fielding evidently expected the play to be popular (or wished to give the impression that it would be), for he announced early on the day of its first performance that "none will be admitted after the House is full; for which Reason, the sooner you come, or secure your Places, the Better."[37] Fielding's expectations proved to be well founded, as the *Daily Advertiser* reported the next day: "Last Night the two new Performances at the Hay-Market . . . were receiv'd with the greatest Applause ever shown at the Theatre." That night Egmont attended the play (having seen *A Rehearsal of Kings* there on the previous Tuesday) and noted, "It is a good satire on the times and had a good deal of wit."[38] The play was an extraordinary success. Through the remainder of the season it was performed on thirty-five of the thirty-nine evenings the Haymarket was open, holding the stage without interruption (except for Wednesdays and Fridays during Lent, and Passion Week) until the first week in May.[39]

Two days after *The Historical Register* had its first performance, the House of Commons again turned its attention to the problems facing Cambridge University. On Wednesday, 23 March, even before the bill they were opposing had reached the floor, a group of former distillers who had set up as vintners in Cambridge presented a petition to the House; they recited the misfortunes they had suffered as a result of the Gin Act and the expenses they had incurred in opening taverns in Cambridge. Their petition ended with the hope "that they shall not a Second time be turned adrift to Seek their Fortunes" at the risk of "the utter Ruin of themselves and Families," and prayed that the House would reject the university's request for legislative authority to suppress them. The House tabled the petition until the bill was ready for consideration in committee.[40]

Then, on Thursday, 24 March, Townshend presented to the House, pursuant to its order, the bill that he and Walpole had drafted in response to the two petitions from the university. Its title, reflecting the priorities it gave to its two purposes, was

> a Bill for the more effectual preventing the unlawful Playing of Interludes within the Precincts of the University of *Cambridge*, and the Places adjacent; and for explaining and amending so much of an Act, passed in the last Session of Parliament, intituled, An Act for laying a Duty upon the Retailers of spirituous Liquors, and for licensing the Retailers thereof, as may affect the Privilege of the University of *Cambridge* with respect to the licensing Taverns, and all other publick Houses, within the Precincts of the same.

The bill was received, had its first reading, and was ordered for a second reading, which occurred a little more than a week later.[41]

In the meantime, however, the question of regulations dealing with the stage was raised in the press. On Friday, 25 March, the day before the second part of "The Vision of the Golden Rump" appeared in *Common Sense*, the *Daily Journal* warned that legislative restrictions were a sure forerunner to an attack on the liberty of the press. The *Journal*'s essay seems to have been based more on a general apprehension of official interference with the stage and the press than on opposition to any specific legislation, pending or contemplated, but its appearance may suggest that some sort of national restrictions were being rumored.

That conclusion is supported by a reference to the anxiety of London players reported in the *Daily Post* on the following Tuesday (29 March). "The Actors of the several Theatres," it said, "are in no small Pain about the present Act depending in the House of Commons call'd the Vagrant Act, for fear of being deem'd Vagabonds; and are therefore perpetually soliciting their Friends for a Clause in their Favour."[42] The "Vagrant Act" was the "Bill for the more effectual punishing Rogues and Vagabonds, and for the better Relief of such poor Persons as are therein mentioned," written by the select committee headed by Hay and Pollen, which had had its first reading on 9 March; it was scheduled to be considered in a Committee of the Whole House during the week of 21 March, but it was put off until Wednesday, 30 March, instead.

The *Daily Post* report presumably reflected actors' fears that the bill would be amended in committee the next day in a way that would overturn the court ruling involving Harper in 1733 and make any actor not directly under the protection of a patentee (and through him, of the Lord Chamberlain) liable to arrest, fine, and imprisonment. Such a provision would affect not only players at the independent theaters and in the country, but also those employed at Drury Lane and Covent Garden, because it would make it impractical for them to use the threat of another "revolt" (of the kind led successfully by Theophilus Cibber in 1733–34) as a tactic in negotiations with their managers. A return to the legal conditions that had existed before Harper's trial, in other words, would have restored the practical monopoly of the patent theaters; a more restrictive definition of "Rogues and Vagabonds" could even shut the theaters entirely if it specifically and without exception classified all actors as vagrants. The same concern was evident in an article, recently attributed to Fielding, that had appeared in the *Daily Journal* on 25 March. Publication of the article, "Some Thoughts on the Present State of the Theatres, and the Consequences of an Act to Destroy the Liberty of the Stage," was probably timed to coincide with the consideration of the bill by the House in committee. The writer argued that the creation of a new theatrical monopoly threatened to put players, dramatists, and audiences alike at the mercy of arbitrary, cowardly, and tasteless managers. A similar apprehension was again voiced in the *Grub-Street Journal* on 7 April; the paper opposed the new vagrancy bill, warning that it would become a source of arbitrary power and "a scourge to the People" by giving to justices of the peace unprecedented power to punish anyone it classified as a rogue or vagabond.[43]

It is difficult to determine with any certainty the degree to which these fears were justified. The definition of vagrancy included in what appears to be the bill printed at the end of the 1735–36 session (which presumably formed the basis for the House's deliberations in March and April 1737, if it was not in fact the bill then considered) is substantially the same as that contained in the existing statute (12 Anne 2, ch. 23) and would therefore not have materially changed the legal status of London actors: it states that "all Fencers, Bear-Wards, common Players of Interludes, Minstrels, Jugglers, . . . shall be deemed Rogues and Vagabonds."[44]

From a manuscript among Walpole's papers in Cambridge, however, it appears possible that either in the preceding session, or, more probably, in the 1736–37 session, the ministry intended to propose an amendment to the vagrancy bill then under consideration that would have restored the monopoly of the patentees and consequently would have increased the control that the Lord Chamberlain could exercise over acting companies. The relevant portion of the manuscript reads: "All Fencers Bear-Wards Common Players of Interludes (Except such as Act or Play under Letters Patent or Licenced granted or to be granted by His Majesty His Heirs or Successors) And all Minstrels and Juglers shall likewise be deemed Rogues and Vagabonds."[45] It was probably this provision (or one like it) that the actors feared might be added to the vagrancy bill scheduled for committee on Wednesday, 30 March. In the event, however, the bill was put off again, from Wednesday to Thursday, and then postponed seven more times before it was removed from the calendar on 5 May and sent back to a select committee that was revising a bill dealing with the related issue of the relief and employment of the poor.[46]

On Friday, 1 April, the Cambridge bill had its second reading and was ordered to a Committee of the Whole House for consideration two weeks later. Two petitions dealing with the bill's prohibition of dramatic performances were also announced on 1 April. Although neither petition appears to have survived, a summary in the House *Journals* of the first, from Joseph Kettle, the owner of the new permanent theater in Cambridge, indicates that he opposed the bill because it would prevent him from using the playhouse that he had gone to considerable expense to erect. The second petition, from "several Gentlemen and Inhabitants of the Town and County of *Cambridge*, and . . . Owners of Estates in *Sturbridge* Fair," also opposed the bill and emphasized, as Kettle's had, that the recently completed theater was intended for use only during the annual fair. Kettle and the city residents asked that they be heard by the House, through their respective counsels, against the pending bill.[47]

The printed case corresponding to the city residents' petition indicates the grounds on which they defended the new playhouse (see App. C-4). They pointed out that plays and other entertainments had always been popular at the fair but that "common Wooden Booths and Boarded Places" had had to be used for them, "to the great Hazard and Inconveniency of the Spectators"; Kettle's "commodious and convenient Playhouse" allowed plays to be performed "in a much more orderly, decent and convenient

Manner, than had been before usually done." The case opposes passage of the new bill not only because it is "unreasonable" in itself but also because it would prohibit an activity in one town that was legal everywhere else in the nation, thereby placing the inhabitants of Cambridge under a restriction "which no other Part of the Kingdom is liable to," and from which "the rest of his Majesty's Subjects . . . in all other places" were and would be free.[48]

The case, the petition that it represented, and Kettle's own petition objected to the new bill on many of the same grounds that the petitioners against Barnard's bill had cited two years earlier. They defended the theater as a lawful economic enterprise, the suppression of which would inflict a severe hardship on those directly engaged in it and unreasonably prevent those who wished to patronize it from doing so.

The petitions may have been a prelude to comments from other groups and individuals interested in having their views on the bill considered by the House. But they were not to receive as full a hearing there as similar petitions had two years earlier. Separate motions were made, and the question called to a vote, for each petition to be brought up to the bar for presentation to the House. In both instances the question failed, and so the petitions objecting to the restriction of "Plays and Interludes" were thrown out.[49]

The following week (3–10 April) was Passion Week. The theaters were all dark, except for Covent Garden, where several musical entertainments were performed, including one on Wednesday by command of the king and queen.[50] The prince and princess had provided a different sort of entertainment at court that same day when it was declared, after Frederick had made broad hints about it, that the princess was then in her fourth month of pregnancy. The announcement was received at St. James's with something less than thanksgiving, and even with some skepticism. During the preceding autumn, when the queen had "expressed open doubts" that her son's marriage had ever been consummated, Hervey told her that Miss Vane, the prince's mistress, had described the prince as "ignorant to a degree inconceivable, but not impotent," but the event proved the degree of his ignorance to have been exaggerated.[51]

After Easter, the theaters resumed a full schedule. At the Haymarket, Fielding's company performed *The Historical Register* every night during the week of 11 April. On Wednesday, 13 April, Fielding moved it to first place in the evening, displacing Lillo's *Fatal Curiosity* as the main play for the rest of the month, and added a new afterpiece. The new play had first been advertised under the title *The Damnation of Euridice* on 15 March as part of the double bill with *The Historical Register* a week before the latter's first performance, but on 21 March the Haymarket offered *Fatal Curiosity* instead. On 4 April another notice appeared, advertising a "very short, but very merry Tragedy, call'd EURIDYCE HISS'D: or, A WORD *to the* WISE" for performance on 13 April, when it finally appeared.[52]

Like *The Historical Register*, the new play exploited parallels between the theater and politics.[53] The ostensible target of Fielding's play is his own farce *Eurydice; or, The Devil Henpeck'd*, which had been offered only once, at Drury Lane on Saturday, 19 February, but had been prevented by rioting in the footmen's gallery.[54] In Fielding's new play, the historical and literary background is represented by the rehearsal of a tragedy (written by "Spatter") that dramatizes the damnation of a farce titled *Eurydice* (written by "Pillage"). At the same time this rehearsal that forms the matter of the play has political overtones. Pillage represents not only a dramatist (Fielding) but also a great man (Walpole) who is "at the very top and pinnacle of poetical or rather farcical greatness" when suddenly "his farce" is damned and he becomes "the scorn of his admirers"(lines 25–31): the "great man" was a conventional designation for Walpole, and the term "farce" had already been established in *The Historical Register* (I.95) as a metaphor for politics.

The connection with *The Historical Register* is emphasized in Pillage's first speech. It refers to the "crowd of actors, / Gaping for parts and never to be satisfied," who daily surround the "author of a farce" (lines 40–41), reiterating the parallel between the theater and politics that Medley had previously established in *The Historical Register* (II.293–96) and that underlies the scene between Apollo and the prompter (III.35–71) in the earlier play. Pillage goes on to make the analogy inherent in his role even more explicit:

> . . . Wolsey's self, that mighty minister,
> In the full height and zenith of his power,
> Amid a crowd of sycophants and slaves,
> Was but perhaps the author of a farce,
> Perhaps a damned one too. 'Tis all a cheat,
> Some men play little farces and some great.
> (44–49)

Spatter then explains that he has made his "Great Man not only a poet but a master of a playhouse," and shows Pillage (whom he and Sourwit refer to as a "great man" four times in six lines) holding a levee for actors who are "soliciting for parts, printers for copies, boxkeepers, scene-men, fiddlers and candle-snuffers"; in the dialogue that follows, Pillage solicits "claps" for his farce from various actors, in return for his promises of parts or favors. The "house" in which his farce is to be tested suggests both a playhouse (Drury Lane, with Pillage in the role of Fleetwood) and the House of Commons, and the "claps," both votes and applause. After the members of the levee have left the stage, Pillage assures himself of the success of his scheme:

> Then I defy the town, if by my friends,
> Against their liking, I support my farce,
> And fill my loaded pockets with their pence,
> Let after-ages damn me if they please.
>
> (122–25)

Pillage echoes the greed displayed by Apollo in *The Historical Register*, who admits to Ground-Ivy's claim that "things [have] carried in the House against the voice of the people before today" but says disdainfully, "Let them hiss. Let them hiss and grumble as much as they please, as long as we get their money." In both cases, as Medley says of Apollo's remark, it is "the sentiment of a Great Man" (III.117–22).

Spatter's "catastrophe," the reception given to *"Eurydice"* (281, 304), occurs in the penultimate scene of the play. "Description" arrives from the house with the news that "all's lost, Eurydice is damned." Although at first "the benches" rang with "loud applauses," "a gentle hiss arose" as the "shallow plot" "began to open more," and "was quickly seconded" "by a catcall from the gallery."

> Then followed claps,
> And long 'twixt claps and hisses did succeed,
> A stern contention: victory hung dubious.
> So hangs the conscience, doubtful to determine,
> When honesty pleads here and there a bribe.

But when "the damnation of the farce was sure," all those who had been engaged to clap "strove who first should hiss / and show disapprobation" (304, 308–17, 328–29).

The "example" (368) here, as in *The Historical Register*, is clearly intended to apply to both the political and theatrical worlds. But the satire of *Eurydice Hissed* is in many respects sharper and more partisan than that of the earlier play. *The Historical Register* undercuts patriots as well as politicians and attacks Walpole under terms that could apply generally to others who abused power. In *Eurydice Hissed*, however, there can be little doubt that the satire is meant to apply specifically to Walpole's method of governing, particularly to his maneuvers in trying to force the excise bill through Parliament. He had introduced the subject in a speech in the House of Commons on 18 March 1732/33, the bill had had its first reading on 4 April, and its second was scheduled one week later. But on 11 April, on account of violent and widespread demonstrations outside and rapidly declining support inside the House, he postponed the second reading "to a later date," a tactic that deliberately killed the bill. Its defeat was noisily celebrated in London, and a year later the anniversary of its defeat was marked by riotous celebrations.[55] The lines in *Eurydice Hissed* referring to Pillage's interest in "pence" and in "raising" his prices probably point to the excise bill; Honestus's remark that he is "most impolitic to affront / The army in the beginning of your piece" (156–57) is almost certainly a reference to the report (made to Walpole by Lord Scarborough) that the army feared that the excise bill would lead to an increase in the price of tobacco, as well as a reference to the scene in *Eurydice* involving the ghost of a military beau.[56] The description of the preparations for and the reaction to *Eurydice* in Fielding's later play (307–29) also parallels the progress of the excise bill, and it seems likely that Fielding offered *Eurydice Hissed* in mid-April to coincide with the fourth anniversary of its defeat. Moreover, contemporary comment leaves no doubt that the play was publicly received, whatever Fielding's intentions may have been, as an allegory on the defeat of the excise.[57] The day after the first performance of *Eurydice Hissed*, in fact, the ministry's newspaper attacked the Opposition for what it claimed was its new practice of enlisting dramatists to criticize the government. In the *Daily Gazetteer* for 14 April, "Lord Littledone" admits that he has persuaded London dramatists "to put into their Plays all the strong Things they can think of against Courts and Ministers, and Places and Pensions, and all that; and they have hit my Humour to a Tittle."[58]

At the end of the week in which *Eurydice Hissed* had its premiere, Parliament was asked to extend the provisions of the pending bill on theaters to include the other university town. On Friday, 15 April, the day on which it had resolved to consider the measure in committee, the House of Commons received a petition from the chancellor, masters, and scholars of Oxford University, adopted there in convocation on 7 April, seeking the same powers that were to be granted to Cambridge (see App. C-5).[59] The petition was presumably presented by the members for the university, Henry Hyde (Viscount Cornbury), long a leading Jacobite, and Edward Butler, "an extreme Tory" who had entered the House in succession to William Bromley on 31 March.[60]

In Cambridge the university authorities had to contend every year with the entertainments offered at Stourbridge Fair, but in Oxford after about 1713 they were generally able to prevent performances: the few existing references suggest that what little drama there was appeared during times of vacation.[61] As late as 1733 companies had attempted to set up in the city, but the authorities were more successful in enforcing their prohibitions than their counterparts at Cambridge had been.[62] Nevertheless, the university decided to petition Parliament to extend the provisions of the bill it was considering for Cambridge to Oxford as well.

After the petition was read it was referred to the Committee of the Whole House which was scheduled to be held that day, and the committee was advised that it had the "Power to extend the Provisions of the . . . Bill to the University of *Oxford*" without having to discharge the bill and draft a new one. But the House later postponed the meeting of the committee once again, to the following Wednesday morning.[63]

Meanwhile, *The Historical Register* and *Eurydice Hissed* continued to play to full houses every night. On Monday, 18 April, while Giffard was offering "a new *Ball Dance*, Dedicated to the Princess of Wales," as part of the entertainments at Lincoln's Inn Fields, the Prince and Princess of Wales themselves and (separately) Egmont were in the audience at the Haymarket. Egmont, presumably like most of those who saw the afterpiece, concluded that the "farce . . . called *Eurydice First*, [was] an allegory on the loss of the Excise Bill. The whole was a satire on Sir Robert Walpole." This remark was much more specific than the one he had recorded after first seeing *The Historical Register*. But Egmont's attention was not exclusively on the stage, and he "observed that when any strong passages fell, the Prince . . . clapped, especially when in favour of liberty."[64] The *Daily Post* soon afterward reported that the prince had "seem'd so pleas'd" that he could be expected to return to see another performance of the plays.[65] The presence and behavior of the prince, of course, did more than help to point the satiric lines of the play. They could also be construed as public expressions of the prince's rejection of—even hostility to—his father's minister, and as public endorsements of the play's political sentiments. They highlighted the growing interaction between the drama and politics that was to lead to the Licensing Act less than six weeks later.[66]

On 19 April, the day after that performance, still another petition from a former distiller was presented in Parliament in opposition to the Cambridge theater bill. It was referred to the committee scheduled to meet on it the following morning, but the committee was postponed yet again, to Wednesday, 27 April.[67] At the same time it became an issue in local politics when, on 22 April, the mayor of Oxford reported to the city council accounts he had received from the city's parliamentary representatives about Oxford University's petition to have its interests incorporated in the Cambridge bill. This news from the capital was the first official notice the council had that the university was seeking legislative action to confirm its authority. In reaction to the report, the council, evidently apprehensive that its own jurisdiction might be infringed by the university's, drafted a petition, "praying that the rights and privileges of the City of Oxford be preserved," and agreed that it "be sealed and sent up immediately by a special messenger to our representatives in Parliament and that it be at their discretion to present it or not as they think fit."[68] The members for the city evidently felt the petition was unnecessary, and it was never presented to either House, although the relief it sought was included in the final version of the bill (see App. C-8, Art. V).

On the same day that the Oxford city council was drafting its petition, Giffard's theater in London offered as an afterpiece a play that reflected the influence Fielding's plays (and others performed by his company) had on the other independent playhouse in London. *The Mad-House*, a "New Ballad-Opera burlesqu'd" written "After the Manner of Pasquin," was advertised as having been "first intended for the Little House in the Haymarket," but it became instead one of the several new plays offered by the company at Lincoln's Inn Fields during the season. Despite its novelty (the epilogue, for example, was spoken by an actor "leading in an Ass"), the play never reached the third night, but it is important as an instance of Giffard's willingness to experiment with new plays written in imitation of Fielding's, his frequent demonstrations of loyalty to the royal family notwithstanding.[69]

April ended with little more official activity affecting the theaters. On Saturday, 23 April, the day after *The Mad-House* was first performed, two footmen stood trial for their roles in the riot at Drury Lane on 5 March. The trial was vigorously contested, with "30 Witnesses examin'd on both Sides," and it "lasted near 7 Hours." When the jury brought in a conviction, both men were "committed to Bridewell" "to be kept to hard Labour for six months."[70] In Parliament, the committee to consider the bill to prevent plays in Cambridge had been ordered for Wednesday, 27 April, but was postponed until the following Monday; the vagrancy bill was scheduled for hearings in committee on Monday, 25 April, and again on Thursday, but both were put off.[71] The House of Commons ended the month with the rejection of a bitterly disputed economic measure. Sir John Barnard, who had led the popular movement to limit the number of playhouses two years earlier, had sponsored a bill to reduce the interest rate of the public funds from 4 to 3 percent, a move that the ministry opposed, predicting it would lead to economic paralysis. The price of stocks fell, there was a run on the Bank, and popular sentiment began to rise against the plan. Finally, on Friday the bill was "flung out of the House of Commons" on a division late in the evening. Outside Parliament, the mob reacted quickly, rejoicing in "a general illumination," and with great difficulty was prevented from pulling down or setting fire to Barnard's house. Instead, it burned Barnard in effigy, all the while shouting "Long live Sir Robert Walpole for ever." As Egmont noted, the reaction marked a significant change in popular opinion from that of four years earlier, when Barnard had been praised in the streets for defeating Walpole's excise.[72]

When the House returned to business on Monday, it at last took up the bill to prohibit plays in Cambridge in a Committee of the Whole House.

Although Townshend had originally introduced the bill, the committee on 2 May was chaired by Walpole himself, who had drafted the bill with Townshend.

Since no detailed records of the committee's deliberations have survived, it is difficult to determine the extent to which the bill was debated. In his preliminary report to the House after the Speaker resumed the chair, Walpole indicated that the committee had considered the relevant petitions, had gone through the bill, and had made several amendments to it: it was almost certainly in this meeting that the bill was amended to extend to Oxford University the same authority it granted to Cambridge University. The House, after hearing the chairman's brief report, ordered the formal report to be received the next morning.

The next day Walpole delivered his report to the House. The amendments proposed by the committee were read, and some of them were further amended; after these and several new amendments had been agreed to, the bill was ordered engrossed. As the Cambridge theater bill moved closer to passage, however, the vagrancy bill came closer to being thrown out: although the latter had been set for consideration in committee on 3 May, late in the day it was postponed again until Thursday.[73]

The action of the House on the universities' bill early in May marked a turning point in the history of theater law: meeting as a committee with Robert Walpole in the chair, it approved legislation that would directly prohibit the performance of any plays in the vicinities of the two universities. Such a proscription, had it been first proposed for London or for the nation in general, would probably have provoked (as Barnard's bill had at various stages two years before) a flood of petitions and substantial opposition in the House. But the bill for Cambridge and Oxford was limited both geographically and politically; it purported to legislate a prohibition that did not exceed the traditional authority of the universities, but only one that their authority had proved inadequate to enforce. Despite these special circumstances, the bill was the first instance of a parliamentary restriction on the theaters since the Commonwealth and in effect set a kind of precedent: members in the House might find it difficult to raise objections based on libertarian principles to legislative suppression of the stage after the House had approved a measure to impose just such a prohibition. Approval seems to have been almost routine. On the same day (3 May) that the House received the formal report from the committee, John Byrom was present at a discussion in which the bill was mentioned: Sir Thomas Aston, an outspoken critic of Walpole (and sometimes of the king), it was said, had been "very abusive upon the Universities" during the deliberations in the House (on what day is not clear), but the consensus seemed to be "that the Cambridge bill had been carried pretty well."[74] The remark suggests that whatever opposition there had been to the bill had probably not been widespread.

As Parliament was moving closer to adopting legal restrictions on theaters in the university towns, new topical satires were continuing to appear on stages in London. On Tuesday, 3 May, and again on Wednesday, Fielding's company performed new plays for the first time since the premiere of *Eurydice Hissed* in mid-April. Of the first new piece, *The Sailor's Opera; or, An Example of Justice to Present and Future Times*, nothing is known beyond the information in newspaper notices, which described it as "A new Ballad Opera" written "by a Female Politician" "in Honour of the Gentlemen of the Navy."[75] Somewhat more is known about the "new Satyrical, Allegorical, Political, Philosophical Farce" titled *Fame* attributed to James Lacy. The last of the play's four subtitles suggests that its satire aimed at very recent political events in Parliament ("Queen Elizabeth's Trumpets; or, Never Plead's Hopes of being a Lord Chancellor; or, The Lover turn'd Philosopher; or, The Miser's Resolve upon the lowering of Interest"). The second may also have referred to Sir John Barnard in connection with contemporary rumors of the plans for major changes in the ministry; earlier in the spring, before Barnard led the movement to lower the interest rate, Walpole had reportedly offered him the chancellorship (but of the Exchequer, not the position of Lord Chancellor), which he refused. Other descriptions in the list of characters likewise suggest that the play was a satire directed in some way at the issue of lowering the interest rate on the funds, and that it bore certain resemblances to Fielding's *Historical Register*: the characters included "Sir Hardheart Pelf, an usurer, and Justice of the Peace; Counsellor Pleadwel, a man of Honour, . . . ; Counsellor Never-plead of Brick-Court in the Temple; an Original Fustian turn'd Auctioneer, preparatory to a Presbyterian Parson; . . . a Pack of Fashionable Ladies and Beaux." Walpole was probably represented by "Mr. Quidnunc, a very deep-headed Man," and conceivably the satire aimed even higher, at the model for the character listed in last place in an advertisement for the play, "George, Counsellor Never-plead's Chief Clerk."

Although the details of the farce are obscure, Lacy himself provided at least a partial description of the action in a letter published in the *Daily Advertiser* on the last day of April, in which he praised the play he had seen "accidentally" the day before in rehearsal. In a statement that may have included a veiled reference to Never-plead's Chief Clerk, he praises the characters for being "strong, lively, majestic, and just," and says he found "the Stile sublime; the Sentiments grand, full of Patriotism; and the Catastrophe so masterly wrought up, that . . . no Farce whatever, now acting will draw more Tears than this." Lacy's description of the part of this "Catastrophe" that affected him "beyond all" indicates that the farce alluded to the possibility (first publicized on 29 March) that Parliament might include in its vagrancy bill (scheduled, again, for committee on Thursday, 5 May) a clause that would reverse the precedent set in the Harper trial by the decision of then Lord Chief Justice, now Lord Chancellor, Philip Yorke: the farce displayed "the Zeal, the exemplary Zeal of a worthy Magistrate [Sir Hardheart Pelf], who so strictly adheres to the very Letter of the Law, as to send a rich and honest Merchant, and Freeholder [Mr. Jamaica] to the House of Correction, as a sturdy Beggar, or Loiterer."[76] The farce was performed only once, as the afterpiece to *Pasquin*, on Wednesday, 4 May, for Lacy's benefit, when, for the first time since its premiere on 21 March, *The Historical Register* was not included in the Haymarket's bill.[77]

A few hours before the Haymarket performances began on Wednesday, the House of Commons took up the Cambridge bill for its third and last reading. The third reading of a bill was usually followed by a motion that the bill pass, but on 4 May the House adopted several minor amendments to its wording after the bill had had its final reading.[78] It was then resolved, evidently without a division,

> That the Bill do pass: And that the Title be, An Act for the more effectual preventing the unlawful Playing of Interludes within the Precincts of the Two Universities in that Part of *Great Britain* called *England*, and the Places adjacent; and for explaining and amending so much of an Act, passed in the last Session of Parliament, intituled, An Act for laying a Duty upon the Retailers of spirituous Liquors, and for licensing the Retailers thereof, as may affect the Privilege of the said Universities with respect to the licensing Taverns, and all other Publick Houses, within the Precincts of the same.

After passing the bill, the House, according to custom, ordered the member who had introduced it, Thomas Townshend, to carry it to the House of Lords for "their Concurrence."[79]

The bill consisted of six clauses (see App. C-8). One (the fifth) provided that nothing in the act would be construed to affect in any way the liberties and privileges of the city of Oxford; this clause suggests that the council's petition of 22 April was considered by the House even though it was never formally introduced. The last clause provided that the act was to be deemed a public act in all judicial proceedings.[80] The second, third, and fourth clauses attempted to achieve a compromise between the traditional right of the two universities to license taverns and public houses, and the pleas by former distillers (who had been forced out of business by the Gin Act and had set up as vintners in their vicinities under the authority of a clause in the same act) that Parliament not deprive them of their livelihood a second time. In the second clause the bill restored the right of the universities to license taverns and public houses, the provisions of the Gin Act notwith-standing. The third clause, however, provided that any qualified distillers who, in accordance with the provision of the Gin Act, had become vintners or wine sellers in Cambridge[81] without licenses from the university could continue in that trade if they took out licenses by 24 June and paid fees proportional to those paid annually by the regular establishments for their licenses; they would thereafter be subject to the same regulations as the other vintners and wine sellers. The fourth clause prohibited Oxford University from collecting any money from any of its licensees apart from fees equal to those usually collected by Cambridge University.

The first clause of the bill dealt with the issue of theaters, the subject of the first petition from the University of Cambridge introduced in Parliament. The clause provided the relief the petitioners had sought, but not by prohibiting the establishment of playhouses, the remedy suggested in the original petition. Instead, the House revived what had been until 1733 the traditional device for suppressing unwanted theaters: it simply revised the definition of "rogues and vagabonds" in such a way as to overturn the precedent established by Harper's acquittal. The House noted that "doubts have arisen or may arise, whether" the universities were "sufficiently im-powered to correct, restrain or suppress common Players of Interludes, settled, residing or inhabiting within the Precincts of either of the said Universities, and not wandering abroad." To remove those "doubts," the bill provided

> That all Persons whatsoever who shall for Gain . . . exhibit any Stage Play
> . . . or other theatrical or dramatical Performance . . . within the Precincts
> of either of the said Universities, or within five miles of the City of
> Oxford, or Town of Cambridge, shall be deemed Rogues and Vaga-
> bonds; and that it shall and may be lawful to and for the Chancellor
> thereof or his Deputy respectively, to commit any such Person to any
> House of Correction within either of the Counties of *Cambridge* or
> *Oxford* respectively, there to be kept to hard Labour for the Space of
> one Month, or to the Common Gaol of the City or County of Oxford, or
> Town or County of Cambridge respectively, there to remain without
> Bail or Mainprize for the like Space of one Month.

Under this provision, anyone taking part in any dramatic performance within five miles of Oxford or Cambridge was subject to imprisonment as a vagrant without trial or bail. Moreover, and most importantly, such persons were to be classified and acted against as vagrants exclusively on account of their involvement in a dramatic performance, irrespective of any settlement, residence, or habitation they might maintain there. The clause was pro-phetic. In less than a month Walpole's government would introduce legislation built around a nearly identical provision; in that case, however, its effects would not be confined to two towns but would extend to the whole country.

The next day, Thursday, 5 May, Townshend carried the bill to the bar in the House of Lords. In accordance with the traditional ritual, Philip Yorke, who as Chief Justice had handed down the decision in Harper's case and who was now Lord Chancellor, met Townshend at the bar, took the bill from him, and carried it into the House of Lords, where it had its first reading as the first item of business of the day.[82] In the Commons, meanwhile, the vagrancy bill came up again for consideration in committee, but this time the order referring it to committee was discharged, and it was sent to yet another select committee (headed by Hay and Pollen) named that day to write a new version of the bill for the better relief and employment of the poor.[83]

On the same day, the *London Daily Post and General Advertiser* published an announcement that highlighted another major change in theatrical activity in London: Henry Giffard, for at least the third time within a year, was advertising to sell his interest and the properties in his theater on the east side of London, a playhouse that had been idle since 13 May 1736.[84] It is not clear whether Giffard, having taken up the management of the more spacious Lincoln's Inn Fields Theatre, was attempting to rid himself of the encumbrance of another house or whether he was in need of money. The three advertisements suggest that whatever his motives or circumstances, however, Giffard had no intention of taking his company back to Goodman's Fields.

There were to be only about a half dozen performances at Lincoln's Inn Fields after Giffard's advertisement appeared, and only nine at the Haymarket. But while the season seemed to be nearing an end, an intense debate was about to open in the press over the plays the London theaters had offered to audiences during the past several months.

The debate began with an ominous attack on Fielding in the *Daily Gazetteer* on Saturday, 7 May, in the form of a letter from "An Adventurer in Politicks."[85] The letter carefully distinguishes between the "Liberty of publickly reasoning on Affairs, or canvassing a Minister's Conduct," which the correspondent associates with the clearly established "*Liberty of the Press*," and "the bringing of POLITICKS on the STAGE," a practice that "no Argument whatever, can be alledged to support." The proper vehicles for criticism are "private Conversation, or . . . Print"; the stage is an improper medium because of three special effects of dramatic satire which the writer goes on to enumerate, taking most of his examples from the Little Theatre in the Haymarket.

"The Election" (the first play rehearsed in *Pasquin*), like Gay's *Beggar's Opera* before it, only exposed "with *Wit*, what ought to be punished with *Rigour*," and thus encouraged, as Gay's play had, the practices it ridiculed. Yet the letter-writer absolves *Pasquin* from "the Fault" its author "has since committed" in *The Historical Register* and *Eurydice Hissed* of "coming so near" in a dramatic representation "as to point *any Person out.*" *The Historical Register* could "make a *Minister appear ridiculous to a People*" and expose him "to publick Resentment" (the hallmarks of seditious libel); *Eurydice Hissed* is even more objectionable because it "insinuate[s] . . . that *all Government is but a Farce (perhaps a damned one too).*" Moreover, such satires have a third effect, the dimensions of which are international and so, the writer suggests, far more dangerous to the nation. "Will the exposing the Ministry before the Eyes of the REPRESENTATIVES of all the Princes in EUROPE," he asks, "give their Masters a *higher* Idea of the *Court of England?* Will it give Us a greater Weight Abroad?"

Having argued that the stage may encourage emulation of the vices it ridicules, public resentment of the ministry at home, or of government generally, and contempt for the nation's leadership abroad, the "Adventurer" describes the proper function of the theater: to provide "a general Mirror, where the Beauties and Deformities of human Nature are represented Impartially; whence we either *copy* or *reject*, as we find our Resemblance *good* or *bad.*"

The lesson ominously suggests the consequences of deviating from the legitimate purpose of drama. "Those who abuse [the] . . . LIBERTY of the Subject," he warns, "give the greatest Shock that can possibly be given to LIBERTY ITSELF, by shewing *how much* the ABUSE *of it, might make a* RESTRAINT *necessary.*" In his reply less than a week later, Fielding showed that he understood this to have been a ministerial threat of repressive measures aimed at the stage.

Despite its dogmatic tone of intimidation, the letter contains—perhaps unintentionally—a note of irony. The "Adventurer" attributes the composition of *Eurydice Hissed* to Fielding's greed, the "*Auri sacra fames.*" By using the same Virgilian phrase (*Aeneid* III.57) that was embroidered in gold characters on the cassock worn by the Chief Magician in "The Vision of the Golden Rump," the "Adventurer" attributes to Fielding the very characteristic that had distinguished the figure of Walpole, his main target, in the satire in *Common Sense* seven weeks earlier. Readers of the *Gazetteer* on that Saturday would not have had far to look for a reminder of the Magician's role in "The Vision": the *Craftsman* for 7 May announced, "This Day is publish'd (price 1s.) A new PRINT, representing the Festival of the GOLDEN RUMP. . . . Design'd by the Author of Common Sense" (see above, Fig. 2).[86]

Fielding's reply to the *Daily Gazetteer*'s "Adventurer in Politicks" was part of a "Dedication to the Public" prefaced to the first editions of *The Historical Register* and *Eurydice Hissed*, published together five days later, on Thursday, 12 May.[87] In his "Preface to the Dedication," Fielding explains his decision to depart from custom by not providing his work with a proper patron (as a good parent, he says, should provide his children with a godfather): instead, in what was probably seen as a reference to the affairs in St. James's, Fielding resolves to throw "the following piece on the public, it having been usual for several very prudent parents to act by their children in the same manner."

Much of the "Dedication" consists of an ironic defense against "the iniquitous surmises of a certain anonymous dialogous author who, in the *Gazetteer* of the 17th instant, has represented *The Historical Register* as aiming, in conjunction with *The Miller of Mansfield*, the overthrow of the M——y."[88] Fielding insists, however, that his play is in fact "a ministerial pamphlet, calculated to infuse into the minds of the people a great opinion of their ministry." The critics in the *Gazetteer* who would have "the scene of politicians" in *The Historical Register* represent the ministry, Fielding says, show a suspicious "eagerness . . . at applying all manner of evil characters to their patrons." Their manner of making the libel by applying it brings to Fielding's mind "a story I have somewhere read" involving "two gentlemen," a "witty spark," and "Bob," his "extremely short-sighted" "grave companion," who while walking come upon "the figure of an ass hung out," which Bob's companion tells him is his picture. Bob falls "into a violent rage" and threatens to prosecute "the master of the house" "for exposing his features in that public manner." The landlord denies the accusation, but the mob "smoked the jest and agreed . . . that the sign was the exact picture of the gentleman." Someone finally takes "compassion of the poor figure . . . [and] whisper[s] in his ear, 'Sir, I see your eyes are bad and that your friend is a rascal and imposes on you. The sign hung out is the sign of an ass, nor will your picture be here unless you draw it yourself.' " Bob may here represent Walpole, as he certainly does in the section that follows shortly thereafter, where Fielding insists that "it is so plain who is meant by the *Quidam* that he who maketh any wrong application thereof might as well mistake the name of . . . Old Nick for Old Bob." At the same time, however, the ambiguity inherent in the word "ass" suggests that Bob may as well be the king; his "friend," Walpole; and "the master of the house" displaying "his features," the manager to whom the dramatic version of "The Vision of the Golden Rump" was delivered at about this time. Such a reading would make ironic sense out of Fielding's otherwise curiously insistent description of this "impertinent story, which," he says, "can be applied only in the above-mentioned instance to my present subject."

The "Dedication" concludes with Fielding's vow to continue to exercise whatever talents nature has given him for "ridiculing vice and imposture . . . while the liberty of the press and stage subsists, that is to say, while we have any liberty left among us." In part because of the consequences of the plays that followed the "Dedication," however, it was soon impossible for Fielding to keep his promise.

Two days later, on Saturday, 14 May, *Common Sense* renewed its offensive against Walpole in another allegorical satire titled "The Rat and the Statue: A Chinese Allegory," involving *"Hoen Kong,"* "his *Chinese* Majesty," and "his Minister *Koan Tchong."* The story describes "what was the most to be fear'd in a Government," the invasion by "a Rat" of the hollow wooden statue erected "to the Genius of the Place." The statue is identified with Hoen Kong in a context that extends its significance to Britain and also suggests a resemblance between it and the wooden-headed Pagod[89] in "The Vision of the Golden Rump": "I could have wish'd our Author had inform'd us, how his *Chinese* Majesty relish'd the Similitude; for, in reality, it was making no Difference between an *anointed* Head and a *wooden one."* The writer wonders how such "a Minister" can "nibble himself into his Prince's Favour, and the Prince not *smell a Rat?"*

Koan Tchong concludes from the allegory that "the Regard one has for the Statue, saves the Rat that's got into it," since whatever action is taken to drive out the rat will invariably damage the statue. The author, however, disagrees, and recommends whatever measures are necessary to prevent the rat from entirely devouring the statue from within. At the same time, the author explains that Koan Tchong's

> Way of Reasoning . . . was a Piece of ministerial Logick, which has been used in other Countries besides *China.* For he so closely connects the Rat and the Statue, and, consequently, the King and the Minister, that, in effect, he makes them but one Flesh, and one would think they grew together like the two *Hungarian* Girls; by this Way of Reasoning, whoever attack'd this all devouring Rat, *alias* Minister, was an Enemy to the Statue, *alias* King.

The footnote, which emphasizes the connection between this allegory and the one in *Common Sense* nearly two months earlier, explains that the *"Two* Hungarian *Girls,* . . . shewn some Years ago as a fine Sight, . . . were fasten'd together by the Rump."[90] Koan Tchong's "Way of Reasoning" proved to be prophetic of "ministerial Logick": Walpole himself argued in very much the same terms within a fortnight before the House of Commons to persuade its members to approve the Licensing Act.

During the week in which Fielding's plays and "The Rat and the Statue" were published, the House of Lords gave all but final approval to the bill to prevent dramatic performances in Cambridge and Oxford. On Monday, 9 May, the bill was read the second time and then referred to a Committee of the Whole House for consideration on Thursday. Joseph Kettle tried once again to petition Parliament for permission to be heard "by Counsel" against the bill (see Apps. C-6 and C-7). In substance, and in most respects even in its wording, his argument this time was identical to that of the case published earlier by the group of gentlemen from Cambridge in connection with their own petition to the Commons on 1 April. In fact, Kettle's petition may have been drawn up at about the same time: it refers to the bill under its old title, which had been formally changed just before it passed the Commons five days before. Kettle's attempt to secure relief from the prohibitions of the bill had no more success in the Lords than it had had a month earlier in the Commons: the petition was presented, read, and promptly rejected.[91] That same evening the Haymarket offered *Pasquin*. It was the last time the play was to be performed in London in the eighteenth century.[92]

The next day the Haymarket offered a public rehearsal of Henry Carey's *Dragon of Wantley* in place of regular performances.[93] Carey had evidently taken the idea for his ballad opera from James Ralph's *Touchstone*, published in 1728, which had recommended Dick Whittington and his cat, Robin Hood, the dragon of Wantley, and Tom Thumb as native subjects for British drama.[94] At the center of the action is a huge dragon who preys on the people of Wantley and is finally dispatched by the heroic knight, Moore. While the dragon was a familiar part of the machinery in farces and pantomimes, especially *Harlequin Doctor Faustus*, during the 1730s it was often used to symbolize the excise bill. In a 1733 ballad titled "An Excise Elegy; or, The Dragon Demolish'd," for example, the bill is represented as "the *Wantley* great Dragon, / Which poor helpless Children did not leave a Rag on." Fielding used the same device in *Tumble-Down Dick*, and the reference to the dragon in "The Vision of the Golden Rump" may have been similarly significant.[95] Carey's play, which was to have its first formal performance on 16 May, almost certainly included a mechanical flying dragon, a device that would have added to its popularity.[96]

On Thursday, 12 May, the day that *The Historical Register* and *Eurydice Hissed* were published, the Lords sat as a Committee of the Whole House to consider the bill dealing with Cambridge and Oxford, and made (in addition to one minor amendment in wording) a change in the first clause affecting the prohibition of dramatic performances. The clause had declared any persons who assisted in a performance for hire to be rogues and vagabonds without providing for any special exceptions, but the Lords acted formally to exclude exceptions. As a result of their amendment, the clause applied its definition of rogues and vagabonds to all persons involved in performances for hire, "any Lycense of the Chancellor Masters and Scholars of either of the said Universities of Oxford or Cambridge or any thing herein or in any other Statute, Law, Custome, Charter or Priviledge to the contrary notwithstanding" (see App. C-8). The amended clause removed any doubt about the extent to which the bill would prevent theatrical performances in or near either of the universities. The committee considered part of the next clause in the bill, and then adjourned until the following Monday (16 May).[97]

Upon reconvening, the committee completed its review of the bill without proposing any new changes. After the third reading on Wednesday, 18 May, "the Question was put 'Whether this Bill, with the Amendments, shall pass?' " and the question "was resolved in the Affirmative." A message was sent to the House of Commons to announce passage of the bill and to ask the lower House to concur with the Lords' amendments.[98]

Although the end of the season was approaching, the theaters continued to offer new pieces during the week of 16 May. On Monday the Haymarket presented two new plays, *The Lordly Husband*, a two-act farce, and *The Dragon of Wantley* in its first public performance; and on Tuesday Drury Lane included as the afterpiece to *Cato* a new farce, *The Eunuch; or, The Darby Captain*. Older plays, a number of them with satiric overtones, continued to be offered as well: *The King and the Miller of Mansfield* was part of a benefit night for Dodsley at Drury Lane on Monday and was repeated on Thursday; *King Charles the First* appeared with *The Honest Yorkshireman* at Lincoln's Inn Fields on Wednesday; while Drury Lane offered *The Beggar's Opera* with *The What D'Ye Call It* the same night. The king, evidently for the first time since his return to London in January, attended the opera at the King's Opera House on Tuesday and probably went to Covent Garden on Wednesday, when Handel's new opera *Berenice* was presented "By His Majesty's Command." Meanwhile, *The Historical Register* and *The Dragon of Wantley* were offered again on Tuesday and Wednesday: although a report published less than a year later indicated that Carey's play had "little Success" at the Haymarket and that the audience had to be dismissed "on the Third Night" (Wednesday), both it and *The Historical Register* were performed again on Thursday.[99]

The same day Parliament passed the first bill dealing with the stage in nearly a century. On Thursday, 19 May, the House of Commons agreed to the amendments made by the Lords to the universities' bill, and Townshend was instructed to carry the bill back to the other House and inform the Lords of the Commons' approval.[100] As a result of the act (10 Geo. II, ch. 19; reprinted in part in App. C-8) no dramatic performances were given in Cambridge, with the exception of puppet shows (about the legality of which there was apparently little agreement) in Stourbridge Fair, for at least eight years. A company from Sadler's Wells that played at a music booth also offered entertainments, but they were limited to "rope dancing; tumbling, postures, singing, balancing and serious and comic dancing."[101]

6

PASSAGE OF THE LICENSING ACT

Parliamentary action on the bill that a month later was to become the Licensing Act began on Friday, 20 May. There seems to be nothing to show a direct connection between it and the universities' bill, but the proposal to the House of Commons, less than twenty-four hours after passage of that bill, of a measure which in its provisions was so similar to the earlier bill makes improbable the assumption that the two bills were completely unrelated. In fact, because the original version of the second bill was apparently so similar to the section in the universities' bill dealing with players, it seems likely that had the second theater bill been proposed before the first had passed, its original provisions would have been added as new clauses to the bill still under consideration, or both bills would have been referred back to committee for consolidation into a single bill. Either procedure would not only have delayed passage of the universities' bill, but would also have meant that further amendment, especially of the sort the ministry intended to make, would have so complicated and so delayed the measure that it almost certainly would have had to be put over until the next session. For reasons that became clear as the second bill made its way through Parliament, the ministry considered such a delay unacceptable.

INTRODUCTION IN THE HOUSE OF COMMONS

On Friday, 20 May, in the House of Commons it "was moved, That the First Section of an Act, made in the Twelfth Year of the Reign of Queen *Anne*, intituled, An Act for reducing the Laws relating to Rogues, Vagabonds, sturdy Beggars, and Vagrants, into One Act of Parliament, . . . might be read," and the motion was approved. The first section of 12 Anne 2, ch. 23 (see App. A-2), included the clause classifying actors as vagrants under which Harper had been unsuccessfully prosecuted in 1733. After the section had been read, the House granted "leave . . . to bring in a Bill to explain and amend so much of [12 Anne 2, ch. 23] . . . as relates to the common Players of Interludes."[1]

Although the bill that was subsequently brought in has always been associated with Robert Walpole,[2] there is no official evidence that he was involved in proposing the measure. The records of the House of Commons do not identify the member who moved that the first section of the old vagrancy act be read, although the standard parliamentary history indicates that it was Walpole who "obtained leave to bring in" the bill.[3] Moreover, Walpole was not even included in the select committee named to draft the bill, which consisted of Henry Pelham, Walpole's "deputy"; George Bubb Doddington; Sir Joseph Jekyll, the Master of the Rolls; John Howe, Walpole's "confidential friend"; Sir Dudley Ryder, the attorney general; and John Strange, the solicitor general.[4] It was apparently not until nearly a week later that Walpole took public action that was thereafter to link him directly to the censorship provisions of the bill.

Although the newspapers the next day (Saturday, 21 May) contained no mention of the parliamentary order for a bill dealing with players, one of them, *Common Sense*, published a letter that defended the stage from recent press attacks.[5] Signed "Pasquin," the letter was a reply to the arguments of the "Adventurer in Politicks" in the *Daily Gazetteer* two weeks earlier. The identity of "Pasquin" is uncertain: the letter has been attributed to Fielding, although Horace Walpole thought Chesterfield had written it.[6]

The stage, "Pasquin" contends in his letter, has not disclosed "Secrets of Government which, like the *Mysteries* of the *Bona Dea*, are improper to be beheld by vulgar Eyes, such as Secret Service, &c." There is consequently little of the danger, which the "Adventurer" had apprehended, that the stage might interfere in some way with Britain's foreign affairs. "I do not believe foreign Ministers to be so weak," "Pasquin" continues, "as to remain in an entire stupid Ignorance of what we are doing; nor do I think, if well-considered, a more ridiculous Image can enter into the Mind of Man, than that of all the Ambassadors of *Europe* assembling at the *Hay-Market* Playhouse to learn the Character of our Ministry." Bringing "Politicks on the Stage" is beneficial to society and good government, he argues, when it exposes "a general Corruption," as the plays of Aristophanes had, and produces that sort of laughter which "Mr. *Hobbes* will tell you . . . is a Sign of Contempt."

"Pasquin" concludes his letter with a reply to another of his opponent's objections, using an extended scatological simile that was especially suggestive in light of the events of the spring. The "Adventurer" had ended his letter with the prophecy that the author of *The Historical Register* and *Eurydice Hissed* might very well turn his talents against "future Administrations" (presumably of those now in the Opposition who support him), but "Pasquin" is confident that even in that event

> they will be able to triumph over, and trample upon all the Ridicule which any Wit or Humour could level at them: For Ridicule, like *Ward's* Pill, passes innocently through a sound Constitution; but when it meets

with a Complication of foul Distempers in a gross corrupt Carcase, it is
apt to give a terrible Shock, to work the poor Patient most immoder-
ately; in the Course of which Working, it is ten to one but he bes—ts his
Breeches.

The first notice in the newspapers of the renewed parliamentary interest
in the theaters appeared in the *Daily Post* on Monday, 23 May. "We hear,"
the paper said,

that a Bill is ordered into Parliament for suppressing the great Number
of Play-Houses or Players of Interludes, so justly complained of, and for
the future no Persons shall presume to Act any Play, &c. without first
obtaining a License from the Lord Chamberlain of his Majesty's
Houshold for the Time being, any Persons acting without such Licence
to be deemed Vagrants and Punished as such, according to the Act of the
12th of Queen Anne.

If this represents an accurate summary of the substance of the bill,[7] then it
must have required actors to obtain licenses (for themselves, not the plays
they performed) from the Lord Chamberlain. The report is especially
significant because it purports to reveal the terms of a bill before the
measure itself was brought in to Parliament. On Tuesday the *London
Evening Post* also reported that a bill affecting the theaters had been
ordered into Parliament,[8] but by the time this notice appeared, the bill had
already had its first reading.

On Monday morning, parliamentary attention to the universities' bill
formally ended when, immediately after prayers in the House of Lords,
Townshend, pursuant to the order of the lower House, returned the bill to
the Lords and informed them of the concurrence of the Commons in their
amendments.[9] Ironically, twenty-four hours after official action ended on a
bill that a number of Cambridge residents had opposed because it imposed
a special restriction against dramatic performances there that did not apply
in the rest of the country, the ministry brought in a bill that would, in its final
form, extend the same prohibition to the nation as a whole.

That Monday night (23 May) the Haymarket offered *The Historical Register* and *Eurydice Hissed*. According to an item in the *Daily Advertiser* that
day, the "Dutchess Dowager of Marlborough" was expected to attend that
evening to see *The Historical Register*.[10] She and the rest of the audience saw
the last performance at the Haymarket that season[11] and also the last performance of *The Historical Register* and *Eurydice Hissed* in London during
the eighteenth century.

The next day, Tuesday, 24 May, "Mr. *Pelham* presented to the House,
according to Order," the bill that was to become known as the Licensing Act.
Its full title suggested that its aim was to control actors and actresses by the

same means that had just been used to prohibit theatrical performances in the two university towns: it was called "a Bill to explain and amend so much of an Act, made in the twelfth Year of the Reign of Queen *Anne*, intituled, An Act for reducing the Laws relating to Rogues, Vagabonds, sturdy Beggars, and Vagrants, into One Act of Parliament; and for the more effectual punishing such Rogues, Vagabonds, sturdy Beggars, and Vagrants, and sending them whither they ought to be sent; as relates to the common Players of Interludes."[12]

The speed with which the bill was brought in, and the earlier coincidence of its having been moved the day after consideration of the universities' bill ended, suggest that it, like the bill that followed it, may actually have been drawn up sometime before 20 May. The only measure introduced in the House after this theater bill was one to settle £50,000 annually on the Prince of Wales and a jointure of the same amount annually on the princess in the event that she survived her husband. The latter bill was first called for in the House on Tuesday, 24 May, just before the theater bill was introduced, but its provisions had been a major factor in the resolution of the dispute over the prince's allowance in February, and Ryder and Strange had begun work on the bill by 25 March.[13] Although the bill for the princess's jointure (as it was often called) was probably ready on 24 May, the practice of the House prevented its being brought up immediately after leave for it had been given,[14] and so its introduction was delayed until Wednesday.

Since the princess's jointure had been a concession by the king, it is perhaps understandable that its introduction in Parliament was delayed nearly two months, until the last possible moment. The reasons why the theater bill was not introduced until so late in the session, however, are not clear. Chesterfield suggested about a week later that the ministry hoped by bringing it in late in May to be able to "hurry" it through both Houses at a time when there would be few members present and when reluctance to delay adjournment through prolonged debates or procedural maneuvering might be strongest.

Besides a hope that the prospect of a prolonged session would discourage scrutiny of the bill, and besides its wish to keep its new proposal separate from the universities' bill, the ministry may have had another reason for waiting until 20 May to bring the matter before Parliament. The introduction of new legislation—even of bills the government wanted to "hurry" through—was apparently useful as a stratagem for delaying the end of the session and thereby preventing the king from leaving the country. Although he had earlier declared his intention to be in Hanover by mid-May, he had remained in London during the first part of the month because Parliament was still considering action against Edinburgh for the murder of Captain Porteous. He felt a strong personal interest in a legal reprisal for the insult the affair had offered to the queen's authority, and the ministry, wishing to delay or prevent his departure (which was certain to provoke unrest—probably violent—in England), reportedly succeeded in prolonging discussion of the Porteous bill.[15] When that measure finally passed the House of Lords on 11 May,[16] however, the ministry once again had to deal with pressure from the king to conclude business in Parliament and so allow him to return to Hanover. Sometime during May Walpole apparently acquainted the king with one or two plays he had acquired in manuscript, the substance of which was so defamatory to the king and queen that the king's interest in the passage of a new playhouse bill[17] made him willing to remain in London long after the day he had set for his departure. Probably for the same reason the ministry waited until the end of May to introduce the bill settling a jointure on the Princess of Wales, a measure that had been part of the compromise Walpole had proposed in February to defeat the motion on the prince's allowance. The king was thereby obliged by an agreement he had never formally approved to wait out an extended parliamentary session until its terms were satisfied.

Another explanation for the timing of the introduction of the theater bill, and one that has been accepted almost universally, is that the measure was drafted in an attempt to block performance of a dramatic farce based on "The Vision of the Golden Rump." Wilbur Cross, for example, reports that once "in possession of the farce, Walpole made immediate use of it for the enactment of a law placing the stage under strict censorship."[18] When it was brought in on 24 May, however, the bill apparently dealt exclusively with players and theaters, and made no provision for any sort of censorship.

CONSIDERATION IN THE COMMONS

Except for the notice in the *Daily Post* on 23 May, there is no direct evidence of what provisions the theater bill contained when it was introduced for its first reading. But on the basis of the final text of the act and of inferences from contemporary evidence and secondary sources, it is possible to reconstruct a tentative outline of the bill on its introduction and to trace the process of its amendment over the next week.

After reviewing the definition in 12 Anne 2, ch. 23, which declared "that all . . . Common Players of Interludes and other persons therein named and Expressed shall be deemed Rogues and Vagabonds," the bill noted, presumably in reference to the Harper decision, that "some Doubts have arisen concerning so much of the said act as relates to Common Players."[19] To remove those doubts, the bill set out a more detailed definition, according to which, beginning on 24 June 1737,[20]

> every person who shall for hire Gain or Reward act represent or
> perform . . . any Interlude Tragedy Comedy Opera Play ffarce or other
> Entertainment of the Stage . . . in case such person shall not have any
> Legal Settlement in the place where the same shall be . . . performed
> without authority by vertue of Letters Patent from his Majesty . . . or
> without Licence from the Lord Chamberlain . . . shall be deemed to be a
> Rogue and a Vagabond within the intent and meaning of the said recited
> act . . .

and subject to its penalties. Moreover, the bill extended this definition of
vagrancy to apply to managers, prompters, and anyone else who might have
a hand in dramatic performances.

Although the intent of this clause was clear, its wording did not resolve
the central question of whether "Letters Patent from his Majesty" or a
"Licence from the Lord Chamberlain" was necessary for all players, or was
required only by those having no "Legal Settlement" where they performed.
It also was not clear whether the Lord Chamberlain's license was to be
granted to players individually, or to a playhouse. The next clause in the bill,
however, completely overturned the precedent established by Harper's
case in 1733. It enacted "that if any person having or not having a Legal
Settlement as aforesaid shall without . . . authority [of Letters Patent] or
License [from the Lord Chamberlain] . . . perform . . . for hire Gain or reward
any . . . Play . . . every such person shall for every such offence forfeit the sum
of fifty pounds" in lieu of suffering the penalties imposed by 12 Anne 2, ch.
23. The wording of the second clause clearly suggests that elsewhere in the
bill the Lord Chamberlain was authorized to license either players or
theaters, or both.

The rest of the original bill probably dealt with the enforcement of these
clauses. It stipulated that in the event that an offender did not pay the fine
and the "distress and sale" of his belongings did not raise the required £50,
he would be committed to the local house of correction at hard labor for six
months, or to the common jail for the same period. Furthermore, the bill
provided that any play performed "where Wine Ale Beer or other Liquors"
were sold would "be deemed to be . . . performed for Gain Hire and
Reward."

In substance, the bill as originally drafted was probably similar to that part
of the universities' bill which had dealt with players. In this case, however,
the prohibition extended everywhere in the nation, excepting only persons
performing under the protection of letters patent or a license from the Lord
Chamberlain; and it imposed the severe penalties of 12 Anne 2, ch. 23, or a
fine of £50, or six months' imprisonment, in place of the one month
imposed by the universities' bill. Had the bill been enacted in this form, it
would have closed the Little Theatre in the Haymarket and every other

theater in the country except those operating under the authority of a patent or those whose company had been or would be licensed by the Lord Chamberlain. Although its provisions were quite different in form, the practical consequences of the original bill would have been virtually identical to those anticipated from Barnard's bill in 1735. It would have legislated a theatrical monopoly in which, in London, only Fleetwood and Rich were likely to participate.

According to a contemporary report, after the bill was read on 24 May, there was "a debate of about two hours upon it, but no Division." This debate may have concerned the kinds of performances recently offered at the independent London theaters, especially at the Haymarket, for the member observed immediately afterwards, "Never was there more occasion for" the regulation of playhouses "sure than at present, for the Stage is scurrilous to the last degree."[21] After the two-hour debate, the bill was ordered for a second reading the next morning, at which another debate occurred.

"THE GOLDEN RUMP"

It was probably either during the debate on Tuesday, 24 May, or on Wednesday that Walpole announced to the House that he intended to move an additional clause to the bill that would empower the government to censor dramatic performances. Before the debate began, Walpole had "made extracts of the most exceptionable passages" in a play he had recently received, and, to illustrate the need for such a clause, "submitted them to several members of both parties, who were shocked at the extreme licentiousness of the piece, and promised their support to remedy the evil. With their advice, concurrence, and promise of cooperation,"[22] Walpole "pull'd this Play out of his Pocket" in the course of the debate, "and read some Passages of it in the House, which disgusted the Members so much, that . . . [e]ven the strongest Opposers of [the bill] . . . were ashamed that the Liberty of the Stage and Press should be prostituted to such vile Purposes, and so much infamous Scurrility."[23] As a result, "a general conviction prevailed, of the necessity of putting a check to the representation of such horrid effusions of treason and blasphemy."[24] This conviction prevailed especially in St. James's, where the new bill became "a favourite point" after Walpole read the play to the king.[25] The first minister evidently exploited the play, and the bill to ban it and similar performances, in order to restore himself in the king's favor.

The play was a farce titled *The Golden Rump*. Although it was apparently never printed or performed, and although the manuscript version used by

Walpole has since disappeared,[26] it is possible to reconstruct enough of the play to confirm that it was based in substance as well as title on "The Vision of the Golden Rump" that had appeared in *Common Sense* two months earlier.

Like its published counterpart, the play "was fraught with treason and abuse upon the government," "abounding in profaneness, sedition, and blasphemy." Its "abuse was vented not only against the parliament, the council, and ministry, but even against the person of Majesty itself."[27] Hervey, who seems to have been acquainted with it at firsthand, described the play as "the most barefaced and scurrilous abuse on the persons and characters of the King and Queen and the whole Court."[28]

There is indirect evidence in contemporary press accounts that at least two parts of "The Vision" (parts that were also represented in the print, *The Festival of the Golden Rump*, which may have been issued to publicize the play) were incorporated in the dramatic version. On Saturday, 28 May, the *Craftsman* published a letter which indicated that Sacoma had had a major role in the farce. The letter was from the same anonymous correspondent who "about two Years ago . . . sent [Caleb D'Anvers] . . . some Remarks on a *Bill*, for the better Regulation of *Play-houses*; which seem'd calculated to destroy a numerous Body of Men, call'd *Strollers*, both *theatrical* and *political*; between whom I drew a short Parallel, and endeavour'd to do Justice to a *certain eminent Stroller*." What had renewed the contributor's interest in this topic, he says,

> was the ill Treatment, my *Hon. Friend* hath lately received from several Authors. . . . They . . . proceeded so far at last, that a *Farce* was actually in Rehearsal, at one of our Theatres, in which the *same excellent Person* was to have been introduced upon the Stage, as we are inform'd, with a *Pair of Scales* in one Hand, to scandalize his *Office*, and *lugging up his Breeches* with the other, to reflect upon his *Politeness*. But *this abominable Design* was happily discover'd by the Vigilance of *another great Personage*, nearly related to him, who hath not only prevented the Execution of it, but is determined to take ample Vengeance upon all *such audacious Authors* and *Players*, by putting an effectual Restraint upon the *Stage*.[29]

Another indication of a specific similarity between "The Vision" and *The Golden Rump* appeared in "An Essay on Kicking" in *Common Sense* on 11 June. The writer says that he has "often observ'd a Kicking to be the most diverting Scene in a modern Comedy." After citing Farquhar's *Trip to the Jubilee*, Congreve's *Old Batchelor*, and Shadwell's *Squire of Alsatia* as examples, he points out that

> Hitherto . . . these Kickings have been only the Support and Ornament
> of the Comick Scene; I wish with all my Heart some Poet of a sublime
> Genius would venture to write a Kicking in a Tragedy; I am very well
> persuaded, if an Author was to introduce a King kicking a first Minister,
> it would have a very good Effect: Such an Incident must certainly give
> great Pleasure to the Audience, and contribute very much to the Success
> of the Play.[30]

Although "The Vision" itself had contained a number of details that easily
lent themselves to representation in a theatrical performance—including a
mechanical dragon, the wand of the Chief Magician (a stock prop for
Harlequin), and even the Tapanta's bell (the device used by the prompter to
cue background music to accompany action or dialogue)[31]—it is unclear
whether the author of the dramatic version adapted the essay with the
intention of having the adaptation performed. This question is directly
related to the identity of the playwright, which was so frequently and
inconclusively disputed in the eighteenth century that the *Biographia Dramatica* assigned the play simply to "somebody or other."[32]

The earliest attribution of the play apparently appeared in the letter to the
Craftsman published on Saturday, 28 May. The correspondent insinuates
that the farce was written specifically to provoke passage of a censorship law
in Parliament: "No other Reasons have been yet given for . . . [the censorship
clause] than what are founded upon an *obscure Piece*, which was never
exhibited upon the Stage, and pretended to be suppress'd; so that it may
have been written on Purpose, for ought we know, and with such a particular Design."[33] The hypothesis was similar to that proposed in the *Prompter*
in mid-May 1735 to explain the advertisement for a "new theatre" in
London, only in this later case the primary purpose was alleged to be the
creation of censorship rather than the statutory restoration of a theatrical
monopoly, and the provocateur was presumed to be, not one of the
patentees, but the king's first minister. The attribution, whatever its merits,
clearly implied that Parliament and the nation were duped into accepting a
law imposing dramatic censorship, and that Walpole himself had been
secretly responsible for "greasing its progress."[34]

Three years later the accusation was repeated in a mock autobiography of
Theophilus Cibber. "Suppose Sir," the author writes, that the "*Golden
Rump* Farce was wrote by a certain great Man's own Direction, and as much
Scurrility and Treason larded in it as possible."[35] Ironically, this "autobiogra-
phy" of Theophilus Cibber has often been attributed to Henry Fielding,[36] the
playwright to whom the ministry repeatedly ascribed authorship of *The
Golden Rump*. If the play had been closely modeled on "The Vision" in
Common Sense, it would have easily found a place in the repertory of

Fielding's theater: its setting and its Oriental flavor were eminently compati-
ble with the atmosphere surrounding the Great Mogul's Company of Comedians, late servants of Kouli Kan and Theodore, who had promised to
entertain the town in the "Eastern manner" earlier in the season.

The first suggestion that Fielding had been involved with the farce
appeared in an "Appendix" by "X. P." to "An Essay on Kicking," published in
the *Daily Gazetteer* on 13 July. "I cannot, indeed, at present, recollect any
Kicking in the *Tragic Drama*," "X. P." admits, echoing the observation of the
anonymous writer in *Common Sense* a month earlier, "but if the Author of
the *Tragedy of Tragedies* had not had his *sublime Genius* cramp'd by an *Act
of Parliament*, I am certain he would immediately embraced the Hint of a
King's kicking his Prime Minister, and wrote a Tragedy of Five Acts, for the
Sake of that single Scene . . . [,] and I doubt not but on this Occasion, he
would have exhibited the kicking Character, *propria Persona*."

The Golden Rump was explicitly attributed to Fielding three years later by
a writer who, if he was not a member of the government or under its
direction, was at least sympathetic to it.[37] "F——ng, . . . Author of several
Pieces that had some Success on the Stage," "Marforio" writes,

> is a strong Instance of Ingratitude to the Ministry as he lies under the
> strongest Obligations to Sir *R——rt W——ple*. . . . I have some Reasons
> to know particular Obligations he lies under to the Minister, who once
> generously reliev'd him by sending him a considerable Supply of ready
> Money when he was arrested in a Country-Town some Distance from
> *London*, and must have rotted in Prison had it not been for this
> Generosity in the Minister. . . . He [later] . . . set up for a Play-Writer, and
> push'd his natural Turn for Ridicule and Satyr so far, that upon the
> Ministry getting into their Hands a Play in Manuscript wrote by him, it
> was thought proper to pass the Act by which the Stage was subjected to a
> Licencer.[38]

Fielding quickly denied the attribution in the preface to "Of True Greatness" (7 January 1741): "I have been often censured for Writings which I
never saw. . . . I can truly say I have not to my Knowledge, ever personally
reflected on any Man breathing, not even One, who has basely injured me,
by misrepresenting an Affair which he himself knows, if thoroughly disclosed, would shew him in a meaner Light than he hath been yet exposed
in."[39]

Some years later Horace Walpole (Sir Robert's son) reaffirmed the
attribution to Fielding in his account of the circumstances that led to passage
of the playhouse bill. "The opposition to the Court," he wrote,

> had proceeded so far, as to be on the point of ridiculing the King
> publicly on the stage of the little theatre in the Haymarket, in a dramatic
> satire, called the "Golden Rump," written by Fielding. Sir R. Walpole,

having intelligence of this design, got the piece into his hands—[I have in my possession the imperfect copy of this piece, as I found it among my father's papers after his death]—and then procured the act to be passed for regulating the stage.[40]

Despite these accusations, however, there is as little direct evidence to show Fielding's responsibility for the farce as there is to show Walpole's.

The manner in which Walpole acquired the manuscript of the play has also never been satisfactorily explained. Chesterfield, speaking in the House of Lords against the theater bill early in June, complained that although he had "made all possible Enquiry," he had been unable to learn any details of "the great Occasion" for the new bill. "I have, 'tis true," he admitted, "learned from common Report without Doors, that a most seditious, a most heinous Farce had been offered to one of the Theatres. . . . But what was the Consequence? The Master of that Theater behaved as he was in Duty bound, and as common Prudence directed: He not only refused to bring it upon the Stage, but carried it to a certain honourable Gentleman in the Administration, as the surest method of having it absolutely suppressed."[41]

In 1740, one of the standard collections of parliamentary debates briefly described the circumstances surrounding the delivery of the farce to Walpole, including the identity of the manager involved: "a farce called the *Golden-Rump* . . . had been brought to the then master of the theatre in *Lincoln's-Inn-Fields*, who, upon perusal, found it was designed as a libel upon the government, and therefore, instead of having it acted, he carried it to a gentleman concerned in the administration." Two years later, a footnote in another standard history of parliamentary proceedings identified the manager by name: "One Mr. *Giffard*, who had removed thither [to Lincoln's Inn Fields] with a Company of Players, from *Goodman's-Fields* where he had a Theatre."[42] Also in 1740, the anonymous author of Theophilus Cibber's "autobiography" repeated the story in greater detail in a way that suggested that most of the information was by then common knowledge:

> Mr. *Giffard* had remov'd about this Time from *Goodman's Fields* to *Lincoln's Inn Fields* House . . . ; His Removal had not answer'd his End, and his Affairs began to grow desperate. He had never as yet given any prejudicial Offence to the Court, yet was suppos'd not to have such Obligations to it, as to deny, at this Juncture, the performing a Farce which might bring him a large Sum of Money. At this Time, in . . . *Common Sense*, there was a libellous Production call'd the *Golden Rump*, which the Town and the Mob were Fools enough to think Wit and Humour: Now as the hitting in with the Humour of the multitudinous Mob is very advantageous to a Theatre, a Dramatick Piece was wrote on the *Golden Rump* Subject, and call'd the *Golden Rump*, which was given Mr. *Giffard* to be perform'd; but before it was rehears'd it so happen'd, no Matter how or why, but so it happen'd, that Mr. *Giffard*

went to *Downing-Street* with this Satirical Farce in his Pocket, which
was delivered to a *great Man* for his Perusal. . . . This . . . is notoriously
certain, that the Farce of the *Golden Rump* was carried to a great Man,
and the Master of the Playhouse, who carried it, was promised something, which he has been some Time in a vain Expectation of, but will
now, in all Probability, end in nothing at all.[43]

Despite the absence of evidence to confirm this account, it has continued
to be repeated in various forms. In 1743 James Ralph claimed that "the
Projector got Possession of [the manuscript] at a high Price," and Coxe,
Walpole's biographer, offered the additional information that Walpole
"paid the profits which might have accrued from the performances, and
detained the copy." An "Anecdote of . . . Walpole . . . [and] Gifford" published
in 1787 indicates that although the minister promised the manager "an
employment equal in its emoluments to 600 *l. per annum*," he never
fulfilled the promise; the *Biographia Dramatica* also mentions the promise,
but implies that it was honored.[44]

In the spring of 1737, Giffard may well have been pressed by financial
necessity to undertake such a scheme in the hope of a reward from the
government. He was still bound by the lease from Sir William Leman for
Goodman's Fields, as well as by the lease for Rich's theater in Lincoln's Inn
Fields, where his company was then performing; he had offered the former
lease, and his interest in the Ayliffe Street theater and its properties, for sale
or auction several times during the 1736–37 season, most recently at the
beginning of May, but apparently without success. Moreover, his attempts in
November 1736 to support the theater in Lincoln's Inn Fields by subscriptions may have indicated financial difficulties: the prompter at Drury Lane
suggested that Giffard's "Success" at Rich's old house "did not answer his
Merit" as well as he had expected.[45]

According to the author of Theophilus Cibber's "autobiography," Giffard's expectation of a reward was a more decisive factor in his delivery of
the manuscript to the ministry than was commonly supposed. He suggests
not only that Giffard acted out of motives unconnected with the impulses of
"Duty" and "Prudence" that Chesterfield had praised, but that his reward
had been arranged before he ever received the manuscript. "Suppose," the
author says, "*Giffard* had a private Hint how to act in this Affair, and was
promis'd great Things to play a particular Part in this Farce. —Suppose he
was promis'd a *separate Licence*, or an Equivalent: —You may then suppose
the M....... a thorough Politician, who knew to manage bad Things to the best
Advantage."[46]

This supposition seems to be confirmed by a letter from Henry Giffard
now among Walpole's papers at Cambridge (see App. C-9). Although the
letter is not dated and does not mention *The Golden Rump* by title, it seems

reasonable to assume in view of the testimony of contemporaries linking Giffard and the farce that the letter was written sometime in the spring of 1737 and probably accompanied the manuscript of the play when Giffard delivered it to Walpole.[47] Giffard acknowledges that it has been "with the greatest Difficulty" that he has "prevaild with" himself "to entertain a Thought of receiving any thing for the Stage, wch might carry in it the remotest Construction against any part of the Conduct of the present happy Administration." Nevertheless, despite his patriotic scruples, Giffard reveals that he has undertaken precisely what his "Principle disclaims," and now must "do a Violence" to his "Inclination, in being oblig'd to receive a Premium" for it, which he instead "shou'd reject" were he not "bound by Fatal Necessity." He concludes with the assurance that "if any thing in my little Power, cou'd contribute to the Welfare of this Government, no Man has it more sincerely at Heart, than . . . Y^r Honour's most Obedient, & Devoted, Humble Ser' Hen^y Giffard."[48] The letter implies that Walpole had arranged in advance to pay Giffard for "receiving" a play critical of the government, and that Giffard had, however reluctantly, subsequently done so.

The report that *The Golden Rump* came to Walpole through the manager of the Lincoln's Inn Fields Theatre has been cited as evidence to refute Horace Walpole's claim that the play was "written by Fielding," on the grounds that he "would never have given to another theatre a political farce certain to draw away from his own house the very audience on which he was depending for the support of his company."[49] Both Drury Lane and Lincoln's Inn Fields, however, performed Fielding's plays during the 1736–37 season; it had, in fact, been Fielding's practice earlier in the decade to offer his political satires to Drury Lane "or another larger theatre" before trying to produce them at the Haymarket.[50]

There may have been special reason for Fielding to seek a different theater for such a play. Although as the manager Fielding was in control of his own company, he did not have exclusive control over the Little Theatre in the Haymarket. The playhouse itself was held by John Potter, who had built it about 1720. Fielding apparently took a lease on the theater about 8 March 1736/37, when the *Daily Advertiser* announced that "the Great Mogul" had just concluded a "Treaty" for the house. Details of the arrangement are not known, but it appears that Potter retained some degree of control over what was performed there, and in May he acted to suppress the performance by Fielding's company of an unidentified play. His intervention was at the request of the Lord Chamberlain, who in turn was acting on the instructions of Walpole. Potter had evidently gone to the Lord Chamberlain when he learned of plans to perform this play and had thereupon been promised a reward if he prevented it. At the end of the first week in January 1738, Potter wrote to the Duke of Grafton to remind him and Walpole of his cooperation with the government. The letter bears several similarities, in phrasing and structure as well as substance, to Giffard's: "As my inclination lead me to my duty to obtain Leave to waite on you and also to aply to the Rt Hon Sir Robt Walpole. In order to prevent what was Intended to be Represented in my theatre in May last it was your Grace's pleasure to declare I should meet with a Reward for such dutifull Behaviour." Moreover, Walpole had put his assurances in writing, for Potter says he has "read the promise of Sir Robt Walpole to the same purport with this adition Soe soon as your Grace and Sir Robt should taulk on that head I should with the Rest of mankind, find due incurragement to bear an honnest mind." Potter concludes his letter with a reiteration of his opposition "to the utmost of my Power against all scandall and defamation," apparently prominent qualities of the piece he had succeeded in keeping off the Haymarket stage.[51]

If it was not *The Golden Rump* to which Potter referred, it was almost certainly a play—or perhaps two plays—Fielding advertised on 25 May, the day on which the new theater bill had its second reading."The Great Mogul's Company of Comedians" was preparing

> MACHEATH turn'd PYRATE: or, POLLY in INDIA. An Opera. Very much taken, if not improv'd from the famous Sequel of the late celebrated Mr. Gay. . . . And after the Run of that, the Town will be entertain'd with a new Farce of two Acts, call'd The KING and TITI: or, The MEDLARS. Taken from the History of King Titi. Originally written in French, and lately translated into English.[52]

The plays were to be performed on 30 May, the anniversary of the restoration of the monarchy in 1660.

Neither of these two plays was performed or printed, but the first, based on Gay's banned play *Polly*, undoubtedly would have been offensive to the government. The second, *The King and Titi*, was almost certainly based on Hyacinthe Cordonnier de Saint-Hyacinthe's *Histoire du Prince Titi*, published in Paris in 1735, a work offensive not only to the government but also to the royal family. The *Histoire* capitalized on the quarrel between the Prince of Wales and his parents; it portrayed the king and queen (King Ginguet and Queen Tripasse in the play) as intending to disinherit Prince Titi in favor of their younger son, Triptillon (the Duke of Cumberland, whom his parents wished to make Elector of Hanover and ultimately king in succession to his father).[53] If either or both of the plays advertised by the Haymarket on 25 May constituted the "scandall and defamation" that Potter had suppressed, it may have been that a copy of one or the other of them came into Walpole's possession and, with *The Golden Rump*, made up the "two plays in manuscript, which were the most barefaced and scurrilous abuse on the persons and characters of the King and Queen and the whole Court," that Hervey reported "Walpole had got into his hands."[54]

Walpole's payments to persons involved in the theaters for suppressing certain plays may have extended beyond Giffard and Potter to Fielding himself. In the preface to "Of True Greatness" early in 1741, Fielding confesses, "I have been obliged with Money to silence my Productions, professedly and by Way of Bargain given me for that Purpose," in a context that is clearly political and that suggests that he received the money from Walpole or someone close to him.[55]

These three pieces of testimony from Giffard, Potter, and Fielding probably each refer to separate incidents. They clearly suggest that Walpole was actively involved in silencing plays through direct but secret negotiations with the two major independent London theaters: Potter was offered money to refuse a play or plays; Giffard was offered money to accept one; and Fielding was offered money to silence his "productions." They illustrate what the *Biographia Dramatica* says Walpole claimed, in regard to *The Golden Rump*, was "the necessity of employing the public money to prevent even absolute treason from appearing on the open stage, unless some authority of another kind could be found for stopping her mouth."[56]

When Walpole distributed portions of *The Golden Rump* to the members of the House of Commons and then read them from the floor, he reportedly did not complain of the attacks against himself and his ministry that they contained so much as of the "insults on Their Majesties,"[57] who were portrayed in a most offensive way. Despite the impropriety of referring to the king in order to affect the outcome of the debate,[58] the impression this scene made on the House must have been comparable to that created a quarter-century later, when "the reprobate Earl of Sandwich read in hushed tones, though with evident relish, the printed text of the 'Essay on Woman' " to the House of Lords. " 'Nobody,' wrote Halifax [the secretary of state] the same evening to the King, 'spoke against the motions [condemning Wilkes] or seem'd desirous of protecting [him].' "[59]

With the exception of the clause creating legal censorship, the other provisions of the playhouse bill had been approved in principle by the Commons two years earlier, and yet had been thrown out for the sake of avoiding such a clause. The use to which Walpole put *The Golden Rump* effectively neutralized the last objections to censorship, objections which, as Chesterfield later implied, had in any event been declining in the face of the increasingly offensive satiric plays of the two previous seasons.

FURTHER CONSIDERATION IN THE COMMONS

At least nominal resistance to the theater bill continued even after Walpole had presented extracts from *The Golden Rump*. According to a letter from a member of the House, it was objected during debate on 25 May that the bill was opposed by many who were absent from the House that day. But "the Master [of the Rolls, Sir Joseph Jekyll] was strong for the suppression of Playhouses &c. and said that thô it was a thin house, yet he thought if those Gentlemen who were absent, as had been urged, should differ in opinion with him & be against the Bill, he thought they were better employed in looking after their own private Affairs."[60] A recorded division (on a motion for the second reading of the Edinburgh bill), the last business that same day, however, shows that there were then at least 245 members present, far more than the 40 required for a quorum and considerably more than what might be said to constitute a "thin" House.[61] Jekyll's comments provoked Pulteney to "roast him most violently," and Pulteney went on to attack three other members who presumably had spoken in support of the bill. He "fell upon Winnington [a staunch supporter of Walpole's] . . . without mercy, & spared not Sr Robt^t [Walpole], nor Sr Wm Yonge [another supporter]."[62]

Pulteney's chief objection to the bill indicates that the Opposition had decided to try to defeat it on the grounds that "this restraint upon the Writers for the Stage, was a certain preamble to the taking away the Liberty of the Press in general." This link between the freedom of the stage and the freedom of the press, which Fielding had emphasized at the conclusion of his "Dedication" to *The Historical Register* two weeks earlier, was to be used again, with greater eloquence but as little effect, in the House of Lords a week later.[63]

Pulteney added "a story" to suggest the motives he believed lay behind the ministry's determination to impose censorship, first on the stage and then on the press: "Charles ye 2^d seeing a man in the Pillory, asked the crime, 'Twas libelling Lord Clarendon, odds fish! crys the King, why did not the Fool go on libelling of mee, he must now certainly suffer for libelling this great man."[64] The letter which is the unique source of information about this debate leaves some doubt as to whether there was a division on the motion to refer the bill to a Committee of the Whole House for consideration the next morning,[65] but the *Journals* show none on the bill during its consideration by the House of Commons.[66]

The next day, Thursday, 26 May, four years to the day after John Highmore had locked his acting company out of Drury Lane and thereby helped to precipitate the chain of events that was finally reaching its conclusion, the House resolved itself into a Committee of the Whole House to take up the playhouse bill.[67] The debate in committee may have been protracted, since it was the only item of business the House considered that day apart from the second reading of the princess's jointure bill. Outside Parliament, the *Grub-Street Journal* reprinted the substance of the announcement about the theater bill that had appeared in the *Daily Post* on Monday, and added only, "This Bill *has very much allarmed our Society.*"

When the committee had finished its deliberations, Pelham, who had been in the chair, reported that its members "had gone through the Bill, and made several Amendments thereunto." According to Coxe, one of the changes, the clause "which occasioned so much obloquy, empowered the lord chamberlain to prohibit the representation of any theatrical performances, and compelled all persons to send copies of any new plays, parts added to old plays, prologues and epilogues, fourteen days before they were acted, and not to perform them, under forfeiture of £50, and of the licence of the house."[68] Copies of new dramatic pieces were to be sent to the Lord Chamberlain "together with an account of the Playhouse or other place where the same shall be and the time when the same is intended to be first acted . . . signed by the . . . Manager or one of the Masters . . . of . . . [the] Company of actors."[69] Although no official record survives of the proceedings in committee on 26 May, a French report from London on 30 May (10 June NS) indicates that the clause was brought to a vote in the committee and was adopted, with 185 members in favor of it and only 63 against.[70]

The clause did not authorize the Lord Chamberlain to grant permission for performances or licenses for plays: its only requirement in respect to plays or other dramatic performances was that, on penalty of a £50 fine and revocation of the theater's license, a copy of every new piece, together with an indication of the place and time intended for its first performance, signed by the manager of the playhouse, had to be sent to the Lord Chamberlain at least fourteen days in advance of the performance. But the clause did empower the Lord Chamberlain "to prohibit the acting performing or representing any Interlude Tragedy Comedy Opera Play ffarce or Other Entertainment of the Stage or any Act Scene or part thereof or any Prologue or Epilogue." His power extended not only to every play, old or new, but to every performance of every play, whether the play itself had been licensed by him or not. Moreover, the Lord Chamberlain's power to censor was entirely unrestricted: he was to exercise it "from time to time and when and as often as he shall think fit," and from his decision there was no provision for an appeal in law.

A second clause, probably added to the bill in committee, restricted the location of playhouses by providing that letters patent from the king, or "the License of the Lord Chamberlain" authorizing dramatic performances for payment, could not extend to "any part of Great Britain Except in the City of Westminster and within the Liberties thereof and in such places where his Majesty his heirs or successors shall in their Royal Persons reside and during such residence only." The clause abridged the prerogative of the king to authorize theaters by letters patent anywhere in the country, restricting that power, and consequently the presence of theaters, to Westminster. This clause, which closely resembled one of the main provisions of the unsuccessful theater bill of 1735, was reportedly proposed by the sponsor of the earlier bill, Sir John Barnard.[71]

The bill, as amended, would once again make players subject to a virtual monopoly on the part of the patentees by exposing actors to arrest as vagrants or to a fine if they acted for payment in an independent theater. Second, it would restrict theaters to Westminster, thereby limiting the king's traditional prerogative to grant letters patent.[72] Third, it would impose unrestricted dramatic censorship by force of law; and by requiring managers to submit new plays to the censor, it would particularly empower him to exercise prior restraint over contemporary dramas. Its heavy penalties in each of the three areas would apply equally to everyone involved in a violation, managers and players alike. It would mean the immediate end of provincial theaters, of the independent theaters in London and Westminster, and of the relative independence of players that had been established by the verdict in Harper's trial in 1733. It would mean the prohibition—or, what in some ways might be more significant, the unpredictable threat of prohibition—of every dramatic performance that the Lord Chamberlain thought "fit" to interdict. It would mean that no new play critical of the government could be performed in the future except with the government's official permission, which, if granted, would show that the government did not think the play worth prohibiting. For the theaters, it would formalize the monopoly of the patentees under the control of the Lord Chamberlain. For the drama, it would make every performance of every play liable to prohibition at any time and for any reason, or for none.

After the committee completed its work on the bill, Pelham indicated to the House of Commons that he was ready to deliver its report, and the House ordered that it be received the next morning.[73] The next day, Friday, 27 May, he delivered the bill, with its amendments, to the clerk. The House voted on each amendment (one of which "was disagreed to") and then added several more amendments.[74] Finally, the bill, with its amendments, was ordered to be engrossed prior to the third reading.

By the end of the deliberations that Friday, it was clear that the bill would be approved. The next day, 28 May, Cope observed in a letter to Edmund Weston that "ye Bill will pass & no playhouse be allowed but in the Libertys of Westminster, & those to be licens'd & under the direction of the Lord Chamberlain."[75]

PASSAGE IN THE COMMONS AND INTRODUCTION IN THE LORDS

While passage of the bill may have seemed all but a certainty in Parliament, disagreement over the measure was just beginning to appear in the press.

On Saturday, 28 May, the *Craftsman* printed an anonymous letter purporting to be from a person who had written to the *Craftsman* in 1735 (issue of 28 June) opposing Barnard's bill. In this case, however, he claimed to support the new bill as a measure necessary to protect his *"honourable Friend," "a certain eminent Stroller,"* from "the ill Treatment . . . [he] hath lately received." The letter describes "a *Farce*," probably *The Golden Rump*, that "was actually in Rehearsal, at one of our Theatres," in which his "Friend" was represented in the posture in which Sacoma is portrayed in the print of *The Festival of the Golden Rump*. *"This Abominable Design,"* the letter reports, "was happily discover'd by the Vigilance of *another great Personage*, nearly related to Him, who hath not only prevented the Execution of it, but is determined to take ample Vengeance upon all *such audacious Authors* and *Players*, by putting an effectual Restraint upon the *Stage*."

The letter goes on to quote the same report of the bill that had appeared in the *Daily Post* on Monday and in the *Grub-Street Journal* on Thursday. From it the correspondent concludes that the bill under consideration "will effectually keep the *Stage* within due Bounds, and remedy the Evil, *so justly complain'd of*," since the Lord Chamberlain will never "suffer any Thing to be brought upon the *Stage*, which is not intirely agreeable to the *Court*; much less such obnoxious Performances as the *Beggar's Opera, Pasquin*, the *historical Register*, and other Pieces of the like Kind. He may likewise prohibit the Representation of any *old Plays*, which breathe the same factious Spirit; or, at least, without being duely gutted and modell'd to the *present Times*."

Sunday was the anniversary of Charles II's birth; Monday (the day advertised for the first performance of *Macheath Turn'd Pyrate; or, Polly in India* at the Haymarket) was the celebration of his restoration; and according to custom, Parliament did not meet over the "Holydays."[76] On Tuesday, 1 June, the playhouse bill was read for the third time in the Commons. During the recess the bill had been engrossed by being copied out in a distinctive "engrossing hand" on five presses, skins of parchment about eighteen inches long and twelve inches wide, which were then sewn together head to tail: this fair copy of the bill became the "original act" after it passed the House of Lords and received the royal assent (see Frontispiece). Since the playhouse bill was to be a public act and had been treated as such from the beginning, it was never officially printed (as Barnard's had been).[77]

After the third reading the Speaker, according to form, asked of the House, "Is it your pleasure that the bill do pass?" The House, on a voice vote, indicated its assent. At the top of the bill was written "Soit baillé aux Seigneurs" to indicate approval by the lower House, and Pelham was ordered to carry the bill to the Lords and to "desire their Concurrence."[78] The bill was delivered the same day to the House of Lords, where it immediately had its first reading and was ordered for second reading the following day.[79] The *Daily Post* reported its passage by the House of Commons the day after it occurred. Only nine days—four of them holidays—had elapsed from the first reading of the bill to its passage in the Commons.

It is not clear how much opposition to the measure was registered in the lower House. William Coxe was apparently the first to claim "that not a single petition was presented against [the bill] . . . , and not a single division [on it] appears in the journals of either house. Striking proofs," he notes, "if any were still wanting, to shew the general opinion in favour of its necessity."[80] Although no record of any petition appears in the *Journals*, Sir John Hawkins reports that Giffard himself petitioned against the bill. Coxe believed that Hawkins was referring mistakenly to Giffard's petition against Barnard's bill two years earlier,[81] but Hawkins may have had in mind "The Case of the Proprietors of the Theatre in *Goodmans-Fields*," which was evidently written sometime during the last week in May 1737 to oppose the playhouse bill while it was in the House of Commons (see App. C-10). The 1737 case resembles the one the subscribers to the Goodman's Fields Theatre wrote in 1735 (although the 1737 case of the proprietors sets the amount of the 1731 theater subscription at £2,500, or £200 more than the figure in the earlier case and petition).[82]

The proprietors of the vacant Goodman's Fields Theatre were not the only group outside Parliament to raise objections to the bill and to seek "some Provision" for themselves while it was under consideration in the House of Commons. Eight "lessees of the Theatre-Royal in Drury-Lane"—all of those named as lessees in the case from Drury Lane in 1735 except John Mills and Mary Heron—repeated in 1737 the objections they had raised to Barnard's bill two years earlier (see App. C-11). Once again their chief fear was that Fleetwood might leave the theater, taking the patent with him and leaving them with a playhouse that could not be used, along with what was then an eleven-year lease on it, the expenses of which exceeded £1,000 annually. As a contemporary observed three years later, the "actors were . . . alarm'd [over the provisions of the bill], and imagin'd this Act would lay them under Oppressions, from which they could gain no proper Redress; for the constant immemorial Way of redressing Grievances, in the Government of a Theatre, is to raise a Revolt, and bring about a Revolution."[83] Like the proprietors of Giffard's old theater, the lessees of Drury Lane clearly recognized the major issue involved in the new bill, and they went so far as to endorse the proposal to regulate dramatic performances. But, like their counterparts at Goodman's Fields, they added a paragraph to their case to convince the legislature that their theater was not one of those that needed to be silenced. The lessees, the case says, "have in all Instances *demonstrated* their *Duty, Affection* and *Loyalty* to HIS MAJESTY, and the present HAPPY

ESTABLISHMENT, and ever have (AS FAR AS LAY IN THEIR POWER) *discountenanced* any thing that had the *least Tendency* to *Vice, Immorality* or *Disaffection.*"

Contemporary reports and modern histories have agreed that the London patentees actively supported the bill. Three years after it became law an anonymous writer recorded what he said "was known to all. The Masters of the two Houses acting under the Patent made no Opposition to this Bill; they did all in their Power to promote it, because it would suppress, for the present, all Theatres but their own."[84] Charles Fleetwood petitioned the Lord Chamberlain directly to express his less-than-enthusiastic support for the bill. Fleetwood's "Memoriall" in the Walpole papers at Cambridge (reprinted in App. C-12), like the cases of the lessees of his theater and of the proprietors of the house in Goodman's Fields, deplores recent trends in drama and recognizes the need "to suppress immediately this pernicious growing Evil." But Fleetwood also reveals an anxiety about the bill that seems at first appropriate only to someone like Giffard, who was almost certain to face ruin if it passed: "Somethings, contain'd in this Bill, may possibly bear too hard, upon a *Large Intrest, & property*, he has *from a patent Granted by his present Majesty*, which might reasonably induce him to *petition*, for such provisoes, as might *Establish*, & *exempt*, his *Grant*, . . . but [instead he] throws *himself* & *property* entirely upon *his Majesty's* know Goodness and under his *protection.*"[85]

One possible explanation for Fleetwood's attitude may lie in the clause that would revoke a theater's "Grant License and Authority" if it performed a prohibited play, or a new play before it submitted a copy to the Lord Chamberlain. A more satisfactory explanation of his position, however, as well as of the otherwise puzzling references in the engrossed bill to the Lord Chamberlain's authority to "license" theaters, may be suggested by a paragraph in the *Craftsman* on 28 May. Having noted earlier that under the bill the Lord Chamberlain "is to have the absolute Power of Licensing *Playhouses*," the writer goes on to complain that "the *Theatre* should be made a *meer Tool of the Court*, by the Abolition of Patents . . . and converting them into *temporary Licence's, during Pleasure.*" This comment suggests that one provision of the bill would abolish patents and replace them with temporary, revocable licenses; such a provision would account not only for Fleetwood's anxiety over the bill, but also for references within the bill itself to licenses for theaters granted by the Lord Chamberlain, licenses which the bill did not authorize him to issue, and which, later in the century, were to become a matter of considerable dispute.[86] It may be that before the bill passed the House of Commons a clause in it was eliminated that would have abolished the patents then in force, replaced them with licenses, and given the Lord Chamberlain absolute authority not only to prohibit any dramatic performance, but also to close any theater at any time simply by revoking his license for it; the same clause presumably authorized the Lord Chamberlain to issue licenses for theaters. Whether such a clause was the amendment that the House apparently adopted in committee on 26 May and then dropped the next day, or was part of the original bill on 24 May, or was ever part of the bill at all, can only be matters of speculation. But Fleetwood's memorial, as well as the reference to licenses in the case of the proprietors of Goodman's Fields and the comments that appeared in the *Craftsman* the day after the Commons completed work on amendments to the bill, all point to the existence of such a clause, which was probably eliminated from the bill by 26 or 27 May.

That no petitions on the bill were presented to either House of Parliament, however, suggests either that opposition to it by those outside Parliament was not nearly so strong as it had been against Barnard's bill, or that those who objected to some of its provisions considered it fruitless to carry their opposition to the legislature. There is, in fact, some evidence that the bill met with little real opposition in either House. The frequent claims that its progress "caus'd great Debates in both Houses," or that in "both Houses . . . there were long debates, and great opposition to this Bill in every step it made," are probably exaggerated.[87] Hervey reported that in "the House of Commons little opposition was made . . . by anybody of note but Mr. Pulteney, nor in the House of Lords but by Lord Chesterfield." So little resistance did the bill meet with that one of the other leaders of the Opposition in the Lords, "Lord Carteret, . . . pleaded great merit at Court from his having said nothing against this Bill, which he knew was a favourite point at St. James's."[88] Neither of the speeches against the bill for which there is evidence seems to have had much effect on its passage; moreover, there is no indication that those who may have opposed it made any attempt to hinder its passage indirectly by parliamentary maneuvering.[89]

CHESTERFIELD'S SPEECH

The most famous and well-documented objection to the bill occurred in the House of Lords, where Chesterfield argued against it in debate. Unlike Pulteney's speech in the Commons, Chesterfield's speech in the Lords has survived to become a classic statement of opposition to censorship. Hervey, who heard it, called it "one of the most lively and ingenious speeches . . . I ever heard in Parliament, full of wit, of the genteelest satire, and in the most polished, classical style that the Petronius of any time ever wrote. It was extremely studied, seemingly easy, well delivered, and universally admired. On such occasions nobody spoke better than Lord Chesterfield."[90] While Hervey was listening on the floor of the House, Colley Cibber was evidently sitting in the gallery[91] and was moved to similar admiration: never, Cibber claimed, "did Orator command more deep Attention:—His charmed Auditors stood motionless, and silent as calm Night;

> They were all Ear. —
> The raptured Soul absorb'd in deep Attention,
> Caus'd every other Sense to drop its Function,
> As Hearing were it's only Faculty."[92]

The very popularity of the speech may have led to an impression of widespread opposition to the bill; it "is most probably," Coxe observed, "that lord Chesterfield alone spoke against the bill, and that his speech . . . has been repeated by subsequent writers who copy each other, until a violent opposition to the measure has been supposed, which never existed."[93] Despite the rapture produced in some parts of the House by the speech, which Chesterfield reportedly wrote out at length and memorized in advance,[94] events four days later indicated that it stirred little, if any, opposition to the bill.

The speech was probably delivered in the House of Lords during the only debate on the bill recorded in the *Journals,* which occurred after the second reading on Thursday, 2 June, over the question of whether the bill should be referred to committee.[95] Despite Chesterfield's general opposition to the playhouse bill, his speech contained few passages directly defending the stage. In fact, much of it was given over to arguments that, while ostensibly showing that a new law was unnecessary, admitted that many recent dramas deserved to be prosecuted under existing laws.

Chesterfield insisted that he was "as much for restraining the Licentiousness of the Stage . . . as any of" the other members of the House, and that "our Stage ought certainly . . . to be kept within due Bounds," but, he added, "for this, our Laws, as they stand at present, are sufficient," at least "for punishing those Players who shall venture to bring any seditious Libel upon the Stage, and consequently sufficient for deterring all Players from acting any Thing that may have the least Tendency towards giving a reasonable Offence." As examples of the sort of drama that deserved prosecution, he described two plays, Fielding's *Pasquin* and Havard's *King Charles the First,* "which, one would have thought, should have given the greatest Offence, and yet both were suffered to be often represented without Disturbance, without Censure. How these Pieces came to pass unpunished, I do not know: If I am rightly informed, it was not for Want of Law, but for Want of Prosecution; without which no Law can be made effectual." Such a prosecution, he implied, would be a relatively simple matter: "If a Play appears to be a Libel upon the Government, or upon any particular Man, the King's Courts are open, the Law is sufficient for punishing the Offender; and in this Case the Person injured has a singular Advantage; he can be under no Difficulty to prove who is the Publisher; the Players themselves are the Publishers, and there can be no Want of Evidence to convict them."[96]

Besides joining in the general condemnation of Fielding's satire, Chesterfield dealt specifically with *The Golden Rump*: "I have," he said, "learned from common Report without Doors, that a most seditious, a most heinous Farce had been offered to one of the Theaters, a Farce for which the Authors ought to be punished in the most exemplary Manner."[97] But Chesterfield could find no grounds in the incident of *The Golden Rump* to justify the bill then before the House:

> The Master of that Theater behaved as he was in Duty bound, and as common Prudence directed: He not only refused to bring it upon the Stage, but carried it to a certain honourable Gentleman in the Administration, as the surest Method of having it absolutely suppressed. . . . The dutiful Behaviour of the Players, the prudent Caution they shewed upon that Occasion, can never be a Reason for subjecting them to . . . an arbitrary Restraint: It is an Argument in their Favour, and a material one, in my Opinion, against the Bill.

The bill, he contended, could not be enforced effectively. Old plays might be applied to satirize contemporaries, and so used not by managers or actors but by "the People who [point] . . . the Satyr," and "the Audience will apply what never was, what could not be designed as a Satyr on the present Times." Moreover, the bill would tend "towards a Restraint on the Liberty of the Press, which will be a long Stride towards the Destruction of Liberty itself." Plays would be written "on Purpose to have a Refusal," since it "will be much easier to procure a Refusal than it ever was to procure a good House, or a good Sale." Once banned, the play "will be printed and published . . . with the Refusal in capital Letters on the Title Page," which will "certainly procure a good Sale."[98] Thereupon, Chesterfield predicted, Parliament will be asked for a bill to prevent such libelous plays from being printed and published, and, when to escape that law, satires are written "by Way of Novels, secret Histories, Dialogues, or under some such Title," it will be asked finally for a bill putting "the Press under a general Licence, and then we may bid adieu to the Liberties of *Great Britain*."[99] That the playhouse bill would lead to general censorship of the press was, Chesterfield implied, the secret intention of those who had introduced it.

He argued that for these reasons the bill "ought to be maturely considered, and every Clause, every Sentence, nay every Word of it well weighed and examined." "There can," he said, "be no great and immediate Danger from the Licentiousness of the Stage: . . . it will not be pretended that our Government may, before next Winter, be overturned by such Licentiousness, even tho' our Stage were at present under no Sort of legal Controul." Consequently, he objected that the bill "ought not to be introduced at the Close of a session, nor ought we, in the Passing of such a Law, To depart from any of the Forms prescribed by our Ancestors for preventing Deceit and Surprize." He disapproved of the bill's having "been brought in at a very extraordinary Season, and pushed with most extraordinary Dispatch . . . [at] the End of the Session." Since then, the charge that the bill was "hurried" through Parliament has been a commonplace of theatrical history; but while the speed with which it was adopted was unusual, it was hardly unprecedented, and the *Journals* show that its progress through each House followed scrupulously each of the "Forms" required by parliamentary procedure.[100]

The next day, Friday, 3 June, the House of Lords, in accordance with its usual practice, adjourned into a Committee of the Whole House on the playhouse bill. Although the *Journals* do not record what occurred in committee, the manuscript minute book in the House of Lords Record Office reveals that Chesterfield's eloquence had had little practical effect. The minutes show that after Lord Delawarr took the chair of the committee, the bill was read, clause by clause; each was "agreed to, to the end of the Bill," and the House then resumed in regular session. Delawarr "reported from the . . . Committee, 'That they had gone through the Bill, and directed him to report the same to the House, without any Amendment.'" The bill was ordered for its third and last reading the following Monday.[101]

THE NEWSPAPERS REACT

In the meantime the debate moved from Parliament to the newspapers, where the issue of press censorship gradually replaced the Licensing Act as the principal topic. On Saturday the *Daily Gazetteer* printed another essay by "An Adventurer in Politicks" that rebutted the arguments put by "Pasquin" in *Common Sense* three weeks earlier (21 May). The "Adventurer," using a method that was quickly to become standard in the newspaper war, bases his attack on historical parallels. He extends his adversary's reference to Aristophanes to a discussion of the merits of Greek comedy, implying at each point an analogy to contemporary drama. Exactly the same method is adopted by "R. F." (almost certainly "R. Freeman," Ralph Courteville's pseudonym)[102] in the *Daily Gazetteer* of 10 June, which consists of an extended history of the stage and its regulation in Greece and Rome.

The argument presented by the "Adventurer" underlines the concern the ministry had about "particular" satires, an issue that the *Gazetteer* debated with the opposition papers week after week throughout most of the summer. "There is something peculiarly absurd," the "Adventurer" writes to "Pasquin,"

> in your quoting *Aristophanes* in your own Justification; . . . whose licentious Abuse of the Stage, put the *Athenians* upon the very Thing our Legislature is now passing into a Law. Every Body that has the least Acquaintance with Literature, knows what *Vetus Comoedia* was; and that the Licentiousness of it took in not only private Life, and as near as was possible, the very exact Figure of Persons; but exposed on the Scene, the principal Men of the Republick by Name.

Aristophanes portrayed even Alcibiades and Pericles in

> their ministerial Characters, as well as their private ones, with the same Licentiousness. . . . This Abuse of Comedy at length stirr'd up the Indignation of the *Athenians*, who thought the *Minister* as well as the private Man accountable to them for his Actions, and not to the Poet; and finding, as *Horace* tells us, the Grievance fit to be restrained by Law, they did restrain it by Law.[103]

The same day *Common Sense* carried a letter from "A. Z." dealing with the playhouse bill. Several of its arguments resemble those advanced by Chesterfield two days earlier in the House of Lords, and the letter itself has sometimes been attributed to him.[104] Although "A. Z.," like Chesterfield, agrees that the "Design" of the bill ("the Regulation of Theatrical Entertainments") "is certainly worthy the Care of the Legislature," he also objects that the bill will "be ineffectual to the End proposed." Just as the bill will put playwrights at the mercy of the arbitrary power of the licenser, the writer argues, it will lay a similar "Restraint on the Actor" by subjecting "him to the arbitrary Will of an insolent Patentee." On all accounts, the bill will injure rather than improve the stage, and will simultaneously threaten other liberties: "A. Z." adds, rather cryptically, that he "need not mention the Infringement attempted by this Act on the Liberty of the Press."[105]

An essay in the *Craftsman* the same day (Saturday, 4 June) shares the same apprehension that the bill is "a Point of much greater Consequence than it seems to be generally imagined." Nothing will "be wanting to compleat *such a Scheme*," the writer says, "could I suppose any Man so wicked as to entertain the Thoughts of it, but putting the *Press* under the same Restraint; and that, I am afraid, is too natural a Consequence of the other." He ends with the observation that since the bill has been "carried through one House with so much Expedition, and even Precipitancy, . . . I shall hardly have any Opportunity of speaking my Mind freely upon it again, unless it should be rejected in the *other*."[106] His fear that the paper would not be able to comment again on the bill proved to be unfounded, however.

The *Craftsman* as well as other papers continued to debate the merits of the bill and the question of censorship generally throughout the summer.

On Monday, 6 June, the *Daily Gazetteer* renewed its defense of the bill in an essay that was the first in a series of six essays over the next nine days tracing the history of the regulation of the stage and explaining why the new bill was reasonable and necessary. The essay that appeared in the *Gazetteer* on 6 June is one of the clearest statements of the ministry's claim that modern dramatic performances were directly related to, and in fact were a primary cause of, the disturbances and unrest that had prevailed in the capital during the previous year. "I appeal," "R. F." says, "to every sober *Housekeeper* in *London* and *Westminster*, for the *Truth* of this Proposition, *That the present* Spirit *of* Tumult, Contempt *of* Laws, Sacred *and* Civil, *and that* Proneness *to* sensual Pleasures, which deform *the* Manners *of the* present Age, *could ever have taken Place, but from the* Licentiousness *of the* Stage *for many Years past.*" Under existing law, the essay points out, only actors are subject to restraints; no penalties can be "laid on the *Wits.* . . . *Libels* may be *Written, Sung,* and *Said,* nay *Printed* and *Published,* too, with tolerable *Impunity.*"

PASSAGE IN THE LORDS

The debate that was rapidly growing between the government's newspaper and the papers sympathetic to the Opposition was overtaken by events that same day. The House of Lords gave a third reading to the playhouse bill on Monday, 6 June, and when the "Question was put, 'Whether this Bill shall pass?' It was resolved in the Affirmative." "Aceste Bille les Seigneurs sont assentus" was written at the top of the engrossed bill to signify the agreement of the upper House, which it had taken only four days to grant. Messengers were then sent to the House of Commons to announce that the playhouse bill had been agreed to by the Lords without any amendment. After the message was delivered to the Commons on Wednesday, nothing remained except the king's assent to put the new law into effect.[107]

An entry in the House of Lords manuscript minute book for 6 June indicates that Chesterfield's eloquence in debate and the arguments in the press opposing the bill had had little effect on members of the upper House. Despite the frequently repeated belief that no divisions on the bill occurred in either House, this and other documents in the House of Lords Record Office show that one was called in the Lords on the question of whether the bill should pass. Cholmondeley is listed as the teller for the "Contents" (those voting for passage), and "Stanhope" (the Earl of Chesterfield) as teller for "Not Cont." (The latter entry, however, is overwritten: another name, apparently "Rockingham," was erased from the minute, and Stanhope's written in its place.) Since the tellers were usually named from among those who had actually participated in the debate on a bill, the record suggests that Cholmondeley may have spoken for the government on 2 June, as Chesterfield (and perhaps Rockingham) had for the Opposition.[108] In any event, the result of the vote tends to confirm reports that while Chesterfield's "Speeches are admired, and his Wit . . . matchless, . . . both have no other Effect but upon the Ear," and that his arguments on this occasion "had no effect, though the house admired his elocution."[109] After only two routine items of business that day, the number of members in attendance had dwindled from fifty-eight, the number present during prayers, to forty-two when the division was called on the playhouse bill. The vote was a complete defeat for those opposing the bill: thirty-seven members voted for passage, and only five (including Chesterfield) voted against it.[110]

7

PUBLIC REACTION AND THE
ROYAL ASSENT

On Wednesday, 8 June, the *Daily Gazetteer* resumed its series of essays on the theaters. "There is not one sober, impartial Man," the writer insists ominously, "but must see and acknowledge, that the *personal* Abuse of *Majesty* itself, as well as the encouraging and promoting all manner of Vice and Immorality, is carried to such a Length, that if some speedy and effectual Stop be not put to such daring Licentiousness, we can expect nothing less, than to fall a Sacrifice to *those*, who lie in wait to destroy us." The essay refutes the argument advanced by the *Craftsman* (and Chesterfield) that a new law is unnecessary in view of the existing laws against libel. "It is very true," this writer says, quoting the *Craftsman*, that

> "all dramatick Writers and *Players* are subject to the same Prosecution as other *Libellers*." But how fallaciously is this argued? He [the essayist in the *Craftsman*] would insinuate to his Readers, what he cannot but know to be utterly false and impossible in Fact; that *Players* and *Libellers*, because they are under the Cognizance of the Law, and subject to Prosecution, may, for that Reason, be restrained from transgressing their Bounds; or in other Words, That *Libelling*, whether by writing, or acting on the *Stage*, may be prevented by Prosecutions at Law.

Actions against printed libel, he says, have been completely unsuccessful: since "it is impossible to put a Stop to this Evil by any Prosecutions at Law," the intervention of Parliament is urgently needed to establish a system of prior censorship over offensive plays.[1]

The next day, Thursday, 9 June, the *Gazetteer* printed a letter from "Appius" that insists that the new measure is vitally necessary for the security of the nation. His argument rests on the assumption that the country faced the imminent threat of a Jacobite revolution, for which the stage would provide the catalyst in the form of a play in which "the *Royal Family* was struck at, and the *King upon the Throne* made the Object of . . . Attack." The essay probably refers to *The Golden Rump* (although it may instead be another play, perhaps *The King and Titi*) as the piece that "designed to carry" the "Abuse of the Stage," already at "an enormous Height, . . . still higher; to confine it within no Bounds; to strike at the Root of all Government; to subvert all Authority; to let loose the Dogs of Malice at *Majesty itself*; to sow, if possible, Division in that Family, on whose Harmony our Happiness is founded, and who can never be divided without Ruin to themselves, and Destruction to the Publick." This play was "conceiv'd with as wicked a Design as ever enter'd the Heart of Man. . . . Does any Man in his Senses think," "Appius" writes, "that they who would rob us of the Protection of the *present Royal Family*, have any other Resource to recommend to us, but what must come from *Rome?*" As it had during the previous summer, autumn, and winter, the government justified its action in dealing with dissent and growing opposition to its policies by finding in those circumstances evidence of a Jacobite conspiracy that threatened to destroy the nation.

Two days later (11 June), *Common Sense* published "A Dissertation on Kicking" that, like "The Vision of the Golden Rump" before it, ridiculed the king's behavior. It proposed that kicking replace bribery as a device for "carrying on the Designs of Ministers of State," and imagines that "it would be pleasant enough, when a great Imployment became vacant, to see a Parcel of impudent Fellows in Lace and Embroidery, pressing and elbowing to be kick'd." All titles, the author suggests, might be conferred in this way, so that it would become a fashion to "see a Fellow at Court, who had just receiv'd a most gracious Kick . . . , return as proud as a Citizen from being Knighted."[2] The writer associates this behavior with scenes of kicking on stage, alluding almost certainly to *The Golden Rump* itself. The essay extends the connection between the stage and the government by introducing the Cibbers, who are here presumably meant to represent not only themselves but the Walpoles. "No one," the writer observes, "has taken a Kicking with so much Humour as our present most excellent Laureat, and I am inform'd his Son does not fall much short of him in this Excellence."

The *Common Sense* essay was probably something more than a spontaneous stroke against the ministry and the king, a public reminder of *The Golden Rump* that might irritate its targets as a partial retaliation for the imposition of dramatic censorship. The resurrection of this reference to the king's notorious habit coincided with the tenth anniversary of his accession to the throne and demonstrated that personally defamatory satire could still be published even if the stage was no longer to be allowed an equal liberty.[3]

On 25 June the *Craftsman* returned to the themes of stage and press censorship. "There is not one Argument," the paper says, "for restraining the *one*, which will not equally extend to the *other*; for if the *Stage* is shut up, on *one Side*, Men will naturally resort to the Press." Furthermore, the essay argues, in a passage that also echoes Chesterfield's speech, "may not *satirical Pieces* be drawn up in the Form of *Plays*, on Purpose to be prohibited?

. . . And if They should have Dexterity enough to evade the *common Course of the Law*, will it not be equally justifiable to put a Stop to such Writings by *extraordinary Methods?*"

The essay anticipates the process that might lead to the imposition of these "methods." The events the writer imagines here are strikingly similar to those that the *Craftsman* (on 28 May) had insinuated had led to the proposal for dramatic censorship: "If any *wicked Minister* should hereafter think it necessary to screen his Actions from publick Notice by . . . a Restraint upon the *Press*, He would certainly cloak it under the Pretence of Zeal for his *Master*." "It was very well observed, in a *certain Place*," the writer continues, apparently referring to Pulteney's speech in the Commons against the bill a month earlier, "that a Man, who had often libell'd King *Charles* the 2d. with Impunity, was at last put in the Pillory for reflecting upon *one of his Ministers*; upon which the *King* express'd Himself to this Effect. —*The Fellow is a Fool. Had He stuck to* ME, *He had been safe enough; but if He takes the same Liberty with* GREAT MEN, *He must expect to be severely punish'd.*" The *Craftsman* also suggests, in another parallel to the circumstances surrounding *The Golden Rump*, that besides arguing the need to restrain the press for the sake of protecting "his *Master*," such a minister, if he needed "a plausible Handle to put his Design in Execution, . . . would probably instruct some of his most trusty Creatures, or Hirelings, to abuse the *just Liberty of the Press*, in order to justify a Restraint upon it."[4] Ironically, the next issue of the *Craftsman* was itself prosecuted by the government for abusing the liberty of the press.

The prosecution involved Henry Haines, who was indicted and convicted for printing a seditious libel that consisted of passages from Shakespeare and from Shakespearean adaptations. The excerpts, along with passages from several non-Shakespearean plays, were part of a letter signed "*C. C. P.L.*" (Colley Cibber Poet Laureate),[5] who advised the new licenser to accept his assistance in identifying the "Multitude of Passages in Plays now in Being, which will be proper to be left out in all future Representations of them." The "Hint" that old plays could be applied to contemporary events, the correspondent acknowledges, had been made earlier by the *Craftsman* (on 8 March 1728/29), which had recommended (as Samuel Johnson was to do in *A Compleat Vindication of the Licensers of the Stage* in 1739) that an *index expurgatorius* be made of objectionable passages; the poet laureate could then be employed to fill in the resulting gaps in the plays.[6]

Of the fifteen passages cited in the letter as deserving the notice of the licenser, eight were included in Haines's indictment,[7] four of them from Cibber's own *Life and Death of King John*. Those passages allude to King John's "having entirely lost the Affections of his People" by behavior that led "the discontented Lords" first to conspire with the French to invade England, and finally to desert them and join "with Prince *Henry*, their new Sovereign, in the Defence of their Country, which his *Father* had brought to the very Brink of Destruction. —Dost not Thou think, *Caleb*," the correspondent asks, "that this Moral requires a different Turn; or that very invidious Constructions may not be put upon it, as it stands at present?"

He goes on to quote four passages from *Richard II*, three of which are cited in the indictment, and one (also cited) from *Henry IV, Part 2*. One of them, John of Gaunt's speech concerning "this royal throne of kings, this sceptered isle" (II.i.40–66), the correspondent notes, was "formerly quoted . . . in one of your Papers," and so he repeats "only the Conclusion of it." The lines had appeared in the *Craftsman* on 13 January 1732/33. Even then they had come under official scrutiny. The Treasury solicitor, Nicholas Paxton, had marked the quotation and sent it to Charles Delafaye, the under secretary of state, along with a memorandum noting that it was libelous and recommending it to the consideration of the secretary for prosecution, but the matter evidently went no further.[8]

The *Craftsman* for 2 July, which was intended as part of a series on the new law restricting the liberty of the stage, sparked a debate in the newspapers over the freedom—or licentiousness—of the press that lasted into the winter. The prosecution of Haines quickly became a *cause célèbre*. It was frequently cited by the Opposition press as evidence that the government was, as it had warned, bent on suppressing all criticism and dissent, and was cited by the government to show that licentiousness and attacks on the king had become intolerable.[9] After 2 July, the debate in the newspapers over the playhouse bill continued, but it was overshadowed by the related, and by then more controversial, issue of the freedom of the press.

When the *Craftsman* had begun its series of essays on the new theater law, which were temporarily interrupted by the prosecution for the issue of 2 July, the editor had feared that even the first installment on 18 June would appear too late: "I am afraid," he wrote, that "the *Playhouse Bill* will receive the *Royal Assent*, and so become an *Act of the Legislature*, before this Paper sees the Light." A week earlier, the *Craftsman* had reported that "Parliament, 'tis now said, will rise on Friday next," 17 June. The end of the session was put off until the following week, however, and on 18 June the *Craftsman* carried the news "that Tuesday next is fix'd for the Rising of the Parliament."

The session ended, as expected, on 21 June. The king, with both Houses and the Prince of Wales present, gave royal assent to the playhouse bill. At the head of the engrossed bill (now the "original act") were written the words "Le Roy le Veult," the form of assent used for public acts, and the bill thereupon became a law, 10 Geo. II, ch. 28 (see App. C-13).[10] The court then retired to Richmond; the king, who had been expected to leave for Hanover, remained in England, content with a new mistress, Lady Deloraine.[11] It has been widely assumed that the new act was immediately applied with vengeance against Fielding, the ministry's most famous dramatic opponent.[12] In fact, however, the Haymarket had been shut up for almost a month before the bill received the royal assent. During June there were only two or three dramatic performances in London (one on 11 June at Drury Lane, one at Lincoln's Inn Fields on 15 June, and another advertised there for 22 June) in addition to nine operas or musical entertainments, most of them at Covent Garden. The law took effect on Friday, 24 June, the date specifically designated in the act itself, but there were then no London theaters in operation or plays in production for it to affect.

In his speech at the close of the session on 21 June, the king thanked Parliament for its loyal efforts during the past five months. "I return you my Thanks," he said, "for the particular Proofs you have given me of your Affection and Regard to my Person and Honour, and hope the Wisdom and Justice which you have shewn upon some extraordinary Incidents, will prevent all Thoughts of the like Attempts for the future." His gratitude was not just his own, however, but the nation's.

> You cannot be insensible what just Scandal and Offence the Licentious- ness of the present Times, under the Colour and Disguise of Liberty, gives to all honest and sober Men; and how absolutely necessary it is to restrain this excessive Abuse, by a due and vigorous Execution of the Laws. Defiance of all Authority, Contempt of Magistracy, and even Resistance of the Law, are become too general, although equally prej- udicial to the Prerogative of the Crown, and the Liberties of the People; the Support of the one being inseparable from the Protection of the other. I have made the Laws of the Land the constant Rule of My Actions; and I do with Reason expect, in Return, all that Submission to My Authority and Government which the same Laws have made the Duty, and shall always be the Interest, of My Subjects.[13]

Those who heard him may have been uncertain whether he was referring to the Licensing Act, or to the act to punish the city of Edinburgh for its insult to the Crown, or even to the act that postponed the open division between the prince and the rest of the royal family. The king's remarks could have been applied to any of them, and may have applied to all, for the govern- ment saw them all as reflections of domestic turmoil that challenged its authority and threatened its stability. But however prescient the govern- ment may have been , it could not have foreseen that the main provisions of the Licensing Act would endure for more than two centuries, far longer than either the ministry that created it or the perils it was meant to guard against.

APPENDIXES
NOTES
WORKS CITED
INDEX

APPENDIXES

Since this study relies to a considerable extent on unpublished material and on material once published but no longer easily accessible, I have included transcriptions of the most important items in the appendixes.

The end of a page or leaf in the original is here indicated by the symbol #.

The acts in Appendix A are from *The Statutes of the Realm (1101–1713)*, ed. A. Luders et al. (London: Record Commission, 1810–28), Vols. I–VII; and *Acts and Ordinances of the Interregnum*, comp. and ed. C. H. Firth and R. S. Rait (London: HMSO, 1911), Vol. I. Several of the items in Appendixes B and C are transcribed from printed sheets or pamphlets bound in a volume labeled *"Dramatic Tracts and Papers* collected by Mr. [Joseph] Haslewood" (British Library, 11795.k.31), hereafter cited as Haslewood; several others are from sheets bound in a volume labeled "Sir John Barnard's Bill and Related Papers—1735" (Harvard Theatre Collection, TS 297.25.35F), hereafter cited as Harvard. The source of the text for items in Appendixes B and C is indicated after each item.

PRINCIPAL STATUTES AFFECTING DRAMATIC PERFORMANCES BEFORE 1737

A-1. ACTS AFFECTING THEATERS AND PLAYS

1542/43   34 & 35 Hen. VIII, ch. 1. An acte for thadvauncement of true religion. Forbids printing or selling of books, or playing of "interludes, song, or rime," of anything contrary to religious doctrine as stipulated by the king.

1558/59   1 Eliz., ch. 2. Act of uniformity. Against "any psone or psones whatsoever ... [who] shall in anye Enterludes Playes Songes Rymes or by other open Woordes, declare or speake anye thing in the derogation depraving or despising of the same Booke [of Common Prayer], or of any thing therin conteyned, or any parte therof."

1605/6   3 Jac. I, ch. 21. An acte to retraine abuses of players. "For preventing and avoyding of the greate Abuse of the Holy Name of God in Stageplayes Interludes Maygames Shews and such like; Be it enacted by our Soveraigne Lorde the Kings Majesty, and by the Lordes Spirituall and Temporall, and Comons in this present Parliament assembled, and by the authoritie of the same, That if at any tyme or tymes, after the end of this present Session of Parliament, any pson or psons doe or shall in any Stage play Interlude Shew Maygame or Pageant jestingly or prophanely speake or use the holy Name of God or of Christ Jesus, or of the Holy Ghoste or of the Trinitie, which are not to be spoken but with feare and reverence, shall forfeite for everie such Offence by hym or them comitted Tenne Pounde. . . ."

1625   1 Car. I, ch. 1. An acte for punishing of divers abuses comitted on the Lords day called Sunday. Forbids plays on Sundays.

1642   (2 Sept.) Order for stage-plays to cease. "Whereas the distressed Estate of Ireland, steeped in her own Blood, and the distracted Estate of England, threatened with a Cloud of Blood by a Civil War, call for all possible Means to appease and avert the Wrath of God, appearing in these Judgements; among which, Fasting and Prayers, having been often tried to be very effectual, having been lately and are still enjoined; and whereas Public Sports do not well agree with Public Calamities, nor Public Stage-plays with the Seasons of Humiliation, this being an Exercise of sad and pious Solemnity, and the other being Spectacles of Pleasure, too commonly expressing lascivious Mirth and Levity: It is therefore thought fit, and Ordained, by the Lords and

Commons in this Parliament assembled, That, while these sad causes and set Times of Humiliation do continue, Public Stage Plays shall cease, and be forborn, instead of which are recommended to the People of this Land the profitable and seasonable considerations of Repentance, Reconciliation, and Peace with God, which probably may produce outward Peace and Prosperity, and bring again Times of Joy and Gladness to these Nations."

1647 (22 Oct.) An ordinance for the Lord Mayor and City of London, and the justices of peace to suppress stage-playes and interludes. Players to be treated as vagrants.

1647/48 (11 Feb.) An ordinance for the utter suppression and abolishing of all stage-plays and interludes, with the penalties to be inflicted on the actors and spectators therein expressed.

1654 (28 Aug.) An ordinance for ejecting scandalous, ignorant and insufficient ministers and schoolmasters. "Such Ministers and School-masters shall be deemed and accompted scandalous in their Lives and Conversations, as shall be proved guilty of . . . and such as . . . do incourage and countenance by word or practice any Whitson-Ales, Wakes, Morris-Dances, May-poles, Stage-plays, or such like Licentious practices, by which men are encouraged in a loose and prophane Conversation. . . ."

A-2. VAGRANCY ACTS AFFECTING PLAYERS OF INTERLUDES

1285 13 Edw. I, Stat' Wynton, ch. 4.

1331 5 Edw. III, ch. 14.

1349 23 Edw. III, ch. 7.

1383 7 Richard II, ch. 5.

1495 11 Hen. VII, ch. 2.

1503/4 19 Hen. VII, ch. 12.

1530/31 22 Hen. VIII, ch. 12. Defines a vagrant as anyone able to work who is not working, has no visible means of support, and cannot give a reckoning of how he gets his living; offenders to be tied to the end of a cart, naked, and whipped through the town until bloody, then sent to their place of birth or last residence; class includes begging scholars, shipmen, proctors, pardoners, those pretending to "Physyke, Physnamye, Palmestrye," fortunetellers, and those "usyng dyvers & subtyle craftye & unlawfull games & playes."

1535/36 27 Hen. VIII, ch. 25.

1547 1 Edw. VI, ch. 3. Defines a vagrant as anyone without work and without land or income, loitering, idly wandering, and not applying himself "to some honnest and allowed arte Scyence s^rvice or Labour"; offender to be "marked with an whott Iron in the brest the marke of V. and adjudge the said parsone living so Idelye to such presento^r to be his Slave" for two years.

1549/50   3 & 4 Edw. VI, ch. 16.

1572   14 Eliz., ch. 5. Includes "all Fencers Bearewardes Comon Players in Enterludes & Minstrels, not belonging to any Baron of this Realme or towards any other honorable Personage of greater Degree . . . which . . . shall wander abroade and have not Lycense of two Justices of the Peace"; offender "to bee grevouslye whipped, and burnte through the gristle of the right Eare with a hot Yron of the compasse of an Ynche about"; second offense: felony; third: felony without benefit of clergy. (Acts before Elizabeth did not specifically enumerate actors in their scope.)

1575/76   18 Eliz., ch. 3.

1597/98   39 Eliz., ch. 3.

1597/98   39 Eliz., ch. 4. Includes "all psons calling themselves Schollers going about begging, all Seafaring-men pretending losses of their Shippes or Goods on the Sea going about the Country begging or using any subtile Crafte or unlawfull Games and Playes, or fayning themselves to have knowledge in Phisiognomye Palmestry or other like crafty Scyence, or pretending that they can tell Destenyes Fortunes or such other like fantasticall Ymagynacons; all psons that be or utter themselves to be Proctors Precurors Patent Gatherers or Collectors for Gaoles Prisons or Hospitalls; all Fencers Bearewards comon Players of Enterludes and Minstrells wandring abroade, (other then Players of Enterludes belonging to any Baron of this Realme, or any other honorable Personage of greater Degree, to be auctoryzed to play, under the Hand and Seale of Armes of such Baron or Personage)"; repeals all former laws relating to the punishment of rogues and vagabonds; offender to be stripped naked to the waist and whipped openly until bloody, then sent to place of birth or of last residence.

1597/98   39 Eliz., ch. 17.

1601   43 Eliz., ch. 9.

1603/4   1 Jac. I, ch. 7. Recites that since 39 Eliz., ch. 4, "divers Doubts and Questions have bene moved and growen by diversitie of Opinions taken in and upon the letter of the saide Acte: For a plaine Declaration whereof be it declared and enacted, That from henceforthe no Authoritie to be given or made by any Baron of this Realme or any other honourable Personage of greater Degree, unto any other person or psons, shall be availeable to free and discharge the saide psons, or any of them, from the Paines and Punishments in the saide Statute mentioned"; and in the margin (*Statutes of the Realm*, Vol. IV, Pt. 2, p. 1819): "No Licence by any Nobleman shall exempt Players."

1609/10   7 Jac. I, ch. 4.

1662   14 Car. II, ch. 12. An act for the better relief of the poor. Recites that enforcement of 39 Eliz., ch. 4, and 1 Jac. I, ch. 7, has been neglected.

1698/99   11 Wm. III, ch. 18.

1706   6 Anne, ch. 32. Continues 11 Wm. III, ch. 18.

1714   12 Anne 2, ch. 23 (also designated as 13 Anne, ch. 26). An act for reducing the laws relating to rogues vagabonds sturdy beggars and vagrants into one act of Parliament and for the more effectual punishing such rogues vagabonds sturdy beggars and vagrants and sending them whither they ought to be sent. "Whereas many Parts of this Kingdom are extremely oppressed by the usual Method of conveying Vagabonds or Beggars from County to County by having such Persons conveyed as Vagrants who ought not so to be Be it enacted by the Queens most Excellent Majesty by and with the Advice and Consent of the Lords Spiritual and Temporal and Commons in this present Parliament assembled and by the Authority of the same That all Persons pretending themselves to be Patent Gatherers or Collectors for Prisons Gaols or Hospitals and wandring abroad for that Purpose all Fencers Bearwards Common Players of Interludes Minstrels Juglers all Persons pretending to be Gipsies or wandring in the Habit or Form of counterfeit Egyptians or pretending to have Skill in Physiognomy Palmestry or like crafty Science or pretending to tell Fortunes or like phantastical Imaginations or using any subtile Craft or unlawful Games or Plays all Persons able in Body who run away and leave their Wives or Children to the Parish and not having wherewith otherwise to maintain themselves use Loytring and refuse to work for the usual and common Wages and all other idle Persons wandring abroad and begging (except Soldiers Mariners or Seafaring Men licensed by some Testimonial or Writing under the Hand and Seal of some Justice of Peace setting down the Time and Place of his or their Landing and the Place to which they are to pass and limiting the Time for such their Passage while they continue in the direct Way to the Place to which they are to pass and during the Times so limited) shall be deemed Rogues and Vagabonds . . ."; offender may be whipped until bloody, or sent to House of Correction to hard labor, then sent to place of birth or last residence; or justice may order seven-year apprenticeship in Britain or in British factories beyond the sea; repeals 39 Eliz., ch. 4, and 1 Jac. I, ch. 7.

APPENDIX B

DOCUMENTS RELATING TO
SIR JOHN BARNARD'S BILL, 1735

B-1. A BILL FOR RESTRAINING THE NUMBER
OF HOUSES FOR PLAYING OF INTERLUDES

[Contemporary manuscript notations, printed here within brackets, appear in the Harvard copy at the points indicated.]

A Bill for Restraining the Number of Houses for Playing of Interludes, and for the better Regulating Common Players of Interludes.

Whereas his Majesty King *Charles* the Second, did, by Letters Patent, bearing Date the twenty-fifth Day of *April*, in the ___ Year of his Reign, give and grant unto *Thomas Killigrew*, his Heirs and Assigns, full Power, Licence and Authority of erecting one Theatre or Play-house, and of keeping Players and other Persons for acting Tragedies, Comedies, Plays, Operas, and other Entertainments of the Stage, with several Powers and Provisoes therein mentioned.

And whereas his said Majesty, did by other Letters Patent, bearing Date the fifteenth Day of *January*, in the fourteenth Year of his Reign, give and grant unto Sir *William Davenant*, his Heirs and Assigns, the like full Power, Licence and Authority of erecting one Theatre or Play-house, and of keeping Players and other Persons for acting Tragedies, Comedies, Plays, Operas, and other Entertainments of the Stage, with the like Powers and Provisoes; by both which Letters Patents aforesaid, it is declared and enjoined, that all Companies of Players # other than the two above-mentioned, should be silenced and suppressed, and that no Play should be acted by either of the said Companies, containing any prophane, obscene or scurrilous Passage, or other Passage offensive to Piety or good Manners: Both which said Letters Patents have since, by several mesne Conveyances, been assigned to, and are now vested in *John Rich*, his Heirs and Assigns.

And whereas his present Majesty, by Letters Patent bearing Date the third Day of *July* in the fifth Year of his Reign, did give and grant unto *Robert Wilks, Colley Cibber*, and *Barton Booth*, Esquires, their Executors, Administrators and Assigns, for the Term of Twenty-one Years, to commence from the first Day of *September* One thousand seven hundred and thirty-two, the full Power, Licence and Authority, to form, entertain and keep a Company of Comedians to act Tragedies, Comedies, Plays, Operas, and other Performances of the Stage, with other Powers therein mentioned; which said Letters Patent, are by several mesne Conveyances, now vested

164

in *Charles Fleetwood* and *Henry Giffard*, their Executors, Administrators and Assigns.

And whereas his said present Majesty did, by Letters Patent bearing Date the seventh Day of *July*, in the fifth Year of his Reign, incorporate several Persons therein named, for the Term of Twenty-one Years from the Date thereof, for carrying on Operas, and other Entertainments of Musick, by the Name of The Royal Academy of Musick, with several Powers and Privileges therein mentioned: Notwithstanding which said Letters Patent, diverse ill-disposed and disorderly Persons, have of late taken upon themselves, without any legal Authority, to act and represent Tragedies, Comedies, Plays, Operas, and other Entertainments of the Stage, within the Cities of *London* and *Westminster*, and the Suburbs thereof; and also in several other Places of this Kingdom; for which Purposes, several Theatres, Play-houses, or other Houses, have been erected for carrying on the same, in Defiance of the Laws of the Land; by Reason whereof great Mischiefs have already arisen, and much greater are likely to ensue, unless the same be timely prevented; and the Laws now in being, have been found insufficient for preventing this great and growing Evil: #

For Remedy thereof, and to the End that an Effectual Stop may be put to these pernicious and illegal Practices, Be it Enacted,

By the KING's most Excellent MAJESTY,

By and with the Advice and Consent of the Lords Spiritual and Temporal, and Commons, in this present Parliament assembled, and by the Authority of the same, That from and after the   [29th day September in the year of our Lord 1735]   no Person or Persons shall act, represent or perform any Tragedy, Comedy, Opera, Play, Farce, or other Entertainment of the Stage, for Gain, Hire or Reward, other than, and except such Person or Persons in whom the Right and Property of, in, and to the said several Letters Patents, granted as aforesaid, to the said *Thomas Killegrew*, Sir *William Davenant, Robert Wilks, Colley Cibber*, and *Barton Booth*, and the said Charter of the Royal Academy of Musick, is vested, and their respective Deputies and Servants, during the Continuance of the Powers and Privileges to them by their several Letters Patents respectively granted.

Provided always, That whenever [& as often as] any of the said Letters Patents [or other Letters Patent] shall expire or be determined [& not otherwise or o[n] any other occasion], it shall and may be lawful for his Majesty, his Heirs or Successors, by new Letters Patents under the Great Seal of *Great-Britain*, to authorize and impower any Person or Persons to act, represent, and perform Tragedies, Comedies, Operas, Plays and other Entertainments of the Stage, in the Room and Place of such Person or Persons, whose Letters Patents shall so expire or be determined, [which saids Letters patents hereafter to be granted shall be declared to endure] so that there shall not exceed the Number of   [f]   Theatres or Play-houses, at one and the same Time; that is to say,   Theatres or Play-houses, for acting or representing Plays Comedies, Tragedies, Operas, and other Entertainments of the Stage, and   other Theatre or Opera-house for exercising and acting Operas, and exhibiting all other Entertainments of Musick; which said Theatres or Play-houses and Opera-house shall be situate within   [the City of Westminster or the Liberties]   # thereof, and not elsewhere; [one—] nor shall any [*preceding 3 words struck out; replaced by*: & that no] Tragedies, Comedies, Operas, Plays, or other Entertainments of the Stage, [shall] be acted, performed, or represented in the said [three] Theatres or Play-houses, or Opera-house [*preceding 4 words struck out*], or any of them, which shall contain any prophane, obscene, [seditious] or scurrilous Passage, or any Passage offensive to Piety, or good Manners: And if any Person or Persons [/] not authorized by this Act, or by Letters Patents from his Majesty, his Heirs, and Successors above-mentioned, shall presume to [/] act, represent or perform any Tragedy, Comedy, Opera, Play, or other Entertainment of the Stage, for Gain, Hire, or Reward, such Person or Persons shall, notwithstanding any Settlement, be deemed adjudged and taken as   [Rogues Vagabonds and Sturdy Beggars within the intent]   And if any such Person or Persons shall be found offending against this Act, the Mayor, Bailiff, or other Head-Officer of any City, Borough, or Town Corporate, or any Justice of the Peace of the same County, Riding or Division, within the Limits of their respective Jurisdictions, are hereby impowered and required to order such Person or Persons to forbear acting, representing, or performing any Part in any Tragedy, Comedy, Opera, Play, or other Entertainment of the Stage; and if any such Person or Persons, shall, after such Order served on him, her, or them, act, represent, or perform any Part in any Tragedy, Comedy, Opera, Play, or other Entertainment of the Stage, within the Limits aforesaid, and shall be thereof convicted, by Confession, or the Oath of   [one or more credible Witness or Witnesses]   shall

And in Case any Mayor, Bailiff, or other Head-Officer [or Justice of the Peace] of any City, Borough, or Town Corporate, or Justice of Peace of any County, Riding or Division, shall, upon # Complaint or Information to him or them made, neglect or refuse to put this Law in Execution, every such Mayor, Bailiff, Head-Officer or Justice of the Peace, shall, for every such Neglect or Refusal, forfeit   [the sum of 50£.]   And if any Person or Persons, Body Politick or Corporate, authorized or to be authorized by this Act, or [*preceding 4 words struck out*] by Letters Patent from his Majesty, his Heirs and Successors, as above-mentioned, shall act, perform, or repre-sent, or suffer to be acted, performed, or represented, any Tragedy, Comedy, Opera, Play or other Entertainment of the Stage, containing any prophane, obscene [sedi-tious] or scurrilous Passage, or [Ld Chamberlains power] any Passage offensive to Piety and good Manners, or shall act, perform, or represent, or suffer to be acted, performed, or represented, any Tragedy, Comedy, Opera, Play, or other Entertain-ment of the Stage, in any House or Place not within

such Person or Persons, Body Politick or Corporate, shall for such Offence, forfeit

And every House or Place, not situate within
                                                      wherein any Tragedy, Comedy, Opera, Play, or other Entertainment of the Stage shall be acted, repre-sented, or performed for Gain, Hire, or Reward, shall be deemed and adjudged

And be it further Enacted, That no Person or Persons authorized or to be authorized, as aforesaid, shall, by themselves, their Deputies, Agents or Servants, upon any Pretence or Occasion whatsoever, take or receive from any Person or Persons who shall resort to, or be admitted into any Play-house, Theatre, or other Place, to see or hear any Tragedy, Comedy, Opera, Play, or other Entertainment of the Stage, any more or greater Price, Hire, or Reward than what hath hitherto been usually and customarily taken and received for the same, upon common and ordinary Occasions; and if any Person or Persons shall take, or cause to be taken or received for the same, any greater Price, Hire, or Reward than as before-mentioned, such Person or Persons shall

#

Provided always, and be it Enacted, That if any Tragedy, Comedy, Opera, Play, or other Entertainment of the Stage, shall be acted, represented, or performed in any House or Place where Wine, Ale, Beer, or other Liquors shall be publickly sold and retailed, the same shall be deemed, adjudged, and taken to be acted, represented, and performed for Gain, Hire, and Reward.

And be it Enacted, That all shall be recovered by Bill, Plaint, or Information, in any of his Majesty's Courts of Record at *Westminster*, in which no Essoin, Protection or Wager of Law, shall be allowed, or in a summary Way, before   Justices of the Peace of the County, Riding, or Division, where such Offence shall be committed; and if any Person or Persons, shall think him, her, or themselves aggrieved by the Order or Orders of such Justices of the Peace, it shall, and may be lawful for such Person or Persons, to appeal therefrom to the next General Quarter-Sessions to be held for the said County, Riding, or Division, whose Order therein, shall be final and conclusive; and all   for any Offence or Offences against this Act, shall go and belong

Provided always, and it is hereby Declared, That nothing in this Act contained, shall extend, or be construed to extend to any Person or Persons, on Account of his, her, or their acting, representing or performing any Tragedy, Comedy, Opera, Play, or other Entertainment of the Stage, within any of his Majesty's Royal Palaces, during such Time as his Majesty, or any of the Royal Family shall reside therein.

And be it further Enacted, That no Person or Persons, shall be liable to any   by Reason of any Offence or Offences committed against this Act, unless such Person or Persons be sued, prosecuted, or informed against, within the Space of   next after such Offence or Offences committed. # And if any Action or Suit shall be commenced or brought against any Justice of Peace, or other Person, for doing, or causing to be done, any thing in Pursuance of this Act, such Action or Suit shall be commenced within   Months next after the Fact committed, and not afterwards; and the Defendant and Defendants, in such Action or Suit, may plead the General Issue, and give the special Matter in Evidence; and if upon such Action or Suit, a Verdict be given for the Defendant or Defendants, or the Plaintiff or Plaintiffs become Nonsuit, or discontinue his or their Action, then the Defendant or Defendants shall have   Costs, and have the like Remedy for the same, as any Defendant or Defendants hath, or have in other Cases by Law.

Be it also Enacted, by the Authority aforesaid, That this Act shall be deemed a publick Act, and shall be so adjudged and taken in all Courts of Justice, without special Pleading of the same   *[Entire last paragraph struck out]*
#

(endorsed:) A BILL *for Restraining the Number of Houses for Playing of Interludes, and for the better Regulating Common Players of Interludes.*
From Haslewood; 7 pp., printed bill; lacunae appear as indicated. Manuscript notations from Harvard copy.

B-2. THE CASE OF THE SUBSCRIBERS TO GOODMAN'S FIELDS

THE / CASE / OF / *The Several Persons upon whose Subscription the / Theatre at* Goodman's-*Fields hath been built, in / relation to a Bill now brought into Parliament to / restrain the Number of Playhouses,* &c.

IN the Year 1731, a Subscription being opened to build a New Theatre in *Goodman's-Fields*, twenty-three Persons became Subscribers at One hundred Pounds each, with which, the said Theatre was built, and was by Indentures assigned in twenty-three individual Shares to the Subscribers, to secure to each of them One Shilling and Sixpence for every acting Day.

That by virtue of the said Indentures, the Subscribers are advised that each of them is *legally entituled* to receive the aforesaid One Shilling and Sixpence every acting Day; and that the said Theatre is thereby *legally* vested in them by way of Mortgage to secure such daily Payments.

That in regard the said Subscribers are by the LAW *of the Land* entituled to, and interested in the said Theatre, and Performances therein exhibited, (nothing being there exhibited contrary to Law) they humbly presume and hope, from the Honour and Justice of Parliament, that nothing will be inserted in the said Bill, which may destroy their *Legal Right* by suppressing the said Theatre, especially inasmuch as there is no Precedent where the private Interest of any Subject has been taken away by Parliament, without an Equivalent being given for the same.

(endorsed:) The Case of the Subscribers who have built the Theatre in *Goodman*'s-Fields.
From Haslewood; sheet is numbered "12" in MS; endorsed, in MS, "1735." No subscribers' names are included.

B-3. THE CASE OF HENRY GIFFARD

The CASE *of* HENRY GIFFARD, *Proprietor / of the Theatre in* Goodman's-Fields, *in relation / to a* BILL *now depending in Parliament, for restraining the Number of Play-Houses,* &c.

In the Year 1729, Mr. *Odell* erected a *Theatre* in *Goodman's Fields*, wherein

Performances of the Stage were exhibited; some time after, in the said Year, a Representation was made by the then Lord Mayor and Court of Aldermen, to his Majesty, in order to suppress the same; whereupon an Order was sent by my Lord Chamberlain for shutting up the said House.

Hereupon Mr. *Odell* took the Opinions of several of the most eminent Lawyers, concerning the said Order, and the Legality of the said Theatre; who having advised, that the said Mr. *Odell* had a *Right by the Law of the Land*, to proceed in his said Undertaking, he continued to carry on the Business of the said Theatre a Year and a Half, without any *Complaint* or *Interruption*; and then being minded to quit the Business, the said *Henry Giffard purchased his Right, and became the Proprietor* of the said Theatre; and being in himself persuaded and convinced, that the said Undertaking was a *lawful* and *honest* Profession, and no further *Opposition* or *Complaint* having then been made, he believed all Persons *agreed* or *acquiesced* therein: Hereupon the said *Giffard* acted one Season in his own Right, during which time he opened a Subscription to erect a new Theatre in the Place of the old one, which was published all over the Town, (the Parliament then sitting) and was so well received, that several substantial Merchants and Citizens of *London* became Sub-scribers to the building thereof; and the said *Giffard* having entred into a Contract with Sir *William Leman* for a Lease of the Ground for the Term of Sixty one Years, the present Theatre was erected; and during the whole Time the same was erecting, and until now, for several Years since, *not the least Complaint* has been made; upon which, the said *Giffard* having no Doubt, but that he was as *lawfully* and *honestly* employed as the Followers of other Business or Professions are, invested all his Fortune in the said Business, *and has applied many thousand Pounds in the Purchase of Cloaths, Scenes, Decorations, and other Necessaries for the same, and contracted thereby Debts to a great Amount*; so that in case a Law should pass to suppress the said Theatre, it will absolutely divest the said *Giffard* of his *Legal Property*, which is very large, and be the utter Ruin of him and his Family. Therefore he hopes, from the Honour and Justice of Parliament, such will not be his hard Fate; but on the contrary, that he may be protected in his *Legal Property*, and follow this his Business and Employment therein; if not, he hopes an Equivalent will be made him, as has always been done where Property has been taken away.

If it be suggested, that this House may be a Detriment, by Apprentices frequenting the same, the Answer, it is presumed, is obvious, That such Apprentices as will frequent Play-Houses contrary to their Master's Intentions, will not go to this House, where they may be seen either by the Masters, or some of the Master's Acquaintance; but will go to those at the other End of the Town, where they are less liable to be known.

N.B. Goodman's-Fields *Play-House is in the County of* Middlesex, *and not in the City of* London, *as the Play-House formerly in* Dorset-Gardens *was; and that Play-House was not put down by any Authority, but abandoned because of its prejudicial Situation close to the River of* Thames.

(endorsed:) CASE OF HENRY GIFFARD, In relation to a BILL now depending in Parliament, for the restraining the Number of Play-Houses, &c.

From Haslewood; sheet is numbered "9" in MS; endorsed, in MS, "1735."

B-4. THE CASE OF THE COMEDIANS
OF GOODMAN'S FIELDS

THE / CASE / OF THE / COMEDIANS, &c. belonging to the / *Theatre* in *Goodman's-Fields*, / In Relation to a BILL for Restraining the / Number of Play-Houses, &c.

WHEREAS, by a Bill now depending in Parliament, the *Suppression* of the *Theatre* in *Goodman's-Fields* is intended, which if it should take Place, in the present Form, would absolutely deprive above 300 Persons of the *Common Necessaries* of *Life*, whose *sole Dependance* is upon the *Existence* of the *said Theatre*, not having been bred to any other Business; exercising this under the *Certainty* of its being *Lawful*.

BY the passing of this into a *Law*, they, the present Actors, &c. of *Goodman's-Fields Theatre*, will be excluded even the *Prospect* of a *Livelyhood*, it being improbable, nay almost impossible, that they should be admitted into the Two remaining Play-Houses, as they are already *over-burthen'd* with People, and are more likely to *discharge* some of their present Actors, than *receive* any Additional.

IN this *melancholly* Exigence, where can they more *properly apply*, than to those HONOURABLE MEMBERS, who compose THAT AUGUST ASSEMBLY, whose *Humanity*, as well as *Justice*, may find out some *Expedient* to *relieve* those, who in such Case, have the *Certainty* of being *Undone*, and, as they conceive, without even the *Prospect* of the *least Advantage*, accruing to *any Person*.

(endorsed:) The Case of the Comedians, &c. belonging to the *Theatre* in *Goodman's-Fields*; in Relation to a Bill for Restraining the Number of Play-Houses.

From Haslewood; sheet is numbered "10" in MS; endorsed, in MS, "1735."

B-5. THE SAME, TO THE HOUSE OF COMMONS

To the Honourable / House of Commons. / The CASE of the Company of Comedians, belonging to the *Theatre* in *Goodman's-Fields*.

IF the BILL, now depending in Parliament, should, in the present Form, pass into a Law, the Actors of *Goodman's-Fields* will be deprived of the Means of Life; unless the known *Justice* and *Humanity* of this HONOURABLE HOUSE should immediately interpose, by admitting a Clause or Clauses, for tolerating them, the present *Actors* of *Goodman's-Fields*, to Act in some of the several Counties of *England*, and thereby enable them to Support Themselves and Families, in the Manner they have hitherto done.

They humbly conceive, that to render any Man incapable of getting his *Bread*, in the *Business* or *Occupation* which he has been train'd up to from his *Youth*, and what he has follow'd for several Years without Interruption, (having always presum'd it *Lawful*) is depriving him of *Life* in the most terrible Manner, and is consequently more *Fatal*, than the taking away any Particular Part of his *Property*, while he has a Competency still left for his *Subsistence. All which is humbly Submitted to the tender Consideration of this* Honourable House.

(endorsed:) The Case of the Company of Comedians belonging to the Theatre in *Goodman's-Fields*.
From Haslewood; sheet is numbered "11" in MS.

B-6. MR. RICH'S CASE

Mr. *RICH*'s / CASE / ON THE / BILL / For Restraining the / Number of PLAY-HOUSES, *&c.*

[*In right margin:* 15 *January*, / 14 K. *Charles* II.] KING *Charles* the Second did, by Letters Patent under the Great-Seal, grant unto Sir *William Davenant*, his Heirs and Assigns, full Power, Licence and Authority to erect one Theatre, or Play-house, and of keeping Players and other Persons for the acting of Tragedies, Comedies, *&c.*

THE said Letters Patent, by several Mesne Assignments, became vested in *Christopher Rich*, Esq; and others.

THE said *Christopher Rich* having rebuilt the Theatre in *Lincoln's-Inn-Fields* at a very great Expence, and most of the other Persons who were interested in the Patent, refusing to contribute any Money towards getting together a Company of Actors, or for the purchasing of Cloaths, Scenes, Machines, and other Things necessary for Acting; the said *Christopher Rich*, in order to raise Money for these Purposes, in the Year One thousand seven hundred and fourteen divided the said House into Thirty-six Parts or Shares, and in Consideration of the Payment of One hundred and twenty Pounds, by each of the Persons who bought such Share, the said *Christopher Rich* agreed to pay to each of them Two Shillings a Night for every Night that any Play should be acted in the said Theatre, *and when not therein, if elsewhere under the Authority of the said Letters Patent.* #

The said *Christopher Rich* afterwards died, and by his Will he devised his Interest in the said Letters Patent and Theatre, to his two Sons, *John* and *Christopher Rich*.

IN Pursuance of the above Agreement, they acted at the Theatre in *Lincoln's-Inn-Fields*, and have paid each of the Purchasers of the said Thirty-six Shares, Two Shillings each Night there has been any Play acted under the said Letters Patent, which, with the Ground-Rent of the said House, being One hundred Pounds a Year, amounts to Seven hundred and twenty Pounds a Year. [*In right margin:* 25 *April*, / 14 *Car.* II.] King *Charles* the Second, by Letters Patent, granted the same Priviledges of erecting a Play-house to *Thomas Killigrew*, his Heirs and Assigns.

Mr. *John Rich* intending to erect a Theatre in *Covent-Garden*, purchased the said Letters Patent, which by several Mesne-Assignments, are now become vested in a Trustee for him.

IN Order to purchase this Patent, Mr. *Rich* was obliged to borrow a large Sum of Money; for the securing the Repayment of which, this last-mentioned Patent is actually mortgaged. [*In right margin:* 1731.] Mr. *John Rich*, at his own Expence, erected the Theatre in *Covent-Garden*, and has divided it into Fifty Shares, and he has convenanted to pay for each of them Two Shillings for each Night of his Acting there, or in any other Place, which, with the Ground-Rent of the said House, amounts to One Thousand Pounds a Year at least.

IF the Bill should take away one of the Patents, Mr. *John* and Mr. *Christopher Rich* will lose the Benefit of the Play-house in *Lincoln's-Inn-Fields*, if Mr. *John Rich* should act in *Covent-Garden* Play-House: Or if they act in *Lincoln's-Inn-Fields*, then Mr. *John Rich* will lose the Benefit of *Covent-Garden* House, besides the Value of one of the Patents; which, if to be sold, with the Scenes, Machines, &c. according to the Rate, and in Proportion to what was given for the Patent, Scenes, Machines, &c. of *Drury-Lane* Play-House, would be worth a considerable Sum; by which means that Sum will be lost, and the Rent of Shares in both the Houses must be paid, though but one of them can be used.

THIS being a true State of the Case, it is submitted to the Consideration of this Honourable House, whether, if the Bill should pass as it now stands, it is not much more reasonable to make Mr. *Rich* Satisfaction for the Loss of the Rent of one of the Houses, and one of the Patents, than to oblige him to contribute to make up the Losses # which may be sustained by others; and when compared with his own, are inconsiderable, especially considering that he has acted and laid out his Money under the Authority of two legal Patents and the Sanction of the Law: Whereas the others have acted, if not in open Defiance of the Law, yet upon a very Precarious and Doubtful Footing, and after a Declaration made by the late Lord-Chancellor, the late Lord *Raymond*, and Mr. Baron *Comyns*, that if they should act, such Acting would be illegal, after a Petition from the City of *London* to his Majesty, and an Address moved for in the House of Lords to suppress them, and and after an Order sent by his Majesty's Command from the Lord-Chamberlain to forbid their Acting.

(endorsed:) Mr. *RICH's* CASE On the BILL For Restraining the Number of PLAY-HOUSES, &c.

From Harvard.

B-7. THE CASE OF THE COMEDIANS OF DRURY LANE AND COVENT GARDEN

THE / CASE / OF / John Mills, Benjamin Johnson, James Quin, Josias Miller, Theophilus Cibber, John Harper, Benjamin Griffin, William Mills, William Milward, Charles Shepard, Thomas Walker, Lacy Ryan, John Hippisley, Dennis Delane, Thomas Chapman, Samuel Stephens, Mary Heron, Elizabeth Butler, Christiana Horton, Anne Hallam, Jane Bullock, and Elizabeth Buchanan, in Behalf of *Themselves* and the *Rest* of the *Comedians* of the *Theatres-Royal* of *Drury-Lane* and *Covent-Garden*.

DRAMATICK COMPOSITIONS have ever been esteem'd among the finest Productions of Human Genius; and the Acting them has, by some of the *Wisest Men* in *all Ages*, been countenanc'd, as greatly serviceable to the *Cause* of *Virtue*: Wherever *Learning* is *encourage'd*, or *Arts* and *Sciences flourish*, DRAMATICK POETS, and ACTORS, who *excel*, meet not with Protection only, but with *Publick Honour* and *Reward*. It is therefore humbly conceiv'd, it can never be intended to *destroy* the Stage altogether, but to put it under proper *Regulations*. #

In the Bill now depending in Parliament for restraining the Number of Houses for playing of Interludes, &c. there is a Clause of the following Purport.

"No Person or Persons shall Act, Represent, or Perform any Tragedy, Comedy, Opera, Play, Farce, or other Entertainment of the Stage, for Gain, Hire, or Reward, other than, and except such Person or Persons in whom the Right and Property of, in, and to the said Letters Patents, granted as aforesaid, to the said *Thomas Killegrew*, Sir *William Davenant, Robert Wilks, Colley Cibber,* and *Barton Booth,* and the said Charter of the Royal Academy of Musick, is vested, and their respective Deputies or Servants, during the Continuance of the Powers and Privileges to them by their several Letters Patents respectively granted."

Shou'd the Bill pass as it now stands, it will subject all These who have from their *Infancy* dedicated themselves to the *Profession* of *Acting*, to the *Arbitrary* Will of any One who is pleas'd to *buy* the *Patent* under which they at Present *Act*: For, no doubt, there may be soon (AS HAS HERETOFORE BEEN PRACTIS'D) *Cartels*, as *they* call 'em, establish'd between the *Patentees,* that *one House shall never receive an Actor who has left the other, let the Motive be Ever so just.*

The *Purchaser* of a *Patent* may thus oblige the present *Actors* to submit to the *hardest Terms*, or reduce them to *Beggary*, by taking from them the Exercise of their Profession: and there will hardly be found others who have any Degree of Merit, Imprudent enough to engage in the Profession with such a Prospect, to study an Art with that Application which is necessary to attain to any Kind of Perfection, when the *Fruit* of their *Labour* is being *reduced* to a State of the most *abject Slavery,* to be *bought* and *sold* in a *Market,* and to depend absolutely upon the Pleasure of any One who has Money enough to lay out in such a Purchase.

If not for the Sake of the Actors, yet for the *Honour of the Nation,* it is hoped, shou'd this Bill pass into a Law, and any *Differences* or *Disputes* hereafter happen between the *Patentees* and *Actors,* That the Arbitration thereof shall be placed in the Hands of some *Men* of *Fortune, Learning* and *Ability* (to be # appointed as the Legislature shall think fit) who will be *Impartial Judges* between the *Patentees* and *Actors* in their Disputes.

There is no Possibility the Stage shou'd ever subsist in this Kingdom, if *Authors* and *Actors* are *subjected,* without Controul, to the *Caprice* or *Ignorance* of *any Men who may hereafter look upon a Patent only as a proper Security upon which to lay out their Money.*

John Mills, Benjamin Johnson, Josias Miller, Theophilus Cibber, John Harper, Benjamin Griffin, William Mills, William Milward, Mary Heron, and *Elizabeth Butler,* Part of the abovenamed Performers, have taken a *Lease* of *Drury-Lane Play-House* for FIFTEEN YEARS, for which they are to pay NINE HUNDRED and TWENTY POUNDS *per Annum,* besides *Taxes* and *Repairs,* and *as the Law now stands, they run no Risque.* But should the Bill now depending, pass into a Law, the *Patentees* may go to *another House,* and the LESSEES will be forc'd to *pay* this *great Rent* without daring to make any Use of the Play-House, which must necessarily end in THEIR RUIN.

The LEGISLATURE has *never yet* thought it *just* to affect *private Property* by a Law EX POST FACTO, and therefore the *Lessees* of *Drury-Lane* Play-house *hope* if this Bill shou'd pass, that *Provision* will be made for *their Case,* and that *they* are as much entitled to be *protected* in the *Rights* which they now by *Law* enjoy, as the *Patentees*, &c.

(endorsed on back of p. 3:) THE CASE OF His Majesty's Company of COMEDIANS, &c.

From Haslewood; sheet is numbered "8" in MS.

B-8. THE CASE OF LEE AND SYMES

THE / CASE / OF / CHARLES LEE Esq; Master / AND / LESTRANGE SYMES Esq; Controller / of his Majesty's Revels, / *Sheweth*,

THAT the said *Charles Lee* and *Lestrange Symes*, Esquires, are by Royal Letters Patent from King *Charles* II. and his present Majesty, respectively appointed Master and Controller of all and singular Drolls, Revels, and Masques within the Realm; and respectively hold and enjoy the Offices of Master and Controller of the Revels, and all Fees, Profits, Privileges, and Advantages appurtenant thereto.

THAT the said Offices of Master and Controller of the Revels have, time immemorial, been held and enjoyed under Royal Letters Patent; and the Patentees have, by virtue thereof, always Licensed and Authorized Players of Interludes, Drolls, Country Shews, and Entertainments, to the Encrease of the Publick Revenue, each Licence being subject to a Stamp-Duty, and by which Licences Players are restrained from every thing tending to Profaneness and Obscenity, or which may be any ways offensive to Piety and good Manners.

THAT great Expence hath attended the Patentees of the said Offices, in procuring and passing their respective Patents; and there being at present a Bill depending in Parliament, "For restraining the number of Houses for Playing of Interludes, and for the better regulating common Players of Interludes"—It is apprehended such Bill, if passed into a Law, may affect the Right and Interest of the said Patentees, unless a saving Clause be therein provided, That nothing in the said intended Law shall extend to prejudice the Right or Interest of the said Master and Controller of his Majesty's Revels:

> *IT is therefore humbly hoped, That such or some other Provision will by the said intended Law be made, for preserving the Right and Interest of the said Patentees respectively, as shall be agreeable to the Wisdom of Parliament.*

(endorsed:) CASE OF The Master AND Controller of the REVELS, In relation to the BILL for restraining the number of Houses for Playing of Interludes, and for the better regulating common Players of Interludes.

From Harvard.

B-9. TONY ASTON'S PETITION AND SPEECH

Tony Aston's / PETITION / AND / SPEECH / (With his Deportment / BEFORE THE / Honble H——se of C——ns / In Behalf of Himself and the ACTORS / in TOWN and

COUNTRY. / To which is Prefix'd, / His VISIONARY INTRODUCTION, &c. / *Fir'd with the Thoughts of Truth and Liberty,* / (*Like* Aristides) *humane ANTHONY*! / *Pleads in the Publick Cause without a Fee.* / LONDON, / Printed for the AUTHOR. MDCCXXXV. #

TO THE / Lords and Commons / OF / GREAT BRITAIN, / THIS / MEDLEY ORATORY, &c. / Is most Humbly DEDICATED / *By their most Grave, Facetious,* / *Profound, Whimsical, Humourous,* / *Serious, Open and Occult* / *Humble Servant,* / Anthony Aston. #

THE / Visionary Introduction. / ON the 28th of *January* last at *Leeds* in *Yorkshire*, I was seized with an involuntary irresistible Motive of hastening to *London*, where (through dismal Roads, soaking Weather, with an old Chair and a blind Horse) I arriv'd, tir'd in Body and perplex'd in Mind, ruminating by what Instinct I was urged to come to a Place (though my native) which was always fatal to my Ease and Purse, when, next Morning, after I had quench'd my Thirst in Bed with three Dishes of Bohea, and corrected it with a Dram of Gin, I fell into a deep Sleep, when lo! a prodigious motly Vulture with *Ninety* Wings and *Seventy four* Claws, (for I number'd 'em) with a terrible *BILL*, open'd at me, raving out in furious Screams in a *Quaker-like* Agony, "*Regulation! Destruction! Acting inconsistent with Christianity! Down with the Players!*"—If it had not been for the *Ninety* Wings bearing it aloft, the *Seventy four* Claws had tore me in pieces. On the Wings was dispos'd most curiously in white Feathers the Word *NO*, (a Comfort to me;) on the Claws, in bloody Characters, the Word *YEA*, (horrible!) when on a sudden it vanished—And Fancy presented a Roly-poly Table, whereat Five Hundred and odd Gentlemen were playing at *Pass and no Pass*; they were a little hot about their Bets, when I went Half a Crown with an honest *Lincolnshire* Gentleman on the Side of *No Pass*; and the Dispute growing high, I was pitch'd on, to have leave to speak in Decision of the Stakes—but they were still divided in their Sentiments—when an elderly Man at the Door, with a Mutton-Chop in one Hand, and a Crust of Bread in the other, cry'd out, (with a Voice as terrible as a Turnkey) *Clear the Room*! when bustling to get out, I fell down the Stairs, and wak'd out of my Dream; when by my Bed-side sat a Friend to welcome me to Town: You have been sound asleep, # said he, I was loth to 'wake you; though I saw you in a violent Agony, uttering unintelligibly, (like a Boy counting Half-pence, or an Actor bit in a Benefit;) then, your convulsive Jaw open'd, and threw out, *Old England! Liberty! Smoak the Quaker*! I told him my Dream—Gracious! (said he) this is portentous! why, there is a *Bill* advancing to ruin all the Actors: You are by this Dream pointed at to be the Man that must boldly Plead for Yourself and others: Be brisk and indefatigable, I warrant you Success. Although Parson B——df——rd should preach *Leviticus* against you, you'll have *Numbers* on your Side: Throw in a Petition, be early. Faith, said I, 'tis very dangerous medling; I am (through many Misfortunes) grown poor, and if I should gain any Point for my Brother Actors, they are many of 'em ungrateful mean-spirited People, and won't thank me for't. Preserve (said he) thy wonted noble Soul; heap Coals of Fire on their Head. I dare not stir, said I, I must make either the Patentees or Players my Enemies, and they hate me enough already, tho' they don't love one another; and as soon as some Nobleman becomes my Friend, their Slander takes him off. Well, said he, if you don't be quick, the Co——ns in four Days will *commit* the Bill: I had rather (said I) they should *Commit* the *Bill* than me: However, said I, I'll try if my noble Friend my Lord *T——c——l* will assist me: so I drew up the following Petitiou, which was carried in by his Lordship, the Patriot of Liberty and Property. **#**

THE / PETITION. / *To the Honble. the C——m——s of* Great / Britain *in P——t Assembled.* / The HUMBLE PETITION of / *Anthony Aston*, Comedian, / *Most Humbly Sheweth,* /

THAT whereas there is a Bill now depending in this Honourable H——se for lessening the Number of Playhouses, and Regulating Common Players of Interludes.

Which Bill, if it should pass into a Law, in the Form it is, your Humble Petitioner will be inevitably ruin'd.

That he is by many Misfortunes become Poor, and hath not Money to Fee Council.

Wherefore he humbly craveth to be heard before this Honourable H——se personally;

And Your Humble Petitioner, &c. **#**

Then I was presently inform'd by my good Lord *G——ge,* that I should be immediately heard before the Com——t——e of the whole House. Then my Heart danc'd, caper'd, and frisk'd as quick as a Pea on a Pin's Point on the small End of a Tobacco-Pipe; my Lips biver'd, my Throat gulpt, my Spirits sunk like *South-Sea* Stock; and if I had had a *Drachm,* should not have *Scrupled* to have drank it——when the noble Assertor of Liberty took me by my Left Hand, and introduced me before the H——b——e House; so after my bowing as low as a Chaplain to a good Dinner, I was removed from Place to Place as often as a Sharper does his Lodging, and laugh'd at a great while, (upon my Soul I can't tell for what not I) I sat down in a rare Sweat for two Hours, while Council talk'd, (*I say hem, hem,* &c.) prodigious fine—I began.

THE / SPEECH. / *May it please this H——b——e H——e,*

The Joy which I conceive on this your exuberant Condescention, pumps from my Heart a Deluge of Gratitude; but I humbly hope, that the Lacrymatic Issue of the Ocular Effusion will be totally absorb'd by the Sunshine of Your *Goodness.*

Then Tears flow'd down to molify the Laws,
Stretch'd out my Hand and pleaded for the Cause.

I shall humbly endeavour to modify my Speech into three Branches, First, of the Laudability, Use, and Lawfulness of Acting; Secondly, Generally in the Behalf of my Brethren wheresoever dispers'd; and lastly, in behalf of my self.

I humbly observe to Your Honours, That among the various Petitions, Cases, &c. not one of them but what have snug regard only to their own identical Interest, and (not in the least) in or for any or all of my Brethren, although most of those Actors have been itinerant; but

Non Nobis solum nati sumus. **#**

Acting in itself hath, by all eminent Lawyers, been judged no *Malum in se,* and that Diversion hath been encouraged by good and great Men, before, in, and from the State of the *Roman* Empire; in the Decrease of it, indeed, Sense, Learning, Wit, and

Plays were discountenanc'd; then the Age became deprav'd, and the People *Dissented* from rational Entertainments, to flock to bestial, inhumane Sights:

> *Beasts killing Beasts, Men shedding Blood of Men,*
> *And Beasts with Men contending.*

And now if sensible Diversions are depress'd, it will be a fine Sight to have our Quality and Gentry bespeak Boxes at the *Bear Garden*;

> *Then Butchers may tread upon the Necks of Nobles.* Rowe's J. Shore.

Plays, if rightly adapted in Sense and Words, are of extreme good Use, the Clergy, the Lawyers, &c. may from the Stage learn beautiful Position, decent Action and Face, Cadence of Voice, and force of Energy;

> *How to awake the drowsy Bench of Justice,*
> *Or how to soften Rigour into Mercy.*

Your unthinking Youths who hate dull Forms and Trammels of Rules, that pull up their Noses at a Right Reverend, are often caught by fair Guile at a well wrote instructive Play; as the divine *Herbert* hath it,

> *A Verse may find him who a Sermon flies,*
> *And turn Delight into a Sacrifice.*

So, in fine Satyr, and also in Low Life, many will not be severely documented, who are often in Comedy jeer'd out of their Vices, by seeing their Images expos'd.

As to a Regulation of Plays, Players, and Playhouses, it is devoutly to be wish'd; but this Bill points directly at a total rural Extirpation: Whereas it is humbly to be presum'd, the prime Intention of it was only to destroy *Goodman's Field* Playhouse, under the Title of *Common Players of Interludes*, which is a *Misnomer in Terminis.* For there are no such Persons now in being as were at the time of making that first Act against *Common Players of Interludes.* That Act took its rise in the biggotted papistical Times, when an idle Set of scandalous People (with as many Cloaths, &c. as thrust into a Sack and lie on a Jack Ass) went # into Villages, presenting divers Interludes, particularly one call'd, *King John and the Abbot of Unreason*, exposing the Ignorance, Pride, Hypocrisy, and Lewdness of the Monks, Friars, &c. but now the Country is regularly entertain'd at great Expence with good Plays, and Waggon Loads of Scenes and adapted Habits.

So that it would be a great Loss to the Country Gentry to be depriv'd of seeing Plays elsewhere than at the two Patent Playhouses; their purposely coming to *London*, would put them to a vast Expence and Inconveniency—Besides, what an Outcry would there be through all the Counties in *England*, if Sister *Abigail*, Cousin *John*, and *Cicely*, &c. should be hinder'd at Marts, Fairs, Horse Races, and Cock Matches, of their usual Dramatic Diversion? —The Country 'Squire, and Half-farmer, must lose many a Day's Ploughing to put Horses to his Coach to drive to *London*, to see a Play, and then go directly back again.

As I was saying (I ask the Council's pardon) a Regulation is necessary, to lop the vicious Branches, but not eradicate the Whole, that wou'd be to destroy the *Pious* with the *Wicked*; but if all Country Actors must promiscuously suffer by this Act, I question if there is Wood enough in *England* to hang them all on; What Recourse for their Bread must most of them take, who, for many Years, have addicted themselves solely to Acting, and especially those who from their Infancy have been trained up in it? If silenc'd, "they cannot dig, and to beg they'll be "ashamed, being capable in no other way to subsist honestly.

To avoid being prolix about a Regulation, I humbly refer to my Memorial, given in to the *Gentlemen order'd to prepare the Bill, which I humbly conceive both Masters and Actors, &c. would have acquiesced in.

But the †Punishment specified in this Bill is so severe, the Thoughts of it makes my Shoulders smart; it is giving the *Magistrates* the *Whip-hand* of us all, except the Patentees, who are or should be good and impartial Judges, and Encouragers of Actors; yet altho' I am esteem'd through the Kingdom as a Top Proficient, especially by many Gentlemen of this H——b——e House (if they don't remember me, I do them by the half Crowns I have had of them) yet these worthy Patentees refuse me my Livelihood under them, altho' I was initiated there, and have often been with them; and am now (without Gaul to any Actor) willing to contend from the *Ghost* in *Hamlet*, to *Hob* in the *Country Wake*.

Wherefore, most humbly, I beg Your Honours will be Commiserately touch'd for all Actors, especially my self. #

Since for Twenty-five Years past, *My Medley*, void of Immorality, Scurrility, Prophaneness, and ill Manners, hath been admitted and applauded throughout *Great Britain*, when and where common Players have been rejected; nay, I have been invited often into the private Apartments of the Heads of Colleges, and Noble, and Gentlemens Houses: So that if it had not been for accumulated Misfortunes, I had been in easy Circumstances; and ought I not to be rather encouraged than distress'd? considering too, that there is a Bill advancing to secure to Inventors of Engraving, &c. and to Authors, &c. for investing in them their several Properties in their Designs.

I humbly beg, that I only, and none else, may be allow'd to exhibit a Medley throughout *Great Britain*, or be otherwise provided for, that I may not starve in my declining Years.

But if it shall be the Will of this H——b——e H——e, that this Bill must pass, and I and thousands must Perish—*Fiat*!

Non meum est contra Authoritatem Senatus dicere.

FINIS.

N.B. My Memoirs of the STAGE will be publish'd early next Winter.

> *Jam Seges ubi Troja fuit.*
> *I shall not look upon the like again.* Hamlet.

From Haslewood (title page, dedication page, then the speech) and the Folger Shakespeare Library (introduction and petition); 12 pp. In Haslewood, MS note on

---

*By Sir *E*——*w*——*d St*——*n*——*y*.
†*Whipping*

page between 1735 bill and this: "It Did belong to Mr Kemble. Not perfect wanting two leaves, at least, for the visionary introduction: but considered the fragment too rare and singular not to be secured." Folger copy is complete.

B-10. THE PLAYER'S LAST REFUGE

The PLAYER'S LAST REFUGE: Or the STROLLERS in DISTRESS.

(1) a Strolling *Hannibal* in Distress. (2) the Ghost of *Lunn* executed at Kingston with a Halter about his Neck offering Him his Masque and Pistols. (3) Despair and Poverty exciting him to receive the same. (4) a strolling *Sophonisba* who rather than Submit to the Power of the C[omo]n C[ounci]l, heroically deprives herself of Life by a Draught of pure *Hollands*. (5) Hob having no more to do with his Well is Employ'd in Digging a Grave for *Pistol*. (6) the Corps of *Pistol* supported by *Hamlet, Sr John Falstaff, Harlequin, Orpheus,* &c. (7) H[i]pp[es]ly a *Retailer* of *Coffee,* F[iel]d[in]g a *Retailer* of *Wine,* chief Mourners. (8) S^r J[oh]n B[arnar]d, riding in Triumph o'er the ruins of *Troy, Punches Opera* the *Sausage* and *Black pudding* stalls, &c Pointing to a Black Cloud which hangs over G[oo]dm[an]'s F[iel]ds pl[a]yh[ous]e.

[1735]

'Mourn *Smith field Muses* Mourn! Your Fall's Decreed,
And now the Starch'd Enthusiast doth succeed,
With *Quaker's* Coat beneath Close Girt about, —
Full bottom Wigs, Gold chains and *Furs* without,
Press'd on by Holy Zeal or Worldly Pride—
(He knows not which, they are so near Ally'd)
Fond to be Talk'd of he'll reform the Age—
—Tis done—he stands the *Terror* of the *Stage,* —
See *Fritters* fall a Victim to his Wrath—
And see him tumble Down the long stew'd Broth
The ratt'ling platters the scar'd Dames appall
—But *Tragedy* & they are Doom'd to *Fall*—
'Nay ev'n at *Royall Ensigns* see him strike—
Crowns & Black puddings are to him alike—
Raptur'd a Gloomy Low'ring Cloud He Sees—
And *Goodman's* fall he with a smile Decrees—
Vows that he'll banish thence y^e *Rake & Fop*—
And Turn it once more to a *Throwster's shop*—
Forth from the Fair the *Hero* Stalks Dismay'd—
Doubtfull to take ye Road or Learn a Trade—
Despair & Poverty near him Attend,—
And *Lunn* with Masque & 'Pistols stands his friend
F[ieldin]g Whom once did Gods with *Nectar* cheer
Pawns his full Bottom for a *Pot* of *Beer*—
And *Maw-mouth'd H[ippes]ly* o'er ye Coffee's smoke,
Casts forth askew, a dismall Shocking Look,—
See M^{rs} L[e]e to her last Coag retires—

Takes a full Quartern & with Grief Expires
Hark from th' ecchoing Booths a Dismall Roar
Proclaims aloud, that *Pistol is no more.* —
Falstaff [Griffin] & *Hamlet* Lay him on the Bier—
And *Orpheus* [Rich] *Harlequin* brings up the Rear—
Industrious *Hob* finding no more *Fair room*
Converts his useless Well into a Tomb.—
Down Drop ye Booths the Grubstreet *Bards* Undone
These *Are thy Triumphs, thy Exploits S^r I[oh]n.* —

[Sir John Barnard, Lord Mayor.]

Printed for B. Dickenson at Inigo Iones's Head against Exeter Change in ye Strand & published according to Act of Parliament 1735. [May 1730 Goodmans fields Theatre supresed for a short time.]

From British Museum, Political and Personal Satires No. 2146; roman and italic in this transcription are reversed from the print; brackets indicate contemporary MS additions. The print which this text accompanies is shown in Fig. 1.

APPENDIX C

DOCUMENTS RELATING TO THE
LICENSING ACT, 1737

C-1. CAMBRIDGE UNIVERSITY SENATE
RECORDS (1736)

Whereas a Play Booth is intended to be erected within the Precincts of the Town & Jurisdiction of the University of Cambridge, contrary to the good Order & Discipline of the said University, May it Please you, that if any Member of this University of what Standing or Degree soever, shall presume to be present at any Play or Interlude there to be acted, he shall suffer the Penalty of Forty Shillings for each Transgression of this Order.

Read Aug. 10. Granted Aug. 11. [1736]

From Cambridge University Archives, MS. Grace Book I (1718–44), IX, 412.

May it Please you to grant Procuratorial Power to the Masters of Arts undernamed to continue untill the Feast of St Michael, And more particularly to be exercised at Sturbridge ffair & at the Playhouse lately built within the Precincts of ye Town and Jurisdiction of the University; And that all Scholars under Tuition may be obliged to pay the same Obedience in Points of Discipline to Them as to the Proctors themselves is due.

Lect. Sept. 6   Concess Sept. 7 1736.

From Cambridge University Archives, MS. Grace Book I (1718–44), IX, 412. Seventeen names are listed after the entry.

C-2. CAMBRIDGE UNIVERSITY PETITION TO
PARLIAMENT (TAVERNS)

To the Honble the Knights / Citizens & Burgesses assembled in Parliam^t / The Humble Petition of the Chancellor / Masters & Scholars of the University of Cambridge

Sheweth

That the University by ancient Custom & Charters confirmed by Acts of Parliam^t hath long enjoyed the Sole Right of Licenceing Taverns and all other Publick Houses within the Precincts of the same

181

That this Right hath from time to time been reserved to U[s by spe]cial Clauses in all # Acts of Parliam[t] relating to y[e] Regulation of Taverns & other Publick Houses.

That for want of such Reservation in an Act passed in the last Session of Parliament Intituled an Act for laying a Duty upon the Retailers of Spirituous Liquors & for Licensing the Retailers thereof Several Persons Distillers have set up the Trade of Vintners in the Town of Cambridge without being Licenced by the University in prejudice to the Ancient Rights & Priviledges thereof

May it therefore Please this Honourabl[e] House to take the Premisses into Consideration & grant such Relief as to them in their great Wisdom shall seem meet

And your Petitioners shall ever pray &c.

Lect. & Concess. Placeat Vobis ut Petitio modo lecta

Mart. 3° 1736/7 Sigillo vestro communi Sigelletur & vestro
Nomine praesentetur.

From Cambridge University Archives, MS. Grace Book I (1718–44), IX, 418–19. Letters in brackets are partially torn.

C-3. CAMBRIDGE UNIVERSITY PETITION TO PARLIAMENT (PLAYHOUSES)

To the Hon[ble] the Knights Citizens & / Burgesses assembled in Parliam[t] / The Humble Petition of the Chancellor Masters / & Scholars of the University of Cambridge

Sheweth

That a House hath lately been built within the Precincts of the University for the Acting of Plays and Interludes & hath accordingly been made Use of for that Purpose notwithstanding the Vicechancellor & Heads of Colleges did discourage & to the Utmost of their Power endeavour to prevent the Building the said House

That many Inconveniencies & Mischiefs will arise & the Manners of y[e] Youth Committed to our Care be in great Danger of being corrupted if Play Houses should be established amongst Us #

That your Petitioners are not impowered by any Law now in being effectually to prevent the Establishm[t] of such Houses

May it therefore please this Honourable House to take the ptmes into Consideration & grant such Relief as to them in their Great Wisdom shall seem meet

And your Petitioners shall ever pray &c.

Lec. & Concess. Placeat Vobis ut Petitio modo lecta

Mart:5° 1736/7. Sigillo vestro communi sigilletur & vestro
Nomine praesentetur.

From Cambridge University Archives, MS. Grace Book I (1718–44), IX, 419–20.

C-4. REASONS HUMBLY SUBMITTED AGAINST THE UNIVERSITY BILL

REASONS / HUMBLY SUBMITTED / Against passing the Bill, *For the more effectual preventing the unlawful / playing of Interludes within the Precincts of the University of* Cam- / bridge, *and the Places adjacent; and for explaining and amending so / much of an Act passed in the last Session of Parliament, intituled,* An / Act for laying a Duty upon the Retailers of Spirituous Liquors, and for / licensing the Retailers thereof, *as may affect the Privilege of the Uni- / versity of* Cambridge, *with respect to licensing Taverns, and all other / publick Houses, within the Precincts of the same.*

THERE hath been, Time out of Mind, an ancient Fair called *Sturbridge* Fair, annually held in *September*, for about the Space of a Fortnight, within the Precincts of the Town and University of *Cambridge*.

The Commerce of this Fair, and the Entertainment of Plays and Interludes which have been usually acted for the Diversion of Persons resorting to the same, have occasioned a great Concourse of the Gentlemen and Inhabitants of the adjacent Counties, as also from divers other Parts of *England*, to the great Benefit of the Inhabitants of the Town and County of *Cambridge*, and the Owners and Proprietors of Estates in the said Fair.

These Plays and Interludes having been acted in a Number of common Wooden Booths and Boarded Places, to the great Hazard and Inconveniency of the Spectators, *Joseph Kettle*, an Owner of Land in the said Town, for the more regular and convenient Performing of Plays during the Time of *Sturbridge* Fair only, at his own considerable and sole Expence, erected and built upon his own Ground a commodious and convenient Playhouse in the Precincts of the Town of *Cambridge*, upon his own Land, for the Entertainment of the Company who should come to *Sturbridge* Fair; and in which Plays were perform'd, during the Time of the last Fair, in a much more orderly, decent and convenient Manner, than had been before usually done.

By the said Bill, should the same, as it now stands, pass into a Law, all Plays and Interludes would be absolutely prohibited within the Town and Precincts of *Cambridge*, and that even during the Time of *Sturbridge* Fair.

But it is humbly hoped the said Bill shall not pass into a Law, amongst many others, for the following REASONS:

I. With regard to the said *Joseph Kettle*, as it would absolutely restrain him from making use of the said Playhouse, and in Consequence thereof greatly and prejudicially affect him in his Property.

II. For that the erecting the said Playhouse was no Infringement of any Law then or now in being; and the said *Joseph Kettle*, in erecting the same, made a lawful Use of his own Property; and it is therefore hoped, no Law shall be now made to restrain him from the free Use and Enjoyment thereof, or to make that illegal now, which was a lawful Act at the Time of doing it.

III. For that the said *Joseph Kettle*, at the Time of erecting the said Playhouse, did not mean or intend to have Plays acted therein but during the Time of *Sturbridge* Fair only; and he is ready and willing to undertake and engage, in the most effectual Manner, That the said Playhouse shall not be opened, or any Plays or Interludes acted therein, but during the Continuance of *Sturbridge* Fair only.

IV. Should therefore this Bill pass into a Law, it would lay a Restraint on the Precincts of the Town of *Cambridge*, which no other Part of the Kingdom is liable to; and it is humbly hoped, there will be no other Restraint by Law to hinder Plays or Interludes being acted within the said Town, or the Precincts thereof, during the Time of such Fair, than what already extends, or shall extend, to the Kingdom in general.

V. For that the acting such Plays and Interludes, at the Time of the said Fair only, can be of no Prejudice to any of the Members of the said University of *Cambridge*; the said University having sufficient Power and Authority, by their own Constitutions, By-laws, and Customs, to prevent any of their own Members, if they see proper, from frequenting or going to the same, and have accordingly effectually restrained and prevented them from going to the same by such their By-laws and Customs, whenever the Governors of the said University have thought proper to do so: But the Governors of the said University have for many Years past been so far from thinking such Plays and Interludes any improper Entertainment for the Members of the said University, that they have, as far as in them lay, encouraged the same.

VI. For that the said Fair happens in Vacation-time, when the Scholars, or younger Part of the said University, are absent, and not within the University during the Time of the said Fair.

VII. For that, whatever the Sentiments of the Governors of the said University may be at present, as to Plays and Interludes during the Time of *Sturbridge* Fair being an improper Entertainment or not for their own Members; it is humbly hoped, others, who are no Members, shall not be restrained from having such Plays and Interludes acted during the said Fair, otherwise, or in any other manner, than the rest of his Majesty's Subjects are in all other Places.

VIII. For that such Restraint is unreasonable in itself, and will be of great Prejudice to the Inhabitants of the said Town and County, and Owners of Estates in the said Fair.

For all which, amongst many other Reasons, it is humbly hoped, the said Bill shall not pass into a Law.

(endorsed:) REASONS HUMBLY SUBMITTED Against passing the Bill, *For the more effectual preventing the unlawful playing of Interludes within the Precincts of the University of Cambridge, and the Places adjacent; and for explaining and amending so much of an Act passed in the last Session of Parliament, intituled,* An Act for laying a Duty upon the Retailers of Spirituous Liquors, and for licensing the Retailers thereof, *as may affect the Privilege of the University of Cambridge, with respect to licensing Taverns, and all other publick Houses, within the Precincts of the same.*

From Lincoln's Inn Library, MP 103, fol. 295.

C-5. OXFORD UNIVERSITY PETITION
TO PARLIAMENT

Die Jovis (viz.) Septimo Die Mensis Aprilis Anno Domini 1737°. Causa Convocationis ut legatur Libellus Supplex Inferiori Domo Parliamenti Acadamia nomine praesantandus [?sumi infinem?] et Privilegia in quadam Billa nunc temporis coram Senatu agitata ab Academia Cantabrig: petita, ad Universitatem Oxon extendentur.

To the Honourable the Commons of Great Britain / in Parliament assembled / The Humble Petition of the Chancellor Masters and / Scholars of the University of Oxford

Sheweth, —

That, Whereas your Petitioners are informed that a Bill, intituled A Bill for the more effectual Preventing the unlawful Playing of interludes within the Precincts of the University of Cambridge, and the Places adjacent, and for explaining, and amending so much of an Act Pass'd in the last SeSsions of Parliament intituled An Act for laying a Duty upon the Retailers of Spirituous Liquors and for Licensing the Retailers thereof, as may affect the Privilege of the University of Cambridge with respect to Licensing Taverns and all other Publick Houses within the Precincts of the same is now depending in this Honourable House tending to the better Preservation of the Discipline and good Government of the University of Cambridge in the several instances recited in the said Bill, And Whereas your Petitioners apprehend that the several Powers and advantages propos'd to be granted to the Univerity of Cambridge will be equally serviceable and necessary both with the regard to the order, Discipline and better Government of the University of Oxford and also to other good purposes intended by the said Bill: They therefore Humbly Pray that by the favour of this Honourable House they may be included in the said Bill, and that the several Powers and Benefits therein granted may be extended to the University of Oxford in the same manner as they are propos'd to be granted to the University of Cambridge

And your Petitioners as in Duty bound shall ever Pray
Dated in Convocation under the Seal of the University (which we use in these cases) the 7th day of April 1737.

From Bodleian, Oxford University Archives, MS. Register of Convocation, 1730–41, N.E.P. / *subtus* / Reg. Be., fol. 71.

C-6. JOSEPH KETTLE'S PETITION

A Petition of Joseph Kettle Esquire was presented and Read, setting forth, "That he hath, at his own great Expence, built a commodious Playhouse, on his own Land, within the Precincts of the Town of Cambridge, for the Entertainment of the Company who should come to Sturbridge Fair; and that, by the last mentioned Bill, the Petitioner will be restrained from making Use of the said Play-house, which will greatly affect his Property"; and praying, "That he may be heard, by Counsel, against the said Bill, and have such Relif as to the House shall seem meet."

From House of Lords Record Office, H.L. MS. Minute Book No. 83, for 9 May 1737.

C-7. THE SAME, ANOTHER COPY

To the Right Honble the Lords Spiritual / and Temporal in Parliament Assembled / The Humble Petition of Joseph Kettle Esquire

Sheweth

That Plays and Interludes have for many years past been constantly acted during the Time of Sturbridge Fair within the Town and precincts of Cambridge and the same having been Acted in a Number of Comon Wooden Booths and Boarded Places to the great Hazard and Inconveniency of the Spectators your Petitioner for the more regular and Convenient performing of Plays during the Time of Stourbridge Fair only, at his own great and sole Expence Erected and Built a Commodious and Convenient Playhouse in the Precincts of the Town of Cambridge upon his own Land for the Entertainment of the Company who should come to Sturbridge fair and in which Plays were performed During the time of the last Fair in a much more orderly decent and Convenient manner than had been before usually done.

That a Bill is now depending before your Lordships Entitled "An Act for the more Effectual preventing the unlawful playing of Interludes within the Precincts of the University of Cambridge and the places adjacent and for explaining and amending so much of an Act passed in the Last Session of Parliament Intitled An Act for Laying a Duty upon the Retailers of Spirituous Liquors and for Licensing the Retailers thereof as may Affect the Priviledge of the University of Cambridge with respect to Licencing Taverns and all other Publick houses within the Precincts of the same" By which Bill should the same be passed into a Law your Petitioner will absolutely be restrained from making use of the said Playhouse and will be greatly and prejudicially Affected in his property

Therefore and as the Erecting of the said Playhouse was as your Petitioner humbly apprehends no Infringement of any Law then or now in being And your Petitioner in Erecting the same made a Lawful use of his own property. Your Petitioner humbly hopes no Law shall be now made to restrain him from the Free use and Enjoyment thereof or to make that illegal now which was a Lawful Act at the Time of doing it and as your Petitioner at the Time of Erecting the said Playhouse did not mean or Intend to have Plays acted in the said House but during the Time of Stourbridge Fair only so your Petitioner most humbly assures your Lordships That the said playhouse shall not be opened or any Plays or Interludes acted therein but during the continuance of Sturbridge Fair only

Your Petitioner therefore humbly Prays your Lordships That he may be heard by his Councel against the said Bill and to have Such Releife in the premisses as to your Lordships shall seem Meet

And your Petitioner shall ever Pray &c.

Jo: Kettle

(endorsed:) Petition of Joseph Kettle Esqr to be Heard by Councel ag^t the Bill to prevent Unlawful Playing of Interludes in the Universities   Read 9^t Maÿ 1737. Order'd to be Rejected. Bill read 5th   1737. May 9.

From House of Lords Record Office, H.L. MS. Main Papers, for 5 May 1737. Petn. of Joseph Kettle to be heard against 9 May.

C-8. THE UNIVERSITIES' ACT

An Act for the more effectual preventing the unlawful playing of Interludes within the Precincts of the two Universities, in that Part of *Great Britain* called *England*, and the Places adjacent; and for explaining and amending so much of an Act passed in the last Session of Parliament, intituled, *An Act for laying a Duty upon the Retailers of Spirituous Liquors, and for licensing the Retailers thereof*, as may affect the Privilege of the said Universities, with respect to licensing Taverns, and all other Publick Houses within the Precincts of the same.

'WHEREAS the Letters Patent of King *Henry* the Eighth, made and granted unto the Chancellor and Scholars of the University of *Oxford*, bearing Date the first Day of *April* in the fourteenth Year of His Reign; and the Letters Patent of Queen *Elizabeth*, made and granted unto the Chancellor, Masters and Scholars of the University of *Cambridge*, bearing Date the twenty sixth Day of *April* in the third Year of Her Reign; and also all other Letters Patent by any of Her Progenitors or Predecessors made to either of the corporated Bodies of the said Universities, and all manner of Liberties, Franchises, Immunities, Quietances and Privileges, View of Frank Pledge, Law Days, and other Things, whatsoever they were, the which either of the said corporated Bodies of the said Universities had, held, occupied or enjoyed, or of Right out to have had, used, occupied and enjoyed, were by Authority of Parliament in the thirteenth Year of Her Reign, confirmed to the Chancellor, Masters and Scholars of either of the said Universities, and their Successors, for the great Love and Favour that Her said Majesty bore towards Her said Universities, for the great Zeal and Care that the Lords and Commons had for the Maintenance of good and godly Literature, and the various Education of Youth, within either # of the said Universities; and to the Intent that the ancient Privileges, Liberties and Franchises of either of the said Universities, granted, ratified and confirmed by the Queen's Highness, and Her most noble Progenitors, might be had in greater Estimation, and be of greater Force and Strength, for the better Increase of Learning, and the further suppressing of Vice: And whereas Doubts have arisen or may arise, whether by any of the said Letters Patent, Liberties, Franchises, Immunities or Privileges, or by any subsequent Charter or Charters, or by the Laws and Statutes of this Realm, the Chancellor of either of the said Universities, or the Vice Chanceller thereof, or his Deputy, or any other Person or Persons, be sufficiently impowered to correct, restrain or suppress common Players of Interludes, settled, residing or inhabiting within the Precincts of either of the said Universities, and not wandering abroad: And whereas the Erection of any Playhouse within the Precincts of either of the said Universities, or Places adjacent, may be attended with great Inconveniences,' May it please Your Most Excellent Majesty that it may be enacted, and be it enacted by the King's Most Excellent Majesty, by and with the Advice and Consent of the Lords Spiritual and Temporal, and Commons, in this present Parliament assembled, and by the Authority of the same, That all Persons whatsoever who shall for Gain in any Playhouse, Booth or otherwise, exhibit any Stage Play, Interlude, Shew, Opera, or other theatrical or dramatical Performance, or act any Part or assist therein, within the Precincts of either of the said Universities, or within five Miles of the City of *Oxford*, or Town of *Cambridge*, shall be deemed Rogues and Vagabonds; and that it shall and may be lawful to and for the Chancellor thereof or his Deputy respectively, to commit any such Person to any House of Correction within either of the Counties of *Cambridge* or *Oxford* respectively, there to be kept to hard Labour for the Space of one Month, or to the Common Gaol of the City or County of *Oxford*, or Town or County of *Cambridge* respectively, there to remain without Bail or Mainprize for the like Space of one Month; any Licence of the Chancellor, Masters and Scholars of either of the said Universities of *Oxford* or *Cambridge*, or any Thing herein or in any other Statute, Law, Custom, Charter or Privilege, to the contrary notwithstanding.

[Sections II, III, and IV deal with the regulation of taverns.]

V. Provided always, That this Act, or any Thing herein contained, shall not in any wise be construed to prejudice or confirm any of the Liberties, Privileges, Franchises, Jurisdictions, Powers and Authorities appertaining or belonging to the Mayor, Bailiffs and Commonalty of the City of *Oxford*, or to any of them, but that they and every of them and their Successors, may have, hold, use and enjoy, all their Liberties, Privileges, Franchises, Jurisdictions, Powers and Authorities, in such large and ample wise as though this present Act had never been had or made.

VI. And be it further enacted by the Authority aforesaid, That this Act shall be deemed a Publick Act, and shall be judicially taken Notice of as such by all Judges, Justices and other Persons whatsoever, without specially pleading the same.

10 Geo. II, ch. 19

From *Statutes at Large, of England and of Great-Britain: From Magna Carta to the Union of the Kingdoms of Great Britain and Ireland* (London, 1811), IX, 508–12; printed marginalia are omitted.

C-9. HENRY GIFFARD'S LETTER

Sir

'Tis with the greatest Difficulty, I have prevaild with my self to entertain a Thought of receiving any thing for the Stage, wch might carry in it the remotest Construction against any part of the Conduct of the present happy Administration—& I intreat your Honour, to believe, I do a Violence to my Inclination, in being oblig'd to receive a Premium, for what my Principle disclaims, & on that Score shou'd reject, were I not bound by Fatal Necessity, And give me leave, to assure you, Sir, if any thing in my little Power, cou'd contribute to the Welfare of this Government, no Man has it more sincerely at Heart, than

Sr Y^r Honour's most Obedient, +
Devoted, Humble Serv'
Hen° Giffard

(endorsed:) M. Giffard

From Cambridge University Library, Cholmondeley (Houghton) MS. Corr. 3253.

C-10. THE CASE OF THE PROPRIETORS
OF GOODMAN'S FIELDS

the County of *Middlesex*.

IN the Year 1731, *Henry Giffard* open'd a Subscription for Two Thousand five hundred Pounds, to erect a *Theatre* on a Building-Lease, from Sir *William Lemon*, for the Term of Sixty one Years, and subject to a Ground-Rent of Forty five Pounds *per Annum*.

THAT the said *Proprietors* being well informed by their *Council* learned in the *Law*, that the said Undertaking was *lawful*, did severally subscribe and pay the Sum of One Hundred *Pounds* for each *Share* of the said *Theatre*, with Scenes, &c. Each *Sharer* being intitul'd to One Shilling and Sixpence every acting Night, and the Privilege of seeing the Play *gratis*. For Security of which, the *Lease* was assign'd over to *them* by the said *Giffard*.

THAT ever since (except this present Year) Plays have been exhibited there with all possible Decorum; and constant Regard hath been had, that nothing should be represented, which was offensive to the Laws, Religion, or Moral Vertue.

THAT if the *Bill* now depending in this Honourable *House* for *explaining* and *amending* an *Act* of the 12th of Queen *Anne*, so far as it relates to common *Players* of Interludes, should pass into a Law, (unless some Provision be made for the *Proprietors* therein) it will entirely deprive them of all the improv'd Rent of the said *Theatre*, and subject them to lose their whole Subscription-Money, being Two Thousand and Five Hundred Pounds. Because,

AS the *Bill* now stands, it excludes the *Bills of Mortality*, in which is compris'd the said *Theatre* in *Goodmans-Fields*, and lays the *Proprietors* under an impossibility of obtaining at any Time a *Licence* from the Lord Chamberlain.

The Proprietors *therefore most humbly hope, this Honourable House will take the Premises into Consideration, and grant them such Relief as shall seem meet.*

(endorsed:) THE CASE OF THE PROPRIETORS of the THEATRE in *Goodmans-Fields*, in the *Tower* Division, in the County of *Middlesex*.

From Public Record Office, SP 36/25, fol. 256; title cropped; "Theatrical" in MS above printed endorsement. There is a MS note on the reverse concerning a living in county of Anglesey that has become vacant on death of bishop of Bangor, desired for "a friend of your grace's humble servant."

C-11. THE CASE OF THE LESSEES
OF DRURY LANE

THE / CASE / OF / Benjamin Johnson, Josias Miller, Theophilus Cibber, John Harper, Benjamin Griffin, William Mills, William Milward, *and* Elizabeth Butler, LESSEES *of the* THEATRE-ROYAL *in* Drury-Lane.

That in 1733 they took a *Lease* from the Renters or Proprietors of the said Theatre (for the Term of Fifteen Years) at the *yearly Rent* of 920 *l*. which, together with *Taxes* and *Repairs*, make the *whole* above 1000 *l*. a *Year*.

That if the Bill now depending in this Honourable House, for Explaining and Amending so much of the Twelfth of Queen *Anne* as relates to common Players of Interludes (which they apprehend is designed only to regulate the Stage) should pass into a Law, and they be restrain'd thereby from acting Plays at *the said Theatre*, and should the *Person* who *now occupies* the same (as Tenant at will) happen to die, or dispose of his Clothes, Scenes, &c. or be *minded to quit the same*, then in such Case the Lessees will be *liable* to that *great Rent*, without the Means of doing any Performance whereby to enable them to pay it, *to the inevitable Ruin of themselves and Families*.

They are well persuaded a REGULATION of the STAGE not only may be of *great Use* to them, but of great *Advantage* to the *Stage* in *general*, by preventing the exhibiting any licentious or scandalous Piece, &c. But as THEY have in all Instances *demonstrated* their *Duty, Affection* and *Loyalty* to HIS MAJESTY, and the present HAPPY ESTABLISHMENT, and ever have (AS FAR AS LAY IN THEIR POWER) *discountenanced* any thing that had the *least Tendency* to *Vice, Immorality* or *Disaffection*, they therefore humbly hope they shall be so far considered in the said Bill, as that they may be enabled to perform Plays, &c. at the said Theatre under the Restrictions and Regulations in the Bill, or in such other manner as to this Honourable House shall seem meet.

(endorsed:) THE CASE OF Benjamin Johnson, Josias Miller, Theophilus Cibber, John Harper, Benjamin Griffin, William Mills, William Milward, *and* Elizabeth Butler, LESSEES *of the* THEATRE-ROYAL *in* Drury-Lane.

From Haslewood; sheet is numbered "7" in MS.

C-12. CHARLES FLEETWOOD'S PETITION

To his Grace the Duke of Grafton Lord / Chamberlain of his Majesty's houshold / The Memoriall of Charles Fleetwood Esq'

Sheweth

That, your Lordships memorialist is apprised, a bill is now depending in parliament for the restraining of Playhouses.

That, he is very sensible the audacious liberties, taken by those who consult, their own private lucre, preferable to all other considerations, makes it now highly necessary, to suppress immediately this pernicious growing Evil.

That, notwithstanding it may so happen, that somethings, contain'd in this Bill, may possibly bear too hard, upon a *Large Intrest, & property*, he has *from a patent Granted by his present Majesty*, which might reasonably induce him to *petition*, for such provisoes, as might *Establish*, & exempt, his *Grant*, yet assured of his Majesty's Candour, Justice, & humanity and considering, how near the sessions of Parliament, is drawing to a conclusion, and that his Majesty's Honour, and Dignity, and the welfare of all honest men is concern'd in passing this into a Law; your Lordships *Memorialist determines*, to do nothing that shall tend to obstruct, or even retard, This bill, but throws *himself* & *property* entirely upon *his Majesty's* know Goodness and under his *protection*.

From Cambridge University Library, Cholmondeley (Houghton) MS. Class 80/206; the *n* in "own"(paragraph 2) is crossed out; "yet" (between "Grant" and "assured") is written over the word "Intrest," which is crossed out.

C-13. THE LICENSING ACT

Le Roy le Veult.

Soit baillé aux Seigneurs
Aceste Bille les Seigneurs sont assentus.

Whereas by an act of Parliament made in the Twelfth Year of the Reign of her Late Majesty Queen Anne Intituled an act for reducing the Laws relating to Rogues Vagabonds Sturdy Beggars and Vagrants into one act of Parliament and for the more effectual punishing such Rogues Vagabonds Sturdy Beggars and Vagrants and Sending them whither they ought to be sent It was Enacted that all persons pretending themselves to be Patent Gatherers or Collectors for Prisons Gaols or hospitals and wandring abroad for that purpose all ffencers Bear Wards Common Players of Interludes and other persons therein named and Expressed shall be deemed Rogues and Vagabonds **And Whereas** some Doubts have arisen concerning so much of the said act as relates to Common Players of Interludes **Now** for Explaining and Amending the same **Be it Declared** and **Enacted** by the Kings Most Excellent Majesty by and with the Advice and Consent of the Lords Spiritual and Temporal and Commons in this present Parliament assembled and by the authority of the same that from and after the twenty fourth day of June One Thousand seven hundred and thirty seven every person who shall for hire Gain or Reward act represent or perform or cause to be acted represented or performed any Interlude Tragedy Comedy opera Play ffarce or other Entertainment of the Stage or any part or parts therein in case such person shall not have any Legal Settlement in the place where the same shall be acted represented or performed without authority by vertue of Letters Patent from His Majesty His Heirs Successors or Predecessors or without Licence from the Lord Chamberlain of His Majestys Household for the time being shall be deemed to be a Rogue and a Vagabond within the intent and meaning of the said recited act # and shall be Liable and Subject to all such penalties and punishments and by such methods of Conviction as are inflicted on or appointed by the said act for the punishment of Rogues and Vagabonds who shall be found wandring Begging and Misordering themselves within the intent and meaning of the said recited act **And** Be it further **Enacted** by the authority aforesaid that if any person having or not having a Legal Settlement as aforesaid shall without such authority or License as aforesaid act represent or perform or cause to be acted represented or performed for hire Gain or reward any Interlude Tragedy Comedy opera Play ffarce or other Entertainment of the Stage or any part or parts therein every such person shall for every such offence forfeit the sum of fifty pounds and in case the said⌃ ↑ sum of ↓ fifty pounds shall be paid Levied or recovered such offender shall not for the same offence suffer any of the Pains or penalties inflicted by the said recited act **And** Be it further **Enacted** by the authority aforesaid that from and after the said twenty fourth day of June one thousand seven hundred and thirty seven no person shall for hire Gain or reward act perform represent or cause to be acted performed or represented any new Interlude Tragedy Comedy Opera Play ffarce or other Entertainment of the Stage or any part or parts therein or any new act scene or other part added to any old Interlude Tragedy Comedy Opera Play ffarce or other Entertainment of the / Stage or any new Prologue or Epilogue unless a true Copy thereof be sent to the Lord Chamberlain of the Kings Household for the time being fourteen days at least before the acting representing or performing thereof together with an account of the Playhouse or other place where the same shall be and the time when the same is intended to be first acted represented or performed signed by the Master or Manager or one of the Masters or Managers of such Playhouse or Place or Company of actors therein # 3 **And** Be it **Enacted** by the authority aforesaid that from and after the said twenty fourth day of June one thousand seven hundred and thirty seven it shall and may be Lawful to and for the said Lord Chamberlain for the time being from time to time and when and as often as he shall think fit to prohibit the acting performing or representing any Interlude Tragedy Comedy opera Play ffarce or Other Entertainment of the Stage or any act scene or part thereof or any Prologue or Epilogue and in case any person or persons shall for hire Gain or reward act perform or represent or cause to be acted performed or represented any new Interlude Tragedy Comedy Opera Play ffarce or other Entertainment of the Stage or any act scene or part thereof or any new Prologue or Epilogue before a Copy thereof shall be sent as aforesaid with such account as aforesaid or shall for hire Gain or reward⌃ ↑ act ↓ perform or represent or cause to be acted performed or represented any Interlude Tragedy Comedy opera Play ffarce or other Entertainment of the Stage or any act scene or part thereof or any Prologue or Epilogue contrary to such Prohibition as aforesaid every person so offending shall for every such Offence forfeit the sum of fifty pounds and every Grant License and authority in case there be any such by or under which the said Master or Masters or Manager or Managers set up formed or continued such Playhouse or such Company of actors shall cease determine and become absolutely void to all intents and purposes whatsoever   **Provided** always that no person or persons shall be authorized by virtue of any Letters Patent from His Majesty His Heirs successors or Predecessors orby the Licence of the Lord Chamberlain of His Majestys Household for the time being to act represent or perform for hire gain or reward any Interlude Tragedy Comedy Opera Play ffarce or other Entertainment of the Stage or any part # 4 or parts therein in any part of Great Britain Except in the City of Westminster and within the Liberties thereof and in such places where His Majesty His Heirs or successors shall in their Royal Persons reside and during such residence only any thing in this act contained to the contrary in any wise notwithstanding   **And** Be it further **Enacted** by the authority aforesaid that all the pecuniary penalties inflicted by this act for offences committed within that part of Great Britain called England Wales and the Town of Berwick upon Tweed shall be recovered by Bill Plaint or Information in any of His Majestys Courts of Record at Westminster in which no Essoign Protection or Wager of Law shall be allowed and for offences committed in that part of Great Britain called Scotland by action or summary Complaint before the Court of Session or Justiciary there or for offences committed in any part of Great Britain in a summary way before two Justices of the Peace for any County Stewartry Riding Division or Liberty where any such offence shall be committed by the Oath or Oaths of one or more credible Witness or Witnesses or by the confession of the offender the same to be levied by distress and sale of the offenders Goods and Chattels rendring the Overplus to such offender if any there be above the penalty and charge of Distress and for want of Sufficient Distress the offender shall be committed to any House of Correction in any such County Stewartry Riding or Liberty for any time not exceeding Six months there to be Kept to hard Labour or to the common Gaol of any such County Stewartry Riding or Liberty for any time not exceeding Six months there to remain without Bail or Mainprize and if any person or persons shall think him her or themselves aggrieved by the Order or Orders of such Justices of the Peace it shall and may be lawful for such person or persons to appeal therefrom to the next General Quarter Sessions to be held for the said County # 5 Stewartry Riding or Liberty whose Order therein shall be final and conclusive and the said penalties for any offence against this act shall belong one moiety thereof to the Informer or person suing or prosecuting for the same the other moiety to the Poor of the Parish where such offence shall be committed   **And** Be it further **Enacted** by the authority aforesaid that if any Interlude Tragedy Comedy opera Play ffarce or other Entertainment of the Stage or any act scene or part thereof shall be acted represented or performed in any House or place where Wine ale Beer or other Liquors shall be sold or Retailed the same shall be deemed to be acted represented and performed for Gain Hire and Reward   **And** Be it further **Enacted** by the authority aforesaid that no person shall be Liable to be prosecuted for any offence against this act unless such Prosecution shall be commenced within the space of Six Calendar Months after the offence committed and if any action or suit shall be commenced or brought against any Justice of the Peace or any other person for doing or causing to be done any thing in pursuance of this act such action or suit shall be commenced within Six Calendar months next after the fact done and the Defendant or Defendants in such action or suit shall and may plead the General Issue and give the special matter in Evidence and if upon such action or suit a Verdict shall be given for the Defendant or Defendants or the plaintiff or plaintiffs or Prosecutor shall become Nonsuit or shall not prosecute his or their said action or suit then the Defendant or Defendants shall have Treble Costs and shall have the like remedy for the same as any Defendant or Defendants have in other cases by Law. /

For more effectual punishment of Rogues and Vagabonds

(endorsed:) **An Act** to explain and amend so much of an Act made in the Twelfth Year of the Reign of Queen Anne Intituled An Act for reducing the Laws relating to Rogues Vagabonds Sturdy Beggars and Vagrants into one Act of Parliament and for the more effectual punishing such Rogues Vagabonds Sturdy Beggars and Vagrants and Sending them whither they ought to be sent as relates to Common Players of Interludes. Anno 10° Georg ÿ 2ᵈⁱ

From House of Lords Record Office, MS. Original Act, 10 Geo. II, ch. 28; 5 presses; press numbers and virgules appear in original as indicated.

NOTES

The following abbreviations have been used throughout the notes:

BL	British Library
Bod.	Bodleian Library
CLRO	Corporation of London Records Office
CUA	Cambridge University Archives
CUL	University Library, Cambridge
G.B., Parl.	Great Britain, Parliament
GLRO	Greater London Record Office
GM	*Gentleman's Magazine*
HLRO	House of Lords Record Office
HMC	Historical Manuscripts Commission
JHC	*The Journals of the House of Commons*
JHL	*The Journals of the House of Lords*
LIL	Lincoln's Inn Library
LM	*London Magazine*
LS	Emmett L. Avery et al., *The London Stage, 1660–1800*, 5 parts in 11 vols. (Carbondale: Southern Illinois Univ. Press, 1960–68)
PRO	Public Record Office

PREFACE

1 G.B., Parl., *Sessional Papers* (Commons), *1831–32*, Vol. VII, 2 Aug. 1832, "Report from the Select Committee on Dramatic Literature: with the Minutes of Evidence," p. 218.

2 Jean B. Kern, *Dramatic Satire in the Age of Walpole, 1720–1750* (Ames: Iowa State Univ. Press, 1976), p. 47.

INTRODUCTION

1 Charles B. Woods, rev. of *LS*, pt. 3, *1729–1747* (1961), ed. and introd. Arthur H. Scouten, *Philological Quarterly*, 41 (July 1962), 558.

2 C. H. Rolph, *Books in the Dock* (London: Andre Deutsch, 1969), pp. 40–41.

3 *The Usefulness of the Stage to Religion, and to Government* (London: Thomas Harper, 1738), pp. 36–37.

4 Bertrand A. Goldgar has pointed out that the Licensing Act "must be viewed as the government's response to the whole complex of events in the spring of 1737, the most important element of which was the decision of the prince to move openly into Opposition to Walpole." *Walpole and the Wits: The Relation of Politics to Literature, 1722–1742* (Lincoln: Univ. of Nebraska Press, 1976), p. 156.

CHAPTER 1:
DEREGULATION OF THE THEATERS, 1729–1734

1 Patent quoted in Richard Findlater, *Banned! A Review of Theatrical Censorship in Britain* (London: MacGibbon & Kee, 1967), p. 18.

2 For the authority of the Lord Chamberlain, the Master of the Revels, and others to regulate plays before the seventeenth century, see Findlater, *Banned*, pp. 17–21; G.B., Parl., *Sessional Papers*, "Dramatic Literature," p. 21; and Phyllis Hartnoll, "The Theatre and the Licensing Act of 1737," in *Silver Renaissance: Essays in Eighteenth-Century English History*, ed. Alex Natan (London: Macmillan, 1961), p. 166.

3 Findlater, *Banned*, pp. 27–29; and G.B., Parl., *Sessional Papers*, "Dramatic Literature," pp. 22, 34.

4 William P. Williams, "Sir Henry Herbert's Licensing of Plays for the Press in the Restoration," *Notes & Queries*, NS 22 (June 1975), 255–56.

5 Findlater, *Banned*, pp. 30–35; John Genest, *Some Account of the English Stage, from the Restoration in 1660 to 1830* (Bath: H. E. Carrington, 1832), III, 24–27; and Scouten, Introd., *LS, 1729–1747*, p. lxii.

6 Findlater, *Banned*, pp. 31–32; and Scouten, Introd., *LS, 1729–1747*, pp. xxix, lxii–lxiii.

7 Scouten, Introd., *LS, 1729–1747*, pp. lxiii, cxlix; Colley Cibber, *An Apology for the Life of Colley Cibber*, ed. B.R.S. Fone (Ann Arbor: Univ. of Michigan Press, 1968), pp. 151–52; James J. Lynch, *Box, Pit, and Gallery: Stage and Society in Johnson's London* (Los Angeles: Univ. of California Press, 1953), p. 86; and G.B., Parl., *Sessional Papers*, "Dramatic Literature," p. 64.

8 PRO, MS. LC 5/153, fols. 433–34.

9 Emmett L. Avery, Introd., *LS, 1700–1729*, p. cl.

10 Cibber, *Apology*, ed. Fone, pp. 152–53. See also Genest, *English Stage*, III, 24–28; Findlater, *Banned*, pp. 34–35; and John Loftis, *Steele at Drury Lane* (1952; rpt. Westport, Conn.: Greenwood Press, 1973), pp. 48–49.

11 The information on patents in this study is based on the copy of letters patent to Robert Wilks, Colley Cibber, and Barton Booth (1732) in CUL, Cholmondeley (Houghton) MS. Class 91/73; Francis Hargrave, "Mr. Hargrave's Observations in Respect to the Objection to the Patent to Killigrew on the Ground of Merger and Dormancy" (copy), BL, Add. MS. 12,201; G.B., Parl., *Sessional Papers*, "Dramatic Literature," p. 16; Percy Fitzgerald, *A New History of the English Stage from the Restoration to the Liberty of the Theatres* (London: Tinsley Bros., 1882), II, 66; Watson Nicholson, *The Struggle for a Free Stage in London* (Boston: Houghton,

Mifflin & Co., 1906), pp. 1–19; Allardyce Nicoll, *A History of Early Eighteenth Century Drama, 1700–1750* (Cambridge: Cambridge Univ. Press, 1929), pp. 271–76; Emmett L. Avery and Arthur H. Scouten, Introd., *LS, 1660–1700*, pp. xxi–xxiv, xxxi–xliv; Avery, Introd., *LS, 1700–1729*, pp. xxii–xxxvi, xxxix–xlii, lxxx–lxxxviii; Scouten, Introd., *LS, 1729–1747*, pp. lxxxix–xcvi; P. J. Crean, "The Stage Licensing Act of 1737," *Modern Philology*, 35 (February 1938), 242; Aaron Hill and William Popple, *The Prompter: A Theatrical Paper (1734–1736)*, ed. William W. Appleton and Kalman A. Burnim (New York: Benjamin Blom, 1966), p. 180, n. 9; Hartnoll, "Licensing Act," p. 168; Loftis, *Steele*, pp. 33–52, 121–58; and Judith Milhous, "Company Management," in *The London Theatre World*, ed. Robert D. Hume (Carbondale: Southern Illinois Univ. Press, 1980), pp. 1–34.

12 John Rich and his company remained in Lincoln's Inn Fields until the 1732-33 season, when they moved to the new theater Rich had built in Covent Garden; from that time until 1741, both Covent Garden and Lincoln's Inn Fields were apparently operated under Rich's patents. Hargrave ("Patent to Killigrew," BL, Add. MS. 12,201, pp. 3, 8; see also GLRO MS. E / BER / CG / E8 / 10 / 1–4) concludes that after 1732 the two patents were exercised separately, one covering Covent Garden and the other Lincoln's Inn Fields. Rich himself makes the same assertion in "Mr. Rich's Case on the Bill for Restraining the Number of Play-Houses, &c." (n.d.), p. 2, Harvard Theatre Collection, TS 297.25.35F (see App. B-6). But see John Loftis, *The Politics of Drama in Augustan England* (Oxford: Clarendon Press, 1963), p. 99, n. 3; Crean, "Licensing Act." p. 242; and Hill and Popple, *Prompter*, ed. Appleton and Burnim, p. 180, n. 9.

13 John Gay, Pref., *Polly: An Opera* (London: For the Author, 1729), p. i; rpt. in *The Stage and the Licensing Act, 1729–1739*, ed. Vincent J. Liesenfeld (New York: Garland, 1981).

14 See John, Lord Hervey, *Some Materials towards Memoirs of the Reign of King George II*, ed. Romney Sedgwick (London: Eyre & Spottiswoode, 1931), I, 98; [J. Mottley,] "A Compleat List of All the English Dramatic Poets, and of All the Plays Ever Printed in the English Language to the Present Year 1747," in *Scanderbeg; or, Love and Liberty*, by Thomas Whincop (London: W. Reeve, 1747), p. 239; Charles E. Pearce, *Polly Peachum: The Story of Lavinia Fenton and "The Beggar's Opera"* (London, 1913; rpt. New York: Benjamin Blom, 1968), p. 248; James R. Sutherland, "*Polly* among the Pirates," *Modern Language Review*, 37 (July 1942), 291; and David H. Stevens, "Some Immediate Effects of *The Beggar's Opera*," in *The Manley Anniversary Studies in Language and Literature* (Chicago: Univ. of Chicago Press, 1923), p. 188.

15 Cibber, *Apology*, ed. Fone, pp. 191–94; Fitzgerald, *New History*, II, 435–36; and Hargrave, "Patent to Killigrew," BL, Add. MS. 12,201, p. 16.

16 "Translation of the Informd" [26 August 1724?], CUL, Cholmondeley (Houghton) MS. Class 81/20 (a six-page MS., apparently incomplete).

17 For prosecutions under William and Anne, see Joseph Wood Krutch, *Comedy and Conscience after the Restoration* (New York: Columbia Univ. Press, 1949), pp. 169–77.

18 *State Law; or, The Doctrine of Libels, Discussed and Examined*, 2nd ed. (London: T. Wotton & J. Schuckburgh, [1729–30?]), p. 68.

19 See R. v. Tutchin, 14 Howell's St. Tr., 1094 (1704), cited in W. Blake Odgers, *A Digest of the Law of Libel and Slander*, ed. W. Blake Odgers and Robert Ritson, 6th ed. (London: Stevens & Sons, 1929), pp. 371, 419–20; see also Fredrick Seaton Siebert, *Freedom of the Press in England, 1476–1776: The Rise and Decline of Government Controls* (Urbana: Univ. of Illinois Press, 1952), p. 275.

20 Holt's Rep. 424, St. Trials, V, 527, quoted in Francis Ludlow Holt, *The Law of Libel: In Which Is Contained a General History of This Law*, 2nd ed. (London: J. Butterworth & Son, 1816), p. 108, n. s.

21 William Hawkins, *Pleas of the Crown*, B. I, cap. 73, sec. 4, 5, quoted in *State Law*, p. 62.

22 See Laurence Hanson, *Government and the Press, 1695–1763* (Oxford: Oxford Univ. Press, 1936), pp. 23, 67–68.

23 Warrant to Nicholas Paxton, 5 July 1737, PRO, MS. Money Book 39 (T 53/39), p. 36.

24 See Paul S. Fritz, *The English Ministers and Jacobitism between the Rebellions of 1715 and 1745* (Toronto: Univ. of Toronto Press, 1975), p. 117, n. 28; and Michael Harris, "Newspaper Distribution during Queen Anne's Reign: Charles Delafaye and the Secretary of State's Office," in *Studies in the Book Trade in Honour of Graham Pollard*, ed. R. W. Hunt, I. G. Philip, and R. J. Roberts, Oxford Bibliographical Society Publications, NS Vol. 18 (Oxford: Oxford Bibliographical Society, 1975), pp. 139–51.

25 See Hanson, *Government and Press*, pp. 28–29, 55.

26 Siebert, *Freedom of the Press*, p. 267. But see Chesterfield's assertion (quoted in Chap. 6, above, at n. 96) that performances *were* subject to the law of libel.

27 The government was unusually active against offensive publications from 1733 to the end of 1738, when twenty-one indictments were brought for seditious libel in the Court of King's Bench; in the period from 1739 to 1760, there were only sixteen. See Donald Serrell Thomas, "The Political, Religious, and Moral Censorship of Literature in England from the Seventeenth to the Nineteenth Centuries," Thesis Univ. of London 1969, p. 69.

28 Justices' order, *Gazette* of 14 October, quoted in Arthur Bedford, *The Evil and Mischief of Stage-Playing: A Sermon Preached . . . on Sunday the Thirtieth Day of November, . . . 1729. Occasioned by the Erecting of a Play-House in the Neighbourhood. Published at the Request of Several of the Auditors*, 2nd ed. (London: J. Wilford, 1735), pp. 39–40. See also Frederick T. Wood, "Goodman's Fields Theatre," *Modern Language Review*, 25 (October 1930), 446; Nicholson, *Free Stage*, pp. 25–26; and Scouten, Introd., *LS, 1729–1747*, p. xxi.

29 Petition (n.d.), PRO, MS. LC 7/3; a MS draft of the petition in CLRO is dated 21 April and endorsed "presented 28 Aprl 1730" (Shelf 552, Small MS. Box 7, No. 5). Other records in the CLRO show that on 7 April the Court of Aldermen had sent Sir Gilbert Heathcote to Townshend, one of the secretaries of state, for advice and help in suppressing the theater; Heathcote reported to the court a week later that both Townshend and Walpole had promised their "best Assistance" and suggested that the Court should petition the king for relief. MS. Repertories, Court of Aldermen, Vol. 134 (1729–30), pp. 216, 232, 240, 262, 263–65.

30 PRO, MS. LC 5/160, p. 130.
31 Nicholson, *Free Stage*, p. 28; and see James T. Hillhouse, Introd., *The Tragedy of Tragedies; or, The Life and Death of Tom Thumb*, by Henry Fielding (New Haven: Yale Univ. Press, 1918), p. 13.
32 Scouten, Introd., *LS, 1729–1747*, pp. xxii, xlviii; and see Crean, "Licensing Act," pp. 239–40.
33 *London Journal*, 23 Dec. 1721, quoted in Avery, Introd., *LS, 1700–1729*, p. xxxvi.
34 Scouten, *LS, 1729–1747*, pp. 54–68; Hillhouse, Introd., *Tragedy of Tragedies*, pp. 12–13.
35 Walter Aston, "To the Reader," in *The Restauration of King Charles II* (London: R. Walker, 1732), p. ii; rpt. in Liesenfeld, *The Stage and the Licensing Act*; and see *Read's Weekly Journal*, quoted in Crean, "Licensing Act," p. 253, n. 50. Loftis (*Politics of Drama*, p. 103) suggests the play was disapproved on account of Jacobite tendencies.
36 Rpt. in Liesenfeld, *The Stage and the Licensing Act*. See Loftis, *Politics of Drama*, p. 105; Kern, *Dramatic Satire*, p. 45; Wilbur L. Cross, *The History of Henry Fielding* (New Haven: Yale Univ. Press, 1918), I, 107–8; Milton Percival, Introd., *Political Ballads Illustrating the Administration of Sir Robert Walpole*, Oxford Historical and Literary Studies, Vol. 8 (Oxford: Clarendon Press, 1916), p. xx; Mary Dorothy George, *English Political Caricature to 1792: A Study of Opinion and Propaganda* (Oxford: Clarendon Press, 1959), p. 81; and *Remarks on an Historical Play, Called, "The Fall of Mortimer": Shewing Wherein the Said Play May Be Term'd a Libel against the Present Administration* (London: E. Rayner, [1731?]).
37 See Cross, *Fielding*, I, 105–11; and L. J. Morrissey, Introd. and Note on the Text, *The Grub-Street Opera*, by Henry Fielding (Edinburgh: Oliver & Boyd, 1973), pp. 5, 13–18.
38 *Grub-Street Journal*, 24 June 1731, quoted in Morrissey, Note, *Grub-Street Opera*, p. 15; and David Erskine Baker, *Biographia Dramatica; or, A Companion to the Playhouse*, continued by Isaac Reed and Stephen Jones (London: Longman, Hurst, 1812), II, 217, citing *GM*, 1731, p. 286.
39 Nicholas Paxton to [Walpole], 21 July 1731, PRO, MS. SP Geo. II, SP 36/23, fol. 252. Acts of Parliament are identified by the regnal year of the sovereign under whom they were passed, then by chapter number.
40 The phrase "sturdy beggars," customarily applied to vagrants in the statutes, acquired even greater political significance after Walpole used it on 14 March 1732/33 to refer to the crowds of petitioners who had come to Parliament to protest the excise bill. The Opposition quickly—and defiantly—adopted the phrase to describe its members; see Percival, *Political Ballads*, p. 79.
41 Paxton to [Walpole], 21 July 1731, PRO, MS. SP Geo. II, SP 36/23, fols. 252–53.
42 PRO, MS. Letter Book 19 (T 27/25), p. 76 (dated 20 Oct. 1731). The ministry seems to have used the vagrancy law in several ways to suppress criticism. Paxton's letter also mentions his expenses "in taking up & Punishing idle persons who hawk seditious Papers & Ballads about the streets." Like actors, these "mercuries" could be committed to Bridewell as vagrants without a

warrant from the secretary of state, but simply on an order of a justice of the peace, under the terms of the same statute Paxton had used against the Haymarket Theatre. See Hanson, *Government and Press*, p. 50; and the *Craftsman*, 29 May 1731, quoted in Percival, *Political Ballads*, p. 53.

43 See the *Daily Courant*, 25 Aug. 1731, quoted in Scouten, *LS, 1729–1747*, p. 151; and see Loftis, *Politics of Drama*, pp. 103–4. This raid is dated a day earlier by Edgar V. Roberts, Introd., *The Grub-Street Opera*, by Henry Fielding (Lincoln: Univ. of Nebraska Press, 1968), p. xvi; and by Morrissey, Note, *Grub-Street Opera*, p. 18. Morrissey (quoting the *Daily Advertiser*, 22 Aug.) says that several of the actors were taken into custody.

44 This may account for the difficulty most critics have had in explaining why *Hurlothrumbo*, first performed with considerable success in 1729, suddenly seemed to come under ministerial censure in the summer of 1731. See Cross, *Fielding*, I, 78–79, 111–12; Scouten, Introd., *LS, 1729–1747*, p. xlix; Nicholson, *Free Stage*, pp. 22–24; Roberts, Introd., *Grub-Street Opera*, p. xvi; and Malcolm F. Largmann, "Stage References as Satiric Weapon: Sir Robert Walpole as Victim," *Restoration and Eighteenth-Century Theatre Research*, 9 (May 1970), 39.

45 Copy of Letters Patent, CUL, Cholmondeley (Houghton) MS. Class 91/73; see also orders for the letters, PRO, MS. LC 5/160, pp. 175, 179–80; and see Fitzgerald, *New History*, II, 66; and Scouten, Introd., *LS, 1729–1747*, p. lxxxix.

46 For details of the changes, see *The Theatre Royal Drury Lane and the Royal Opera House Covent Garden*, Vol. XXXV of *The Survey of London*, ed. F.H.W. Sheppard (London: Athlone Press, 1970), p. 14; Cross, *Fielding*, I, 147–48; Loftis, *Politics of Drama*, p. 100; and Scouten, Introd., *LS, 1729–1747*, p. lxxxix.

47 In September Hester Booth sold what was left of her share to Henry Giffard, the manager of the new theater in Goodman's Fields. Sheppard, *Drury Lane and Covent Garden*, p. 14; Scouten, Introd., *LS, 1729–1747*, p. lxxxix; Loftis, *Politics of Drama*, p. 100; Fone, Introd., *Apology*, p. xiii; Wood, "Goodman's Fields Theatre," pp. 450–51; and Benjamin Victor, *The History of the Theatres of London and Dublin, from the Year 1730 to the Present Time* (London: T. Davies, 1761), I, 6–11. During March, Aaron Hill had tried to buy what was left of Booth's share and the share owned by Mary Wilks, and take over management of the theater with Highmore, but he had lost so much money during 1726–30 in a timber enterprise for the York Buildings Company that he lacked sufficient funds. See Michael R. Booth, "An Edition of the Theatrical Numbers of the *Prompter*, with Critical Introduction and Notes," Thesis Univ. of London 1958, pp. iv, xlvi–xlvii; Victor, *History*, II, 186; and Fitzgerald, *New History*, II, 75.

48 Scouten, Introd., *LS, 1729–1747*, pp. xc, xcii; Sheppard, *Drury Lane and Covent Garden*, p. 14; Fitzgerald, *New History*, II, 79, 86–87, 91. See John Laguerre's and Hogarth's prints on *The Stage Mutiny* (1733), and the discussion of them by Ronald Paulson, *Hogarth: His Life, Art, and Times* (New Haven: Yale Univ. Press, 1971), I, 322–23.

49 Scouten, Introd., *LS, 1729–1747*, p. xcii; and Sheppard, *Drury Lane and Covent Garden*, p. 14. The record of the ejectment action appears in PRO, MS. KB 122/148, Roll 311 (Mich. 7, Geo. 2); Yorke's bench notes made during the case

are in the Hardwicke Papers, BL, Add. MS. 36,031, fol. 4; and a courtroom note by an anonymous reporter is in LIL, Misc. MSS. Vol. 55, p. 335.

50 Victor, *History*, I, 20–22; and Nicholson, *Free Stage*, p. 36.

51 Nicholson, *Free Stage*, pp. 36–37; Fitzgerald, *New History*, II, 82–83.

52 Fitzgerald, *New History*, II, 83; and W. J. MacQueen-Pope, *Haymarket: Theatre of Perfection* (London: W. H. Allen, 1948), p. 46. See also Nicholson, *Free Stage*, pp. 37–38; Loftis, *Politics of Drama*, p. 101; and Scouten, Introd., *LS, 1729–1747*, p. xcii.

53 Fitzgerald, *New History*, II, 85; and see Cibber, *Apology*, ed. Fone, p. 343, n. 19.

54 Victor, *History*, I, 24n. That *all* players not protected by the Crown, even those "not wandring, &c.," were deemed to be rogues and vagabonds and subject to the penalties of the act of Queen Anne seems to have been the prevailing opinion: [Samuel Carter,] *Legal Provisions for the Poor*, 4th ed. (London: Walthoe and Walthoe, 1718), p. 194; the same argument was advanced in [Samuel Richardson,] *A Seasonable Examination of the Pleas and Pretensions of the Proprietors of, and Subscribers to, Play-Houses, Erected in Defiance of the Royal Licence* (London: T. Cooper, 1735), p. 6.

55 *An Apology for the Life of Mr. T ... C ..., Comedian: Being a Proper Sequel to "The Apology for the Life of Mr. Colley Cibber, Comedian"* (London: J. Mechell, 1740), p. 90; see also Cibber, *Apology*, ed. Fone, p. 154; and Scouten, Introd., *LS, 1729–1747*, p. xcii. A report of the case (from Mich. 7, Geo. 2) was published by Thomas Barnardiston (Vol. II) in 1744 (usually cited 2 Barn. K.B. 350), rpt. in *The English Reports*, 94, K.B. Div. 23 (Edinburgh: William Green, 1909), 546–47. Yorke's bench notes are in the Hardwicke Papers, BL, Add. MS. 36,038, fols. 40–44, but the most extensive records of the case are in LIL: Coxe MS. Vol. 47, fols. 296–98; Coxe MS. Book B (No. 29), fols. 101, 103–10; Hill MS. No. 66 (Osborne 11), fols. 135–39; and Misc. MS. Vol. 55, pp. 363–65. See also BL, Add. MS. 32,251, fol. 137, and Egerton MS. 2,320, fols. 60–61; and PRO, MS. KB 16/10.

56 Giffard continued to own the remaining one-sixth share. Sheppard, *Drury Lane and Covent Garden*, p. 14.

57 *Apology for T ... C ...*, p. 90.

CHAPTER 2:
THE BILL TO RESTRAIN THE NUMBER
OF PLAYHOUSES, 1735

1 *The Manuscripts of the Earl of Carlisle, Preserved at Castle Howard*, Historical Manuscripts Commission Series 43: 15th Report, Appendix, Part VI (London: HMSO, 1897), p. 115. The brackets appear in the published letter as indicated.

2 See, for example, Nicholson, *Free Stage*, p. 55 (who acknowledges that "I have found this mentioned in no other place"); Cross, *Fielding*, I, 225; and Scouten, Introd., *LS, 1729–1747*, p. xlix.

3 The marriage had been arranged in October 1733, but the prince was taken ill on 11 November, and the ceremony was put off from 12 November until 14

March 1733/34. The House gave leave for the bill to settle an annuity of £5,000 on the Princess Royal on 8 April; the bill was brought in and had its first and second readings on the same day. *JHC*, XXII, 308.

4 See *Manuscripts of Carlisle*, pp. 102–31, 138, quoted in Romney Sedgwick, *The House of Commons, 1715–1754* (London: HMSO, 1970), II, 153.

5 *JHC*, XXII, 890; the bill for the jointure was brought in the next day, and had passed the House of Lords by 7 June (see the message from the Lords, ibid., p. 896). For a discussion of the 1737 debate over the "million that was taken from the Sinking Fund" see Richard Chandler, *The History and Proceedings of the House of Commons from the Restoration to the Present Time* (London: Richard Chandler, 1742–44), IX, 347. For additional discussion of the Howard letter, see Vincent Liesenfeld, "The 'First' Playhouse Bill: A Stage Ghost," *Theatre Notebook*, 31 (1977), 9–12.

6 It is listed as item 49 in "The Monthly Catalogue for April 1735," *LM*, April 1735, p. 223. Bedford's sermon is almost certainly the target of the essay in the *Prompter* of 4 April (portions of which are reprinted in *LM*, April, p. 182), which defends the stage against "a *Return* of that *Puritannical* Moroseness of Principle, . . . the stupid Malignity of a weak Man's *blind Zeal*, —against *The Evil, and Mischief, of Stage-Playing!*"

7 Sir John Hawkins, *The Life of Samuel Johnson, LL.D.*, 2nd ed., rev. and cor. (London: J. Buckland, 1787), p. 73.

8 *Universal Spectator*, 12 April 1735. This is quoted in a somewhat different form in *GM*, April 1735, p. 191. See also Crean, "Licensing Act," p. 239.

9 Richardson, *Seasonable Examination*, pp. 17–18, quoted in Alan D. McKillop, "Richardson's Early Writings: Another Pamphlet," *Journal of English and Germanic Philology*, 53 (Jan. 1954), 73.

10 See Scouten, Introd., *LS, 1729–1747*, pp. xcvii, cxii; and p. 470.

11 *London Daily Post and General Advertiser*, 11 Feb. 1734/35, quoted in Scouten, *LS, 1729–1747*, p. 459.

12 *Prompter*, 22 April 1735, in Hill and Popple, *Prompter*, ed. Appleton and Burnim, pp. 54–55. According to the *Prompter*, this practice gave rise to "a Town party," which expected too much perfection in plays and so came prepared to damn them, and a "Poet's party," which expected too much indulgence. Feelings sometimes ran equally high among actors: on 10 May two members of the Drury Lane company fought over a wig; one "push'd violently at the . . . [other] with a Crab-Tree Stick, which enter'd his Eye, broke the Socket of it, and pierc'd an Inch into his Head, of which Wound he died the next Night. The Coroner's Inquest brought in their Verdict *Wilful Murder*." *LM*, May 1735, p. 276; cf. the report in the *London Daily Post and General Advertiser* of 13 May, quoted in Scouten, *LS, 1729–1747*, p. 490.

13 Quoted in William Cobbett, *Parliamentary History of England* (London: Hansard, 1811), IX, col. 915; portions of the letter were reprinted in *LM*, March 1735, pp. 117–18.

14 Hawkins, *Life of Johnson*, p. 74. See also Crean, "Licensing Act," p. 241.

15 See the account of the introduction of the bill in *GM*, Dec. 1735, p. 777; Richardson, *Seasonable Examination*, pp. 4–5; and Chandler, *History and*

Proceedings, IX, 93. The project is discussed by Nicholson, *Free Stage*, p. 56; and Crean, "Licensing Act," pp. 242–43. "A. B." was probably the equivalent in the eighteenth century for a post office box number in a blind-reply advertisement: see a similar reference in Sheridan's *The School for Scandal*, V.iii.97.

16 *Prompter*, 13 May 1735, in Hill and Popple, *Prompter*, ed. Appleton and Burnim, pp. 61–62. Theophilus Cibber reached the same conclusion about the advertisements: see his "Address . . . to the *H———ble* Sir *J———— B————*," in *Cibber's Two Dissertations on the Theatres: With an Appendix, in Three Parts* (London: Griffiths, 1756), pp. 70–71.

17 See Robert L. Haig, *The Gazetteer, 1735–1797: A Study in the Eighteenth-Century English Newspaper* (Carbondale: Southern Illinois Univ. Press, 1960), p. 4; and Hanson, *Government and Press*, pp. 109–15.

18 Chandler, *History and Proceedings*, IX, 93. See also Cobbett, *Parliamentary History*, IX, cols. 944–46; and Nicholson, *Free Stage*, pp. 55–56.

19 *GM*, Dec. 1735, p. 777.

20 Ibid.; and see Chandler, *History and Proceedings*, IX, 93–94; and Cobbett, *Parliamentary History*, IX, cols. 947–48.

21 Figures are from an estimate by the *Prompter*, 18 March 1734/35, rpt. in *LM*, March 1735, p. 128; and from the *Daily Advertiser*, 22 March 1734/35 (cited by Scouten, Introd., *LS, 1729–1747*, p. lxxi; and p. 469). Opposition to operas, and especially to Farinelli, was widespread: for a typical example, see *Fog's Journal*, 26 April 1735, rpt. in *LM*, April 1735, pp. 204–5. The company of French players held the Haymarket from 26 October 1734 until the end of the season in June 1735: see Emmett L. Avery and Mildred Avery Deupree, "The New Theatre in the Haymarket, 1734 and 1737," *Notes & Queries*, 171 (July 1936), 41.

22 *JHC*, XXII, 403.

23 William Coxe, *Memoirs of the Life and Administration of Sir Robert Walpole, Earl of Orford*, new ed. (London: T. Cadell, Jun., & W. Davies, 1800), II, 435. See also Frank Fowell and Frank Palmer, *Censorship in England* (London: Frank Palmer, 1913), p. 134.

24 *JHC*, XXII, 403.

25 Sedgwick, *House of Commons*, II, 57–58, 438–39, 462, 540. Lord Gage had some personal stake in the bill, since he had subscribed £300 to Rich's new theater in 1731: see Basil Francis, "John Rich's 'Proposals,'" *Theatre Notebook*, 12 (1957), 17. Jekyll, Pulteney, Willes, Ryder, and Talbot were appointed, on 2 April, to prepare a bill authorizing residents in Lincoln's Inn Fields to levy a tax on themselves to raise money to improve conditions in the area. Since committee members were usually selected because of their interest in the proposed legislation, it may be that some or all of these five were concerned particularly with the deterioration of London neighborhoods. See *JHC*, XXII, 442; and Peter D. G. Thomas, *The House of Commons in the Eighteenth Century* (Oxford: Clarendon Press, 1971), p. 266.

26 Unanimity was rare in the House: see Thomas, *Commons*, p. 243, who cites Egmont's diary for evidence that at the end of the debate on the address on 17 Jan. 1734/35 four or five members voted nay loudly to show that it was not accepted unanimously, although they could do nothing to oppose it. If a bill was

to be opposed, the motion for leave to bring it in was often chosen as the occasion for forcing a division, and more than half of the bills involved in division at this stage were defeated (pp. 48–50).

27 See text of the bill in Appendix B-1. In the copy in the Harvard Theatre Collection this clause has been crossed out, presumably by a House member who recorded on it changes made after it had been introduced, which suggests that at some later stage the bill became a public—that is, a government— measure. Since the only reliable text of private acts (which before 1798 were not printed in their final form) was the original parchment act preserved by Parliament, the law had to be proved in court by reference to the original unless it contained a clause declaring it to be a public act; in that case the proof was unnecessary and litigation was thereby simplified. See Sheila Lambert, *Bills and Acts: Legislative Procedure in Eighteenth Century England* (Cambridge: Cambridge Univ. Press, 1971), p. 106.

28 See O. Cyprian Williams, *The Historical Development of Private Bill Procedure and Standing Orders in the House of Commons* (London: HMSO, 1948), I, 26; Sedgwick, *House of Commons*, I, 6; and Thomas, *Commons*, pp. 57–58.

29 Lambert, *Bills and Acts*, p. 105. For the 1705 order, see *JHC*, XV, 18; Thomas, *Commons*, pp. 57–59; and Williams, *Private Bill Procedure*, I, 26. The standing order requiring all private bills to be printed was occasionally ignored, so the special order by itself cannot be considered conclusive evidence that the bill was treated as a public one.

30 Lambert, *Bills and Acts*, pp. 86–89, 103; Thomas, *Commons*, pp. 59–60; Williams, *Private Bill Procedure*, I, 26.

31 PRO, MS. Treasury Minute Book 27 (T 29/27), p. 310.

32 Lambert, *Bills and Acts*, pp. 73–74. Members of the House named to the small committees to prepare bills often had little to do with the actual drafting: see Lambert, Introd., *House of Commons Sessional Papers of the Eighteenth Century* (Wilmington, Del.: Scholarly Resources, 1975), I, 10.

33 Quoted in Scouten, *LS, 1729–1747*, p. 466.

34 Letter rpt. in Cobbett, *Parliamentary History*, IX, cols. 945–47. The letter was also reprinted in the *Political State of Great Britain*, 49 (April 1735), 362–64; and portions of it appeared in *LM*, March 1735, pp. 117–18, following which the editor refers the reader to extracts "from the *Apprentices Vade Mecum*, on this Subject, Vol. II. p. 618." For the role Samuel Richardson, the author of the *Vade Mecum*, may have had in writing an editorial comment to the "Tradelove" letter, see McKillop, "Richardson's Early Writings," pp. 72–73.

35 Hill and Popple, *Prompter*, ed. Appleton and Burnim, pp. 40–42. A month earlier, on 21 February, the *Prompter* had complained that government ministers were remiss in failing to direct the stage to encourage public virtue and patriotism (pp. 32–33).

36 *Grub-Street Journal*, Thursday, 27 March 1735. Since the *Journal* usually opposed the positions taken by the *Prompter*, their agreement in this instance may suggest that support for the idea was fairly widespread outside Parliament: see Booth, "An Edition of the *Prompter*," p. lxv. I have not seen the "new Epilogue recommending the Support of the English Theatre—To the Beauties of Great Britain," spoken by Cibber at the conclusion of *The Man of Taste* at

Drury Lane on Saturday, 29 March 1735 (Scouten, *LS, 1729–1747*, p. 474), which may have dealt with the theater bill; nor have I seen the long article opposing the silencing of Giffard's theater in the *London Daily Post and General Advertiser* of 31 March (p. 475).

37 Scouten, Introd., *LS, 1729–1747*, pp. xliii–xlv; and pp. 475–76.

38 *JHC*, XXII, 444; and Thomas, *Commons*, p. 94.

39 The order of the House is found in *JHC*, XXII, 444. A facsimile of the British Library's copy (BL, 11795.k.31) appears in Liesenfeld, *The Stage and the Licensing Act*; the first page of the bill appears in Scouten, *LS, 1729–1747*, opp. p. 967, but is mislabeled "The famous Licensing Act of 1737" (the Licensing Act itself was never officially printed). It is this British Library copy that is reprinted in Appendix B-1 above. A second copy of Barnard's bill is in Columbia University Library (Dram. Lib. D824.128/G79) and a third (with contemporary MS notations, printed in brackets in App. B-1) is in the Harvard Theatre Collection (TS 297.25.35F). The detailed manuscript records of the progress of the bill in the House were destroyed in the "tally-stick fire" on the night of 16 October 1834 that consumed most of the House of Commons records deposited in the Palace of Westminster. See Maurice F. Bond, *Guide to the Records of Parliament* (London: HMSO, 1971), p. 4.

40 *Prompter*, 4 April 1735, rpt. in *LM*, April 1735, p. 182; for a report of the essay, see Richardson, *Seasonable Examination*, as summarized by McKillop, "Richardson's Early Writings," p. 75.

41 *JHC*, XXII, 450.

42 Sedgwick, *House of Commons*, I, 13.

43 Thomas, *Commons*, pp. 49–50. Occasionally, opposition to a bill might be delayed until the committee stage, since the sponsoring member did not have to provide a full text to the House until then, and general agreement on principle might change or disappear when the details of the measure were revealed (p. 52).

44 For the order of business on 10 April, see *JHC*, XXII, 452–55.

45 Sedgwick, *House of Commons*, I, 14; and *JHC*, XXII, 452.

46 Applications from merchants seeking this kind of relief were customarily sent by the Treasury to the appropriate trade board for its recommendation before the Treasury gave permission to proceed with legislation, and occasionally permission was denied. See Lambert, *Bills and Acts*, p. 71; Sedgwick, *House of Commons*, I, 13–14; and, on petitions generally, Bond, *Records*, p. 69.

47 *JHC*, XXII, 452–53.

48 Cf. Hill and Popple, *Prompter*, ed. Appleton and Burnim, p. 49.

49 *JHC*, XXII, 453. The House usually showed its displeasure with petitions by letting them lie on the table; outright rejections were relatively rare: see Thomas, *Commons*, pp. 17–18. There can be little doubt that Giffard's theater was popular among some groups of merchants, at whose "desire" performances were sometimes given (see, for example, 16 Jan. 1734/35, reported by Scouten, *LS, 1729–1747*, p. 451).

50 Neither can be dated 1737, since the theater in Goodman's Fields was not active then; see Scouten, Introd., *LS, 1729–1747*, p. xxvi; and p. 597.

51 *JHC*, XXII, 455–56.

52 This is almost certainly the same lease referred to in the petition. See also *Theophilus Cibber, to David Garrick, Esq:, with dissertations on theatrical subjects* (1759), p. 51, quoted in Crean, "Licensing Act," p. 245, n. 23.

53 *JHC*, XXII, 456.

54 *Universal Spectator*, 12 April 1735. Portions of the essay were reprinted in *GM*, April 1735, pp. 191–92.

55 Richardson, appointed the first official printer for the House of Commons in 1733, would obviously have been in a position to know the provisions of Barnard's bill (Lambert, Introd., *Sessional Papers*, I, 15–16). *Seasonable Examination* was published at the end of April or early in May, and was advertised during the first week in May (*Weekly Miscellany*, 3 May: *Daily Advertiser*, 3, 7 May), according to McKillop, "Richardson's Early Writings," p. 72, n. 2, and p. 74. The pamphlet is listed in "A Register of Books, for May, 1735," in *GM*, May 1735, p. 279, item 8. *Seasonable Examination* and the comments appended to the "Tradelove" letter both abridge in much the same way objections contained in Richardson's 1733 pamphlet *The Apprentice's Vade Mecum*, and the editor's remarks on the "Tradelove" letter in the *Weekly Miscellany* and *Seasonable Examination* refer to Barnard's bill as a "seasonable animadversion." See also Alan D. McKillop, Introd., *The Apprentice's Vade Mecum; or, Young Man's Pocket Companion*, by [Samuel Richardson] (London, 1734; rpt. Los Angeles: William Andrews Clark Memorial Library, UCLA, 1975), p. x.

56 *JHC*, XXII, 459; T. H. Graves, "Some Facts about Anthony Aston," *Journal of English and Germanic Philology*, 20 (1921), 394.

57 *JHC*, XXII, 459. Charles Lee was appointed Master of the Revels for life at a salary of £10 per annum in October 1731, succeeding his late father, Francis Henry Lee, who had been appointed to the post in May 1725; Symes' annual salary was £12.3.4. See Stevens, "Immediate Effects," p. 181; PRO, MS. LC 5/160, p. 174; and PRO, MS. Money Book 36 (T 53/36), pp. 153, 250; Money Book 37 (T 53/37), p. 335; and Money Book 38 (T 53/38), p. 291.

58 For the importance of the chairman in controlling the work of committees, see Thomas, *Commons*, pp. 271–75.

59 *JHC*, XXII, 459.

60 Theophilus Cibber, "Appendix: An Epistle from Mr. Theophilus Cibber, to David Garrick, Esq:," in *Cibber's Two Dissertations*, p. 44. The House reportedly wished "to gather the experience of one who had strolled all over the kingdom" (Fitzgerald, *New History*, II, 103n), and Aston "was allowed to represent the provincial actors before Parliament"; see Graves, "Facts about Anthony Aston," p. 392.

61 It was listed as item 18 in "The Monthly Catalogue for May, 1735," in *LM*, May 1735, p. 283.

62 Cibber, "Epistle to Garrick," p. 44; Charles Dibdin, *A Complete History of the Stage* (London: The Author, 1800), IV, 413; see also Fitzgerald, *New History*, II, 102–3; Crean, "Licensing Act," p. 248n. For a description of how paper bills were amended, see Maurice F. Bond, "Acts of Parliament: Some Notes on the Original Acts Preserved at the House of Lords, Their Use and Interpretation," *Archives*, 3 (Michaelmas 1958), 209–10; and Lambert, *Bills and Acts*, p. 106.

63 *JHC*, XXII, 459; and see Thomas, *Commons*, pp. 280–81.

64 Hill and Popple, *Prompter*, ed. Appleton and Burnim, pp. 52–53. Nicholson (*Free Stage*, p. 58, n. 1) attributes this essay to Hill.

65 *Grub-Street Journal*, 17 April 1735, rpt. in *GM*, April 1735, p. 197.

66 *JHC*, XXII, 466; see also Dennis Arundell, *The Story of Sadler's Wells, 1683–1964* (New York: Theatre Arts Books, 1966), p. 11.

67 *JHC*, XXII, 468–70; and see Thomas, *Commons*, p. 19. For the committee minutes and the petition of the Middlesex justices, see GLRO, MS. MJ/OC 4/30–31; for similar records from the City, see CLRO, MS. Journals of the Common Council, Vol. 57 (1717–36), fols. 340–41.

68 Thomas, *Commons*, p. 156.

69 Tindal's belief that the bill "met with great opposition, and was sometimes in danger of being lost" as it "made its progress, though slowly, through the House," seems to have no foundation; see Tindal quoted in Cobbett, *Parliamentary History*, IX, col. 945.

70 See Thomas, *Commons*, pp. 244–58 passim; and Sedgwick, *House of Commons*, I, 2.

71 *JHC*, XXII, 470.

72 *JHC*, XXII, 470–71.

73 *JHC*, XXII, 471–72.

74 *GM*, Dec. 1735, pp. 777–78. There is no conclusive evidence, however, to show the date on which Walpole offered his clause.

75 Chandler, *History and Proceedings*, IX, 94.

76 Coxe, *Walpole*, II, 435.

77 Harvard Theatre Collection, TS 297.25.35F (see App. B-1). The word "seditious" has also been added in this copy to the similar clause at the top of p. 4.

78 See Scouten, *LS, 1729–1747*, pp. 473–81. The only major incident of which I have found a record apparently occurred in mid-January at the Haymarket, when a "Harlequin" handed the king a printed play bill that read: "By permission. This is to give notice to all gentlemen and ladies and others that at the Opera House in the Haymarket this present evening will be presented The Comical and diverting humours of Punch, And on Thursday next by the Norfolk Company of Artificial Comedians, at Robin's great Theatrical Booth, in Palace Yard, will be presented a comical diverting Play of Seven Acts, called Court and Country, In which will be revived the Entertaining Scene of The Blundering Brothers, with the Cheats of Rabbi Robin, Prime Minister to King Solomon. The whole concluding with a Grand Masque called the Downfall of Sejanus, or the Statesman's Overthrow, with Axes, Halters, Gibbets, and other decorations proper to the Play . . . . N.B.—These are a new set of Poppets as big as the life, chief part of which have been brought up from all parts of the country at a very great expense." Egmont commented simply, "Those who know the times know the satire of this"; the advertised performances evidently never took place. John Percival, *Manuscripts of the Earl of Egmont: Diary of the First Earl of Egmont (Viscount Percival)* (London: HMSO, 1923), II, 145–46 (the entry is for "Thursday, 27" Jan. 1734/35, but that date fell on a Monday).

79 See Thomas, *Commons*, p. 51.

80 Thomas, *Commons*, pp. 215–16. In February 1736/37, during the dispute over the Prince of Wales' allowance, Sir Thomas Hanmer pointed out that "using the King's name to influence the members' votes was formerly a crime, nor was it suffered that the Crown should be informed of what was transacting in the House." Egmont, *Diary*, II, 359. The threat of a veto by the king would have been unusual in any circumstances.

81 Coxe, *Walpole*, II, 435–36. Chandler also describes the clause as one "for enlarging the Power of the Lord Chamberlain, with Regard to the Licensing of Plays" (*History and Proceedings*, IX, 94). It should be noted, however, that *GM* (Dec. 1735, p. 777) and Cobbett (*Parliamentary History*, IX, col. 948) refer to the clause as one "to ratify and confirm (if not enlarge) the Power of the Lord Chamberlain of his Majesty's Houshold over the players." (Loftis, *Politics of Drama*, p. 139, follows Coxe and Chandler, while Nicholson, *Free Stage*, p. 59, follows Cobbett's description; Scouten, Introd., *LS, 1729–1747*, pp. xlix–l, describes the clause simply as one "strengthening the power of the Lord Chamberlain.") *GM* and Cobbett both make clear that the chief objection to the clause was the fear that by it the Lord Chamberlain would be enabled to prohibit plays (both refer to the case of *Polly* in terms similar to Coxe's), so that all the sources agree in treating the clause as one intended to establish official censorship. The references to *Polly* appear to favor the Chandler and Coxe readings.

82 Scouten, *LS, 1729–1747*, p. 482. Another song (or perhaps the same one) dealing with the theater bill was published shortly thereafter and listed (item 25) in "A Register of Books, for May, 1735," in *GM*, May 1735, p. 279: "A Song on the Bill preferred in Parliament for suppressing of Players and Playhouses. By John Phoenix, Commedian, pr. 3 d." (This is also listed as item 169 in James F. Arnott and John W. Robinson, *English Theatrical Literature, 1559–1900: A Bibliography* [London: Society for Theatre Research, 1970], p. 24.)

83 *JHC*, XXII, 475–77.

84 *JHC*, XXII, 477–78.

85 In the "Visionary Introduction" published with his speech, Aston reported that as soon as he reached London he saw in a nightmare "a prodigious motly Vulture with *Ninety* Wings and *Seventy four* Claws . . . with a terrible *BILL*" that screamed "in a *Quaker-like* Agony, *'Regulation! Destruction! Acting inconsistent with Christianity! Down with the Players!'* " (See Appendix B-9.)

86 *JHC*, XXII, 480–81. The last day for such business was 13 May (pp. 490–92).

87 Coxe, *Walpole*, II, 435. According to Watson Nicholson, *Anthony Aston, Stroller and Adventurer* (South Haven: The Author, 1920), p. 38, the bill was "withdrawn" because the petitions in opposition to it were "so successful," a conclusion shared by Cross, *Fielding*, I, 225. Barnard had asked leave to withdraw a different motion on 8 March 1732/33, but his request was opposed, and the Speaker had to remind the House that under those circumstances the motion had to be taken to a vote and could not be withdrawn: see Thomas, *Commons*, p. 173.

88 Thomas, *Commons*, p. 177.

89 *GM*, Dec. 1735, pp. 777–78; Chandler, *History and Proceedings*, IX, 94.
90 "The Diary of Robert Hunter Morris," ed. Beverly McAnear, *Pennsylvania Magazine of History and Biography*, 64 (1940), 189. Walpole's name is in brackets in McAnear's edition.
91 Nicholson, *Free Stage*, pp. 58–59; Loftis, *Politics of Drama*, p. 139.
92 Edward Harley, "Parliamentary Diary, 1734–1750," CUL, Add. MS. 6851, p. 26.
93 Divisions on a bill were not common in the eighteenth century (voice votes were usually not challenged), and it was rare to have more than one division on any single bill, since the minority tended to become smaller with each vote. Opponents therefore timed their action against a bill with some care. See Thomas, *Commons*, pp. 259, 261.
94 *Grub-Street Journal*, 1 May 1735.
95 See *JHC*, XXII, 434, 483–84, 487–88; and Thomas, *Commons*, pp. 264–65.
96 Hill and Popple, *Prompter*, ed. Appleton and Burnim, p. 58.
97 *Prompter*, 6 May 1735 (original issue).
98 *Prompter*, 13 May 1735 (original issue). Hill's suspicions in this issue about the advertisements for a new theater in St. Martins le Grand are quoted above in the text of this chapter at note 16.
99 Hill and Popple, *Prompter*, ed. Appleton and Burnim, p. 63.
100 Although Frederic Stephens, following his practice of dating events represented in prints, dates the print 5 March, the day on which the House gave Barnard leave to prepare his bill, the legend it bears ("published according to Act of Parliament 1735") makes it unlikely that it was offered for sale before the end of June, when the act to protect the copyrights of designers and engravers (8 Geo. II, ch. 13) took effect. Frederic George Stephens and Edward Hawkins, *Catalogue of Prints and Drawings in the British Museum, Division I, Political and Personal Satires* (London: Trustees of the British Museum, 1877), III (I), 91.
101 Sybil Rosenfeld, *The Theatre of the London Fairs in the Eighteenth Century* (Cambridge: Cambridge Univ. Press, 1960), pp. 3, 42; Leo Hughes, *A Century of English Farce* (Princeton: Princeton Univ. Press, 1956), p. 222; and Henry Morley, *Memoirs of Bartholomew Fair*, 4th ed. (London: George Routledge & Sons, 1892), p. 326. For action taken against Mrs. Lee by the City, see CLRO, MS. Repertories, Court of Aldermen, Vol. 139 (1734–35), pp. 321–22 (23 Sept. 1735).
102 Stephens had first appeared at Rich's theater in the role of Othello during October 1734, caused a sensation in Shakespearean roles that season, and in the next season received £200, the highest salary paid an actor at the theater. See Scouten, Introd., *LS, 1729–1747*, pp. cxxx, lxxvi.
103 Scouten, Introd., *LS, 1729–1747*, p. cxxix; Fitzgerald, *New History*, II, 28; and Hugh Phillips, *Mid-Georgian London: A Topographical and Social Survey of Central and Western London about 1750* (London: Collins, 1964), p. 193.
104 Rosenfeld, *London Fairs*, pp. 38–39, 42, 97, 125, 157. On the confusion of Henry Fielding with Timothy Fielding, see Frederick Latreille, "Henry Fielding and Timothy Fielding," *Notes & Queries*, 5th ser., 3 (26 June 1875), 502–3; and Morley, "Epilogue, 1892," in *Bartholomew Fair*, pp. vii–ix.

CHAPTER 3:
POLITICS, SOCIETY, AND THE
THEATERS, 1736

1 Henry Fielding, "Dedication to the Public," *The Historical Register for the Year 1736 and Eurydice Hissed*, ed. William W. Appleton (London: Edward Arnold, 1968), p. 6.

2 See Kern, *Dramatic Satire*, p. 45; Loftis, *Politics of Drama*, p. 128; and Scouten, Introd., *LS, 1729–1747*, pp. xlix–l.

3 See Goldgar, *Walpole and the Wits*, p. 154.

4 Hervey, *Memoirs*, II, 565.

5 Ibid., p. 567.

6 *The Tryal of Robert Nixon, a Nonjuring Clergy-Man, for a High Crime and Misdemeanour* (London: Ed. Cook, 1737), p. 9. For other accounts of this affair, see Hervey, *Memoirs*, II, 567–69; and Thomas Phillibrown, "A Chronological & Historical Account of Material Transactions & Occurrences In my Time," Bod., MS. Eng. Hist. c. 50, pp. 66–67.

7 Robert Walpole to Horace Walpole, 29 July 1736, quoted in Cobbett, *Parliamentary History*, IX, col. 1283. See also Philip C. Yorke, *The Life and Correspondence of Philip Yorke, Earl of Hardwicke* (Cambridge: Cambridge Univ. Press, 1913), pp. 139–40. Walpole's constant fear of Jacobite plots, whether justified or not, was undoubtedly genuine. See J. H. Plumb, *Sir Robert Walpole: The King's Minister* (London: Cresset Press, 1960), p. 46.

8 *Tryal of Nixon*, pp. 5–7. Hervey, however, who was presumably privy to the case, described Nixon as "a Non-juring parson, half mad, and quite a beggar, whom the lawyers should have sent to Bedlam, would have sent to Tyburn, and could only send to rot in jail." *Memoirs*, II, 569.

9 Robert Walpole to Horace Walpole, 29 July 1736, quoted in Cobbett, *Parliamentary History*, IX, col. 1283–85. See also George Rudé, *The Crowd in History: A Study of Popular Disturbances in France and England, 1730–1848* (New York: John Wiley & Son, 1964), pp. 51, 55, 59–60.

10 Hervey, *Memoirs*, II, 569.

11 See Basil Williams, *The Whig Supremacy, 1714–1760*, rev. and ed. C. H. Stuart, 2nd ed. (Oxford: Clarendon Press, 1962), p. 134; and George Rudé, " 'Mother Gin' and the London Riots of 1736," *Guildhall Miscellany*, No. 10 (1959), pp. 53–63.

12 Scouten, *LS, 1729–1747*, p. 593; Cross, *Fielding*, I, 203; and Kern, *Dramatic Satire*, pp. 29–30, 144.

13 BL, Add. MS. 35, 875, leaves 325ᵛ–326ʳ. See also Hervey, *Memoirs*, II, 567; and Rudé, *Crowd in History*, p. 35.

14 See Hervey, *Memoirs*, II, 571; Phillibrown, "Account of my Time," pp. 66–68; BL, Add. MS. 35,875, leaf 326ʳ; and H. T. Dickinson and K. Logue, "The Porteous Riot, 1736," *History Today*, 22 (April 1972), 272–81.

15 Robert Walpole to Horace Walpole, 30 Sept. 1736, quoted in Cobbett, *Parliamentary History*, IX, col. 1287.

16 CUL, Cholmondeley (Houghton) MS. P/70, file 2/1, quoted in Rudé, " 'Mother Gin,' " p. 62. On the Gin Act riots, see also Fritz, *Jacobitism*, pp. 135–36.

17 Hervey, *Memoirs*, II, 569.

18 George, *Political Caricature*, p. 85; and Scouten, *LS, 1729–1747*, p. 603.

19 See Robert Walpole to Horace Walpole, 30 Sept. 1736, postscript (dated 1 Oct.), quoted in Cobbett, *Parliamentary History*, IX, col. 1287; and Hervey, *Memoirs*, II, 569.

20 Hervey, *Memoirs*, II, 539; see also Phillibrown, "Account of my Time," p. 66; and Sedgwick, *House of Commons*, I, 132.

21 Hervey, *Memoirs*, II, 597.

22 Egmont, *Diary*, II, 307.

23 Ibid., p. 305, and see pp. 304–10 passim; see also Hervey, *Memoirs*, II, 597, 609.

24 Hervey, *Memoirs*, II, 610. On the king's extravagance and Walpole's outburst, see Egmont, *Diary*, II, 308, 311.

25 The date on which the queen was hissed is unclear; see Egmont, *Diary*, II, 308; Robert Halsband, *Lord Hervey: Eighteenth-Century Courtier* (Oxford: Clarendon Press, 1973), p. 204; and Scouten, *LS, 1729–1747*, p. 614.

26 Hervey, *Memoirs*, II, 611.

27 Egmont, *Diary*, II, 307–8; Hervey, *Memoirs*, II, 553–56, 611–14, 621; and Charles Chenevix Trench, *George II* (London: Allen Lane, 1973), p. 181.

28 See *London Daily Post and General Advertiser*, 8 Nov. 1736, quoted in Scouten, *LS, 1729–1747*, p. 613; and see pp. 599–621 passim.

29 Egmont, *Diary*, II, 311. The queen herself was reportedly not enthusiastic over her husband's imminent return; see Hervey, *Memoirs*, II, 623–24.

30 Phillibrown, "Account of my Time," p. 69. See also PRO, MS. TS 11/1027; and Hanson, *Government and Press*, pp. 18, 69.

31 PRO, MS. SP 36/39, fol. 274; and *Tryal of Nixon*, p. 10.

32 *The Country Correspondent . . . and An Essay towards the Character of 'Squire Flash,'* No. 1 (London: T. Cooper, 1739), pp. 18–19 (quotation is in italic in original); see also the letter in the *Daily Journal*, 31 Dec. 1736; Scouten, *LS, 1729–1747*, pp. 610, 611, 627; and Hughes, *English Farce*, p. 113.

33 Scouten, *LS, 1729–1747*, p. 591; and Sybil Rosenfeld, "Theatres in Goodman's Fields," *Theatre Notebook*, 1 (Oct. 1945), 49.

34 *London Daily Post and General Advertiser*, 26 July, 16 Sept., 13 Oct., 13 and 22 Nov. 1736, quoted in Scouten, Introd., *LS, 1729–1747*, pp. xxvi–xxvii, lxxv; and pp. 603, 606, 615, 617. Goodman's Fields Theatre remained dark all season.

35 Covent Garden was also disrupted. See Phillibrown, "Account of my Time," pp. 68–69; and Scouten, *LS, 1729–1747*, pp. 603–4, 611. Scouten suggests that Fleetwood himself probably was not involved.

36 This interpretation is proposed by Stephens and Hawkins, *Catalogue of Prints and Drawings*, III (I), 222.

37 Hervey, *Memoirs*, II, 628.

38 Trench, *George II*, p. 187; and see Egmont, *Diary*, II, 321–25.

39 Hervey, *Memoirs*, II, 626–27; and see Alfred James Henderson, *London and the National Government, 1721–1742: A Study of City Politics and the Walpole Administration* (Durham: Duke Univ. Press, 1945), p. 175, n. 47.

40 Hervey, *Memoirs*, II, 624–37; and Sedgwick, *House of Commons*, I, 518. Scouten (*LS, 1729–1747*, p. 624) does not record the queen's presence at an opera this night, but Hervey does.

41 Hervey, *Memoirs*, II, 638–39 (but the toaster was arrested); and see letter from Hervey to Count Agarotti, 16/27 Jan. 1736/37, in *Lord Hervey and His Friends, 1726–38*, ed. Earl of Ilchester (London: John Murray, 1950), p. 263.

42 Hervey, *Memoirs*, II, 636–37.

43 Egmont, *Diary*, II, 325. See also Hervey, *Memoirs*, II, 646.

44 Hervey, *Memoirs*, II, 643. Princess Caroline told Hervey in January that she had heard a report of this incident, which she did not believe, from "her brother or some of his people . . . , about a fortnight ago," and although Hervey did not specify the play at which the outburst was said to have occurred, *King Henry the Eighth* was the first play performed by the prince's command since *Cato* on 3 December; the prince and princess were, however, present at *Porus* on 22 December at Covent Garden, and it may have been there that the alleged incident occurred.

45 Hervey, *Memoirs*, II, 643–44. Hervey is careful here, and in repeating the previous report, to make it clear that the stories originated with the prince and "his people," but admits that the later incident, at least, was "generally believed" to have happened "among all ranks of people through the whole town." For details, not all of them consistent, see also *LM*, Jan. 1736/37, p. 50; *GM*, Jan. 1736/37, p. 59; Phillibrown, "Account of my Time," p. 69; and Trench, *George II*, p. 187. Frederick's father, as Prince of Wales, had raised his own popularity by superintending the suppression of a fire at Spring Gardens in 1716; see *DNB*, VII, 1038.

46 Phillibrown, "Account of my Time," p. 69.

47 Hervey, *Memoirs*, 647–49; Egmont, *Diary*, II, 330; *GM*, Jan. 1736/37, pp. 57–58; and see Trench, *George II*, p. 187.

48 Scouten, *LS, 1729–1747*, pp. 620–21; the *Daily Advertiser*, 14 Jan. 1736/37, quoted in Emmett L. Avery, "Fielding's Last Season with the Haymarket Theatre," *Modern Philology*, 36 (Feb. 1939), 285. (Drury Lane had for several weeks been offering an afterpiece titled *Harlequin Restored; or, Taste a la Mode.*) *The Fall of Bob* was first advertised on 7 January, to be performed with *The Battle of Parnassus* (rehearsed the day before) on 13 or 14 January (Scouten, *LS, 1729–1747*, p. 628). Although there is no record of a performance of *Parnassus*, the title of the main play produced with *The Fall of Bob* suggests a play on the same topic, and *The Defeat of Apollo* may in fact have been a new title for the same play, chosen at least in part to parody the afterpiece at Drury Lane. Similarly, *The Fall of Bob* may have been meant to allude to *The Fall of Phaeton*, an afterpiece performed at Drury Lane frequently from the end of November.

49 Kern, *Dramatic Satire*, pp. 30, 173. Kern, like Nicoll (*Drama, 1700–1750*, p. 340) and the *New Cambridge Bibliography of English Literature* (II, col. 794), titles the play *The Fall of Bob; or, The Oracle of Gin* (both Nicoll and the *NCBEL*, apparently on the authority of the *Biographia Dramatica*, also record the play as "A Tragedy by Timothy Scrub, of Rag Fair, Esq."). Scouten (*LS, 1729–1747*,

pp. 628–31) and Avery, citing the *Daily Advertiser* (of 7 and 14 Jan. 1736/37), give the other version of the title. Appleton (Introd., Fielding's *Historical Register*, p. xii) and the *NCBEL* indicate that no copy of the play has survived.

50 *GM*, Jan. 1736/37, p. 59.

51 Scouten, *LS, 1729–1747*, p. 634, citing the *London Daily Post and General Advertiser*, 1 Feb. 1736/37; copy of letter from Harrington to Paxton, 8 Feb. 1736/37, PRO, MS. SP 44/83, Crim. Warr. Bk., p. 186. Sentinels had also been in attendance during the disturbance at the King's Theatre on 8 February 1734/35.

CHAPTER 4:
DOMESTIC CRISES, SPRING 1737

1 Cobbett, *Parliamentary History*, IX, cols. 1272–74. See also Harley, "Parliamentary Diary," p. 71; Egmont, *Diary*, II, 336; *GM*, Jan. 1736/37, p. 59, and Feb., p. 121; and BL, Add. MS. 35,875, p. 326.

2 Cobbett, *Parliamentary History*, IX, col. 1280. See also *GM*, Feb. 1736/37, p. 109.

3 Cobbett, *Parliamentary History*, IX, col. 1279.

4 Lord Harrington to Nicholas Paxton (copy), 8 Feb. 1736/37, PRO, MS. SP 44/83, Crim. Warr. Bk., p. 186. See also the related proceedings on 14 February at the sessions of the Middlesex justices in GLRO, MS. MJ/SBB 942/35–36.

5 *LM*, June 1737, p. 294. See also Cobbett, *Parliamentary History*, IX, col. 1302.

6 He was also fined 200 marks and required to provide two sureties of £250 each (from others), and one of £500 of his own, to guarantee his "good behaviour" for life. *GM*, Feb. 1736/37, pp. 120, 121.

7 *GM*, July 1737, pp. 374, 401.

8 See Halsband, *Hervey*, p. 211; Leonard W. Cowie, *Hanoverian England, 1714–1837* (London: G. Bell & Sons, 1967), p. 42; Hervey, *Memoirs*, III, 659–60; and Rudé, *Crowd in History*, p. 7.

9 Henderson, *London and the National Government*, pp. 170–71.

10 Trench, *George II*, pp. 142, 179; and see Betty Kemp, "Frederick, Prince of Wales," in *Silver Renaissance: Essays in Eighteenth-Century English History*, ed. Alex Natan (London: Macmillan, 1961), p. 38. For background on the marriage, scheduled so that the king could leave England to rejoin Madame Walmoden at the earliest possible moment in the spring of 1736, see Phillibrown, "Account of my Time," p. 66; and Hervey, *Memoirs*, II, 553.

11 Cobbett, *Parliamentary History*, IX, cols. 1355, 1357, 1358, 1363, 1379; and Kemp, "Frederick," p. 50. The question of the prince's allowance apparently saved the Opposition Whigs from collapse: until the issue presented itself, Pulteney was seriously considering giving up the struggle against the ministry altogether; see Sedgwick, *House of Commons*, II, 515.

12 Hervey, *Memoirs*, II, 620. See also III, 663–65; and A. N. Newman, "Communication: The Political Patronage of Frederick Lewis, Prince of Wales," *Historical Journal*, 1 (1958), 70–71.

13 Phillibrown, "Account of my Time," p. 70. See also Egmont, *Diary*, II, 336–49 passim.
14 Hervey, *Memoirs*, II, 662.
15 See Hervey, *Memoirs*, III, 661–65; Trench, *George II*, p. 189; Cobbett, *Parliamentary History*, IX, col. 1361; Egmont, *Diary*, II, 336–49; and *LM*, Feb. 1736/37, p. 106.
16 Egmont, *Diary*, II, 352. See also Thomas, *Commons*, p. 150; and Cobbett, *Parliamentary History*, IX, cols. 1311–52.
17 Egmont, *Diary*, II, 353.
18 Hervey, *Memoirs*, III, 671–75.
19 Chandler, *History and Proceedings*, IX, 277.
20 See *GM*, Feb. 1736/37, p. 122, and Aug., p. 469; *JHC*, XXII, 759–60; Chandler, *History and Proceedings*, IX, 277–340; Hervey, *Memoirs*, III, 667–92, 769; Cobbett, *Parliamentary History*, IX, cols. 1352–1454; Harley, "Parliamentary Diary," p. 76; Egmont, *Diary*, II, 356–57; and Halsband, *Hervey*, p. 209. In 1742 the Prince of Wales' income from the Civil List was finally increased to £100,000, and he and his father were—at least publicly—reconciled; see Kemp, "Frederick," pp. 38–39.
21 Cobbett, *Parliamentary History*, IX, cols. 1382, 1447–54; but Cobbett's date of 23 February seems to be in error, since all other sources give it as 25 February; see Hervey, *Memoirs*, III, 695–99, 743; *GM*, Feb. 1736/37, pp. 122–23; and Basil Williams, *Carteret and Newcastle: A Contrast in Contemporaries* (Cambridge: Cambridge Univ. Press, 1943), p. 110.
22 Hervey, *Memoirs*, III, 671, 677, 693.
23 Hervey, *Memoirs*, III, 704; and Lady A. Irwin to [Lord Carlisle], 1 March [1736/37], *Manuscripts of Carlisle*, p. 179.
24 Egmont, *Diary*, II, 356. See also Hervey, *Memoirs*, III, 680, 682, 692; and Cowie, *Hanoverian England*, pp. 52, 251.
25 Egmont, *Diary*, II, 356.
26 Hervey, *Memoirs*, III, 653, 703, 708, 715–16, 733–34, 771, 829; Phillibrown, "Account of my Time," p. 70; Thomas, *Commons*, p. 301; and Williams, *Carteret and Newcastle*, pp. 103–4.
27 John Loftis, *Comedy and Society from Congreve to Fielding* (Stanford: Stanford Univ. Press, 1959), p. 111.
28 Cross, *Fielding*, I, 225. See also Ralph Straus, *Robert Dodsley: Poet, Publisher, and Playwright* (London: John Lane, 1910), pp. 57–60; Scouten, *LS, 1729–1747*, pp. 634–76; and Loftis, *Politics of Drama*, pp. 116–17.
29 Egmont, *Diary*, II, 339.
30 "Dedication to the Public," *Historical Register*, pp. 5–6. Fielding cites a letter in "the *Gazetteer* of the 17th instant," which Appleton notes "actually appeared on May 7," but I have not found a direct reference to Dodsley's play in either place.
31 Act II, sc.ii, quoted in Kern, *Dramatic Satire*, p. 158, n. 51; and Act I, quoted in Loftis, *Politics of Drama*, p.118. The title of the play seems to suggest a sequel or rejoinder to the anonymous play *The Patriot*, "a dramatic account of the life of William of Orange" intended primarily as "an open compliment" to the Prince of Wales and "thus an implied criticism of the king," but except for the political

nature of both plays there appear to be no significant similarities. See Kern, *Dramatic Satire*, p. 37.

32 Loftis, *Politics of Drama*, p. 117. See also Kern, *Dramatic Satire*, p. 40.

33 Pref. to 1737 ed., quoted in Scouten, *LS, 1729–1747*, p. 641.

34 Quoted in Emmett L. Avery, "Proposals for a New London Theatre in 1737," *Notes & Queries*, 182 (May 1942), 286–87. See also Scouten, *LS, 1729–1747*, p. 640. J. Paul de Castro assumes that Fielding must have already been bound to a lease at the Haymarket, and so could not have proposed building a new theater at this time; "Proposals for a New Theatre in 1737," *Notes & Queries*, 182 (June 1942), 346.

35 *JHC*, XXII, 786.

36 Scouten, *LS, 1729–1747*, p. 640; and see Cross, *Fielding*, I, 206. For more detailed information about Fielding's play, see Charles B. Woods, "Notes on Three of Fielding's Plays," *PMLA*, 52 (1937), 368.

37 Cross, *Fielding*, I, 207. The *Daily Journal*, 22 Feb. 1736/37, notes "that even when His Royal Highness was there last Week, the Respect due to the Person of the immediate Heir to the Crown could not keep them [the footmen] within Bounds; and for the first and second Acts scarce one Line could be heard distinctly." The earlier incident probably occurred at Drury Lane on Wednesday, 16 February, when *The Twin Rivals* and *The King and the Miller of Mansfield* were offered by command of the Prince and Princess of Wales (Scouten, *LS, 1729–1747*, p. 639). On the problems associated with the footmen and their gallery, see also Woods, "Three Plays," p. 368; Scouten, Introd., *LS, 1729–1747*, pp. lxii–lxiii; Loftis, *Comedy and Society*, p. 16. Farquhar refers to the footmen's gallery in his *Discourse upon Comedy* (1702). Nicoll (*Drama, 1700–1750*, p. 12) places the footmen's riot on 19 February at Covent Garden, but the account in the *Daily Journal* clearly refers to Drury Lane.

38 *LM*, Feb. 1736/37, p. 107; see also Phillibrown, "Account of my Time," p. 70; and Scouten, *LS, 1729–1747*, p. 640.

39 Scouten, Introd., *LS, 1729–1747*, p. cviii. See also Avery, "Fielding's Last Season," p. 286.

40 See James L. Clifford, *Young Samuel Johnson* (London: William Heinemann, 1955), p. 163.

41 *Usefulness of the Stage*, p. 16.

42 Scouten, *LS, 1729–1747*, p. 643; and J. Doran, *Annals of the English Stage from Thomas Betterton to Edmund Kean*, rev. and ed. Robert Lowe (London: John C. Nimmo, 1888), II, 61–62. Lynch (*Box, Pit, and Gallery*, p. 172) observes that Havard's play "met with no success," but that conclusion is not borne out by the record of its twenty performances that season; see Scouten, pp. 643–73. On the Shakespearean revival, see Scouten, p. clxxii; Avery's "The Shakespeare Ladies Club" cited there; and Lynch, p. 91; and for Fielding's exploitation of the new interest in Shakespeare to ridicule Cibber three days after the premiere of Havard's play, see Avery, "Fielding's Last Season," pp. 286–87.

43 Loftis, *Politics of Drama*, p. 120. The play threatened to rekindle the old but still violent controversies over the rights of subjects to oppose monarchic tyranny and to determine the succession. *The Jesuit Unmask'd; or, Some Remarks on a*

Letter in the "Daily Post" of January the 31st (London: T. Cooper, 1737), a stridently pro-administration pamphlet, attacked a letter in the *Daily Post* for comparing (just as Havard does repeatedly in his play) the trial and execution of Charles I to the passion and death of Christ.

44 *King Charles the First: An Historical Tragedy* (London: J. Watts, 1737), p. 5; rpt. in Liesenfeld, *The Stage and the Licensing Act.*

45 Hawkins, *Life of Johnson*, pp. 73–74. Hawkins mistakenly places Havard's play at Giffard's old theater in Goodman's Fields.

46 *GM*, March 1736/37, p. 186.

47 *Common Sense*, 12 March 1736/37. See also *LM*, March 1736/37, p. 163; Genest, *English Stage*, III, 499 (mistakenly dated 5 May 1737); *Daily Advertiser*, 7 and 8 March 1736/37, quoted in Scouten, *LS, 1729–1747*, p. 644. For Wyndham's involvement, see John Byrom, *The Private Journal and Literary Remains*, ed. Richard Parkinson, Remains Historical and Literary Connected with the Palantine Counties of Lancaster and Chester, Vol. 40 (Manchester: Chetham Society, 1856), II (1), 92, journal entry for 27 March 1737. The *Daily Advertiser* of 8 March 1736/37 indicates that Fleetwood received the letter Saturday afternoon, although later reports (e.g., *GM*) imply he received it after the three footmen had been sent to Newgate.

48 *Daily Advertiser*, 8 and 12 March 1736/37, quoted in Scouten, *LS, 1729–1747*, pp. 644, 646.

49 *Daily Advertiser*, 14 March 1736/37, quoted in Scouten, *LS, 1729–1747*, p. 647; and Genest, *English Stage*, III, 499. The *Daily Advertiser* also reported that "the Quality and Gentry are resolv'd in general to discard any Servants that should be known to attempt [any disturbance] . . . , and to give them up to the Rigour of the Law."

50 *Daily Advertiser*, 8 March 1736/37, quoted in Avery, "Fielding's Last Season," p. 288; see also an advertisement in the *St. James Evening Post and London Evening Post* for 8–10 March 1736/37, discussed by Charles W. Nichols, "A New Note on Fielding's *Historical Register*," *Modern Language Notes*, 38 (Dec. 1923), 507–8.

51 *Daily Advertiser*, 10 March 1736/37, quoted in Avery, "Fielding's Last Season," p. 288.

52 *Daily Advertiser*, 23 Feb. 1736/37, quoted in Scouten, Introd., *LS, 1729–1747*, p. cviii.

53 Quoted in Scouten, *LS, 1729–1747*, p. 646.

54 *Usefulness of the Stage*, pp. 16–17.

55 Scouten, Introd., *LS, 1729–1747*, pp. xliv–xlvi; and pp. 641–46.

56 Scouten, Introd., *LS, 1729–1747*, p. xlvi; Fitzgerald, *New History*, II, 436. For the Lord Chamberlain's order itself, see PRO, MS. LC 5/160, p. 318.

57 *JHC*, XXII, 786.

58 *JHC*, XXII, 790.

59 The fair was the most important outside the London area during the eighteenth century, and was said to have been the greatest in Europe in the seventeenth century. See Sybil Rosenfeld, "The Players in Cambridge, 1662–1800," in *Studies*

in English Theatre History in Memory of Gabrielle Enthoven, O.B.E., ed. M. St. Clare Byrne (London: Society for Theatre Research, 1952), p. 24; and Rosenfeld, *London Fairs*, p. xi.

60 Edward Conybeare, *A History of Cambridgeshire* (London: Elliot Stock, 1897), p. 241, citing Carter, "History of Cambridgeshire" (1753); and see Rosenfeld, "Players in Cambridge," p. 24.

61 CUA, MS. Sherlock's Collectanea, c. 1714–80 (ref: Misc. Collect. 17), pp. 77–79, 97 (Thomas Sherlock was vice-chancellor of the university in 1714–15; the collectanea here cited seem to have been written sometime around 1713).

62 Rosenfeld, "Players in Cambridge," p. 25.

63 CUA, MS. Sherlock's Collectanea (17), p. 79.

64 From a grace of 4 Sept. 1701 of the University Senate, quoted in Rosenfeld, "Players in Cambridge," p. 27, and see p. 26.

65 Rosenfeld, "Players in Cambridge," pp. 24, 37. The fair was frequently a source of friction between the town and the university in other ways as well: for several years before 1733, for example, a dispute had arisen between the two over the right to weigh hops (for a fee) in the fair; see Charles Henry Cooper, *Annals of Cambridge* (Cambridge: Metcalfe & Palmer, 1852), IV, 213.

66 CUA, MS. Grace Book I (1718–44), IX, 277–79; Rosenfeld, "Players in Cambridge," p. 27.

67 Rosenfeld, "Players in Cambridge," p. 27.

68 CUA, MS. Grace Book I (1718–44), IX, 412, 419.

69 CUA, Scrap Book II (1735–1827), Misc. Collect. 39, p. 1. The newspaper is not identified; the date of the report is (April ?) "the 9. 1736."

70 Ibid., p. 3. Neither the newspaper nor the date (beyond the month and year) is identified.

71 See CUA MS. Sherlock's Collectanea (17), p. 121.

72 CUA, MS. Grace Book I (1718–44), IX, 418–19.

73 For the petition of 5 March, see ibid., pp. 419–20.

74 Cowie, *Hanoverian England*, p. 247; and *The Historical Register of the University of Cambridge, 1910*, ed. J. R. Tanner (Cambridge: Univ. Press, 1917), p. 31.

75 *JHC*, XXII, 790–91; and see Cooper, *Annals of Cambridge*, IV, 227–29.

76 *JHC*, XXII, 805–6.

CHAPTER 5:
POLITICS, SOCIETY, AND THE
THEATERS, SPRING 1737

1 See Cross, *Fielding*, I, 207; and Appleton, Introd., Fielding's *Historical Register*, p. xiv.

2 *Daily Advertiser*, 23 Feb. 1736/37, quoted in Scouten, Introd., *LS, 1729–1747*, p. cviii and p. 648; and see Hartnoll, "Licensing Act," p. 178.

3 *London Daily Post and General Advertiser*, quoted in Scouten, *LS, 1729–1747*, p. 658.

4 Rpt. in *LM*, March 1736/37, pp. 149–50.

5 See *An Historical View of the Principles, Characters, Persons, &c. of the Political Writers in Great Britain* (London: W. Webb, 1740), pp. 19–20; David Charles Greenwood, *William King: Tory and Jacobite* (Oxford: Clarendon Press, 1969), p. 77; *NCBEL*, col. 796; and Rose Mary Davis, *The Good Lord Lyttelton: A Study in Eighteenth-Century Politics and Culture* (Bethlehem, Pa.: Times Publishing Co., 1939), p. 76.

6 Cross, *Fielding*, I, 219; see also Dane Farnsworth Smith, *Plays about the Theatre in England from "The Rehearsal"... to the Licensing Act* (Oxford: Oxford Univ. Press, 1936), p. 233; *Horace Walpole's Marginal Notes, Written in Dr. Maty's Miscellaneous Works and Memoirs of the Earl of Chesterfield (1777) Communicated by R. S. Turner, Esq.*, Miscellanies of the Philobiblon Society, Vol. 11 (London: Philobiblon Society, 1867–68), note to Chesterfield's *Works*, I, 22, line 21.

7 Greenwood, *King*, p. 77.

8 See Stuart Papers in Windsor Castle, 189/90, 193/133A, 194/10B, 190/12, cited by Greenwood, *King*, pp. 76–77; and George Hilton Jones, "The Jacobites, Charles Molloy, and *Common Sense*," *Review of English Studies*, NS 4 (April 1953), 144–45.

9 *Historical View*, p. 22. The "Vision," according to "Marforio," was written "by Dr. K——g of O——d, a noted Jacobite," but the standard biography of William King (a friend of Swift's and since 1719 principal of St. Mary Hall and a leader of the Oxford Jacobites) points out that "no more than one piece by him can be authenticated," an article on 28 May 1737 in *Common Sense* dealing with Corsica. See Greenwood, *King*, p. 78 (the *Common Sense* article was reprinted in *LM*, May 1737, p. 265). See also Harold Williams, "The Old Trumpeter of Liberty Hall," *Book-Collector's Quarterly*, 4 (Oct.–Dec. 1931), 36, 30–32; Swift, *Correspondence*, ed. Harold Williams (Oxford: Clarendon Press, 1963), IV, 394, and V, 51–54; and Pope, *Correspondence*, ed. George Sherburn (Oxford: Clarendon Press, 1956), IV, 130, n. 2, for additional information on King.

For similar "Oriental" satires see "The Vision of Camilick" (*Craftsman*, 27 Jan. 1726/27), and Lyttelton's *Letters from a Persian in England, to His Friend at Ispahan*, 3rd ed. (London: J. Millan, 1735), pp. 42, 55.

10 See Stephens and Hawkins, *Catalogue of Prints and Drawings*, III (I), 223–27; and Herbert M. Atherton, *Political Prints in the Age of Hogarth* (Oxford: Clarendon Press, 1974), p. 110. Atherton's Plate 19 is identical to the copy reproduced here, except that the price is two-and-six. The print, as much as "The Vision of the Golden Rump," would have been liable to prosecution as seditious libel: see *State Law*, pp. 74–76; and Odgers, *Digest*, p. 126. For prints with a similar theme, see *Idol-Worship; or, The Way to Preferment* (Stephens and Hawkins No. 2447) in Maynard Mack, *The Garden and the City* (Toronto: Univ. of Toronto Press, 1969), p. 148; and *The Punishment Inflicted on Lemuel Gulliver*, in *Hogarth's Graphic Works*, comp. Ronald Paulson (New Haven: Yale Univ. Press, 1965), II, Plate 112.

11 *Common Sense; or, The Englishman's Journal; Being A Collection of Letters ... For the First Year* (London: J. Purser, 1738), p. 49, rpt. in Liesenfeld, *The Stage*

and the Licensing Act. "The Vision" is clearly an example of seditious libel under eighteenth-century law, but it was never prosecuted. See *The Doctrine of Innuendo's Discussed; or, The Liberty of the Press Maintain'd* (London: The Author, 1731), p. 12; Holt, *Law of Libel*, pp. 96–97, n. q; Odgers, *Digest*, pp. 129, 416–17; and Hanson, *Government and Press*, pp. 2, 24.

12 *The Genuine Poetical Works of Charles Cotton, Esq; Containing,* I. *Scarronides; or, Virgil Travestie . . .,* 3rd ed., corrected (London: J. Walthoe et al, 1734), pp. 8–9.

13 The description in "The Vision" combines many details satirically associated with Walpole in other works. See, e.g., "His *Skin* of yellow Damask Hue, / Looks much the worst, when drest in Blue," from "Sir Robert Brass; or, The Intriegues, Serious and Amorous, of the Knight of the Blazing Star" (1731), lines 38–39, quoted in Mack, *Garden and City*, p. 132, n. 11. "Sir Blue-String" (after his Garter ribbon) was Walpole's "commonest nickname"; see Mack, pp. 132–33, and p. 135, n. 19. For Walpole as Harlequin, see Appleton, Introd., Fielding's *Historical Register*, p. xv; and p. 61 (line 187); as magician, see *Craftsman*, 21 Feb. 1735/36, rpt. in *GM*, Feb. 1735/36, p. 88, quoted in Judith Colton, "Merlin's Cave and Queen Caroline: Garden Art as Political Propaganda," *Eighteenth-Century Studies*, 10 (Fall 1976), 16. The portrait may owe something to Swift's "Virtues of Sid Hamet, the Magician's Rod" (1710); see Swift, *Poetical Works*, ed. Herbert Davis (London: Oxford Univ. Press, 1967), pp. 89–91.

14 Pope, *Imitations of Horace*, ed. John Butt, Vol. IV of the Twickenham Edition (London: Methuen, 1969), p. 45 (lines 238–39); and cf. Pope's *Dialogue I*, 157–58 (p. 309). Walpole's son Horace reported that one of the king's mistresses grew so infuriated at having to sit watching him count his money over and over that she publicly scolded him; see Ian Christie, "The Personality of King George II," *History Today*, 5 (1955), 522.

15 Hervey, *Memoirs*, II, 484–85. On the king's similar condition upon his return to England in January 1736/37, see III, 656.

16 Hervey, *Memoirs*, III, 656.

17 E. Smith, *The Compleat Housewife; or, Accomplish'd Gentlewoman's Companion*, 15th ed., with additions (London, 1753; facsimile rpt., n.p.: Literary Services & Production, 1968), p. 361. See also Hervey, *Memoirs*, III, 657; and *Common Sense*, 13 Aug. 1737.

18 Egmont, *Diary*, II, 336–49.

19 CUL, Cholmondeley (Houghton) MS. Corr. 2669; Byrom, *Private Journal*, II, (1), 122.

20 J. H. Jesse, *Memoirs of the Court of England from the Revolution in 1688 to the Death of George II*, 3 vols. (1893), III, 4–5, quoted in Christie, "George II," p. 521. George's behavior seems to have conformed to the "character given to Augustus: *Recalcitrat undique tutus.*" Swift, *Gulliver's Travels*, IV, 12 (the quotation is from Horace, *Sat.*, II.i.20). The king's habit of kicking was so well known that it was frequently discussed in the papers and elsewhere after the spring of 1737. In one (*Fog's Weekly Journal*, 16 July 1737) "Augustus" explains that he had chosen kicking as a diversion because "he had been grievously troubled with the Gravel, and he found this Exercise eased him." Quoted in

Mack, *Garden and City*, p. 138, n. 2. See also *Common Sense*, 11 June 1737, 17 Sept. 1737; Pope's *Dialogue II*, 150–56; and Johnson's "London," lines 129–31, as well as the references noted hereafter to similar allusions during the spring and summer.

21 Hervey, *Memoirs*, II, 484–85, 493–95. For a similar (and perhaps related) spate of kicking provoked in part by frustrated sexual desire, see Apuleius, *The Golden Ass*, VII.

22 Egmont, *Diary*, II, 319.

23 Hervey, *Memoirs*, II, 636–37. Cf. the king's version of the story in his letter that reached the queen the day after Christmas, quoted in the text of Chapter 3, above, at note 42.

24 Stephens and Hawkins, *Catalogue of Prints and Drawings*, III (I), 222; and see Mack, *Garden and City*, p. 130, n. 5. The winds' contumelious salute is a fart. According to Stephens and Hawkins (p. 226), "the printer was taken into custody for this satire."

25 Henry B. Wheatley, *London Past and Present: Its History, Associations, and Traditions* (London: John Murray, 1891), II, 164; see also Arthur L. Dasent, *A History of Grosvenor Square* (New York: Macmillan & Co., 1935). An engraving by Sutton Nicholls of Grosvenor Square about 1731 appears in Phillips, *Mid-Georgian London*, p. 256, Fig. 347.

26 Earl of Ilchester, *Hervey and Friends*, p. 225; Halsband, *Hervey*, p. 188; D. B. Horn, *British Diplomatic Representatives, 1689–1789*, Camden Third Series, Vol. 46 (London: Royal Historical Society, 1932), p. 164; Sedgwick, *House of Commons*, II, 509–10; J. C. Sainty, *Officials of the Secretaries of State, 1660–1782*, Vol. II of *Office-Holders in Modern Britain* (London: Institute of Historical Research, 1973), p. 2; Egmont, *Diary*, II, 174; and Atherton, *Political Prints*, p. 204, n. 37. The *Craftsman*, 28 June 1735 (rpt. in *LM*, June 1735, p. 316), portrays "Marrall" (another name for Horace Walpole) bearing a set of scales nearly identical to those carried by Sacoma. See also Largmann, "Stage References," p. 38.

27 Percival, Introd., *Political Ballads*, p. xlv; and for an early (1727) scurrilous description of Horace's behavior, see ibid., pp. 17–19.

28 Hervey, *Memoirs*, III, 732.

29 Percival, *Political Ballads*, p. 109. Another satire "of the day" (published the same month as "The Negotiators"), Johnson's "London," seems to refer to Horace Walpole under the name of "Balbo," engaged in the same activity (lines 146, 150–51).

30 See Egmont, *Diary*, II, 369–70. In the summer of 1735 the king asked the queen herself to contrive that the Prince of Modera, due to visit England later that year, bring his wife, because he had heard she was free of her person, and he wished to pay his addresses to a daughter of the Duke of Orleans: "—'un plaisir,' ajouta-t'il ... 'que je suis sûr, ma chère Caroline; vous serez bien aise de me procurer, quand je vous dis combien je le souhaite.'" Hervey, *Memoirs*, II, 458–59.

31 Egmont, *Diary*, II, 311, 367, 374; Trench, *George II*, pp. 175–80. The king's impatience with long parliamentary sessions was apparent as early as 1731,

when he ordered Walpole to close the session by 28 April, evidently believing that a session could be ended by command to suit his convenience. See Thomas, *Commons*, p. 90; and Egmont, *Diary*, I, 176.

32 Hervey, *Memoirs*, II, 607.

33 Harley, "Parliamentary Diary," pp. 95–96.

34 Trench, *George II*, p. 191.

35 Scouten, *LS, 1729–1747*, p. 651. The play has frequently been discussed as one of the causes of the Licensing Act: see Loftis, *Politics of Drama*, pp. 134–36; Kern, *Dramatic Satire*, pp. 45–47, 52–53; Hartnoll, "Licensing Act," pp. 178–79; Crean, "Licensing Act," pp. 250–51; Cross, *Fielding*, I, 209 ff.; and the sources cited by Appleton, Introd., Fielding's *Historical Register*. Quotations that follow are from Appleton's edition.

36 Audiences often forced political significance even on innocent passages: see G. B., Parl., *Sessional Papers*, "Dramatic Literature," p. 219; and Lynch, *Box, Pit, and Gallery*, pp. 223, 248.

37 Scouten, Introd., *LS, 1729–1747*, p. lxiii; Appleton, Introd., Fielding's *Historical Register*, p. xii.

38 Egmont, *Diary*, II, 369, 375. See also Scouten, *LS, 1729–1747*, p. 651; Appleton, Introd., Fielding's *Historical Register*, p. xii; and Emmett L. Avery, "An Early Performance of Fielding's *Historical Register*," *Modern Language Notes*, 49 (June 1934), 407.

39 Scouten, *LS, 1729–1747*, pp. 651–61.

40 *JHC*, XXII, 820.

41 *JHC*, XXII, 823. The measure was a private bill and was treated as such throughout the session.

42 Quoted in Scouten, *LS, 1729–1747*, p. 654.

43 *Grub-Street Journal*, 7 April 1737, rpt. in *LM*, April 1737, pp. 192–94. For the attribution and text of "Some Thoughts on the Present State of the Theatres," see Thomas Lockwood, "A New Essay by Fielding," *Modern Philology*, 78 (Aug. 1980), 48–58. With the exception of minor differences in punctuation, capitalization, and spelling, this essay in the *Daily Journal* is identical to the elusive pamphlet with the same title listed by Arnott and Robinson, *Bibliography*, No. 171 (there provisionally and incorrectly dated 1735); for a copy of the pamphlet, see Harvard Theatre Collection, Thr 417.35.

44 Copy of the bill in the University of London Library (No. 7723) labeled "Hanson 5115," referring to the bill so numbered by L. W. Hanson, *Contemporary Printed Sources for British and Irish Economic History, 1701–1750* (Cambridge: Cambridge Univ. Press, 1963). This copy is also labeled "16 Feb. 1739" and has "1739" on its spine, but the bill introduced in that year (on 16 Feb. 1738/39) had a different title (Hanson No. 5374); the dates on this copy of the bill are incorrect.

45 CUL, Cholmondeley (Houghton) MS. Class 64/38. The words "or Licenced" appear above the line, over a caret inserted between the words "Patent" and "granted." The manuscript bears no date or heading and is not endorsed. It contains only one sentence, which begins, "And all Persons pretending to be Gypsies or wandring in the Habit or Form of Counterfeit Egyptians or pretend-

ing to have Skill in Physiognomy Palmestry or like Crafty Science or pretending to tell fortunes or like fantastical imaginations or using any subtle Craft or unlawfull Games or Plays and all Persons being or pretending to be Soldiers Mariners Seafaring Men or Persons going to work in Harvest wandering abroad and begging; and . . .," and ends with the passage quoted in the text. The wording of this draft suggests that it was intended to be the conclusion of a longer clause of definition. Since it proposes a definition of vagrants similar to that contained in 12 Anne 2, ch. 23, and in the bill labeled No. 7723 in the University of London Library (see n. 44, above), and since it exempts one specific set of players from that category, presumably it was meant to be incorporated in a vagrancy bill considered in Parliament during Walpole's administration prior to the Licensing Act. It does not appear, however, in any such bill located by Hanson, or by Sheila Lambert, *List of House of Commons Sessional Papers, 1701–1750*, Special Series, Vol. 1 (London: List and Index Society, 1968). After the 1736–37 session other bills of the same nature were considered in Parliament, but they all contained standard language from the Licensing Act clarifying the definition of "Common Players of Interludes": the only exception is the bill first read on 16 February 1738/39 (BL, 357.c.7[32]), which in the version approved by the Commons and sent to the Lords still has simply the phrase "Common-players of Interludes" without further exception or clarification.

46 *JHC*, XXII, 834, 835, 838, 841, 849, 862, 867, 872, 876.

47 *JHC*, XXII, 836.

48 LIL, MP 103, fol. 295.

49 *JHC*, XXII, 836.

50 Scouten, *LS, 1729–1747*, p. 656.

51 The pregnancy may have been connected with "an operation that was performed upon [the prince] . . . by his Surgeon Valet de chambre Vreid" late in the autumn, the description of which the queen said "I was so far from understanding as believing," and she "begged [the prince] . . . to talk of something else, because he only made me sick and ashamed without comprehending what he meant." Hervey, *Memoirs*, II, 615; and see *GM*, April 1737, p. 250; and Trench, *George II*, p. 184.

52 Avery, "Fielding's Last Season," pp. 288–89. See also A. H. Scouten and Leo Hughes, "The New Theatre in the Haymarket, 1734 and 1737," *Notes & Queries*, 186 (Jan. 1944), 53; Appleton, Introd., Fielding's *Historical Register*, p. xii; and the *London Evening Post*, 7–9 April 1737, cited by Woods, "Three Plays," p. 368, n. 38.

53 For a discussion of *Eurydice Hissed* see Loftis, *Politics of Drama*, pp. 134–35. Quotations that follow are from Appleton's edition.

54 Both Cross (*Fielding*, I, 207) and Woods ("Three Plays," p. 368) indicate that the original play was offered more than once, but the calendar in Scouten, *LS, 1729–1747*, fails to support their view.

55 Kern, *Dramatic Satire*, p. 26; Woods, "Three Plays," p. 370; and Percival, *Political Ballads*, p. 194.

56 Fielding, *Historical Register and Eurydice Hissed*, ed. Appleton, p. 60, n. to lines 156–57; p. 54, n. to line 13; and see Hervey, *Memoirs*, I, 154.

57 See Woods, "Three Plays," pp. 370, 373. The play was timely in another way as well: Parliament was at that time considering another special tax, one to be levied on "all Liquors made . . . from Foreign Fruit or Sugar"; see the *Craftsman*, 2 April 1737, quoted in Woods, p. 370 and n. 43.

58 Quoted in Davis, *Lyttleton*, p. 54; see also Lynch, *Box, Pit, and Gallery*, p. 247.

59 *JHC*, XXII, 846; copy of the petition in Bod., Oxford Univ. Archives, MS. Register of Convocation, 1730–41, N.E.P./*subtus*/Reg. Be. (Acta Convocat: Arch: BE 32), fol. 71.

60 Sedgwick, *House of Commons*, I, 510; and II, 164–65; and *The Historical Register of the University of Oxford, 1900* (Oxford: Clarendon Press, 1900), p. 40.

61 Cibber's company visited Oxford in 1712, but "performances were so arranged as to interfere as little as possible with University life." M. G. Hobson, Pref., *Oxford Council Acts, 1701–1752*, Oxford Historical Society Publications, Vol. 10 (Oxford: Oxford Historical Society, 1954), p. 1. Also see Rosenfeld, "Players in Cambridge," p. 24; and F. S. Boas, "The University of Oxford and the Professional Players," *Times Literary Supplement*, 14 March 1929, p. 206. R. C. Rhodes (*Times Literary Supplement*, 21 Feb. and 11 April 1929) points out that although the 1737 act to prevent plays in Cambridge and Oxford was repealed in respect to Cambridge in 1894, it had not (and apparently has never) been repealed for Oxford.

62 Hobson, Pref., *Oxford Council Acts*, p. 1; and see Marie-Rose Rutherford, "The Abbé Prévost and the English Theatre, 1730–1740," *Theatre Notebook*, 9 (1955), 114.

63 *JHC*, XXII, 846–47.

64 Egmont, *Diary*, II, 390. See also Loftis, *Politics of Drama*, pp. 135–36; Woods, "Three Plays," p. 369; and Appleton, Introd., Fielding's *Historical Register*, pp. xii–xiii. W. R. Irwin, "Prince Frederick's Mask of Patriotism," *Philological Quarterly*, 37 (July 1958), 369, citing Egmont's *Diary*, II, 390, adds that the prince "called with the audience for 'English Roast Beef,' a 'libel on the administration that much entertained the town last winter,'" but no such information or quotations appear there in the *Diary*. Leveridge's song "The Roast Beef of Old England" was performed at Covent Garden on 11 April, 2 and 10 May during the 1737 season. For the dance at Lincoln's Inn Fields, see Scouten, *LS, 1729–1747*, p. 659.

65 Quoted in Scouten, Introd., *LS, 1729–1747*, p. clxxiii.

66 Fielding's two plays "appeared as part of a concerted literary-political campaign during three months of intensive opposition activity initiated by the Prince of Wales, and both Fielding and the stage suffered the consequences of events which had their origin in a family quarrel remote from the Little Theatre at the Haymarket." Goldgar, *Walpole and the Wits*, p. 156.

67 *JHC*, XXII, 849, 855.

68 Act of 22 April 1737, quoted in *Oxford Council Acts*, p. 209.

69 See Valerie C. Rudolph, *"The Mad-House:* A Sane Play in Spite of Its Title,"

Restoration and Eighteenth-Century Theatre Research, 14 (May 1975), 53–60; and Scouten, Introd., *LS, 1729–1747*, pp. lxiii–lxiv; cxliv–xlv; and pp. 661–62.

70 *LM*, April 1737, p. 220; *GM*, April 1737, p. 251; Phillibrown, "Account of my Time," p. 71.

71 *JHC*, XXII, 865–66 (Cambridge); 862, 867 (vagrancy).

72 Egmont, *Diary*, II, 396–97; see also Percival, *Political Ballads*, pp. 104–6.

73 *JHC*, XXII, 869, 871–72.

74 Byrom, *Private Journal*, II (1), 140.

75 Scouten, *LS, 1729–1747*, pp. 666, 668, 670.

76 Quoted in Avery, "Fielding's Last Season," pp. 289–90, and n. 14. See Scouten, *LS, 1729–1747*, p. 667; and Sedgwick, *House of Commons*, I, 436.

77 Scouten, Introd., *LS, 1729–1747*, p. clxx.

78 *JHC*, XXII, 873–74; see Thomas, *Commons*, p. 55, for a discussion of this irregular procedure.

79 *JHC*, XXII, 873–74; and see Thomas, *Commons*, p. 56.

80 For a discussion of this clause, see the text of Chapter 2 at note 27.

81 This provision did not extend to Oxford.

82 The Prince of Wales was sitting in the House of Lords when the bill was brought in. *JHL*, XXV, 105. On procedure, see Lambert, *Bills and Acts*, pp. 104–5.

83 *JHC*, XXII, 876. Both bills remained in that committee until 7 June (p. 895), when the House ordered the poor bill to be printed for the members' use.

84 Scouten, Introd., *LS, 1729–1747*, pp. xxvi–xxvii; and p. 668.

85 Text of the letter reprinted in *Essays on the Theatre from Eighteenth-Century Periodicals*, selected with Introd. by John Loftis, Augustan Reprint Society Publications, Nos. 85–86 (Los Angeles: William Andrews Clark Memorial Library, 1960), pp. 54–57. See also Hartnoll, "Licensing Act," pp. 179–80; Frederick Homes Dudden, *Henry Fielding: His Life, Works, and Times* (Oxford: Clarendon Press, 1952), I, 204; Loftis, *Comedy and Society*, p. 110; and Nicholson, *Free Stage*, p. 61. Loftis (*Politics of Drama*, p. 137) and Appleton (in Fielding's *Historical Register*, p. 5, n. 66) speculate that Lord Hervey may have been the author of the letter.

86 See also Smith, *Plays about the Theatre*, p. 233, n. 143. Although Mack (*Garden and City*, p. 143) indicates that the engraving was published in March, the date assigned to it in the *Catalogue of Prints and Drawings*, III (I), 223, Stephens and Hawkins usually give the date of the incident represented, not the date of publication. I have been able to find no evidence to substantiate any date as early as March; Stephens and Hawkins themselves (p. 227) note the *Craftsman*'s advertisement of 7 May. (Mack, however, argues that "The Vision" in *Common Sense* followed the appearance of the print and was intended to "explain" it.)

87 Fielding, *Historical Register*, pp. 3–10. For the date of publication, see Appleton, Introd., ibid., p. ix; and Avery, "Proposals," p. 286.

88 Fielding errs twice in referring to the letter from the "Adventurer": it appeared on 7, not 17, May, and it contains no discernible reference to Dodsley's *The King and the Miller of Mansfield*.

89 For a discussion of the "old German family called Timberheads," see *Common Sense*, 3 Oct. 1741, rpt. in *GM*, Oct. 1741, pp. 535–36, and cited by Largmann, "Stage References," p. 40.

90 *Common Sense*, 14 May 1737, rpt. in *LM*, May 1737, pp. 252–53. The essay later recommends a novel form of foreign aid by suggesting that the East-India Company send "a Rat-catcher or two next Voyage, for whom they might expect as considerable Returns, as *Whittington* is reported to have made by his Cat," a reference that was perhaps connected in some way with one of the themes Ralph had hit upon earlier in *The Touchstone*. (See the text of this chapter at note 94.)

91 *JHL*, XXV, 108; HLRO, H.L. MS. Minute Book No. 83, for 9 May 1737. The petition, despite its rejection, was preserved among the papers of the House and is now to be found in the Main Papers at 5 May 1737 (9th May, petition).

92 Scouten, *LS, 1729–1747*, p. 670; and Scouten and Hughes, "New Theatre," p. 53. Lacy had concluded his advertisement on 4 May (*Daily Advertiser*) with the note that the performance of the play that Wednesday would "be the last Time of performing Pasquin this season," but it was apparently repeated on the following Monday. Scouten, Introd., *LS, 1729–1747*, p. clxx.

93 *Daily Advertiser*, 11 May 1737, quoted in Scouten, *LS, 1729–1747*, p. 670, and see Scouten's Introd., p. clxxx.

94 See Robert W. Kenny, "James Ralph: An Eighteenth-Century Philadelphian in Grub Street," *Pennsylvania Magazine of History and Biography*, 64 (1940), 221.

95 Percival, *Political Ballads*, p. 75; Kern, *Dramatic Satire*, p. 128.

96 For an example of the danger presented by these machines, see the descriptions of the accident at Covent Garden on 1 October 1736 in Scouten, *LS, 1729–1747*, pp. 603–4.

97 HLRO, H.L. MS. Minute Book No. 83, for 12 May 1737; *JHL*, XXV, 116. The chair was occupied by John West, Lord Delawarr, who acted as chairman of Committees of the Whole House on most bills during the 1730s: see Lambert, *Bills and Acts*, p. 91.

98 *JHL*, XXV, 119, 121, 123; HLRO, H.L. MS. Minute Book No. 83, for 16 May 1737; *JHC*, XXII, 886–87.

99 *Usefulness of the Stage*, p. 18; Avery, "Fielding's Last Season," p. 290; and Scouten, *LS, 1729–1747*, pp. 671–73.

100 Sedgwick, *House of Commons*, II, 464; and *JHC*, XXII, 888. The bill was not yet a law (an "act"). John Byrom noted that day in his journal that after the Commons had agreed to the amendments, William Taylor, a Tory, remarked that "now it was an act of parliament, but I [Byrom] said, Nay, it wants the magical touch of the King." *Private Journal*, II (1), 164.

101 Rosenfeld, "Players in Cambridge," p. 28.

CHAPTER 6:
PASSAGE OF THE LICENSING ACT

1 *JHC*, XXII, 889.

2 During the nineteenth century the Licensing Act was widely referred to simply as "Walpole's Act." See G.B., Parl., *Sessional Papers*, "Dramatic Literature," p. 9;

and G.B., Parl., *Sessional Papers* (Joint Committee), *1909*, Vol. VIII, "On Stage Plays (Censorship)," p. 129.

3 Cobbett, *Parliamentary History*, X, col. 320.

4 Sedgwick, *House of Commons*, II, 155, 330; *JHC*, XXII, 889. One tantalizing piece of evidence suggests that Philip Yorke himself may have helped to draft the Licensing Act. In the Hardwicke Papers immediately after several leaves dealing with the Porteous affair, there is a section of notes (undated but presumably written in the spring of 1737) headed "Plays" consisting of summaries of theatrical patents and other records of the Lord Chamberlain and the Master of the Revels. Yorke's notes may reflect early exploratory work in the government's preparation of the new bill. BL, Add. MS. 35,875, fols. 338–42.

5 *Common Sense*, 21 May 1737, rpt. in *Common Sense; or, The Englishman's Journal* (London: J. Purser, 1738), pp. 114–18, and also in *LM*, May 1737, pp. 261–62.

6 Cross, *Fielding*, I, 220–21; Dudden, *Fielding*, I, 206, n. 1; *NCBEL*, col. 928; Lockwood, "New Essay," p. 50; for Horace Walpole, see his *Marginal Notes*, II, 53–55.

7 Scouten, Introd., *LS, 1729–1747*, p. l, concludes it does.

8 Kenneth D. Wright, "Henry Fielding and the Theatres Act of 1737," *Quarterly Journal of Speech*, 50 (Oct. 1964), 255 and n. 21.

9 JHL, XXV, 127–28.

10 Scouten, Introd., *LS, 1729–1747*, p. clxv; and p. 674.

11 See Scouten, *LS, 1729–1747*, pp. 735–36. The Haymarket was dark from 24 May 1737 until 9 October 1738, when the appearance of a group of French players there provoked the audience to a serious riot.

12 *JHC*, XXII, 890.

13 *JHC*, XXII, 890; *Calendar of Treasury Books and Papers Preserved in Her Majesty's Public Record Office, 1735–1738*, ed. W. A. Shaw (London: HMSO, 1900), p. 368.

14 Thomas, *Commons*, p. 48.

15 See Harley, "Parliamentary Diary," pp. 95–96.

16 The act disabled the provost of Edinburgh, Alexander Wilson, and ordered his imprisonment for a year, abolished the city guard (which had threatened to oppose the national troops), ordered the destruction of the city gate, thereby allowing the king's troops to enter the city at any time without physical obstruction, and fined the city £2,000, which was given to Porteous's widow. See Hervey, *Memoirs*, III, 712, 734–35.

17 Hervey, *Memoirs*, III, 739.

18 Cross, *Fielding*, I, 228–29.

19 Text of the bill is taken from the original act in HLRO, 10 Geo. II, ch. 28. See Appendix C-13. The bill was never officially printed.

20 Until 1793, every new act came into force retrospectively on the first day of the session unless it contained a clause specifically designating a different date on which it was to take effect. Bond, "Original Acts," pp. 210–11.

21 Charles Howard to [Lord Carlisle], 24 May [1737], in *Manuscripts of Carlisle*, p. 115. For a discussion of this letter, see above, Chapter 2 and notes 1–5.

22 Coxe, *Walpole*, II, 437.
23 *Historical View*, pp. 50–51.
24 Coxe, *Walpole*, II, 437.
25 Hervey, *Memoirs*, III, 739. See also *The Town and Country Magazine*, Oct. 1787, p. 467 (this is Mrs. Hardcastle's "Scandalous Magazine"; see Goldsmith, *She Stoops to Conquer*, II.i).
26 *The Golden Rump* has become one of the most elusive pieces of eighteenth-century literature. In 1832, before the fire that destroyed nearly all the eighteenth-century records of the House of Commons, hearings on laws related to the drama failed to turn up any evidence that the play was, or ever had been, among the official parliamentary papers. John Payne Collier, one of the witnesses, said he had "made inquiries on the subject" but had "never been able to procure any intelligence with respect to it. . . . It has never been seen," he said; "I have never heard of anybody that has seen it." G.B., Parl., *Sessional Papers*, "Dramatic Literature," p. 23. On the basis of the note in Holland's edition of the *Memoirs of . . . George the Second* (quoted in the text of this chapter at n. 40), it has been almost universally assumed that Horace Walpole was the last to see *The Golden Rump*, having discovered "the imperfect copy of this piece" among his father's papers. The note, however, does not necessarily support that assumption. The uncertainty arises from the fact that the account of finding "the imperfect copy" is printed in brackets. In his Preface (p. xxvii), Holland says that throughout the *Memoirs* he "has added some notes marked (E), and in some very few instances added or altered a word for the sake of delicacy or perspicuity. On such occasions the word added, or substituted, is printed between brackets of this shape [ ]." The 1846 edition of the *Memoirs* is identical in this respect to that of 1847; in the 1822 edition, however (in Vol. VII of Horace Walpole's *Works*), the material later put in brackets appears in a footnote to the longer footnote (pp. 11–12). It is again not clear whether the secondary footnote is Walpole's or the editor's. Horace Walpole's marginal gloss on this subject in Cibber's *Apology* (see W. B. Coley, "Henry Fielding and the Two Walpoles," *Philological Quarterly*, 45 [Jan. 1966], 167, n. 47) contains no suggestion that he had, or had seen, a copy of the play. Consequently, the "I" in whose possession "the imperfect copy" of the play was last noted might have been Henry Richard Vassall Fox, third Baron Holland, and "my father's papers" may designate, not Robert Walpole's, but those of Stephen Fox, second Lord Holland, the son of Henry Fox, one of Fielding's classmates at Eton and one of Walpole's chief supporters. If that is the case, the "imperfect copy" may have been one of the sheets of passages from the play that Walpole presumably distributed to members of the House before reading them aloud from the floor.
27 Smollett, *The History of England, from the Revolution in 1688, to the Death of George II* (London: J. Wallis, 1805), III, 307; Coxe, *Walpole*, II, 437; Baker, *Biographia Dramatica*, II, 268. The *Apology for T . . . C . . .* (p. 93) calls the play "a scurrilous, ignominious, traiterous, scandalous, &c.&c.&c. Libel against Majesty itself."
28 Hervey, *Memoirs*, III, 738. Hervey's first adjective seems particularly well chosen.

29 Rpt. in *LM*, May 1737, pp. 263–64. See also Nicholson, *Free Stage*, pp. 62–63, n. 2.

30 Rpt. in *LM,* June 1737, pp. 310–11.

31 F. W. Bateson, *English Comic Drama, 1700–1750* (New York: Russell & Russell, 1963), p. 114; Thomas Percy, *Reliques of Ancient Poetry*, ed. Henry B. Wheatley (London: George Allen & Unwin, 1885, 1927), III, 287–88; Sheridan Baker, "Political Allusions in Fielding's *Author's Farce, Mock Doctor,* and *Tumble-Down Dick*," *PMLA*, 77 (June 1962), 229–31; and Hill and Popple, *Prompter*, ed. Appleton and Burnim, pp. 2–3, 176, n. 2.

32 Baker, *Biographia Dramatica*, II, 268.

33 Rpt. in *LM*, May 1737, p. 265.

34 Fowell and Palmer, *Censorship*, p. 135.

35 *Apology for T . . . C . . .*, p. 94. By 1787 the attribution was made explicitly: "Sir Robert . . ., for the purpose of introducing his scheme of a reform to his master . . ., caused a piece of two acts to be written . . . styled the *Golden Rump*." *Town and Country*, Oct. 1787, p. 467. Cross (*Fielding*, I, 227) calls the view that Walpole had the farce written as a provocation "preposterous."

36 Cross (*Fielding*, I, 282–84) concludes that although Fielding was not the author of the "autobiography," he "may have lent his aid here and there."

37 Robert Haig, Introd., *An Historical View of the . . . Political Writers in Great Britain (1740),* Augustan Reprint Society Publications, No. 69 (Los Angeles: William Andrews Clark Memorial Library, 1958), p. iii.

38 *Historical View* (original ed.), pp. 49–50. See also Howard P. Vincent, "Henry Fielding in Prison," *Modern Language Review*, 36 (Oct. 1941), 500. Fielding's arrest may have been for his attempted abduction of the fifteen-year-old heiress Sarah Andrew in 1725. See W. W. Gill, "Early Fielding Documents," *Notes & Queries*, 171 (Oct. 1936), 242; and Cross, *Fielding*, I, 51.

39 Quoted in Cross, *Fielding*, I, 290.

40 *Memoirs of the Reign of King George the Second*, ed., with Pref. and Notes, by the late Lord Holland, 2nd ed., rev. (London: Henry Colburn, 1847), I, 13–14, n. 2. The remark in brackets appears in this form in Holland's edition: see n. 26, above. A marginal gloss by Horace Walpole in his copy of Colley Cibber's *Apology* (pp. 164–65) also recorded that Fielding had written *The Golden Rump* and that Sir Robert had acquired a copy; the gloss may have been the basis for the note in the *Memoirs*; see Coley, "Two Walpoles," p. 166 and n. 45.

41 *LM*, Aug. 1737, p. 402.

42 John Torbuck, *A Collection of the Parliamentary Debates in England* (London: John Torbuck, 1740), XV, 302; Ebenezer Timberland, *The History and Proceedings of the House of Lords* (London: Ebenezer Timberland, 1742), V, 211. See also Cobbett, *Parliamentary History*, X, cols. 323–24.

43 *Apology for T . . . C . . .*, pp. 93–94. Wood ("Goodman's Fields Theatre," p. 453, n. 2) incorrectly claims that the mock *Apology* says that Giffard himself may have written the farce with Walpole's knowledge.

44 [James Ralph,] *A Critical History of the Administration of Sr Robert Walpole* (London: J. Hinton, 1743), p. 312; Coxe, *Walpole*, II, 437; *Town and Country*, Oct. 1787, p. 467; Baker, *Biographia Dramatica*, II, 268. The nature of the reward is unclear: some modern historians have assumed Giffard was paid—or

at least promised—£1,000 instead of £600, although there seems to be no contemporary evidence or testimony to substantiate either figure; see Wood, "Goodman's Fields Theatre," p. 453.

45 W. R. Chetwood, *A General History of the Stage, from Its Origin in Greece down to the Present Time* (London: W. Owen, 1749), p. 167; and see Scouten, Introd., *LS, 1729–1747*, pp. xxvi–xxvii, lxxv.

46 *Apology for T . . . C . . .*, p. 94. This account was repeated by Dibdin (*Complete History*, IV, 409) in 1800, but in a version that indicated that the "hint" to Giffard actually accompanied the play. *The Golden Rump*, Dibdin says, was "full of . . . personal satire against the great," written "for . . . the purpose" of provoking "an interference of the legislature," and "was anonymously sent to Giffard . . . with a private intimation, however, that he should refuse to perform it, and give it up into the hands of government as a thing improper to bring before the public."

47 Like most of the letters to Walpole in the Cholmondeley (Houghton) Collection, the salutation of Giffard's is simply "Sir." G. Allen Chinnery, who issued a handlist of the manuscripts in 1953, identifies the letter as "Henry Gifford [to] Walpole ND," and there seems little reason to believe it may have been addressed to anyone else.

48 CUL, Cholmondeley (Houghton) MS. Corr. 3253.

49 Cross, *Fielding*, I, 227, but see also p. 217.

50 L. J. Morrissey, Introd., *Tom Thumb and The Tragedy of Tragedies*, by Henry Fielding (Los Angeles: Univ. of California Press, 1970), p. 2.

51 The entire letter was first published by J. Paul de Castro, "Proposals," p. 346.

52 *Daily Advertiser*, quoted in Avery, "Fielding's Last Season," p. 290. Also see Loftis, *Politics of Drama*, pp. 136–37, and Scouten, *LS, 1729–1747*, p. 675.

53 Thémiseuil de Saint-Hyacinthe (as he was commonly called), *Le Chef-d'Oeuvre d'un Inconnu*, ed. P. X. Leschevin, 9th ed. (Paris, 1807), I, xcii–xciii, quoted in John B. Shipley, "James Ralph, Prince Titi, and the Black Box of Frederick, Prince of Wales," *Bulletin of the New York Public Library*, 71 (March 1967), 145, 148–57. See also Sir Henry Imbert-Terry, "An Unwanted Prince," in *Essays by Divers Hands*, ed. Hugh Walpole, Transactions of the Royal Society of Literature of the United Kingdom, NS 15 (London: Oxford Univ. Press, 1936), pp. 135–60.

54 Hervey, *Memoirs*, III, 738. It is unlikely that *The Golden Rump*, often described as a two-act farce (perhaps divided along the lines of the two-part essay in *Common Sense*), would have been referred to as "two plays."

55 Quoted in Cross, *Fielding*, I, 291.

56 Baker, *Biographia Dramatica*, II, 268.

57 Hervey, *Memoirs*, III, 738.

58 Egmont, *Diary*, II, 359.

59 George Rudé, *Wilkes and Liberty: A Social Study of 1763 to 1774* (Oxford: Clarendon Press, 1962), p. 33.

60 Colonel Cope to Edmund Weston, 28 May 1737, HMC Series 10: *Reports on the Manuscripts of the Earl of Eglington, . . . C. F. Weston Underwood . . .*, 10th Report, App. I, 10th R. I (London: HMSO, 1885), p. 267.

61 *JHC*, XXII, 892; Thomas, *Commons*, p. 92. Egmont (*Diary*, II, 172) had considered a hundred members to constitute a "very thin House."

62 Cope to Weston, 28 May 1737, p. 267; and see Sedgwick, *House of Commons*, II, 567–68.
63 See also Cobbett, *Parliamentary History*, X, col. 320n.
64 Cope to Weston, 28 May 1737, p. 267. Cross (*Fielding*, I, 229–30) reports that it was in reply to this story that "Walpole read to the House parts of 'The Golden Rump,' saying that he was indifferent to personal ridicule." See also Nicholson, *Free Stage*, pp. 63–65. Pope's "To Augustus" was published about the time that this debate occurred, in the midst of official outrage against attacks on the king, the royal family, and the ministry: see Reginald Harvey Griffith, *Alexander Pope: A Bibliography* (Austin: Univ. of Texas Press, 1927), I (2), No. 458; and D. F. Foxon, *English Verse, 1701–1750* (Cambridge: Cambridge Univ. Press, 1975), II, 130.
65 Cope to Weston, 28 May 1737, pp. 266–67. The confusion arises from the unconventional syntax of the letter. The pertinent passage reads: "The Scotch Bill may be passed in case the North Brittains are not strong enough to throw it out before, for as they divided 99 against 140 odd, on the early or late day for the consideration of the Bill, 'tis imagined they will come pretty near in the progress of the Bill, by many of the Majority going out of Town & such, as the Master, Mr Pulteny & others, I am told, not designing to attend it, they were accidentally in the division for the Comitment of the Only Bill by waiting to flame & exclaim about the Playhouse Bill, I mean Mr Pulteny, for the Master was strong for the suppression of Playhouses &c." A division on the "Scotch Bill" occurred on 25 May and is recorded in the House *Journals*.
    The "Colonel Cope" to whom the letter is attributed may have been John Cope (1690–1760), who was a member of the Commons in 1722–34 and again in 1738–41, but not in 1737. Sir John Cope (not a colonel) served in the House from 1705 to 1741; see Sedgwick, *House of Commons*, I, 575–76.
66 *JHC*, XXII, 891.
67 *JHC*, XXII, 892.
68 Coxe, *Walpole*, II, 438.
69 HLRO, MS. Original Act, 10 Geo. II, ch. 28.
70 Archives Diplomatiques, Ministère des Affaires Étrangères, Paris, MS. Correspondance Politique d' Angleterre (C.P.), Vol. 394, fol. 331.
71 Hawkins, *Life of Johnson*, p. 75; Coxe, *Walpole*, II, 438; Reginald Lucas, *George II and His Ministers* (London: Arthur L. Humphreys, 1910), p. 65. Wright ("Fielding," p. 254) says that Coxe reports that Walpole offered both amendments; in fact, however, Coxe implies, but never states explicitly, only that Walpole proposed the first.
72 Although the bill seemed to suggest that the Lord Chamberlain as well as the king could "authorize" theaters (he by license, the king by letters patent), the act, in its final form, did not empower him to do so.
73 *JHC*, XXII, 892.
74 The whole House apparently voted on 27 May to drop an amendment approved by the whole House in committee on 26 May. Since the *Journals* (XXII, 892) do not show the amendments, and since all other records have evidently been lost, it is impossible to determine conclusively the nature either of this apparently

controversial, and unsuccessful, amendment, or to identify the amendments proposed and adopted on 27 May.

75 Cope to Weston, 28 May 1737, p. 267.

76 See Cope to Weston, 28 May 1737, p. 266; and Thomas, *Commons*, p. 91.

77 For a detailed discussion of the process of engrossment, see Bond, "Original Acts," pp. 205, n. 15, and 206–7.

78 *JHC,* XXII, 893; Thomas, *Commons*, p. 56. Harley ("Parliamentary Diary," p. 97) records the progress of the bill in the Commons: "May 20: A Bill brought in which Subjected all Plays to be acted on the Stage to the examination of the Ld Chamberlain. By this means Several good plays were Suppressed & dull ones Licensed. passed June 1."

79 *JHL,* XXV, 134.

80 Coxe, *Walpole*, II, 439–40. The notion that there was no opposition to the bill outside Parliament, and little inside, has been repeated by Crean, "Licensing Act," p. 253, and Wright, "Fielding," p. 255.

81 Hawkins, *Life of Johnson*, p. 75; Coxe, *Walpole*, II, 439–40n.

82 PRO, SP 36/25, fol. 256. The case is clearly from 1737. It refers to "the *Bill* now depending in this Honourable *House* for *explaining* and amending an *Act* of the 12th of Queen *Anne*, so far as it relates to common *Players* of Interludes" and bears a contemporary manuscript notation, apparently addressed to a bishop, regarding a living in Anglesey that became vacant on the death of the bishop of Bangor; the *Gentleman's Magazine* for June 1737 (p. 371) reports that Dr. Cecil, bishop of Bangor, died on 29 May 1737.

83 *Apology for T . . . C . . .*, pp. 94–95.

84 Ibid., p. 94. For modern comments to the same effect, see, e.g., Nicholson, *Free Stage*, pp. 66–67; Appleton, Introd., Fielding's *Historical Register*, p. xvii.

85 CUL, Cholmondeley (Houghton) MS. Class 80/206. The petition is not dated. Although Fleetwood refers to "a bill . . . now depending in parliament for the restraining of Playhouses," using the phrase that usually designated Barnard's bill, his references to the end of the parliamentary session, and especially to the need to protect the king's "Honour, and Dignity," indicate that the memorial must have been written late in the spring of 1737. Moreover, since Barnard's bill had contained a clause specifically guaranteeing Fleetwood a part of the monopoly, it seems most unlikely that the petition would have been written in 1735.

86 See the legal opinion by "A Magistrate of the County of Middlesex Court" in "*Dramatic Tracts and Papers* collected by Mr. [Joseph] Haslewood" (BL, 11795.k.31). This same "power" of the Lord Chamberlain's is mentioned in the *Apology for T . . . C . . .*, p. 94.

87 *Apology for T . . . C . . .*, p. 90; Cobbett, *Parliamentary History*, X, cols. 326–27. See also the reference to the "vigorous opposition" raised against it in Smollett, *History*, III, 307.

88 Hervey, *Memoirs*, III, 738–39.

89 See W.E.H. Lecky, *A History of England in the Eighteenth Century* (London: Longmans, Green, & Co., 1901), II, 182; and Wright, "Fielding," p. 254, and the sources cited there.

90 Hervey, *Memoirs*, III, 738–39.
91 Cibber, *Apology*, ed. Fone, p. 161.
92 *Cibber's Two Dissertations*, p. 82. See also the praise of Chesterfield's eloquence in the headnote to the speech in *LM,* Aug. 1737, p. 401.
93 Coxe, *Walpole*, II, 440. The speech was first printed in *Fog's Weekly Journal* on 2 July: that text, reprinted with minor typographical variations in the July issue of the *London Magazine*, was immediately recognized to be "very imperfect and erroneous," and so the *London Magazine* provided a "more methodical, and more perfect" text in the August issue as part of its series of parliamentary proceedings and debates. In the meantime the *Gentleman's Magazine* for July published another version in its account of the session's proceedings. The correspondent from whom the *Gentleman's Magazine* purportedly received its copy of the text admitted that he had "added many entire Passages [to *Fog's* version] actually delivered by that Noble Lord," and implied that Chesterfield had given only an abbreviated version of the speech, to which the correspondent had "restored [certain passages] . . . which were absolutely necessary to the Induction of Reasoning; and the Beauty of the Allusions thro' the Whole." The next month, apparently in reaction to an attack by the *Daily Gazetteer* (18 July) on mistakes in *Fog's* version that were later attributed to errors made in transcription, the *London Magazine* similarly confessed to the impurity even of its "more perfect" version: "We cannot pretend," the editor said of the speech that was printed in the August issue, "that it is exactly in the Words made use of by the noble Speaker; and therefore, if we have in the Copy committed any Mistakes either with respect to the Argument or the Expression, we must forewarn the pert Political Criticks of the present, and of every future Age, not to impute them to the original Author." It is this version that "has been repeated by subsequent writers" during and since the eighteenth century. See note (in italic) at the end of the speech in *LM,* July 1737, p. 380; note (in italic) introducing the speech in *GM,* July 1737, p. 409; note preceding the speech in *LM,* Aug. 1737, p. 401; Timberland, *History and Proceedings,* V, 211 ff.; Cobbett, *Parliamentary History*, X, cols. 328 ff.; Philip Dormer Stanhope, *Miscellaneous Works of the Late Philip Dormer Stanhope, Earl of Chesterfield* (London: Edward & Charles Dilly, 1777), I, 228 ff.; and *Cibber's Two Dissertations*, pp. 83–110.
94 Hervey, *Memoirs*, III, 739; see also Walpole, *Marginal Notes*, p. 7.
95 *JHL*, XXV, 137. The text of the speech cited here is from *LM,* Aug. 1737, pp. 401–9.
96 Cibber (*Apology*, ed. Fone, pp. 158–62) later defended the Licensing Act on the contrary grounds, saying that before it was adopted Walpole was defenseless to oppose attacks from the stage.
97 Although Chesterfield's condemnation of *The Golden Rump* is consistent with his later objections to Fielding's and Havard's plays, his tone of moral outrage may have seemed slightly incongruous for one of the founders of *Common Sense*, in which the substance of the "heinous Farce" had been serialized ten weeks earlier.
98 A poem in the January 1736/37 issue of the *Gentleman's Magazine* ("To Mr. Sylvanus Urban, on the Malicious Attacks from His Enemies, 1737") suggests that this notion was applied in various ways: "From Opposition oft great Good

accrues, / The Page suppress'd, were're fondest to peruse." Cf. James Bramston's "The Man of Taste" (1733): "Can Statutes keep the British Press in awe, / When that sells best, that's most against the Law?" Quoted in Hanson, *Government and Press*, p. 68.

99 Cibber (*Apology*, ed. Fone, pp. 156–62) denied that these consequences were inevitable since, he argued, what would incite to sedition if performed before an audience in public might safely—that is, without endangering the state—be read by an individual in private. For a similar distinction, see David Hume, "Of the Liberty of the Press," in *Essays, Moral and Political* (Edinburgh: A. Kincaid, 1741), pp. 15–16; and [Corbyn Morris], *An Essay towards Fixing the True Standards of Wit, Humour, Raillery, Satire, and Ridicule* (London: J. Roberts & W. Bickerton, 1744). Morris's essay is dedicated to Walpole and, according to Kern (*Dramatic Satire*, p. 9), commends him for " 'curbing the theatre' from 'profligate attacks not fairly addressed to the Judgment, but immediately to the Sight and Passions.' " James L. Clifford, however, in his introduction to the pamphlet (in Augustan Reprint Society Publications, No. 10 [Los Angeles: William Andrews Clark Memorial Library, 1947]), says that Morris's dedication (omitted from·the ARS facsimile) praises Walpole "for not curbing the theatre" (p. 6).

100 Complaints of the haste with which a bill moved through Parliament were usually little more than partisan propaganda. Since no particular intervals were required between the various stages of consideration of public bills, such measures could, if necessary, be adopted with very little delay: in 1722 and 1745, for example, bills to suspend the Habeas Corpus Act passed in two days, and most government legislation took less than a month. See Thomas, *Commons*, pp. 60–61 and (for a list of the stages of public legislation in the House of Commons) 63–64.

101 *JHL*, XXV, 138; HLRO, H. L. MS. Minute Book No. 83, for 3 June 1737.

102 See Haig, *Gazetteer*, p. 7.

103 *Daily Gazetteer*, 4 June 1737, rpt. in *LM*, June 1737, pp. 307–8. The *London Magazine* of this month devoted over two pages to "*Extracts from some* Gazetteers, *relating to the Bill for restraining the* STAGE."

104 By Maty (in Chesterfield's *Miscellaneous Works*), who lists it as *Common Sense* No. 19 (it was No. 18) of 4 June; and by Fowell and Palmer (*Censorship*, pp. 136–37).

105 From the original issue, and see *Common Sense; or, The Englishman's Journal* (1738), pp. 127–32, and rpt. in *GM,* June 1737, pp. 358–59.

106 From the original issue, and rpt. in *LM,* June 1737, pp. 304–6.

107 *JHL*, XXV, 139–40; *JHC,* XXII, 896.

108 Although it is virtually impossible to determine why another name was originally written where Stanhope's appears, it is at least conceivable that Rockingham also spoke against the bill on 2 June, the only day of the four on which the bill was considered that he was present.

109 *Historical View*, p. 5; Smollett, *History*, III, 209. Also see Hervey, *Memoirs*, III, 738–39.

110 HLRO, H.L. MS. Minute Book No. 83, for 6 June 1737. The tally was immediately

reported to Paris. Archives Diplomatiques, Ministère des Affaires Étrangères, MS. C. P., Vol. 394, fol. 363. For a list of the fifty-eight members in attendance when the day's session began, see *JHL*, XXV, 139. Manuscript minutes of the House of Lords sessions are also interleaved in the HLRO's copy of the (printed) *Votes and Proceedings of the House of Commons*: the minute there for 6 June (between pp. 302 and 303) records the same tally. See also J. C. Sainty and D. Dewar, *Divisions in the House of Lords: An Analytical List, 1685 to 1857* (London: HMSO, 1976), microfiche 3.

CHAPTER 7:
PUBLIC REACTION AND THE ROYAL ASSENT

1 From the original issue, and rpt. in *LM*, June 1737, p. 308.
2 From the original issue, and rpt. in *LM*, June 1737, pp. 309–11, and in *GM*, June 1737, pp. 361–62.
3 For an "Epigram on the 11th of June" that begins "When *Rumps* were burn'd and *Charles* return'd, / To settle in this *nation* . . .," see *GM*, May 1737, p. 310.
4 From the original issue, and rpt. in *LM*, June 1737, pp. 323–24.
5 Emmett L. Avery's conclusion that "it seems more likely that Cibber did not write it than that he did" is hardly surprising (Avery, "*The Craftsman* of July 2, 1737, and Colley Cibber," *Research Studies of the State College of Washington*, 7 [June 1939], 103). It is borne out by the findings of the government: Yorke wrote to Newcastle on 22 July saying that Nicholas Amhurst should be arrested as the author, since the printing copy was in his handwriting, and since someone ("Perry") who evidently had firsthand knowledge of the affair had sworn that Amhurst was the author (BL, Add. MS. 32,690, fols. 303–4). Amhurst was arrested on a warrant issued by Newcastle on 26 July (PRO, MS. SP 36/39, fols. 112^v–13^r). Haines alone was convicted, and sentenced on 13 May 1738 to twelve months in prison, a £200 fine, and was required to post £2,000 as surety for his good behavior for seven years. He was unable to pay the fine, and so apparently spent the rest of his life in prison, where he wrote *Treachery, Baseness, and Cruelty Display'd to the Full; in the Hardships and Sufferings of Mr. Henry Haines* (London: Henry Haines, 1740), an account of his involvement in the *Craftsman* and of his prosecution.
6 See Loftis, *Politics of Drama*, p. 146. The quotations that follow are from the original issue of the *Craftsman* for 2 July; a transcription of it is printed by Avery, "*The Craftsman* and Cibber," pp. 390–98.
7 PRO, MS. KB 28/144, fol. 26.
8 One of the messengers of the press (see Chapter 1, above) noted in the margin of the *Craftsman*, "Bought Jan. 13th 1732/3 at A Dodd's without Temple Bar." Paxton had then underlined part of the paragraph introducing the passage, indicated by lines in the margins the offensive portions of the passage itself, and sent the paper to Delafaye with his memorandum on 17 January. PRO, SP 36/29, fols. 13–15.

9 See, for instance, *Craftsman*, 16 July, 23 July; *Daily Gazetteer*, 26 July; *Craftsman*, 30 July, 6 Aug.; *Daily Gazetteer*, 18 Aug.; *Craftsman*, 20 Aug., 1 Oct.; *Common Sense*, 8 Oct. The *Craftsman* of 2 July is represented in the satiric print *In Place*, perhaps by George Bickham, published in 1738 in the midst of rising agitation against Walpole's policies toward Spain; see Atherton, *Political Prints*, Plate 23, and Robert A. Smith, *Eighteenth-Century English Politics: Patrons and Place-Hunters* (New York: Holt, Rinehart & Winston, 1972), p. 77, for copies of the print.

10 *JHL,* XXV, 148–51.

11 Hervey, *Memoirs*, III, 743–44.

12 See, for example, Morrissey, Introd., Fielding's *Tom Thumb*, p. 2.

13 *JHL,* XXV, 151. A few days later the king offered a more spontaneous assessment of the preceding months. "Upon Lord Hervey's telling His Majesty that he believed he was very glad, after so long a session, to get a little fresh air in the country; . . . His Majesty very naturally, but very impoliticly, replied: 'Yes, my Lord, I am very glad to be got away, for I have seen of late, in London, so many hungry faces every day, that I was afraid they would have eat me at last.'" Hervey, *Memoirs*, III, 751.

WORKS CITED

MANUSCRIPTS

The Bodleian Library
Archives. Register of Convocation, 1730–41, N.E.P. / *subtus* / Reg. Be.
Eng. Hist. c. 50.
British Library
Add. MSS. 12,201; 32,251; 32,690; 35,875; 36,031; 36,038.
Egerton MS. 2,320.
University Library, Cambridge
Archives. Grace Book I, 1718–44, Vol. IX.
Sherlock's Collectanea, c. 1714–80, Pt. I (ref: Misc. Collect. 17).
Cholmondeley (Houghton). Corr. 2669, 3253. Class 64/38, 80/206, 81/20, 91/73.
Harley, Edward. "Parliamentary Diary, 1734–50." Add. MS. 6851.
Corporation of London Records Office
Repertories, Court of Aldermen, Vol. 134 (1729–30).
Shelf 552, Small MS. Box 7, No. 5.
Journals of the Common Council, Vol. 57 (1717–36).
Greater London Record Office
MJ/OC 4; MJ/SBB 942.
E/BER/CG/E8/10/1–4.
Harvard Theatre Collection
TS 297.25.35F.
House of Lords Record Office
H.L., Minute Book No. 83.
H.L., Main Papers.
Original Act, 10 Geo. II, ch. 28.
Lincoln's Inn Library
Coxe MS. Vol. 47.
          Book B (No. 29).
Hill MS. No. 66 (Osborne 11).
Misc. MS. Vol. 55.
Ministère des Affaires Étrangères
Archives Diplomatiques. Correspondance Politique d' Angleterre, Vol. 394.
Public Record Office
KB 16/10, 28/144, 122/148.
LC 5/153, 5/160, 7/3.
Letter Book 19 (T 27/25).

Money Book 36 (T 53/36); 37 (T 53/37); 38 (T 53/38); 39 (T 53/39).
SP 36/23, 25, 29, 39; 44/83 (Crim. Warr. Bk.).
TS 11/1027.
Treasury Minute Book 27 (T 29/27).

PUBLISHED MATERIAL

Aston, Walter. *The Restauration of King Charles II*. London: R. Walker, 1732.

An Apology for the Life of Mr. T . . . C . . ., Comedian. Being a Proper Sequel to the "Apology for the Life of Mr. Colley Cibber, Comedian." London: J. Mechell, 1740.

Arnott, James F., and John W. Robinson. *English Theatrical Literature, 1559–1900: A Bibliography (with R. L. Lowe's "A Bibliographical Account of English Theatrical Literature," 1888)*. London: Society for Theatre Research, 1970.

Arundell, Dennis. *The Story of Sadler's Wells, 1683–1964*. New York: Theatre Arts Books, 1966.

Atherton, Herbert M. *Political Prints in the Age of Hogarth: A Study of the Ideographic Representation of Politics*. Oxford: Clarendon Press, 1974.

Avery, Emmett L. "*The Craftsman* of July 2, 1737, and Colley Cibber." *Research Studies of the State College of Washington*, 7 (June 1939), 90–103.

———. "An Early Performance of Fielding's *Historical Register*." *Modern Language Notes*, 49 (June 1934), 407.

———. "Fielding's Last Season with the Haymarket Theatre." *Modern Philology*, 36 (Feb. 1939), 283–92.

———. "Proposals for a New London Theatre in 1737." *Notes & Queries*, 182 (May 1942), 286–87.

Avery, Emmett L., and Mildred Avery Deupree. "The New Theatre in the Haymarket, 1734 and 1737." *Notes & Queries*, 171 (July 1936), 41–42.

Avery, Emmett L., et al. *The London Stage, 1660–1800*. 5 pts. in 11 vols. Carbondale: Southern Illinois Univ. Press, 1960–68.

Baker, David Erskine. *Biographia Dramatica; or, A Companion to the Playhouse*. Continued by Isaac Reed and Stephen Jones. Vol. II. London: Longman, Hurst, 1812.

Baker, Sheridan. "Political Allusions in Fielding's *Author's Farce, Mock Doctor*, and *Tumble-Down Dick*." *PMLA*, 77 (June 1962), 221–31.

Bateson, F. W. *English Comic Drama, 1700–1750*. New York: Russell & Russell, 1963.

Bedford, Arthur. *The Evil and Mischief of Stage-Playing: A Sermon Preached in the Parish-Church of St. Butolph Aldgate, in the City of London, on Sunday the Thirtieth Day of November, in the Year of Our Lord 1729*. 2nd ed. London: J. Wilford, 1735.

Boas, F. S. "The University of Oxford and the Professional Players." *Times Literary Supplement*, 14 March 1929, p. 206.

Bond, Maurice F. "Acts of Parliament: Some Notes on the Original Acts Preserved at the House of Lords, Their Use and Interpretation." *Archives*, 3 (Michaelmas 1958), 201–18.

————. *Guide to the Records of Parliament*. London: HMSO, 1971.

Booth, Michael R. "An Edition of the Theatrical Numbers of the *Prompter*, with Critical Introduction and Notes." Thesis Univ. of London 1958.

Byrom, John. *The Private Journal and Literary Remains*. Vol. II, Pt. 1. Ed. Richard Parkinson. Remains Historical and Literary Connected with the Palantine Counties of Lancaster and Chester, Vol. 40. Manchester: Chetham Society, 1856.

Calendar of Treasury Books and Papers Preserved in Her Majesty's Public Record Office, 1735–1738. Ed. W. A. Shaw. London: HMSO, 1900.

Carlisle. *The Manuscripts of the Earl of Carlisle, Preserved at Castle Howard*. Historical Manuscripts Commission Series 43: 15th Report, Appendix, Pt. VI. London: HMSO, 1897.

[Carter, Samuel.] *Legal Provisions for the Poor*. 4th ed. London: Walthoe and Walthoe, 1718.

Chandler, Richard. *The History and Proceedings of the House of Commons from the Restoration to the Present Time*. Vol. IX. London: Richard Chandler, 1742–44.

Chetwood, W. R. *A General History of the Stage, from Its Origin in Greece down to the Present Time*. London: W. Owen, 1749.

Christie, Ian. "The Personality of King George II." *History Today*, 5 (1955), 516–25.

Cibber, Colley. *An Apology for the Life of Mr. Colley Cibber, Comedian*. London: The Author, 1740.

————. *An Apology for the Life of Colley Cibber*. Ed. B.R.S. Fone. Ann Arbor: Univ. of Michigan Press, 1968.

Cibber, Theophilus. *Cibber's Two Dissertations on the Theatres: With an Appendix, in Three Parts*. London: Griffiths, 1756.

Clifford, James L. *Young Samuel Johnson*. London: William Heinemann, 1955.

Cobbett, William. *Parliamentary History of England*. Vols. IX and X. London: Hansard, 1811–12.

Coley, W. B. "Henry Fielding and the Two Walpoles." *Philological Quarterly*, 45 (Jan. 1966), 167–78.

Colton, Judith. "Merlin's Cave and Queen Caroline: Garden Art as Political Propaganda." *Eighteenth-Century Studies*, 10 (Fall 1976), 1–20.

Common Sense; or, The Englishman's Journal. Being a Collection of Letters, Political, Humorous, and Moral; Publish'd Weekly under That Title for the First Year. London: J. Purser, 1738.

Conybeare, Edward. *A History of Cambridgeshire*. London: Elliot Stock, 1897.

Cooper, Charles Henry. *Annals of Cambridge*. Vol. IV. Cambridge: Metcalfe & Palmer, 1852.

Cotton, Charles. *The Genuine Poetical Works*. 3rd ed., corr. London: J. Walthoe et al., 1734.

The Country Correspondent . . ., and An Essay towards the Character of 'Squire Flash. London: T. Cooper, 1739.

Cowie, Leonard W. *Hanoverian England, 1714–1837* London: G. Bell & Sons, 1967.

Coxe, William. *Memoirs of the Life and Administration of Sir Robert Walpole, Earl of Orford*. New ed. Vol. II. London: T. Cadell, Jun., & W. Davies, 1800.

Crean, P. J. "The Stage Licensing Act of 1737." *Modern Philology*, 35 (Feb. 1938), 239–55.

Cross, Wilbur L. *The History of Henry Fielding*. Vol. I. New Haven: Yale Univ. Press, 1918.

Dasent, Arthur L. *A History of Grosvenor Square*. New York: Macmillan & Co., 1935.

Davis, Rose Mary. *The Good Lord Lyttelton: A Study in Eighteenth-Century Politics and Culture*. Bethlehem, Pa.: Times Publishing Co., 1939.

de Castro, J. Paul. "Proposals for a New Theatre in 1737." *Notes & Queries*, 182 (June 1942), 346.

Dibdin, Charles. *A Complete History of the Stage*. Vol. IV. London: The Author, 1800.

Dickinson, H. T., and K. Logue, "The Porteous Riot, 1736." *History Today*, 22 (April 1972), 272–81.

The Doctrine of Innuendo's Discuss'd; or, The Liberty of the Press Maintain'd: Being Some Thoughts upon the Present Treatment of the Printer and Publishers of the "Craftsman." London: The Author, 1731.

Doran, J. *Annals of the English Stage from Thomas Betterton to Edmund Kean*. Ed. and rev. Robert Lowe. Vol. II. London: John C. Nimmo, 1888.

Dudden, Frederick Homes. *Henry Fielding: His Life, Works, and Times*. Vol. I. Oxford: Clarendon Press, 1952.

Egmont. *Manuscripts of the Earl of Egmont: Diary of the First Earl of Egmont (Viscount Percival)*. Vol. II. London: HMSO, 1923.

The English Reports. 94, K.B. Div. 23. Edinburgh: William Green, 1909.

Fielding, Henry. *The Grub-Street Opera*. Ed. Edgar V. Roberts. Lincoln: Univ. of Nebraska Press, 1968.

———. *The Grub-Street Opera*. Ed. L. J. Morrissey. Edinburgh: Oliver & Boyd, 1973.

———. *The Historical Register for the Year 1736 and Eurydice Hissed*. Ed. William W. Appleton. London: Edward Arnold, 1968.

———. *Tom Thumb and The Tragedy of Tragedies*. Ed. L. J. Morrissey. Los Angeles: Univ. of California Press, 1970.

———. *The Tragedy of Tragedies; or, The Life and Death of Tom Thumb*. Ed. James T. Hillhouse. New Haven: Yale Univ. Press, 1918.

Findlater, Richard. *Banned! A Review of Theatrical Censorship in Britain*. London: MacGibbon & Kee, 1967.

Fitzgerald, Percy. *A New History of the English Stage from the Restoration to the Liberty of the Theatres*. Vol. II. London: Tinsley Bros., 1882.

Fowell, Frank, and Frank Palmer. *Censorship in England*. London: Frank Palmer, 1913.

Foxon, D. F. *English Verse, 1701–1750*. 2 vols. Cambridge: Cambridge Univ. Press, 1975.

Francis, Basil. "John Rich's 'Proposals.' " *Theatre Notebook*, 12 (1957), 17–19.

Fritz, Paul S. *The English Ministers and Jacobitism between the Rebellions of 1715 and 1745*. Toronto: Univ. of Toronto Press, 1975.

Gay, John. *Polly: An Opera*. London: For the Author, 1729.

Genest, John. *Some Account of the English Stage, from the Restoration in 1660 to 1830*. Vol. III. Bath: H. E. Carrington, 1832.

George, Mary Dorothy. *English Political Caricature to 1792: A Study of Opinion and Propaganda*. Oxford: Clarendon Press, 1959.

Gill, W. W. "Early Fielding Documents." *Notes & Queries*, 171 (Oct. 1936), 242.

Goldgar, Bertrand A. *Walpole and the Wits: The Relation of Politics to Literature, 1722–1742.* Lincoln: Univ. of Nebraska Press, 1976.

Graves, Thornton S. "Some Facts about Anthony Aston." *Journal of English and Germanic Philology,* 20 (1921), 391–96.

Great Britain. Laws, Statutes. *Statutes at Large, of England and of Great-Britain: From Magna Carta to the Union of the Kingdoms of Great Britain and Ireland.* Ed. John Raithby. Vol. IX. London: George Eyre, Andrew Strahan, 1811.

———. Laws, Statutes. *The Statutes of the Realm (1101–1713).* Ed. A. Luders et al. Vols. I–VII. London: Record Commission, 1810–28.

———. Parliament. House of Commons. *The Journals of the House of Commons.* Vol. XXII.

———. Parliament. House of Lords. *The Journals of the House of Lords.* Vol. XXV.

———. Parliament. *Sessional Papers* (Commons), *1831–32,* Vol. VII, 2 Aug. 1832. "Report from the Select Committee on Dramatic Literature: with the Minutes of Evidence."

———. Parliament. *Sessional Papers* (Joint Committee), *1909,* Vol. VIII. "On Stage Plays (Censorship), together with the Proceedings of the Committee."

Greenwood, David Charles. *William King: Tory and Jacobite.* Oxford: Clarendon Press, 1969.

Griffith, Reginald Harvey. *Alexander Pope: A Bibliography.* Vol. I, Pt. 2. Austin: Univ. of Texas Press, 1927.

Haig, Robert L. *The Gazetteer, 1735–1797: A Study in the Eighteenth-Century English Newspaper.* Carbondale: Southern Illinois Univ. Press, 1960.

———. Introd. *An Historical View of the . . . Political Writers in Great Britain (1740).* Augustan Reprint Society Publications, No. 69. Los Angeles: William Andrews Clark Memorial Library, 1958.

Haines, Henry. *Treachery, Baseness, and Cruelty Display'd to the Full; in the Hardships and Sufferings of Mr. Henry Haines.* London: Henry Haines, 1740.

Halsband, Robert. *Lord Hervey: Eighteenth-Century Courtier.* Oxford: Clarendon Press, 1973.

Hanson, L. W. *Contemporary Printed Sources for British and Irish Economic History, 1701–1750.* Cambridge: Cambridge Univ. Press, 1963.

———. *Government and the Press, 1695–1763.* Oxford: Oxford Univ. Press, 1936.

Harris, Michael. "Newspaper Distribution during Queen Anne's Reign: Charles Delafaye and the Secretary of State's Office." In *Studies in the Book Trade in Honour of Graham Pollard,* ed. R. W. Hunt, I. G. Philip, and R. J. Roberts. Oxford Bibliographical Society Publications, NS 18. Oxford: Oxford Bibliographical Society, 1975.

Hartnoll, Phyllis. "The Theatre and the Licensing Act of 1737." In *Silver Renaissance: Essays in Eighteenth-Century English History,* ed. Alex Natan. London: Macmillan, 1961.

[Hatchett, William.] *The Fall of Mortimer.* 3rd ed. London: J. Millan, 1731.

Havard, William. *King Charles the First: An Historical Tragedy.* London: J. Watts, 1737.

Hawkins, Sir John. *The Life of Samuel Johnson, LL.D.* 2nd ed., rev. and corr. London: J. Buckland, 1787.

Henderson, Alfred James. *London and the National Government, 1721–1742: A*

Study of City Politics and the Walpole Administration. Durham: Duke Univ. Press, 1945.

Hervey, John, Lord. *Some Materials towards Memoirs of the Reign of King George II*. Ed. Romney Sedgwick. 3 vols. London: Eyre & Spottiswoode, 1931.

Hill, Aaron, and William Popple. *The Prompter: A Theatrical Paper (1734–1736)*. Sel. and ed. William W. Appleton and Kalman A. Burnim. New York: Benjamin Blom, 1966.

The Historical Register of the University of Cambridge, 1910. Ed. J. R. Tanner. Cambridge: Cambridge Univ. Press, 1917.

The Historical Register of the University of Oxford, 1900. Oxford: Clarendon Press, 1900.

An Historical View of the Principles, Characters, Persons, &c. of the Political Writers in Great Britain. London: W. Webb, 1740.

Holt, Francis Ludlow. *The Law of Libel: In Which is Contained a General History of This Law*. 2nd ed. London: J. Butterworth & Son, 1816.

Horn, D. B. *British Diplomatic Representatives, 1689–1789*. Camden 3rd ser., Vol. 46. London: Royal Historical Society, 1932.

Hughes, Leo. *A Century of English Farce*. Princeton: Princeton Univ. Press, 1956.

Hume, David. "Of the Liberty of the Press." In *Essays, Moral and Political*. Edinburgh: A. Kincaid, 1741.

Hume, Robert D. *The London Theatre World*. Carbondale: Southern Illinois Univ. Press, 1980.

Ilchester, Earl of, ed. *Lord Hervey and His Friends, 1726–38*. London: John Murray, 1950.

Imbert-Terry, Sir Henry. "An Unwanted Prince." In *Essays by Divers Hands*, ed. Hugh Walpole. Transactions of the Royal Society of Literature of the United Kingdom, NS 15. London: Oxford Univ. Press, 1936.

Irwin, W. R. "Prince Frederick's Mask of Patriotism." *Philological Quarterly*, 37 (July 1958), 368–84.

The Jesuit Unmask'd; or, Some Remarks on a Letter in the "Daily Post" of January the 31st. London: T. Cooper, 1737.

Jones, George Hilton. "The Jacobites, Charles Molloy, and *Common Sense*." *Review of English Studies*, NS 4 (April 1953), 144–47.

Kemp, Betty. "Frederick, Prince of Wales." In *Silver Renaissance: Essays in Eighteenth-Century English History*, ed. Alex Natan. London: Macmillan, 1961.

Kenny, Robert W. "James Ralph: An Eighteenth-Century Philadelphian in Grub Street." *Pennsylvania Magazine of History and Biography*, 64 (1940), 218–42.

Kern, Jean B. *Dramatic Satire in the Age of Walpole, 1720–1750*. Ames: Iowa State Univ. Press, 1976.

Krutch, Joseph Wood. *Comedy and Conscience after the Restoration*. New York: Columbia Univ. Press, 1949.

Lambert, Sheila. *Bills and Acts: Legislative Procedure in Eighteenth-Century England*. Cambridge: Cambridge Univ. Press, 1971.

———, ed. *House of Commons Sessional Papers of the Eighteenth Century*. Wilmington, Del.: Scholarly Resources, 1975.

———, ed. *List of House of Commons Sessional Papers, 1701–1750*. Special ser., Vol. 1. London: List & Index Society, 1968.

Largmann, Malcolm F. "Stage References as Satiric Weapon: Sir Robert Walpole as Victim." *Restoration and Eighteenth-Century Theatre Research*, 9 (May 1970), 35–43.

Latreille, Frederick. "Henry Fielding and Timothy Fielding." *Notes & Queries*, 3 (June 1875), 502–3.

Lecky, William Edward Hartpole. *A History of England in the Eighteenth Century*. Vol. II. London: Longmans, Green, & Co., 1901.

Liesenfeld, Vincent J. "The 'First' Playhouse Bill: A Stage Ghost." *Theatre Notebook*, 31 (1977), 9–12.

———, ed. *The Stage and the Licensing Act, 1729–1739*. New York: Garland, 1981.

Lockwood, Thomas. "A New Essay by Fielding." *Modern Philology*, 78 (Aug. 1980), 48–58.

Loftis, John. *Comedy and Society from Congreve to Fielding*. Stanford: Stanford Univ. Press, 1959.

———. *The Politics of Drama in Augustan England*. Oxford: Clarendon Press, 1963.

———. *Steele at Drury Lane*. 1952; rpt. Westport, Conn.: Greenwood Press, 1973.

———. Introd. *Essays on the Theatre from Eighteenth-Century Periodicals*. Augustan Reprint Society Publications, Nos. 85–86. Los Angeles: William Andrews Clark Memorial Library, 1960.

Lucas, Reginald. *George II and His Ministers*. London: Arthur L. Humphreys, 1910.

Lynch, James J. *Box, Pit, and Gallery: Stage and Society in Johnson's London*. Los Angeles: Univ. of California Press, 1953.

Lyttelton, George, Lord. *Letters from a Persian in England, to His Friend at Ispahan*. 3rd ed. London: J. Millan, 1735.

Mack, Maynard. *The Garden and the City: Retirement and Politics in the Later Poetry of Pope, 1731–1743*. Toronto: Univ. of Toronto Press, 1969.

McKillop, Alan D. "Richardson's Early Writings: Another Pamphlet." *Journal of English and Germanic Philology*, 53 (Jan. 1954), 72–75.

MacQueen-Pope, W. J. *Haymarket: Theatre of Perfection*. London: W. H. Allen, 1948.

Milhous, Judith. "Company Management." In *The London Theatre World*, ed. Robert D. Hume. Carbondale: Southern Illinois Univ. Press, 1980.

Morley, Henry. *Memoirs of Bartholomew Fair*. 4th ed. London: George Routledge & Sons, 1892.

[Morris, Corbyn.] *An Essay towards Fixing the True Standards of Wit, Humour, Raillery, Satire, and Ridicule*. London, 1744; rpt. Augustan Reprint Society Publications, No. 10. Los Angeles: William Andrews Clark Memorial Library, 1947.

Morris, Robert Hunter. "The Diary of Robert Hunter Morris." Ed. Beverly McAnear. *Pennsylvania Magazine of History and Biography*, 64 (1940), 164–217, 356–406.

[Mottley, J.] "A Compleat List of All the English Dramatic Poets, and of All the Plays Ever Printed in the English Language to the Present Year 1747." In *Scanderbeg; or, Love and Liberty: A Tragedy*. By Thomas Whincop. London: W. Reeve, 1747.

Newman, A. N. "Communication: The Political Patronage of Frederick Lewis, Prince of Wales." *Historical Journal*, No. 1 (1958), pp. 68–75.

Nichols, Charles W. "A New Note on Fielding's *Historical Register*." *Modern Language Notes*, 38 (Dec. 1923), 507–8.

Nicholson, Watson. *Anthony Aston, Stroller and Adventurer*. South Haven, Mich.: The Author, 1920.

————. *The Struggle for a Free Stage in London*. Boston: Houghton, Mifflin, 1906.

Nicoll, Allardyce. *A History of Early Eighteenth Century Drama, 1700–1750*. Cambridge: Cambridge Univ. Press, 1929.

Odgers, W. Blake. *A Digest of the Law of Libel and Slander*. Ed. W. Blake Odgers and Robert Ritson. 6th ed. London: Stevens & Sons, 1929.

Oxford. City Council. *Oxford Council Acts, 1701–1752*. Ed. M. G. Hobson. Oxford Historical Society Publications, Vol. 10. Oxford: Oxford Historical Society, 1954.

Paulson, Ronald. *Hogarth: His Life, Art, and Times*. 2 vols. New Haven: Yale Univ. Press, 1971.

————, comp. *Hogarth's Graphic Works*. Vol. II. New Haven: Yale Univ. Press, 1965.

Pearce, Charles E. *Polly Peachum: The Story of Lavinia Fenton and "The Beggar's Opera."* London, 1913; rpt. New York: Benjamin Blom, 1968.

Percival, Milton, ed. *Political Ballads Illustrating the Administration of Sir Robert Walpole*. Oxford Historical and Literary Studies, Vol. 8. Oxford: Clarendon Press, 1916.

Percy, Thomas. *Reliques of Ancient Poetry*. Ed. Henry B. Wheatley. Vol. III. London: George Allen & Unwin, 1927.

Phillips, Hugh. *Mid-Georgian London: A Topographical and Social Survey of Central and Western London about 1750*. London: Collins, 1964.

Plumb, J. H. *Sir Robert Walpole: The King's Minister*. London: Cresset Press, 1960.

Pope, Alexander. *Correspondence*. Ed. George Sherburn. 5 vols. Oxford: Clarendon Press, 1956.

————. *Imitations of Horace*. Ed. John Butt. Twickenham ed., Vol. 4. London: Methuen & Co., 1969.

[Ralph, James.] *A Critical History of the Administration of Sʳ Robert Walpole, Now Earl of Orford*. London: J. Hinton, 1743.

Remarks on an Historical Play, Called, "The Fall of Mortimer." Shewing Wherein the Said Play May Be Term'd a Libel against the Present Administration. London: E. Rayner, [1731].

[Richardson, Samuel.] *The Apprentice's Vade Mecum (1734)*. Introd. Alan D. McKillop. Augustan Reprint Society Publications, Nos. 169–70. Los Angeles: William Andrews Clark Memorial Library, 1975.

[————.] *A Seasonable Examination of the Pleas and Pretensions of the Proprietors of, and Subscribers to, Play-Houses, Erected in Defiance of the Royal Licence*. London: T. Cooper, 1735.

Rolph, C. H. *Books in the Dock*. London: Andre Deutsch, 1969.

Rosenfeld, Sybil. "The Players in Cambridge, 1662–1800." In *Studies in English Theatre History in Memory of Gabrielle Enthoven, O.B.E.*, ed. M. St. Clare Byrne. London: Society for Theatre Research, 1952.

————. *The Theatre of the London Fairs in the Eighteenth Century*. Cambridge: Cambridge Univ. Press, 1960.

————. "Theatres in Goodman's Fields." *Theatre Notebook*, 1 (Oct. 1945), 49.

Rudé, George. *The Crowd in History: A Study of Popular Disturbances in France and England, 1730–1848*. New York: John Wiley & Sons, 1964.

————. "'Mother Gin' and the London Riots of 1736." *Guildhall Miscellany*, No. 10 (1959), pp. 53–63.

———. *Wilkes and Liberty: A Social Study of 1763 to 1774*. Oxford: Clarendon Press, 1962.

Rudolph, Valerie C. "*The Mad-House*: A Sane Play in Spite of Its Title." *Restoration and Eighteenth-Century Theatre Research*, 14 (May 1975), 53–60.

Rutherford, Marie-Rose. "The Abbé Prévost and the English Theatre, 1730–1740." *Theatre Notebook*, 9 (1955), 111–18.

Sainty, J. C. *Officials of the Secretaries of State, 1660–1782*. Vol. II of *Office-Holders in Modern Britain*. London: Institute of Historical Research, 1973.

———, and D. Dewar. *Divisions in the House of Lords: An Analytical List, 1685 to 1857*. London: HMSO, 1976.

Scouten, A. H., and Leo Hughes. "The New Theatre in the Haymarket, 1734 and 1737." *Notes & Queries*, 186 (Jan. 1944), 52–53.

Sedgwick, Romney. *The House of Commons, 1715–1754*. 2 vols. London: HMSO, 1970.

Sheppard, F. H. W., gen ed. *Survey of London*. Vol. XXXV, *The Theatre Royal Drury Lane and the Royal Opera House Covent Garden*. London: Athlone Press, 1970.

Shipley, John B. "James Ralph, Prince Titi, and the Black Box of Frederick, Prince of Wales." *Bulletin of the New York Public Library*, 71 (March 1967), 143–57.

Siebert, Fredrick Seaton. *Freedom of the Press in England, 1476–1776: The Rise and Decline of Government Controls*. Urbana: Univ. of Illinois Press, 1952.

Smith, Dane Farnsworth. *Plays about the Theatre in England from "The Rehearsal" in 1671 to the Licensing Act in 1737*. New York: Oxford Univ. Press, 1936.

Smith, E. *The Compleat Housewife; or, Accomplish'd Gentlewoman's Companion*. 15th ed. with additions. London, 1753; facsimile rpt. n.p.: Literary Services & Production, 1968.

Smith, Robert A. *Eighteenth-Century English Politics: Patrons and Place-Hunters*. New York: Holt, Rinehart & Winston, 1972.

Smollett, Tobias. *The History of England, from the Revolution in 1688, to the Death of George II*. Vol. III. London: J. Wallis, 1805.

Stanhope, Philip Dormer. *Miscellaneous Works of the Late Philip Dormer Stanhope, Earl of Chesterfield*. Vol. I. London: Edward & Charles Dilly, 1777.

State Law; or, The Doctrine of Libels, Discussed and Examined. 2nd ed. London: T. Wotton & J. Schuckburgh, [1729–30].

Stephens, Frederic George, and Edward Hawkins. *Catalogue of Prints and Drawings in the British Museum, Division I: Political and Personal Satires*. Vol. III, Pt. I. London: Trustees of the British Museum, 1877.

Stevens, David H. "Some Immediate Effects of *The Beggar's Opera*." In *The Manley Anniversary Studies in Language and Literature*. Chicago: Univ. of Chicago Press, 1923.

Straus, Ralph. *Robert Dodsley: Poet, Publisher, and Playwright*. London: John Lane, 1910.

Sutherland, James R. "*Polly* among the Pirates." *Modern Language Review*, 37 (July 1942), 291–303.

Swift, Jonathan. *Correspondence*. Ed. Harold Williams. 5 vols. Oxford: Clarendon Press, 1963.

———. *Poetical Works*. Ed. Herbert Davis. London: Oxford Univ. Press, 1967.

Thomas, Donald Serrell. "The Political, Religious, and Moral Censorship of Literature in England from the Seventeenth to the Nineteenth Centuries." Thesis Univ. of London 1969.

Thomas, Peter D. G. *The House of Commons in the Eighteenth Century.* Oxford: Clarendon Press, 1971.

Timberland, Ebenezer. *The History and Proceedings of the House of Lords, from the Restoration in 1660, to the Present Time.* Vol. V. London: Ebenezer Timberland, 1742.

Torbuck, John. *A Collection of the Parliamentary Debates in England.* Vol. XV. London: John Torbuck, 1740.

Trench, Charles Chenevix. *George II.* London: Allen Lane, 1973.

The Tryal of Robert Nixon, a Nonjuring Clergy-Man, for a High Crime and Misdemeanour. London: Ed. Cook, 1737.

The Usefulness of the Stage to Religion, and to Government. London: Thomas Harper, 1738.

Victor, Benjamin. *The History of the Theatres of London and Dublin, from the Year 1730 to the Present Time.* Vol. I. London: T. Davies, 1761.

Vincent, Howard P. "Henry Fielding in Prison." *Modern Language Review,* 36 (Oct. 1941), 499–500.

Walpole, Horace. *Horace Walpole's Marginal Notes, Written in Dr. Maty's Miscellaneous Works and Memoirs of the Earl of Chesterfield (1777) Communicated by R. S. Turner, Esq.* Miscellanies of the Philobiblon Society, Vol. 11. London: Philobiblon Society, 1867–68.

———. *Memoirs of the Reign of King George the Second.* Ed. Lord Holland. 2nd ed., rev. Vol. I. London: Henry Colburn, 1847.

Wheatley, Henry B. *London Past and Present: Its History, Associations, and Traditions.* Vol. II. London: John Murray, 1891.

Williams, Basil. *Carteret and Newcastle: A Contrast in Contemporaries.* Cambridge: Cambridge Univ. Press, 1943.

———. *The Whig Supremacy, 1714–1760.* Ed. C. H. Stuart. 2nd rev. ed. Oxford: Clarendon Press, 1962.

Williams, Harold. "The Old Trumpeter of Liberty Hall." *Book-Collector's Quarterly,* 4 (Oct.–Dec. 1931), 29–56.

Williams, O. Cyprian. *The Historical Development of Private Bill Procedure and Standing Orders in the House of Commons.* 2 vols. London: HMSO, 1948.

Williams, William P. "Sir Henry Herbert's Licensing of Plays for the Press in the Restoration." *Notes & Queries,* 22 (June 1975), 255–56.

Wood, Frederick T. "Goodman's Fields Theatre." *Modern Language Review,* 25 (Oct. 1930), 443–56.

Woods, Charles B. "Notes on Three of Fielding's Plays." *PMLA,* 52 (1937), 359–73.

———. Review of *Part 3 (1729–1747)* of *The London Stage, 1660–1800,* introd. and ed. Arthur H. Scouten. *Philological Quarterly,* 41 (July 1962), 558.

Wright, Kenneth D. "Henry Fielding and the Theatres Act of 1737." *Quarterly Journal of Speech,* 50 (Oct. 1964), 252–58.

Yorke, Philip C. *The Life and Correspondence of Philip Yorke, Earl of Hardwicke.* Cambridge: Cambridge Univ. Press, 1913.

INDEX

COMPOSED BY MODERN TYPOGRAPHERS, INC.
DUNEDIN, FLORIDA
MANUFACTURED BY THOMSON-SHORE, INC.
DEXTER, MICHIGAN
TEXT AND DISPLAY LINES ARE SET IN ITC GARAMOND

Library of Congress Cataloging in Publication Data

Liesenfeld, Vincent J.
The Licensing Act of 1737.

Bibliography: pp. 237–246.
Includes index.
1. Great Britain. Licensing Act (1737) 2. Theater—
Censorship—Great Britain. I. Title
KD3726.A3 1984   344.41'097   84-40153
ISBN 0-299-09810-9   344.10497